INTERACTIVE INDESIGN CS5

INTERACTIVE INDESIGN CS5

TAKE YOUR PRINT SKILLS TO THE WEB AND BEYOND

MIRA RUBIN

Routledge
Taylor & Francis Group

LONDON AND NEW YORK

First published 2011 by Focal Press

This edition published 2015 by Focal Press

Published 2017 by Routledge
2 Park Square, Milton Park, Abingdon, Oxon OX14 4RN
711 Third Avenue, New York, NY 10017, USA

First issued in hardback 2017

Routledge is an imprint of the Taylor & Francis Group, an informa business

Library of Congress Cataloging-in-Publication Data
Application submitted

British Library Cataloguing-in-Publication Data
A catalogue record for this book is available from the British Library.

ISBN 13: 978-1-138-41683-3 (hbk)
ISBN 13: 978-0-240-81511-4 (pbk)

This book is dedicated to the process of awakening,
to the explorations which require us to become more
than we know ourselves to be.

Acknowledgements

This book would never have made it to press if not for the tireless efforts of my dear friend and long-time colleague Kelly McCathran. Her eagle eyes and relentless attention to detail as tech editor for the book have made it a far better product than it would otherwise have been. Kelly, the depth of your commitment, particularly in the face of the extreme demands of motherhood and career, was nothing short of super-human. I can't thank you enough for your friendship, your dedication and your expertise.

When I agreed to write this book, I had no idea what I was in for. At risk of being melodramatic, it's been a journey of the soul. My profoundly dear friend Jacqui Neulinger, who knows me better than anyone else in the world, was a constant beacon, lighting passage for me through sometimes turbulent waters. Jacqui, I am grateful beyond words for your love and wisdom, and for making me see myself and my capabilities through your eyes.

Every athlete needs a coach. Writing this book was the closest thing to running a marathon that I ever expect do, but I couldn't have crossed the finish line without the support of my dear friend and life coach, Dianne Savoie. Dianne, when I lost sight of the light at the end of the tunnel, you showed up with flares to light the way. I am endlessly grateful for your deep commitment, your love, and your tireless reminders to "Get up and dance!"

My parents Lee Rubin and Diane Sovel, both provided support without which the book would have remained no more than a unfulfilled dream. I thank you both from the depths of my heart for making it possible for me to pursue that dream.

Although I've always had visions of being a writer, it was my work writing for Adobe over the last five years that enabled me to take ownership of that vision. Special thanks go to Sally Cox for recommending me, and to Karen LeFever, Lorsen Koo, Janice Lalley, Eric Sahlin, Jason Guerra, Maryann Amado, Bob Bringhurst, Kristine Jensen, Laura Kersell, Jim Ringham, and Alan Mussleman for the opportunity and support you've provided. It's thanks to our business relationship that I was invited to attend a demo days event that inspired the idea for this book in the first place.

A special thanks goes to Sandee Cohen for the inspiration to take my idea for this book and run with it. Sandee, your enthusiasm for the idea was the reassurance I needed to get the ball rolling. I can't thank you enough.

No technically-oriented book gets written without the help of experts. I want to express my deep appreciation to Chris Kitchener, Lorsen Koo, David Helmly, Kelly McCathran all of whom extended themselves in trouble-shooting, problem-solving, and fact-checking. I thank you also on behalf of the readers for making the book a more reliable resource.

Of course, if it weren't for Adobe and all the people behind the extraordinary Adobe applications, there wouldn't have been anything to write about. I am tremendously grateful for the creative power you make available through your products and for the worlds of opportunity they've inspired.

Table of Contents

INTRODUCTION

Breaking the Mold: Interactive InDesign

The release of InDesign CS5 is nothing short of revolutionary. Now you can apply all the tools that have made InDesign the industry standard for print, to design for interactive electronic media too. With the release of Creative Suite 5, InDesign has evolved from print to "printeractive!" Designers expected to meet the demands of a changing media landscape can now design for multiple destinations from one environment, using the same skills, tools, and even the same assets. Right inside InDesign, you can bring your print projects to life with video, audio, interactive navigation, and even animation. And you don't need to read or write one line of code to do so. Hallelujah!

About the Book

The idea for this book was born in a moment of rapturous enthusiasm over the truly revolutionary, and evolutionary direction taken by Adobe with the release of InDesign CS5. This version of InDesign represents a whole new paradigm, bridging the gap between print and interactive design. Now you can bring your print designs to life or your interactive designs to the printed page, all within the same robust and versatile interface – and re-purpose your assets at the same time! You can create documents for publication to interactive PDFs and eBooks, the web and mobile devices, or migrate content to Flash Professional or Dreamweaver for further development. The truth is, the possibilities are so huge and the implementation so easy, that if you don't yet use InDesign, now's the time to start. If you do use InDesign, now's the time to take it to the next level—and that's where this book comes in.

The book is intended to be used both for reference and as a hands-on how-to manual. There's something in here for everyone. If you're new to InDesign, the instructions and illustrations are concise enough that you should be able to follow along without any difficulty. If you're a seasoned user, living daily in InDesign, not only will you learn about its interactive features, but you're bound to pick up lots of tips and tricks that will be a boon to your print work as well.

While you could most likely open to any exercise in any chapter and follow it, you'll get the most out of the book if you start at the beginning and work your way through to the end. Within the topic-based framework, tangential but relevant subjects are often discussed in the context of the exercise workflow. So, for example, a discussion about designing buttons leads to a discussion of effects, which leads to a discussion of object styles. Each chapter builds on the last, and because there are all kinds of productivity gems sprinkled throughout, there's a lot you could miss by skipping around.

The book is divided into the following parts:

- **Part 1: Interactive InDesign!**
  This section provides all the preliminaries: introduction to the concepts and considerations behind interactive design, the interactive interface and customizing the workspace, as well as a preliminary introduction to the output options available for interactive documents.

- **Part 2: Buttons**
  Buttons are at the heart of interactivity, and InDesign buttons have tremendous versatility and power that go well beyond simple interface navigation. In this section you will really dig in and discover the broad range of appearance options and functionality made available by using buttons. You'll start by

modifying buttons from the Sample Buttons library and move on to creating buttons of your own from scratch. From simple buttons to navigation bars and drop-down menus, this section gives you what you need to be a button-making master. Not only will you learn everything you need to know to make your buttons beautiful, but you'll learn to achieve stellar effects by applying InDesign's built-in button functionality in unexpected ways.

- **Part 3: Animation**
  Now you can make your projects more dynamic and engaging by creating Flash animation right in InDesign! Fade in, fade out, grow, and shrink: these are just the beginning of the animation capabilities built into CS5. Learn how to work with animation presets, animate on a motion path, and set animation timing and triggers. Once you've got the basics, you'll expand your skills with advanced techniques that take your projects to the next level, creating complex, timed, interactive presentations; sequenced animations; and animated buttons. With what you can do in InDesign CS5, you won't believe you're working in a print layout application.

- **Part 4: Working with Media in InDesign**
  Adding media to your InDesign projects is simple (and pretty amazing), but making your media files web-worthy is a much more challenging endeavor. Speak with anyone who works with video for more than a few minutes, and you'll learn that video compression is more art than science. This section provides an orientation to the concepts and considerations related to this sometimes dizzying topic and shows you how to use Adobe Media Encoder to prepare video for use in your InDesign projects. Then, with the basics under your belt, you'll actually place your compressed video, audio, and Flash files in your project and view the fruits of your labor.

- **Part 5: Bookmarks, Hyperlinks & Cross-References**
  Bookmarks, hyperlinks, and dynamic cross-references have been familiar interactive features used in multipage PDFs for quite some time. While bookmarks are strictly an Interactive PDF feature, cross-references and hyperlinks carry over to SWF export as well as PDF. In fact, this part of the book explores novel ways to use cross-references as the primary navigation in an interactive project. The tools and skills covered in this section apply equally to print and interactive design.

- **Part 6: Layout**

  This part fills in some of the blanks and includes working with type, setting up multipage interactive documents, and working with master pages. It also includes an assortment of layout and graphic tools and tips. The chapter on working with type runs the gamut from InDesign fundamentals like threading text, to lesser known and more advanced type techniques like creating nested styles. Whether you're a seasoned InDesign professional or a new user, this part has goodies you'll appreciate, and covers several of the new tools and features you'll come to love.

- **Part 7: Output: Processes, Pitfalls and Performance**

  Now that you know how to create a masterpiece, you'll want to ensure that it performs to your expectations. This part is essential to learning how to optimize your files for their intended destination. Perhaps most important, you'll learn how to design around the unanticipated, often quirky behaviors you may encounter as you push the envelope of InDesign's interactive capabilities.

In the interest of smoothing workflow and increasing efficiency, the book is riddled with keyboard shortcuts. If you're not big on shortcuts yet, please just give them a dedicated try, at least as you work your way through the book. While the initial discipline can be a little uncomfortable, the time they save will reward your perseverance.

Conventions Used in the Book

The screenshots in the book were taken using a Mac. In the interest of balance, for keyboard shortcuts and menu commands, Windows shortcuts are given first, followed by a slash, and then by instructions for Mac. A typical example is Ctrl+0/Command+0. The + sign in a shortcut means that the keys are additive rather than sequential; you need to hold them down at the same time. In other words, you hold down Ctrl or Command, add the 0, and then release both keys.

Menu commands are typically preceded by the words "Go to", followed by a hierarchy of menu names separated by a *greater than* sign (>). EXAMPLE: Go to Window > Object & Layout > Align. In this example, "Window" is the parent menu, "Object & Layout" is a submenu and "Align" is the panel being opened.

There are frequent sidebars; some are tips, some are cautions, some are asides. There are lots of pictures too, to provide a visual reference.

In the event that you're not in front of your computer when reading the book, in most cases you'll still be able to get a good idea of what's being discussed. Of course the exercises will make more sense if you're working through them in InDesign.

Exercise steps are blue, and conversational and explanatory text appears in black. Exercise file names are bolded. If a menu item, file name or button name is in lower case in the context of the application or file structure, it appears in lower case in the book. It was a toss-up as to whether to format such things in all lowercase letters, all initial capital letters or mixed for visual emphasis. We decided it made the most sense to stick to the capitalization conventions used in the application and actual file or object name. As a result, there are occasional sentences that may not make total sense until you identify the reference to an interface element, file, or object name.

In Chapter 3, page 27, you'll set up a customized interactive workspace. It's assumed throughout the book that this workspace is in use when reference is made to panels in the Panel dock. If you don't use the Modified Interactive workspace, the next best option is the Interactive workspace preset.

Nearly every exercise is accompanied by files that you can download from http://www.interactive-indesign.com. In most cases, an exercise has both a start and an end file so you can see the final result before going through the step-by-step lesson. Deconstruction of existing projects is a time-honored learning method and the "end" files are provided with that purpose in mind.

The Photographs

All photographs used in the book and the accompanying projects were taken by Mira Rubin, with the exception of 3 purchased stock images: the turkeys, the loon, and the birds playing in a bird bath. The stock images are used as illustration for the audio files included in Part 4: Working with Media in InDesign. The photographs were provided for the purpose of working through the exercises included with the book, and any distribution or commercial use is strictly prohibited without written consent of the author.

It's our hope that in reading this book and working through the exercises, you will experience even a fraction of the excitement and enthusiasm about InDesign that brought the book into being. The excitement is about the worlds of possibility that InDesign puts at your fingertips. Enjoy, and create with abandon!

Part 1

INTERACTIVE INDESIGN!

This section provides the foundation to get you up and running with the rich interactive capabilities of InDesign CS5. You'll learn guidelines for interactive design, become familiar with the interactive design tools, customize the interface, and get a taste of what you can really do when you put InDesign through its paces. Get ready for a wild ride! You're not going to believe the amazing things you can do.

● Chapter 1

SHOWCASE

You're going to be blown away by what you can create with InDesign CS5. This chapter provides a first taste of what can be accomplished with this awesome tool as you tour some of the completed project files from the book. Both in a browser and in Adobe Reader or Acrobat, you'll see video and animation in action, navigate through the pages, send email, and open a web page. Then, when all is said and done, you'll have the rest of the book to learn how to do all it all and more.

Welcome to the PrInteractive Paradigm

THIS JUST IN: InDesign is not just for print anymore! The folks at Adobe have gone way above and beyond, smashing the mold with this release of InDesign. Defying categorization as an application purely for print, InDesign CS5 represents a new category of hybrid technology, making a lunar leap toward seamlessly migrating print content to web and interactive content.

While it's true that this is not the first version of InDesign to include interactivity, it **is** the first version with animation capabilities and media support, which makes all the difference. The previous version of InDesign supported export directly to SWF (the export format for Flash animation), but it created a more static file. In CS5, the combination of new features, with which you'll become intimately familiar, along with Acrobat and Reader 9 support for Flash media, has made *interactive* InDesign a reality that can't be denied.

To orient you to what's in store, you might want to take some time to play with the sample files we've collected for you from the exercises later in the book. Since the next two chapters lay the groundwork for designing for interactivity, this chapter is meant to get you hooked and excited enough to hang in through the foundation stuff. If you prefer surprises, and don't require extra inspiration, feel free to just dive right in and skip to Chapter 2. Otherwise, hang onto your hat and prepare to be amazed—and try to remember, everything you're seeing was created in a "print layout" application.

Exercise 1.1: Kicking the Tires and Taking Her for a Spin

To check out the sample files for this exercise, you'll need to have Adobe Reader or Acrobat 9 (Standard or Professional) as well as a browser with Flash Player installed on your system.

1. Open your browser of choice, go to File > Open, and browse to the chapter1_exercises folder. Open **interactive_indesign_end.html** and marvel at the images flying in from the left of the page. The animation was created entirely in InDesign!

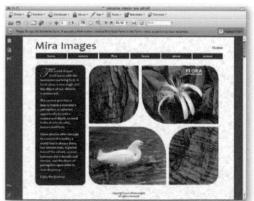

This HTML page contains interactive buttons, Flash animation, video, and audio.

2. Mouse over the large images and then the buttons on the navigation bar at the top of the page to see the dropdown menus. Click the upper left image of the tree bark to navigate to the Texture page.

3. Note the animation of the thumbnail images flying onto the filmstrip as the page loads. Mouse over the thumbnails to see the button rollover effect, and then click the thumbnails to display large versions of their images.

4. Click the Flora button on the navbar (navigation bar) and explore the Flora About page. Mouse over the province names (below the "Pacific Ocean" text on the map) to highlight the Costa Rica provinces. Click the volcano names at the lower right of the page to display popups that tell you more about each volcano. When you're done, click the see Flora slide show text (yet another button) at the lower right of the page.

InDesign allows you to create rollovers and popups that translate to both Interactive PDF and SWF.

5. On the Flora Slide Show page, click the Next and Previous arrow buttons on either side of the flower images to cycle through the slide show. Click the fauna button on the navbar to navigate to the Fauna Scrap Book page.

6. Note how the scrap book images position themselves along an arc as the page loads. Click each of the thumbnail images, and when the large popup image appears, click to close it.

7. Mouse over the fauna button on the navbar to display the dropdown menu, and then click on slide show. Click the thumbnail buttons on the scrolling navbar to display larger versions of the images.

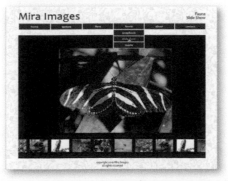

You can even use InDesign's animation features to animate buttons.

From the fauna dropdown on the navbar, choose movie. This page includes Flash video and audio files. Play the movie slideshow by clicking on the photo of the flamingos. Click the gray buttons below the video to jump to preset cue points in the movie. Play each audio clip by clicking on the right-facing arrow below each photo.

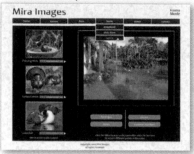

Whether exporting to Flash SWF or Interactive PDF, you can include rich media in the documents you export from InDesign.

8. Click the Contact button on the navbar and mouse over the envelope on the page to see the rollover effect. Click to bring up your email client with a pre-addressed email, and then close your email application without sending.

9. Back in the browser, click the www.miraimages.com link to open the web page in a new browser window. Close the new window and, when you're done exploring, close the file.

   The rich media file you've just seen is 100% InDesign, created with no external development, and not one line of code. The layout, the buttons, the animation—all of it was done directly in the foremost print layout application in the industry. With a few minor adjustments, the same file can be exported to Interactive PDF with similar results: the video, the audio, and even animation. But wait, there's more!

10. Once again, still in the browser, go to File > Open, and from the chapter1_exercises folder, open **banner_ad.html**.

Chapter 11, starting on page 208, is all about banner ads.

   Banner ads are to web as print ads are to magazines and newspapers. Chapter 11, starting on page 208, teaches you how to create a banner ad with the proper dimensions and gives you the skinny on industry standards. The file size of the banners you can create in InDesign is too hefty for commercial placement, but might work perfectly for a local site. In whatever way you choose to use them, the animation skills you'll learn in this chapter will serve you well.

11. Close the file, quit the browser, and open either Acrobat 9 Standard or Professional, or Adobe Reader 9. Go to File > Open, navigate to the chapter1_exercises folder, and open **flower_gallery.pdf.** When the alert pops up, click Yes to allow the file to display in Full Screen Mode. When the file opens, click the flower images to explore the gallery.

InDesign provides a wide assortment of page transitions you can apply to your projects and presentations with just a click.

In real life, you wouldn't want a different transition on every page of your document, but this file is built for demonstration purposes, to familiarize you with InDesign's wide assortment of Page Transitions.

12. When you're finished exploring the document, press Esc on your keyboard to exit Full Screen mode and then close the file. Still in Acrobat or Reader, go to File > Open and, once again, navigate to the chapter1_exercises folder. This time, open **multistate_presentation.pdf**. You may need to scale the document window to see the buttons at the bottom of the screen. Click the octagon buttons in the main content to see an assortment of animations. Click the buttons at the bottom of the screen to navigate to the different "pages" of the presentation.

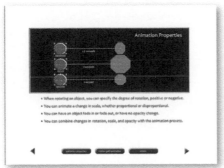

InDesign's interactive capabilities are perfect for creating dynamic and engaging presentations.

13. When you're finished checking out the document, close the file and quit Acrobat or Reader.

The files you've just toured provide you with a taste, just a bit of a tease, and hopefully your mind is churning with ideas of how you might apply some of the effects you've seen to projects of your own. By the end of the book, you'll be able to do all this and more. So, without further ado, let's get started!

CHAPTER SUMMARY

This chapter got you up close and personal with a bunch of really remarkable results you can achieve with InDesign CS5's interactive tools. You viewed documents exported to both Interactive PDF and Flash SWF that included interactive buttons, animation, audio, and video. You interacted with a full screen presentation complete with page transitions, and, hopefully, came away from it all awed and inspired by the possibilities of taking your print skills into the world of interactive design.

The next couple chapters provide a road map for navigating that world, and introduce you to the dynamic design tools in InDesign that make the journey possible.

Chapter 2

DESIGNING FOR INTERACTIVITY

If you're coming from the world of print, and this is your first encounter with the world of interactive design, the landscape may initially feel somewhat upside down. Color model, image resolution, document size, page orientation, and font choices are all different when designing for electronic media. Once you understand the lay of the land though, getting acclimated is easy. This chapter will start you off on the right foot as you begin your adventure into this expansive and exciting terrain.

Print vs. Web and Interactive

It's a good bet that if you're reading this book, you're probably a print designer. And like so many other print designers, you're probably being tasked to expand your skill set to design for the web, and possibly for electronic devices. The beauty of InDesign CS5 is that it allows you to design it all in the very same interface.

The thing is, print and interactive are, by their nature, very different animals. To design effectively for both requires an understanding of the differences. You can then let these differences inform your design choices in order to create an optimal workflow.

Color: RGB vs. CMYK

In doing a point-by-point comparison, the obvious place to start is with color, or, more specifically, how that color is achieved. Color in print is obviously a function of ink on paper. In standard 4-color process printing, cyan, magenta, yellow, and black inks (CMYK) are combined to achieve a multitude of colors. The more ink added, the darker the color becomes. Theoretically, if you added 100% cyan, 100% magenta, and 100% yellow ink together, you would end up with black. In actuality, what you end up with is a muddy reddish brown, so black is added to make a true, rich black.

In the world of digital communications, color is made of light. No doubt you have, at one time or another, seen light split through a prism. White light goes in and a rainbow comes out. Actually, when talking about projected light, the color white is achieved by combining 100% red, 100% green, and 100% blue light to create what is known as the RGB color model. The exact opposite of ink: the more colored light you add, the lighter the color becomes—until, when you've added all the color you can add, you end up with white.

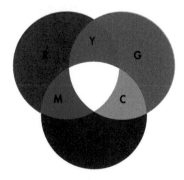

Opposites

Red	⟷	**C**yan
Green	⟷	**M**agenta
Blue	⟷	**Y**ellow
	K Blac**K**	

Blue + Green = **C**yan (opposite **R**ed)

Red + Blue = **M**agenta (opposite **G**reen)

Red + Green = **Y**ellow (opposite **B**lue)

The RGB color space refers to color generated by light, while CMYK refers to color rendered in ink. RGB color is represented by an indexed scale from 0-255, where 0 = 0% light and 255=100% light. CMYK color is represented in ink percentages from 0%-100%.

RGB is the color space for devices that project or measure light, and CMYK is the color space for print. The two color spaces are quite literally opposites. Red is actually the opposite of cyan. So, for example, to reduce the amount of red in an image, you would add cyan. Similarly, to add yellow, you would reduce the amount of blue.

CMYK is measured in ink percentages from 0% - 100%. By contrast, RGB color is represented on an indexed scale of 0 - 255. On this scale, 0 equates to 0 percent light, and 255 equates to 100% light. While higher percentages of ink make color darker, RGB is the opposite. Higher index numbers indicate a greater amount of light, and, generally, the more light, the lighter the color.

If you've been working in print, you know that, traditionally, you are expected to deliver your files to your print provider in CMYK color. What's important to know here is that the RGB color space has a wider gamut than CMYK, meaning it encompasses a broader range of colors. In order to retain the largest possible color palette, Adobe has long recommended that files be kept in RGB until it's time for final print conversion to CMYK. When files are converted from RGB to CMYK, colors outside of the color space are irretrievably lost. Switching back to RGB will not reclaim them. For this reason, ideally, you'll want to stick with the RGB color space up to the last possible moment in your print workflow. If your print provider doesn't use a PDF workflow, most modern RIPs (raster image processors) do an excellent conversion at the time of imaging, which means that most print providers can handle RGB files. This was not true three to five years ago.

In terms of workflow, the good news is that anything destined to be viewed on screen will be viewed in RGB. If you use an RGB workflow, and your print provider prefers PDFs, you can typically do the RGB to CMYK conversion when you do the PDF conversion.This makes it feasible to repurpose the same RGB file for output to both print and interactive documents.

Since you'll be working in RGB for interactive projects, you'll also want to know that there is more than one flavor of RGB to choose from. You can liken the variations in RGB color models to different sized boxes of crayons. ProPhoto RGB is like the big, deluxe box of 128 crayons with more colors in it than you can imagine. sRGB, on the other hand, is more like a crayon box with eight basic colors. Despite the fact that sRGB color is by no means the best possible RGB model, it is unfortunately the one in widest use. We have Microsoft to thank for its prevalence, since sRGB is used in Internet Explorer and the Microsoft Office Suite. Due to the popularity of these applications, Adobe has now assigned sRGB as the default with which Creative Suite documents are tagged. In terms of maintaining consistent color from one application to another, this is a good thing for web or screen. (For high-end print, the more robust RGB flavors are preferred.) It used to be that, without employing color management, files created in Adobe applications would look terrible in Microsoft applications. Now, since the applications speak the same color language, results are more reliable.

While you may never encounter an issue that requires you to delve into color management, and it's not a topic that will be addressed in any great depth here, it's useful to have at least a basic understanding of what it's about (should you come across an issue in the future). Suffice it to say, if you encounter a situation where the color in a file becomes flat or washed out and you can't figure out why, it is most likely a case for color management.

When documents are created in the Creative Suite applications, a color profile that defines the color space is attached to the document by default. Converting a document from RGB to CMYK, is comparable to translating a document from one language to another. The color profile acts as a language definition of sorts. If you were to translate a poem from Italian to English, for example, you would choose different words than you would to translate a scientific paper. You could liken this translation intent to the intent you can choose when converting a file from one profile to another. Without getting into much greater detail here, the thing to be aware of is that sometimes, things get lost in translation, resulting in a mismatch of color that negatively impacts your document. This can sometimes be corrected by properly converting the document color to a new destination color space.

The destination color space is just that: the color space for the ultimate output destination of the document. If an image is destined to be on the web, the destination color space would be sRGB. If it is destined to be printed, its destination color space would be determined by the type of press and paper to be used. The most common high-end print destination color space is Adobe RGB 1998 or ColorMatch RGB (but if you check with your print shop, they should be able to provide recommendations).

Before a PDF print workflow was common, it used to be that every placed image and every element in an InDesign document destined for print had to be CMYK rather than RGB. Since digital images originate in RGB, each and every image had to be converted, and document colors had to be carefully chosen to ensure they used the right color space. Now, when a PDF workflow is implemented, the tedious process of converting files placed in an InDesign document virtually disappears. You can rely on the PDF conversion process to do the conversion for you. You'll learn more about PDF conversion options in Part 7 Output: Processes, Pitfalls, and Performance, starting on page 329.

Color management can be a complex topic and fortunately, by default, the Creative Suite applications are synchronized to pretty much handle it for you behind the scenes, particularly for onscreen or multi-media purposes. If you do want to learn more about color management—and there is quite a lot to know—do a search for it in InDesign Help. You'll find a wealth of information and resources on the topic.

Now that you've had a brief orientation to the concepts governing color management, let's get back to color basics. CMYK colors are defined by the percentages of cyan, magenta, yellow and black inks of which they are comprised. RGB colors are defined in terms of an 8-bit index that goes from 0 to 255 for each of the 3 color channels: red, green, and blue. The 0 in the index indicates 0 light; in other words, black. The 255 at the other end of the spectrum represents 100% light in the channel—so, 255 in the red channel and 0 in the green and blue channels would appear as the color red. If red, green, and blue together each had an index of 255, the resulting color would be white.

In relation to the web, you've most likely encountered the term "web-safe color." When computer monitors displayed 256 colors rather than the millions of colors more common today, web-safe colors represented a color palette of 216 colors that would display uniformly across multiple operating systems. In the past, using web-safe colors was the only way you could ensure that your graphics would appear on the page the way you intended.

One look at the web-safe color palette, and it's clear that its colors were not chosen by designers. After all, how many shades of neon green does a designer really need? The fact is, the web-safe color palette was determined mathematically.

The colors of the web-safe palette are segmented into six groups, each containing a mathematical progression of hue.

Before proceeding with an explanation of how it all works, first a disclaimer. It is in no way essential that you understand the intricacies of how the hexadecimal web colors are defined or how the web-safe colors were determined. When you plug the numbers in, they work, whether you understand exactly what they mean or not. That said, if you're a little queasy about math, feel free to skip this next little bit. (It's really simple math, though.) We just thought it was cool to be able to decode the puzzle and make some sense of those weird hexadecimal values.

To understand it all better, it will be helpful to first understand the hexadecimal, or base 16, system. In a hexadecimal system, the value we know as 16 is represented as 10. Rather than going from 0 to 9 as our base 10 numbers do, additional "digits" are added to represent the values from 10 -15. The count from 0 to 10 in base 16 would look like this: 0, 1, 2, 3, 4, 5, 6, 7, 8, 9, A, B, C, D, E, F, 10.

Web colors consist of three hexadecimal (base 16) values, one for each of the three color channels: red, green, and blue. The hexadecimal values are a translation of the value of the color index for that particular channel (0 - 255), and always comprise two hexadecimal digits. As with the base 10 system, the first digit represents the number of times the base number, in this case 16, goes into a given value (0 - 255) and the second digit represents the remainder. (As an example, in base 10, 10 goes into 35, 3 times with a remainder of 5.) So if the index value for red were 255, to convert that value to a hex value, you would divide 255 by 16 to get 15 with a remainder of 15. 15 is represented in base 16 by the letter F, so the first digit in the hexadecimal pair would be F. To determine the remainder, you would multiply 16 by 15 and subtract the product from the original index value. 15 times 16 equals 240. 255 less 240 is 15, so the remainder is 15, making the second hex value F as well. Therefore, the hex representation of the index value of 255 works out to be FF.

Now that you know how the hex color values are calculated, if you're not too dizzy, we can take a look at how the web-safe colors were determined. Web-safe colors are always and only composed of combinations of the following paired hexadecimal digits: 00, 33, 66, 99, CC, and FF. Here's how it breaks down:

index value	percentage of light	hex value
0	0	00
51	20%	33
102	40%	66
153	60%	99
204	80%	CC
255	100%	FF

Hexadecimal values as they relate to color index and percentage of light. The index value of all the web-safe colors are multiples of 51.

Kinda cool, right? So, any time you see a hex value that has three identical hexadecimal pairs, you know it means the color has equal amounts of red, green, and blue and that, consequently, the color is a shade of gray.

hex value		Red	Green	Blue
#000000		00	00	00
#333333		33	33	33
#666666		66	66	66
#999999		99	99	99
#CCCCCC		CC	CC	CC
#FFFFFF		FF	FF	FF
#FF0000		FF	00	00
#00FF00		00	FF	00
#0000FF		00	00	FF
#FFFF00		FF	FF	00
#FF00FF		FF	00	FF
#00FFFF		00	FF	00

Web-safe colors broken down by color channel.

100% red + 100% green = 100% yellow, etc. (FF means 100%), as you saw in the color model chart in the preceding pages. And so it comes full circle.

Image Resolution and File Size

Another dramatic difference between print and web is the resolution required for the images in the final output. When you send images to press, the image resolution should be no less than 300 ppi (pixels per inch). For the web, resolution of your images should be no less than 72 ppi. As a general rule, if you're creating images for an actual HTML page, their resolution should also be no more than 72 ppi. We'll talk more about output and file optimization at the end of the book, but for now, it's

Note: Just a little trivia: The word pixel is a contraction of the term "PIcture ELement".

important to understand that a constant consideration when designing for the web is the trade-off, or rather the balance, between quality and speed. Since delivery of your content is reliant on electronic transmission, the size of your final file has an inverse relationship with the speed at which it's able to be delivered. While you can pack a high resolution file in an exported SWF or PDF file, this typically adds file overhead that serves to slow delivery and performance without providing any corresponding benefit. The general rule is that, for electronic delivery, you want the most compressed image you can achieve that is still of acceptable quality.

High resolution images can be converted to a lower resolution in the SWF and PDF export process. This makes it feasible, at least theoretically, to design for both print and interactive output at the same time. Because there's a big difference in resolution and color requirements depending upon your final output destination, you'll need to plan accordingly when developing a workflow that includes output to both print and interactive mediums.

Page Orientation and Document Dimensions

The next obvious consideration when designing anything meant to be seen on a computer monitor is page orientation. While print documents most often have a portrait orientation (unless you're designing for devices), your interactive work will most likely have a landscape orientation. This dramatically shifts the balance of the page when conceptualizing your design.

Additionally, you'll need to determine the dimensions of your document pages. To do so, you'll want to take into account the typical screen resolution used by your target audience. As computers have become more commonplace and technology has advanced, there has been a marked trend toward higher screen resolution. Not that many years ago, a typical monitor would have a screen resolution of 800 x 600. At the writing of this book, 1024 x 786 represents the low end of monitor resolution, which more commonly starts at 1280 x 1024 and above. What exactly does this look like in terms of page size?

Three standard screen resolutions and the visual effect of those resolutions as they would appear when displayed on a monitor of the same size.

Screen resolution is expressed in pixels (px). A pixel is essentially a square of color with no inherent dimension of its own. The rectangles in the top row of the diagram on the previous page represent three standard screen resolutions. The rectangles in the bottom row represent the appearance of those screen resolutions on three monitors of the same size. You can see that the text on the monitor with the 1280 x 1024 screen resolution appears much smaller than the text on the one with the resolution of 800 x 600.

The point is, if your target audience is using a screen resolution of 800 x 600, creating a page bigger than that would require them to scroll to see the whole thing. Conversely, if your audience uses a screen resolution of 1680 x 1050, a page that's 800 x 600 will look like a postage stamp on their screens.

Presuming you know who your audience is, how do you determine what monitor resolution they use? This is the million dollar question. Obviously, if you're creating a project for an internal audience, you have a better chance of gathering statistics directly. If you have an existing website, you can frequently get web statistics from a web administrator. In many cases, websites are equipped on the administrative end with the ability to collect information about site visitors: what browser they use, their screen resolution, and their operating system. All this information is useful to inform your design. If you don't have an existing site and have no way to retrieve information specific to your audience, you can use general statistical trends as your guidelines.

A good source of information on user trends is the W3Schools site: http://www.w3schools.com/browsers/default.asp. Keep in mind, however, that the statistics they share have been collected from the traffic to their specific site, and that their visitors are typically a more technically-oriented group than the norm.

At the time of this writing, for delivery to the general public, it's pretty safe to design your project considering a screen resolution of 1024 x 768 as the lowest common denominator. But that doesn't mean you should use those dimensions as your document page size. If your audience will be accessing your content via the web, you need to take into account the browser chrome, as well as the menu bars and browser elements that are part of the container in which your content will be displayed. Browsers typically use more screen real estate at the top of the screen than they do at either side, and to accommodate all the browser bells and whistles, a good page size is somewhere in the range of 900 x 700. However, lots of people design pages over 1000 px wide and have no problems. In other words, without solid statistics, this is not a precise science. For people who have higher-resolution monitors, it's common to have multiple windows open at once, rather than just one page displayed at full screen view. 900 x 700 seems to be a good middle ground to straddle the many possible variables.

Font and Font Size

It used to be conventional wisdom that, on the printed page, serif fonts are easier to read than sans-serif fonts. While the controversy still rages in regard to print, it's pretty solidly accepted that, for general content, sans-serif fonts are preferred for on-screen reading. For small text especially, the low resolution of the screen makes the detail of serif text less intelligible. Serif fonts are fine for headers or typographical accents, but you want to stick with sans-serif fonts for your body text.

Serifs   Sans-serif
          (No serifs)

Serif and sans-serif fonts. Sans-serif font text is easier to road on screen.

What about font size? Well, check back to the monitor resolution diagram on , starting on page 15. The answer is, it depends. Like so many other aspects of designing for web and interactive mediums, there's not one absolute and definitive answer. The recommendation is that you test. In fact, that's the recommendation for any project you create for electronic delivery. Test on multiple computers, multiple operating systems, multiple screen resolutions, multiple browsers. Testing your content is an essential part of designing for web and interactive mediums, and there's just no way around it.

Margins and Bleeds

To start, if you're designing for electronic output only, you have license to forget about margins and bleeds entirely. They can be useful as design guides but, unlike print, with interactive design, whatever you put within the boundary of your page will appear reliably in your finished product. If, however, you want to multi-task your document, whatever margins and/or bleeds you establish for the print end will have no negative impact on your interactive piece.

Interactive Design Guidelines

Certainly, an obvious use of InDesign's interactive capabilities is to bring life to existing print projects, but you can just as easily create purely interactive projects from scratch. Regardless of the starting point, the design of any interactive project demands consideration of the factors that impact the user experience.

The quality of the user experience and the usability of the interactive interface are critical concerns in designing for interactive mediums. There are a number of things that contribute to the quality of this experience some of which we've touched upon already. There's been mention of file size as it influences delivery, and page and font size as they relate to your audience. The colors you choose, the layout of the page, the overall look and feel; all these things, too, are obvious design considerations for interactive design, as they are for a project of any type. Additionally, good interactive design requires attention to information design and information architecture.

The flow of information through your project, and the structure you establish to navigate it, are huge factors in defining the user experience. Unless specifically intended otherwise, the goal is to make the interface as user friendly and transparent as possible. It should be easy for your audience to find their way around visually, and logically, without having to put too much attention on figuring it out. You want them to be able to find what they're looking for quickly and easily.

In service to this objective, before even starting design of the visuals, take some time to think through the intention of the project. Is it informational? Is it for entertainment purposes? What do you want people to come away with? Is there a call to action?

Identify your audience, and then get clear on the content you want to include. The next step is to flow chart and storyboard the project. You can make these steps as detailed and formal as the project demands. You'll find that the effort you invest up front to work things out will reward you well when it comes time for the visual design.

A really valuable technique for working through the details of a project is to create a series of scenario-based case studies. Start with an objective, like finding contact information, and then itemize each step necessary to meet it. Identify the menus used, the buttons clicked, etc. In the process, you will identify the interface elements and the functionality you'll want to build into the project. You'll be surprised by the project requirements you'll expose with this procedural approach, and by how many wrong paths you can avoid by using it. Before getting too far along with filling in the visual details, test a skeletal structure of the project. Test it with people who are unfamiliar with it, to see if they can navigate it effectively. Since it's easy to get too close to a project and to miss otherwise obvious issues in site logic or concept, having outside testers is a really valuable way to get feedback.

If your project has more than one page, you'll need to incorporate some sort of navigation. When designing navigation, make use of the fact that there are certain conventions, certain assumptions, that guide the experience of the audience engaging with your project. If you deviate from these conventions, do so in a way that serves your overall objective. You don't want to burden your audience with figuring things out, when what you really want is for them to retrieve information or take a particular action.

The first rule of navigation is to keep it consistent from page to page; in other words, don't change the location of navigational buttons from one page to the next. You don't want to make your users have to figure things out every time they get to a new page.

By convention, hyperlinks are identified by an underline and the color blue. Navigation bars or links are most often found at the top, bottom, and at either side of an interface (usually the left). Since computer users are generally acclimated to looking for navigation in these locations, it's pretty safe to remove the default underline from such links and to format them with an appearance other than the traditional link blue. If you have links elsewhere in the content, however, think carefully before removing the familiar underline and color. People are accustomed to these identifiers; if you use a different format, you run the risk of losing some of the click-through for which the link was intended.

While dropdown menus are a great way to conserve screen real estate, it's important not to bury critical links where there's a risk they won't be found. Anything important should be easily accessible. Ideally, you want your visitors to be able to access significant site content in two clicks—three at the most.

When using next and previous buttons for page navigation, people expect to find them on the lower right corner of a page, with the next button to the right of the previous button. If you decide to put them somewhere else, be consistent.

Color can be an excellent navigational indicator, providing a visual cue to help in orienting the user. This technique may be familiar from print design, where color is used to distinguish one section of a catalog from the next. Like a catalog, a product site would generally maintain a similar format from one section to another in order to present a consistent overall environment. While you could change the color from one section of a site to another, you'll want to be sure to maintain a consistent framework so your audience can be assured that they're still in the same site.

When there are interface features that aren't obvious, such as clickable elements that trigger pop-ups, for example, include a notation that provides any necessary instructions. Remember, unless the site is deliberately meant to be an explorative experience, you want to give your audience as much assistance as you can to help them have the experience you designed the site to achieve.

Well, that about wraps up the guidelines. Now that you've got a bit of a foundation, it's time to get to know the InDesign tools you'll use to bring your documents to life.

CHAPTER SUMMARY

This chapter provided you with an official introduction to the world of interactive design. You discovered a number of the considerations governing choices related to creating projects for electronic output, including:

- Font choices
- Color models
- Document dimensions
- Monitor resolution
- File size
- Project intent
- Planning a project
- Designing for user experience

Along the way, you learned a lot about color models and color for electronic output including:

- The difference between RGB and CMYK color
- Concepts around color management
- Hexadecimal color and how to interpret it
- Color in print-to-interactive workflow

In considering the user experience, you learned the importance of:

- Consistent navigation
- Using established conventions to inform your design process
- Testing

Now that you've had an orientation, the next step is to get familiar with the tools you'll rely on in your interactive work. Chapter 3 takes you on an extensive tour of the InDesign interface and provides all kinds of ways you can tailor it to the way you work. Whether you're a newbie or a seasoned professional, you're guaranteed to learn something useful and new.

● Chapter 3

THE INTERACTIVE INTERFACE

This chapter will get you cozy with the tools in InDesign that make the magic possible. With two workspaces dedicated to interactive development, there are a plethora of panels to help you bring your projects to life. Once you get familiar, you'll customize the workspace so the necessary tools are right at your fingertips.

The Interactive Workspace

InDesign CS5 is replete with new panels and tools specifically geared toward multimedia and interactive design. In fact, there are two predefined workspaces expressly dedicated to this purpose. In case you're not familiar with workspaces, they are saved arrangements of panels and customized menu settings that make it easy to switch from one category of task to another with only a click. InDesign CS5 comes with eight different task-based workspaces. You can also create your own, tailored perfectly to your needs. In fact, you'll be doing just that after you get a brief tour of the panels in the interactive workspace presets.

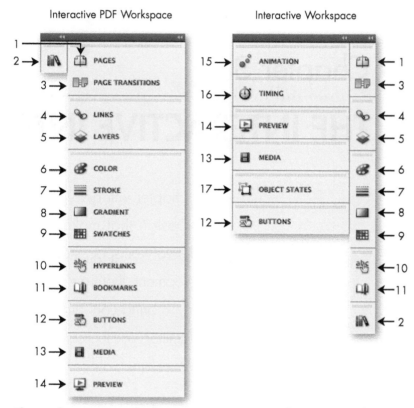

The panel arrangements for the preset Interactive PDF and Interactive workspaces. Click the panel name or icon to expand a panel.

1) Pages.   2) Sample Buttons.   3) Page Transitions.   4) Links.   5) Layers.   6) Color.
7) Stroke.   8) Gradient. 9) Swatches. 10) Hyperlinks.   11) Bookmarks.   12) Buttons.
13) Media.   14) Preview.   15) Animation.   16) Timing.   17) Object States

InDesign CS5 documents can be output to both PDF and SWF. SWF is the output format for Flash, and provides support for InDesign animation, while output to PDF does not. As a result, the three panels that deal with animation—the Animation panel, the Timing panel and the Object States pane—are not included in the Interactive PDF workspace.

There are nine panels dedicated specifically to interactive functions, and what follows is a brief introduction to each of them, in alphabetical order, as they appear in the Interactive section of the Window menu.

Animation Panel

Now you can create animation right in InDesign! From the animation panel, using a wide assortment of provided motion presets, you can animate objects to fade, bounce, zoom, rotate, and much more, simply with the click of a button. A preview window at the top of the panel shows the motion of the preset to help you visually sort through the many preset options. The motion presets in InDesign come directly from Flash, and can be easily interchanged between the two applications. You can even create and save custom presets of your own. To learn what's possible and how to do it, check out Part 3: Animation, starting on page 125.

Animation panel.

Bookmarks panel.

Bookmarks Panel

Bookmarks are essentially internal document links that appear in the Bookmarks tab of Acrobat and Adobe Reader. Each bookmark jumps to a text anchor or a document page. Bookmarks are a PDF-specific feature. Learn more in Bookmarks, starting on page 249.

Buttons Panel

Buttons are the very heart of interactivity in InDesign, and the Buttons panel is where the action is: literally. The Buttons panel enables you to add commands, called *actions*, that allow you to navigate from page to page, open URLs, control animation, and much more. To learn the cool things you can do with buttons and the Buttons panel, check out Part 2: Buttons, starting on page 55. It's *all* about buttons.

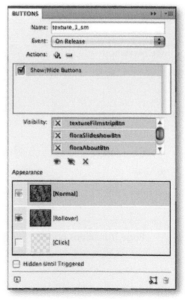

Buttons panel.

Hyperlinks panel.

Hyperlinks Panel

With the Hyperlinks panel, you can create links that jump to other portions of the document, to different documents, and to external websites. Hyperlinks work when exported to both SWF and interactive PDF. For more on hyperlinks, see page 265.

Media panel.

Page Transitions panel.

Media Panel

In addition to adding video files to your InDesign document, you can preview them directly in the Media Panel. The Media panel lets you scrub through your video, and add navigation points that you can later target with button actions. You can also choose a poster to appear on the page when the video isn't on, as well as a controller that appears when it plays. You can add and test audio files too! Video and audio are supported in output to both SWF and PDF. For more on incorporating media into your documents, check out page 233: Adding Media in InDesign.

Object States Panel

With multi-state objects, it's easy to create slide shows, with no limit to the number of slides (or *states*). Each Object State can contain nearly anything you can put on a document page. Unfortunately, though, multi-state objects do not function when exported to PDF. Chapter 10, starting on page 189, is all about multi-state objects.

Object States panel.

Page Transitions

InDesign is great for creating full-screen presentations that work in both SWF and PDF, and page transitions can provide them with a little extra pizazz. The Preview panel lets you choose from 13 pre-built transitions that you can preview in the panel. You can modify both the transition direction and speed, and then apply them to an entire document or to select pages. To see transitions in action, take a look at the Page Transitions chapter starting on page 205.

Preview Panel

With the Preview panel, not only can you *see* what you've created, but buttons work, animations play, and you can even watch included video. The Preview panel lets you view a selection, a spread, or the entire document. An in depth introduction to the Preview panel begins on page 90.

Preview panel.

Timing Panel

The Timing panel works with the Animation panel to keep things in proper order. Use it to change the sequence of your animations, set delays, and group animations to play together. You won't be using this panel except for documents output to SWF, since InDesign animation doesn't translate to Interactive PDF. (But there's a workaround on page 352. You'll start getting familiar with the Timing panel on page 140.

Additional Tools for Interactive Design

There are several additional panels that may not be familiar to you, but that are especially useful when designing for interactivity: the Align, Effects, Object Styles, and Pathfinder panels. You'll also want to get to know Mini Bridge, the Preflight panel, and the Links panel.

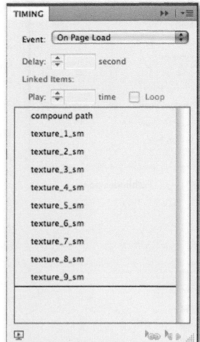

Timing panel.

Align panel.

Align Panel

While InDesign's smart guides are tremendously useful, there are times when only the Align panel can do the job of aligning or distributing multiple objects. The Align panel is nested with the Pathfinder and Transform panels. Go to Window > Object & Layout > Align to open it.

Effects Panel

The Effects panel provides an at-a-glance view of the effects applied to an object, its stroke, fill, and text. It enables you to set opacity and blending mode, isolate effects, and apply a knockout to an object group right in the panel. It also provides easy access to the Effects dialog. While you can also get to the Effects dialog through the Control panel, the visual feedback from the Effects panel makes it easier to see the details of what's going on.

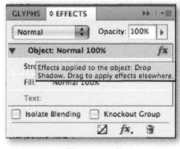

Effects panel.

Object Styles panel.

Object Styles Panel

The Object Styles panel enables the capture of all manner of object attributes that you can then apply at the click of a button. Object styles can incorporate Paragraph styles, drop shadows, Frame Fitting options, and more. You'll find them invaluable in maintaining consistent appearances for buttons and other interface elements.

Pathfinder panel.

Pathfinder Panel

The Pathfinder panel is a great aid in modifying paths and creating shapes that would otherwise be nearly impossible to draw. Its convenient all-in-one interface puts tools for paths, points, and shapes right at your fingertips. The Pathfinder panel is found under Window > Object & Layout > Pathfinder. Learn more about the Pathfinder panel on page 155.

Preflight Panel

For print or interactive design, the Preflight panel is a truly awesome tool for helping you keep your documents error free. It's absolutely indispensable for print work, but also provides a solid benefit for working with documents destined for the screen. It can help you

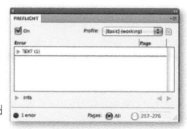

Preflight panel.

keep track of overset text, image resolution, disproportionate scaling, and so much more. What's best about the Preflight panel is that it's dynamic, providing you with feedback as you go, so you don't end up with a host of unpleasant surprises when it's time to output your file. Check out page 37 in this chapter to learn more.

Links Panel

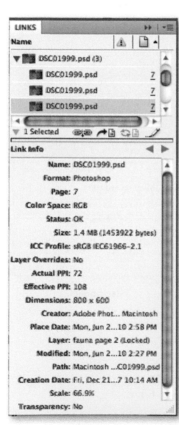

Links panel.

With the release of InDesign CS4, the Links panel evolved from being a simple access point for managing placed files to an at-a-glance source of important information. Clicking a link displays a wealth of file info, including the page and layer on which the file was placed, content dimensions, effective resolution, color space, scaling percentage, and more. Learn more about the Links panel on page 40 of this chapter.

Mini Bridge

A discussion of InDesign panels wouldn't be complete without mention of Mini Bridge. Now you can visually browse for files, sort them, filter them, place them and more, without ever leaving InDesign. Bridge has always been a powerful (and under-used) tool for accessing and organizing files. Now a good bit of that power is harnessed and accessible from within InDesign. Learn to use Mini Bridge in the exercise on page 46 in this chapter.

Mini Bridge.

Setting Up a Custom Workspace

Now that you've gotten a feel for some of the tools you'll be using, let's take a couple minutes to customize the workspace and make it even more conducive to the work of interactive design.

Custom Interactive workspace.

You'll be using the Pages panel to navigate from page to page, and full access to the Layers panel will be essential to select and reorganize objects in your document. You'll also be relying heavily on the Buttons panel. We've found it helpful to stack these three panels in a column of their own in the panel dock so they're always readily available. We've also found it convenient to position the Preview panel in a column to the left of the other panels, and to add the Align and Pathfinder panels to that column. It's great to have the Object Styles panel readily available, and you'll want to have the Character and Paragraph Styles panels close at hand as well. If you'll be doing a lot with Tables, you might as well add the Table and Cell Styles panels to the party. With so many panels in so little space, you can collapse most of them down to icons to conserve your screen real estate. The following exercise shows you how to set things up and get organized.

Exercise 3.1: Setting Up a Custom Workspace

To complete this exercise, you'll begin with the Interactive workspace and then customize the panel selection and arrangement.

1. Before we get started, if you're working on a Mac, you might want to turn on the Application Frame to enclose all the application interface elements in one moveable, scalable window. To do this, go to Window > Application Frame. You'll then be able to drag the application window, and all the tools and panels will travel with it. Also, if you click your desktop, your panels will still show. Without the Application Frame turned on, clicking outside InDesign makes the panels disappear. You can also find the Application Frame in Photoshop & Illustrator.

2. At the right of the Application bar, at the very top of your screen, you should see the word "Essentials". This is the default workspace when you first open InDesign. Click the down arrow next to the word and choose Interactive (not Interactive PDF) from the list of workspaces.

   When the workspace opens, you'll notice that one column of panels is collapsed to icons only, and the other displays both icons and the panel names. You're going to become very familiar with the interactive panels and their icons, so, in the interest of conserving space, you'll collapse the expanded column to show icons only.

3. Position your cursor over the left edge of the expanded panel column. When you see the double-sided arrow, click and hold down the mouse, and drag to the right until the words in the column disappear. Keep dragging until the column snaps to the width of the icons.

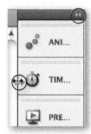

Panels can be expanded and collapsed by dragging from their left edge. To open all the panels in a column, click the double arrow at the upper right of the column. To open an individual panel, click its icon.

Next, you'll drag the Pages and Layers panels into a new column.

4. Click and drag the Pages panel icon ( ) to the left of the existing panel columns. When you see a blue line at the left edge of the column, release the mouse to dock the Pages panel in a column of its own.

To dock a panel in a new location, drag it to its new position and then release the mouse when you see a blue line.

5. Drag the Buttons panel right below the Pages panel icon and release it when you see the blue line between the two panels.

6. Drag the Layers panel icon below the Buttons panel icon and release the mouse when the blue line appears between them.

The stacked Pages panel, Buttons panel, and Layers panel.

7. Click the double arrow at the upper right of the panel column you just created to expand it.

If you expect to have a large number of pages in your document, you may want to maximize the number of pages you can see in the Pages panel without needing to scroll.

8. From the Pages panel menu (the ▾☰ button at the upper right corner of the panel) choose Panel Options, and deselect the Show Vertically checkbox in the Pages section of the panel.

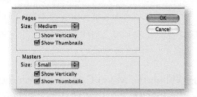

To customize the Pages panel display, choose Panel Options from the panel menu.

9. Drag the Preview panel just to the left of the Pages panel and drop it when you see the blue line at the right edge of the Preview panel.

10. Go to Window > Object & Layout > Align. The Align panel is grouped with the Pathfinder and the Transform panels. Drag and dock the Align panel only, directly below the Preview panel icon.

11. Drag the Pathfinder panel over the Align panel icon and drop it when you see a blue outline around the icon. This will group the Align and Pathfinder panels so, when the panel opens, they will be accessible through separate tabs in the same panel. Since you'll be able to do your transformations from the Control panel, you can close the Transform panel.

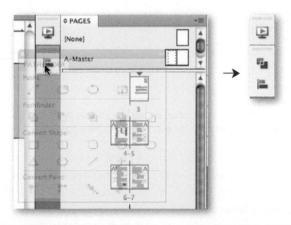

When you group panels in the dock, the panel icons have no dividing line between them. They appear as tabs when the panel is opened.

12. Go to Window > Styles > Object Styles and then drag the Object Styles panel in-between the Swatches and Hyperlinks panels. Do the same for the Paragraph and Character Styles panels, and then add the Table and Cell Styles panels if you'd like.

The suggested arrangement for the first column of stacked panels in the panel dock. The panel sequence from top to bottom is as follows: 1) Page Transitions. 2) Links. 3) Color. 4) Stroke. 5) Gradient. 6) Swatches. 7) Table Styles. 8) Cell Styles. 9) Paragraph Styles. 10) Character Styles. 11) Object Styles. 12) Effects. 13) Hyperlinks. 14) Bookmarks.

13. Go to Window > Effects and dock the Effects panel just below the Object Styles panel.

Note: You can change the default Display Performance setting from the Display Performance category of the Preferences dialog.

By default, InDesign uses a low quality display for placed files in order to conserve system resources and render the files more quickly. You may, on occasion, need to evaluate the quality and detail of a placed file, or, alternatively, choose to speed up the page processing by displaying only placeholders. The appearance of placed files on the page is controlled by the Display Performance settings, which are accessed either through a contextual menu or from the View or Object menus. To make the command easier to find, you'll highlight the menu item as part of the saved workspace.

14. Go to Edit > Menus. When the Menu Customization dialog opens, leave Category set to Application Menus and click the arrow to the left of the word "Object" in the Applications Menu Command section of the dialog.

15. Scroll down until you see the words "Display Performance" and then click the word "None" to the right of the eye icon. This will display the menu highlight colors. Select a color and click OK to close the dialog. Go to the Object menu to see the Display Performance menu item highlighted in the color you selected.

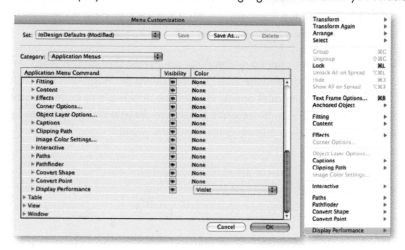

The Menu Customization dialog lets you set the visibility and highlight color for every menu in the application.

The Menu Customization dialog makes it possible to assign colors to every menu in the application, and also to control menu visibility. Unless you're a very advanced InDesign user, familiar with the function of every menu item, we strongly encourage you to leave all menu items visible. There's no better way to learn the application than by digging into each of the available menus and tools. If you can't see them, you'll have no way of knowing what options are available. If you do decide to hide some menu items, you can still access them through the Show All Menu Items command at the bottom of any menu with hidden items. Alternatively, you can choose Window > Workspace > Show Full Menus to show all menus for the active workspace.

16. Last but not least, you'll add Mini Bridge to your customized workspace. Go to Window > Mini Bridge and then dock it below the Align and Pathfinder panels.

17. From the workspace switcher dropdown menu, or from Window > Workspace, choose New Workspace. Name your workspace and check the Panel Locations and Menu Customization checkboxes. Name the workspace "Interactive Modified."

Custom workspaces can include both panel locations and customized menus.

As you become more comfortable with the interface and your own workflow, you will no doubt find certain panels and panel arrangements to be more convenient than others. InDesign retains the changes you make to a workspace until you select Reset (workspace name) from the Workspace dropdown. To redefine the existing workspace with new panel locations, just re-save it with the existing name.

Setting Application Preferences and Defaults

You can further customize your experience with InDesign by redefining application defaults to accommodate your preferences. If you set your preferences with no document open, any tool or menu setting you establish becomes the default for all new documents. You can set default preferences in the other Creative Suite applications in the same way. If you have a document open when you change preferences or tools, most of your setting changes will affect only that one document.

If you have a favorite font, this is the time to select it. Just select the Type tool and enter whatever formatting you prefer in both the Character and Paragraph sections of the Control panel. All the settings you choose will become the default definition applied to new text, including such things as Paragraph Rules, Keep Options, and Hyphenation.

The same principle holds true for fill and stroke color and weight, object reference point, margins and columns, drop shadows, and gradient colors; in short, any settings that you can set without an open document. For example, adding frequently used colors with no document open makes them available in all new documents.

Setting Preferences in the Preferences Dialog

While there are at least three ways to do almost everything in Adobe applications, the Preferences dialog gives you access to a whole set of controls that are, in most cases, available nowhere else in the interface. Found under the Edit menu in Windows and the InDesign menu on Mac, the Preferences dialog is a parent-child type menu with categories on the left that relate to controls on the right. While it may appear a little overwhelming at first, and the default settings for a good number of the Preferences will never change, there are a couple settings that are worth adjusting to ease your workflow.

Exercise 3.2: Working with the Preferences Dialog

In this exercise, you'll enable drag and drop text editing, turn on spell check, set the units of measure for your documents, and learn a very cool way to use the dynamic spelling feature to enhance efficiency.

For text editing, being able to drag and drop text is an incredible efficiency enhancement. Since it's not turned on by default, you'll enable it now in the Preferences dialog.

1. With no document open, go to Edit > Preferences (Windows) or InDesign > Preferences (Mac), and select Type from the left column in the Preferences dialog. Then, in the Drag and Drop Text Editing section of the dialog, check the Enable in Layout View checkbox.

You can set up drag and drop text editing in the Type section of the Preferences dialog.

If you'll be working with a lot of copy in InDesign, dynamic spelling, and possibly auto-correction, can be very useful too. If you've used spell check in other applications, InDesign's spell check will make you feel right at home.

2. Still in the Preferences dialog, to turn on spell check, select Spelling in the column at the left of the dialog. Check the Enable Dynamic Spelling checkbox. Then, choose the colors you'd like to use to indicate misspelled words, uncapitalized words, uncapitalized sentences, and repeated words.

Autocorrection provides an additional spelling aid with its own dedicated Preferences category. If there are words you routinely misspell, you can add them to a customized dictionary. But, you can stretch Autocorrect to become an even more powerful efficiency tool for writing technical terms, company names, or any long words or phrases that you use regularly. Here's how.

Note: Misspelled words, uncapitalized words, uncapitalized sentences, and repeated words are indicated by a squiggly underline in whatever color you set when you enable dynamic spelling in the Preferences dialog.

3. Select Autocorrect from the left column of the Preferences dialog. Check the Enable Autocorrect checkbox and click the Add button. In the Misspelled Word text field, type an easy-to-remember abbreviation for the word or phrase you would like to be able to enter more quickly. For example: ASI (for Adobe Systems Incorporated).

4. In the Correction field, type the full word or phrase you would like InDesign to enter automatically. Then click OK to close the Add to Autocorrect List dialog. For example: Adobe Systems Incorporated.

Note: To remove a word from the Autocorrect word list, select the word and click the Remove button at the lower right of the dialog. To change an existing word in the list, select it and click the Edit button. Make your changes in the Edit Autocorrect List dialog and then click OK to close. To delete the entire list, select the first word, hold down the Shift key, and click the last word. Then click the Remove button.

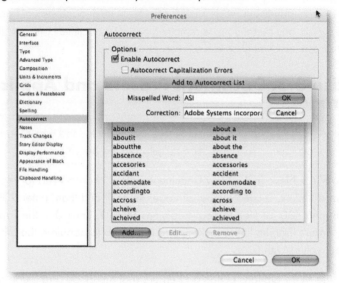

By being just a little clever with the Autocorrect feature, you can get InDesign to enter text for you automatically.

The next time you want to enter the word or phrase, just type the abbreviation you entered in the Correction field. InDesign will fill in the long version for you. Pretty cool, yes?

The spelling controls can also be accessed through the Edit menu and the text-specific context menu. To access the context menu, Right-click/Ctrl-click with the Type tool active in a text frame. From the Spelling menu option, you can choose Check Spelling, Dynamic Spelling, or Autocorrect. You can also access the User Dictionary, or, if applicable, the dictionary specific to the active document.

From the Preferences dialog, you can set the default unit of measure for your document to points, picas, inches, centimeters, ciceros, agates, pixels, or even a custom setting. For interactive design, the obvious choice is pixels. Truth is, pixels and points are effectively the same measure, since there are 72 of either in an inch (at least according to Adobe Postscript). (In actual typesetting, there are 72.27 points per inch and, in fact, the Units & Increments dialog even offers a Traditional points/inch option that is true to that measure.)

5. From the left column of the Preferences dialog, select Units & Increments. Choose Inches from both the Horizontal and Vertical dropdowns.

6. Click OK to close the Preferences dialog.

Creating a Document Preset

A couple minutes here and a couple minutes there can add up to hours and hours over the course of a project. Every little thing that cuts the time spent on routine tasks can result in huge long-term savings. Document presets fall into this time-saving category, capturing all the New Document settings in named and reusable presets that includes the number of pages, page size, margin and column settings, ruler units, bleed, and slug. You can also choose from either a print or web intent, which automatically populates the Swatches panel with either CMYK or RGB colors, respectively. Any presets you create stay in the preset list until you delete them or delete your application preferences. Also, any preset you use remains the default document preset in the New Document dialog, until you choose a different preset.

Exercise 3.3: Document Presets and Application Preferences

In this exercise, you'll set up a document preset, learn how to load and export saved presets, and learn how to set application defaults with no document open.

1. Go to File > New. In the New Document dialog, choose Web for the document Intent. Leave Number of Pages set to 1 and then, enter 900 for Width and 700 for Height. Leave columns set to 1. Enter 0 in the Top Margin field, ensure that the link is locked, and press Tab to populate the other margin values with 0.

2. Click the More Options button and ensure that the Bleed and Slug values are set to 0.

3. Click the Save Preset button and name it "Web 900 x 700". Click OK to close the Save Preset dialog, and then click OK to create your new document.

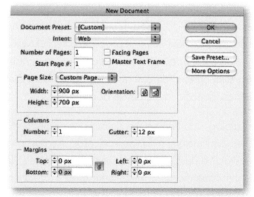

You can create a new document and save a document preset in one step from the New Document dialog.

Note: For print documents, if you need to set a bleed, press the More Options button at the right of the New Document dialog.

You don't need to open a document in order to create a document preset. InDesign has a Document Preset dialog where you can create, save, and edit presets or load any number of saved presets from an external file. In the next step, you'll load a collection of web presets from an external file.

As with other advertising media, web ads are most often sold in conventional sizes. The provided presets are representative of the most popular ad dimensions.

4. Go to File > Document Presets > Define. Click the Load button and browse to the chapter_3_exercises folder. Select the **web_banner_presets.dcst** file and click Open to add a collection of the most common web banner sizes to the presets window. Click OK to close the Document Presets dialog.

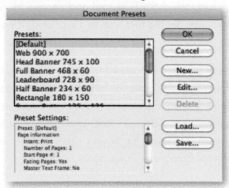

The Document Presets dialog makes it possible to create, save, load, edit, and remove document presets.

5. It's easy to save multiple presets in a collection you can share. If the presets you want to save are listed consecutively in the Document Presets dialog, click the first preset, hold down the Shift key, and click the last preset to select everything in between. (Hold the Ctrl/Command key and click to select non-consecutive files.) Then click Save, name your document, and click OK. The saved preset file will have a DCST extension.

The Document Setup dialog, which looks nearly identical to the New Document dialog, enables you to change the number of pages in an open document, their orientation and dimension, and their bleed and slug. Text frames already on your document pages won't be affected, though, unless you have Layout Adjustment turned on. (For more on Layout Adjustment, see page 290.) The settings you enter in the Document Setup dialog with no document open become the settings that appear in the New Document dialog when the [Default] document preset is selected.

6. With your document still open, go to File > Document Setup. Note that this dialog enables you to enter document intent and page dimensions of your choosing. Values entered with no documents open become the new default settings. Click OK to close the dialog without making any changes.

The Margins and Columns dialog enables you to change the margin settings and the number of columns on a document page or a master page. When you change the margins and columns on a master page, new pages you add to the document that are based on that master will reflect the new settings. As with Document Setup, existing text frames won't be affected unless Layout Adjustment is on. If you set Columns and Margins with no document open, new documents you open will use those settings when the [Default] document preset is active in the New Document dialog.

7. Go to Layout > Margins and Columns and, when the dialog opens, ensure the link icon is linked.

8. For the Top Margin, enter 0 and then press Tab to populate the other fields. Take note that the default number of columns is also set from this dialog. Click OK to close and commit your settings.

9. To set the default font, select the Type tool and choose Myriad Pro from the Font Family dropdown. Set the font size to 12 pt and, if necessary, set the font style to Regular.

   Kerning is the space between a pair of characters. If the kerning is bad (we're looking at you, free fonts), the brain has to work harder to read each letter or word. Optical Kerning is an important and under-used feature that enhances readability by making letter spacing cleaner and more proportional. You can set Optical Kerning as the default for all your type by redefining the [Basic Paragraph] style in the Paragraph Styles panel.

10. To set Optical Kerning, go to Window > Styles > Paragraph Styles or click ▣ in the long first column of the panel dock.

11. In the Paragraph styles panel, double-click [Basic Paragraph]. When the Paragraph Style Options dialog opens, select Basic Character Formats from the left of the window and then select Optical from the Kerning dropdown. Click OK to close the dialog.

Customizing the Control Panel

As part of your customization efforts, you could also choose to hide a number of the controls on the Control panel. Again, unless you are a very experienced user, and are certain that you don't want or need ready access to particular tools, we strongly recommend that you leave them showing. Then take some time to learn what they do.

The Customize Control Panel dialog is actually a good place for that learning to begin. It identifies each control by name, thereby providing a term that you can investigate further in InDesign's Help application. To open the dialog, choose the Customize option from the Control panel menu. Expand the categories and make note of any controls that are unfamiliar. It's a good bet that even if you're a seasoned InDesign user, you'll find things in those lists you didn't know existed.

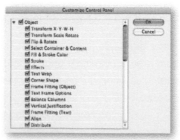

The Customize Control Panel dialog is a good place to familiarize yourself with all the Control panel controls.

Arranging Document Windows

You can have InDesign arrange multiple documents for you from the Arrange option of the Window panel, or the Arrange documents button on the Application Bar.

While not a persisting preference, you can also customize the way multiple documents are displayed in the application window. By default, multiple documents open in tabs that you can reorder by dragging. The tabs can also be dragged away from the tab bar to float in an independent window. You can then add additional documents to the floating window. Each document you add will have its own tab as part of the new document group.

Note: To close the windows for all open documents, press Shift+Ctrl+Alt+W/ Shift+Command+Option+W.

While you can manually arrange the windows, there are some handy controls you can use to automatically arrange things for you. Go to Window > Arrange or click the Arrange Documents button on the Application Bar to choose an arrangement.

The available window configurations in the selection panel will depend on the number of open documents. Just click an available layout to rearrange your documents. To put all the files back into one window, go to Window > Arrange > Consolidate All or choose Consolidate All (▦) from the Arrange Windows selection panel (▦ ▼).

Customizing the Preflight Panel for Interactivity

Whatever work you're doing in InDesign, whether it be for print or for web, the objective is to smooth the workflow and make it as efficient and effortless as possible. The Preflight tool is great in that it can be set up to give you dynamic feedback as you develop your document. The next exercise explores some of the capabilities of the Preflight panel, and walks you through establishing settings tailored specifically to interactive design.

Exercise 3.4: Customizing the Preflight Panel

1. With the document open from the previous exercise, click the down arrow next to the Preflight Error Indicator at the lower left of the document window. Choose Define Profiles from the Preflight menu.

Access the Preflight panel and the Define Profiles dialog through the Preflight menu at the bottom left of the document window.

Live Preflight is active for all documents unless you deliberately turn it off. The default profile is set to detect missing, modified, and inaccessible links, overset text, missing fonts, and unresolved caption variables. While having live feedback to inform you of these things is helpful, it's only the beginning of what the Preflight panel has to offer.

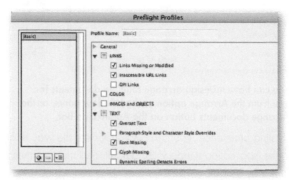

Live Preflight dynamically checks your document against criteria you select.

There are many alerts you can set in the Preflight panel, depending on the requirements of your document. For purposes of this exercise, you'll add just a few of the more critical settings to enhance the default preflight profile.

2. Expand the Images and Objects section of the panel by clicking the arrow at its left, and check the Image Resolution checkbox.

3. When you try to change the default settings, you'll be prompted to save the changes to a new profile. Click OK and name the new profile "Interactive." Note that the list of saved profiles appears on the left of the dialog.

You can set Preflight Profile settings to check for a minimum resolution of 72 ppi and non-proportional scaling.

4. Check the Image Resolution checkbox and enter 72 as the minimum image resolution for each color mode option. Check the Non-Proportional Scaling of Placed Object checkbox to match the image above.

5. Scroll down to the Text section of the dialog, leave the defaults, and check the checkboxes for Glyph Missing and Dynamic Spelling Detects Errors. You may also choose to add a warning for minimum font size and non-proportional type scaling.

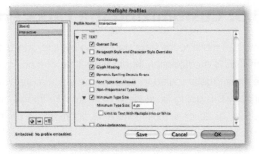

**Text settings in a preflight profile can alert you to missing
fonts and glyphs and also check for spelling errors.**

6. Scroll down to the Document section and check the Blank pages checkbox.

7. When you've finished entering your settings, click OK to save the profile.

   To set a preflight profile as the default for new documents, with no document
   open, go to Window > Output > Preflight to open the Preflight panel. Choose
   Preflight Options from the Preflight panel menu, and then choose your saved
   profile from the Working Profile dropdown. Leave the remaining default settings
   and click OK to close the Preflight Options dialog.

You can change the default preflight profile from the Preflight Options dialog.

Customizing the Links Panel

The Links panel works in concert with the Preflight panel to help you keep on top
of any potential problems with placed files. While the Preflight panel provides an
alert when there's an issue, the Links panel often provides specific detail as to what
caused the error.

Clicking an item in the Links panel displays all manner of metadata (data about
the file) in the panel's bottom pane. The best part of the panel though, is that you
can customize it to display *any* of that metadata in the panel columns. Then, at-a-
glance, you can determine whether your linked images have the necessary image
resolution, whether they are proportionally scaled, what color space they use, and
so much more.

The next exercise walks you through customization of the Links panel.

Exercise 3.5: Customizing the Links Panel

The first adjustment you'll make to the Links panel display is to add a column to show Effective Resolution. This is a calculation that multiplies the original image resolution by the percentage the image is scaled to arrive at the actual output resolution. For the web, any value under 72 is going to create a problem with image quality. If you see that an image has two resolution values in the Links panel, this is an indication that the image has been non-proportionally scaled.

The Links panel can also provide an at-a-glance view of image dimensions and scaling percentages, as well as object color space. Additionally, it can also show the page and layer on which placed content occurs, making it easier to locate. The Links panel can do all of this for you and more.

1. Go to Window > Links or click the 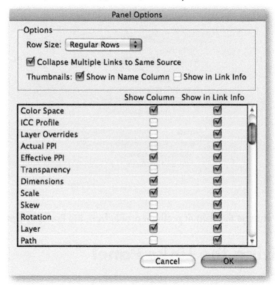 icon in the panel dock to open the Links panel.

2. Choose Panel Options from the panel menu. When the dialog opens, leave the default settings and, in the Show Column, check the checkboxes for Color Space, Effective PPI, Dimension, Scale, and Layer. Click OK to close the dialog.

You can set a wide range of information to display in the Links panel through the Panel Options dialog.

Now that you've set the panel preferences, you'll adjust the columns to better see the information.

3. At the top of the panel, position your cursor over one of the lines dividing the columns. When the cursor changes to a double-sided arrow, drag to adjust the column width. You can also click a column header to sort the column contents. For example, you can click the Name header to sort the linked files alphabetically and numerically. Click again to switch between ascending and descending order.

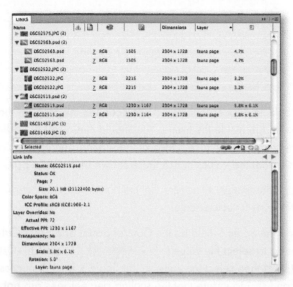

The Links panel: When a document contains multiple instances of the same file, they are grouped under the file name. Twirl down the arrow to see the information for each file instance.

Exercise 3.6: Correcting Preflight Errors

1.   Open **ex3_6_start.indd** and save it as ex3_6.indd.

The Interactive profile you developed in the previous exercise has been embedded in the file. Look at the Preflight Error indicator at the bottom left of the screen and note that multiple errors are present in the document.

2.   Double-click the red error indicator at the bottom left of your document window to open the Preflight panel, twirl down the arrow for Images and Objects, and note that there are two issues with the problem object: non-proportional scaling and resolution. Twirl down the arrow for Image Resolution and double-click the file name to select the image and jump to its location in the document.

3.   With the image selected, open the Links panel.

The link is highlighted in the panel and you can see that the effective resolution of the image is 51 x 50. There are two resolution values, one for the horizontal and one for the vertical. This is additional confirmation that the image has been scaled non-proportionally. You can fix the resolution issue by exchanging the linked file for one that meets your resolution requirements, but you'll need to fix the scaling issue manually.

4.   Click the Relink button ( ) at the bottom of the Links panel and browse to the chapter_3_exercises folder. Select **CostaRicaProvinces.psd** and click Open to replace the existing file with a higher resolution image.

A look in the Links panel confirms that the new file has an effective resolution of at least 106, but the scaling issue is still unresolved. This next bit is a little tricky, in that the scaling percentages for the object that appears on the Control panel show 100% for both Width and Height. How can this be when you have multiple indicators that the object is non-proportionally scaled? Well, the dimensions and scale shown on the Control panel relate to the object *frame*, rather than the placed content. It's the scaling of the content that needs to be corrected.

Note: Be sure that when you double-click, you click the image and not the green map overlays.

5. With the Selection tool, double-click the ocean in the map on the page to access the image inside the frame. You should see a red bounding box line around the image. Now take a look at the scaling percentages on the Control panel to see that the values match those shown in the Links panel.

   For this particular image, it happens that the horizontal scale needs to be adjusted to match the correct vertical scale.

6. Click inside the Scale Y field on the Control panel and press Ctrl+A/ Command+A to select the value (🔢 ⬍ 67.795% ⬍). Press Ctrl+C/Command+C to copy it, and then select the value in the Scale X field. If necessary, click the link icon (🔗) to ensure that the scaling percentages are **not** constrained to scale proportionally. Press Ctrl+V/Command+V to paste the value in the Scale X field, and press Enter/Return to commit your change. Check the Scale and Effective PPI values in the Links panel to see that, now, they each display only one value. Check the Preflight panel to see that the Images and Objects errors have disappeared.

   You still have a couple text errors to correct to make the document error-free.

7. In the Preflight panel, twirl down the Text arrow and then the arrow for Overset text. Click the blue 1 to the right of the first Text Frame error. This is the page number where the error occurs; clicking it will select the overset text frame in your document. Note the red + sign at the lower right corner of the frame that indicates the overset text.

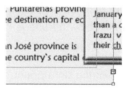

A red plus sign at the lower right edge of a text frame indicates that the frame is not large enough to display all the text in the frame.

8. With the Selection tool, position your cursor over the center resize handle along the bottom of the frame. When the double-sided vertical arrow appears, drag down until the last line of text fits in the frame and the + sign disappears. Note that the first Text Frame entry in the Preflight panel disappears as well.

9. In the Preflight panel, double-click the remaining Text Frame item. Then, with the Selection tool, drag the lower right corner of the selected text frame to the right to widen it. Another error bites the dust.

Unfortunately, the Dynamic Spelling Problem error in the Preflight panel is a notification alert only, and does not link directly to the trouble spots in the document. Not a problem: you can locate the issues easily enough using the Check Spelling command.

Before doing so, however, you'll set some preferences to detect issues with spelling and repeated words, and to ignore other error types.

10. In Windows, go to Edit > Preferences > Spelling; on a Mac, go to InDesign > Preferences > Spelling. In the Preferences dialog, if necessary, deselect the checkboxes for Uncapitalized Words and Uncapitalized Sentences. If it's not already checked, check the Enable Dynamic Spelling checkbox and click OK to close the dialog.

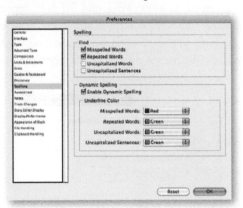

You can customize the spelling preferences to determine the type of errors detected by the Dynamic Spelling feature.

Note: The interactive layouts you'll be working with are likely to have an assortment of buttons using lowercase names. Deselecting Uncapitalized Words and Uncapitalized Sentences from the Spelling Preferences will give you fewer false misspelling indicators.

11. To detect and correct the spelling issue(s) in the document, go to Edit > Spelling, and choose Check Spelling (Ctrl+I/Command+I). When the Check Spelling dialog opens, ensure that Document (not story) is selected from the Search dropdown. Click Start.

12. When the first misspelled word appears, choose "volcanoes" from the Suggested Corrections list, and then click Change. Change the next word to "characteristics" and then click the Done button to close the dialog. Save and close the file.

Note: You can also access the Spelling commands through the context menu when the blinking Type tool cursor is active in a text frame. Just Right-click/Ctrl-click to access the menu.

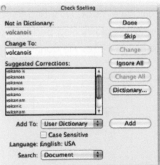

The Check Spelling dialog enables you to check spelling in the remainder of the active Story, the entire Story, the Document or All Documents.

Working with Mini Bridge

Before the release of Creative Suite 5, Bridge was (and actually still is) a *great*, but largely undiscovered, stand-alone application that shipped with the Creative Suite. Like Windows Explorer or File Browser on steroids, Bridge lets you visually browse much more than just image files. You can preview multi-page PDFs and multi-page InDesign files (in Bridge CS5), native Photoshop and Illustrator files, video, audio, 3D files, SWF, FLV, and F4V files, as well as most files supported by the version of QuickTime that's on your computer. But Bridge does way more than browse files. It's also a user-friendly interface for keywording, filtering, sorting, and batch processing. In fact, you can use Bridge to batch rename files of any type, even Word docs! Bridge also contains a sophisticated image processing application called Camera Raw for non-destructive individual and batch correction of RAW, JPEG, and TIFF files. Impressive list of credentials, yes? Hopefully impressive enough to inspire you to learn more. Choose InDesign Help from the Help menu and when the Adobe Community Help window opens, choose Bridge from the Search dropdown. It's worth your time to check it out.

You can search Adobe Community Help for Help on any of the Creative Suite applications including Bridge.

That said, Mini Bridge harnesses a good bit of the power of Bridge and brings it right into the InDesign (Photoshop and InCopy) interface. Bridge and Mini Bridge communicate to keep thumbnails and file data synchronized. It's a short trip to Bridge if you want access to its more robust capabilities, but Mini Bridge lets you browse, filter, sort and batch, and choose from a variety of ways to view your files.

To open Mini Bridge, go to Window > Mini Bridge or click the icon that you added to the 4th column of your Panel dock. Mini Bridge opens to its Home page. From there, you can set preferences for launching Bridge and for the panel appearance. The Browse Files button makes the connection with Bridge that generates the panel thumbnails.

The Mini Bridge Home page is where you set preferences and make the connection to Bridge.

You can place files into your InDesign file either through the Place command in the Mini Bridge Tools menu or by simply dragging the file(s). Dragging a file will either load the Place cursor, or, if you drag over an existing empty frame, will place the file.

Mini Bridge is actually composed of multiple components: the main Content area is complemented by the optional display of the Path Bar, Navigation Pod, and Preview Pod. Access the appearance controls from the Panel View button (▦) at the upper right of the panel.

The View button (▦) at the lower right of the panel lets you choose from four different content views: Thumbnails, Filmstrip, Details, and List. Ratings and labels established in Bridge are visible in all but Filmstrip view, and can be used as criteria by which to sort and filter files.. Details view shows file information including creation and modification date, file size and file type.

You can choose from 4 views of the Content panel: Thumbnails, Filmstrip, Details and List.

By far the coolest feature of Mini Bridge is that it can show you a virtual collection of all the files linked to any selected InDesign document. If you've ever been at a loss to remember where you stashed a particular image, but you *do* remember the name of an InDesign file where you used it, just find that document in Mini Bridge, Right-click/ Ctrl-click and choose Show Linked Files. Mini Bridge will deliver the files for your convenience, in one neat little window.

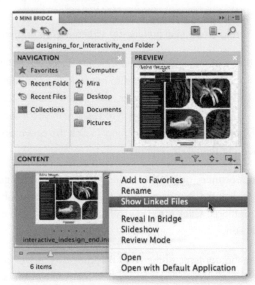

Mini Bridge can display a virtual collection of all the files linked to any InDesign document you select.

Note: You can initiate batch processing and other automated tasks in Photoshop through the Mini Bridge Tools menu. Select one or more documents, click the Tools button, and then choose a task from the Photoshop submenu.

As with most things, the best way to get to know Mini Bridge is to use it. In the next exercise, you'll get a feel for what it can do.

Exercise 3.7: Working with Mini Bridge

1. If you've not already added Mini Bridge to the panel dock, go to Window > Mini Bridge and dock it below the Preview panel.

2. If you haven't used Mini Bridge before, it will open to its Home page. If you've already been using it, click the Home Page button (🏠) at the upper left of the panel to go there.

3. Click the Settings button (📠) and when the new pane appears, notice the Browse Files button (📠) at the upper right of the screen. This button provides one-click access to the browsing window from any other screen in the panel. Click on the words "Bridge Launching" to open the preferences dialog.

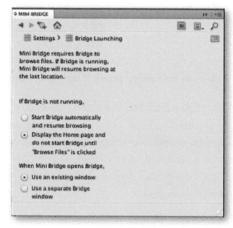

Bridge Launching preferences screen of Mini Bridge.

4. Read the setting options and leave the defaults. Click the Settings breadcrumb in the path bar at the top of the panel to return to the previous screen (📠 Settings > 📠 Bridge Launching). If you don't see the Settings breadcrumb (because the panel is not wide enough to display it) you'll see a down arrow to the left of the words "Bridge Launching". Click the down arrow to open the popup menu, and then click Settings.

5. Click on Appearance, adjust the settings in the Appearance screen as desired, and click the Previous button (◀) at the upper left of the screen to return to Settings. Click the Browse Files button (📠) to open the browsing screen.

6. To better see the contents of the Mini Bridge pods, hover over the left edge of the panel. When the cursor changes to a double-sided arrow, drag to the left to widen the panel. To better see the files displayed in the Navigation pod, hover over the bar between it and the Preview pod. Then drag the bar when the cursor changes to a double-sided arrow.

7. From the second column of the Navigation pod, click the location where you've saved the exercise files. For example, My Documents/Documents or Desktop. You'll see the folder hierarchy appear above the Navigation pane with each folder name separated by a **>**. Click the rightmost **>** to display a list of subfolders. Select the appropriate sequence of subfolders to browse to the **chapter_3_exercises** > **links** folder.

Click the rightmost **>**, and then select from the list of subfolders to navigate through the file hierarchy.

When the links folder is open, you should see a notation at the bottom left of the panel indicating that the folder contains 14 items.

8. Select Grid Lock from the View Button (⊞▾) menu at the bottom of the Content pod. This will ensure that no matter how small Mini Bridge gets, the display will always show complete thumbnails. Drag the slider at the bottom of the Content pod as far to the left as possible, so all the thumbnails fit in the window. If Mini Bridge is too small, mouse over its lower left corner and drag down and to the left to enlarge it. You can also drag the handles (≡) on the dividers between the pods to adjust their size.

Mini Bridge with Grid Lock turned on to display full image thumbnails.

9. Click the **flower6.jpg** image thumbnail, and then press the Spacebar on your keyboard to open it in Full Screen Preview mode. The image should fill the display window. Click it once to zoom to 100% view, and then drag to see its detail. Click again to fit the image back in the window. Try clicking the corners of the image to see what happens.

10. Still in Full Screen Preview mode, navigate to the next and previous images using the right and left arrow keys on your keyboard. When you're done exploring, press Escape to return to InDesign.

11. Select another image in the Content pod and click the down arrow of the Preview button, to the right of the slider at the bottom of the window. Select Preview from the menu options to fill the Content pod with the selected image.

Note: You can drag the slider at the bottom of the Content pod to enlarge and shrink the thumbnails.

Note: The down arrow of the Preview button gives you access to assorted viewing modes.

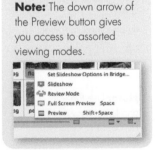

Note: Once you've chosen a setting from the Preview menu, it becomes the new default. You can then click the icon rather than the arrow for one-click access to that preview mode.

Note: You can use the wheel on your mouse to zoom in or out with the Loupe tool. You can also use the + and - keys on your keyboard.

Note: In Review Mode, you can rotate images, rate and label them, and even cull them from the review window to create a saved collection of the remaining files.

No Rating
Reject
★
★★
★★★
★★★★
★★★★★

No Label
Select
Second
Approved
Review
To Do

Rotate 90° Clockwise
Rotate 90° Counterclockwise

Open
Open in Camera Raw...

Note: You can exit Review Mode either clicking on the X at the lower right of the Review window or by pressing Escape on your keyboard.

Note: Use the right and left arrows on your keyboard to cycle through the thumbnails loaded into the cursor. A number on the thumbnail indicates the number of files loaded.

Click the image to zoom to 100% view, and then drag it in the window to inspect it more thoroughly. Click the Close button to return to thumbnail view.

12. With none of the images selected, click the down arrow for the Preview button again and choose Review Mode from the menu.

13. Use the right and left arrow controls at the lower left of the window to move through the images (◄ ► ▼). When a non-insect image appears in the central viewing window, click the down arrow to remove it from the review. (You can also use the right, left, and down arrows on your keyboard.)

14. Notice that when you move the mouse over the image in the central viewing area, the cursor changes to the Zoom tool (🔍). Click the image, and the Loupe tool opens, allowing you to inspect the image detail more closely. Drag the Loupe tool around the image and then click on it to close it.

15. Right-click/Ctrl-click on each of the remaining images. From the context menu, add a star rating and/or label to each of them. (You can also use the numbers 1 - 5 on your keyboard to assign a rating as you review.)

16. Click the New Collection button (▣) at the lower right of the window. In the New Collection dialog, enter the name "Insects". When you save the Collection, you'll get bounced out of Review Mode and back into InDesign.

17. Back in Mini Bridge, in the first column of the Navigation pod, click Collections, and then click Insects (on the right). The insect photos appear in the Content pod.

18. Click Recent Folders in the Navigation pod, and then click the links folder on the right. Then, click the Panel View button (▤) at the upper right of the Content pod. Deselect Path Bar and NavigationPod so Content is the only pod left open.

19. Click the Filter menu button (▼) and try out a couple of the filters. Choose Clear Filter from the Filter menu to restore all the files to view.

20. Click the Sort button (⬍) and choose By Date Created. Sort again By Date Modified.

21. Go to File > New and choose the Web 900 x 700 Document Preset that you saved in Exercise 3.3. In Mini Bridge, select several of the images in the links folder by holding the Shift key and clicking them with the Selection tool. Click the Tools button (▣) at the upper right of the Content pod and choose Place > In InDesign to load the multi-place cursor.

22. Click on the document, and, holding the mouse, drag on a diagonal line, down and to the right, to draw a frame. Release the mouse to place your first image. Repeat for the other loaded images, drawing frames of different sizes until the cursor is empty. Save the file as ex3_7.indd in the chapter_3_exercises folder, and then close it.

23. In Mini-Bridge, click the Panel View menu and turn on the Navigation and Preview pods and the Path Bar.

The Bridge Triple Play: Keywords, Advanced Search, and Smart Collections

To complete your tour of Mini Bridge, you'll take a look at a triple-play combination of three of the most useful and powerful facets of Bridge: keywords, advanced search, and Smart Collections.

While we're not looking to do a deep dive into Bridge in this book, the advanced search feature is just too wonderful a productivity tool to let it slip by without mention. What makes it so powerful is the range of criteria on which you can base a search. From color space to aspect ratio and image resolution, to font face and swatch color, you can search for pretty much any metadata encoded in a file. Your search can contain any number of criteria you like, to make it as granular and specific as you could ever want.

One of the best applications of the search feature is when it's used in conjunction with keywords. Bridge makes it possible to create and apply keyword sets and subsets to your files that you can then leverage as part of your search criteria. While keywords and search are a tremendous productivity enhancer when used together, their power is increased exponentially when you take it one step further and save your search criteria as a Smart Collection. Smart Collections are essentially the result of an ongoing dynamic search. Every time you add a file to your system that matches the criteria specified in your Smart Collection search, it gets added to the collection's virtual folder, no matter where on your system it resides. We *love* this feature!

The organizational strategy of keywording your documents and creating saved searches in the form of Smart Collections can actually be life altering when it comes to your workflow. Just imagine the time you could save if you could actually find your files without having to dig through endless iterations to locate the specific version you're looking for. What a concept! Yes, it takes planning and an investment of some time to put it all together, but the time you'll save in the long run is truly incalculable. The next exercises provide an introduction; it's yours to take it from there.

Exercise 3.8: Advanced Search in Bridge

1. In Mini Bridge, click the Search button (🔍) at the upper right of the panel. Then click the Bridge Advanced Search button to jump over to the full Bridge application.

2. When the Bridge Find dialog opens, the Look in dropdown should be targeting the links folder that you had open in Mini Bridge. Leave the links folder selected and check out the dropdown. You'll see a list of links to your recently visited folders, with a Browse link at the bottom.

Filename
Date Created
Date Modified
File Size
Document Type

Bit Depth
Color Mode
Color Profile
Height
Width

Copyright Notice
Description
Document Title
✓ Keywords
Label
Preserved Filename
Rating
Urgency

Altitude
Exif Color Space
Exposure
Exposure Bias Value
Exposure Mode
Exposure Program
Flash
Focal Length
Focal Lgth in 35mm
ISO
Serial Number
Model
White Balance

Swatch Group
Swatch Name

All Metadata

Although rather unassuming in appearance, the Find dialog is an extremely powerful tool that lets you search based on any metadata encoded into your files.

3. From the Criteria dropdown, choose Keywords, leave the word "contains" and enter "insects" in the value field. If an additional entry appears in the Criteria list, click the ⊖ button at its left to delete it. Don't click Find yet.

Keywords have been added to most of the files in the folder. The insect images have been tagged with two keywords: "Costa Rica" and "Insects". The flower images have been tagged with the words "Costa Rica" and "Flora". If you were to do a search for the keyword "Costa Rica", it would return photos of both the flowers and insects. If you had photos of other insects and wanted only those from Costa Rica, you could refine the criteria to search for the keywords "Insects" and "Costa Rica", and require that the search meet all criteria.

For this example, you want to locate only the insect images that have a width of 800 px. You could search for Width directly, since it's on the criteria list, but for the purpose of illustration, you'll search All Metadata for the number 800 instead.

4. Click the plus sign at the end of the first line to add another search criterion. Choose All Metadata from the criteria list, leave contains selected and enter 800 in the value field. Still don't click Find.

5. Ensure that the selection for Match is: if all criteria are met, and that both the include all subfolders and include non-indexed files checkboxes are checked.

6. Click Find to see the results of your search.

Note that the search returns only the insect images. Click the files returned from the search to see that they are each 800 x 600.

7. Click the Save as Smart Collection button next to the New Search field at the upper right of the Content pod, and name the collection "**Insects 800 x 600.**" Click Save to close the dialog and create the collection.

Smart Collections create virtual folders that update dynamically to include all files that meet your search criteria.

8. Mouse over the Smart Collection button again to see that it's tooltip has now changed to Edit Smart Collection. Click the button and expand the Look in dropdown. If you see chapter_3_exercises in the list of recent folders, select it. Otherwise select Browse, locate and select the chapter_3_exercises folder, and click the Choose button. Click Save and immediately; the window will update to include the additional file that matches your saved search.

9. Keep Bridge open and active for the next exercise.

If this exercise got your attention and your head is spinning with all the ways Smart Collections can revolutionize your workflow, you're probably eager to know how to add keywords to your documents. Check out the next exercise to learn just how easy it is.

Note: Be particularly aware of the folder you select when defining your Smart Collection, since it determines the scope of your search.

Exercise 3.9: Working with Keywords

1. Still in Bridge, select Keywords from the workspace switcher at the upper right of the interface.

2. In the Keywords workspace, you'll find the Keywords panel at the left of the Bridge interface. You'll see that there are already some keyword sets for commonly used categories in the pod. Click to select any one of the insect images, and, if they weren't already there, the parent keyword "Costa Rica" appears with the child or sub keyword "Insects" nested below it.

Note: You can create a keyword to be used only for organizational purposes, by enclosing it in square brackets: [keyword]. Organizational keywords cannot be used to tag files.

The Bridge Keywords panel. When a file is selected, Keywords applied to that file appear in the panel in italics, if they aren't already in the list of existing keywords.

3. To add a keyword, click the New Keyword button (⊛) at the bottom of the panel. Enter "Interactive InDesign" in the text field that pops up at the top of the panel, and press Return/Enter to enter the name.

4. Select the "Interactive InDesign" keyword, click the New Sub Keyword button (⊛) and enter "[Photographs]" in the name field to create an organizational category name. Press Enter/Return to enter the keyword and keep it selected.

5. Click the New Sub Keyword button again, enter "Flora" and press Enter/Return.

6. With Flora selected, click the New Keyword button (⊛), enter "Fauna" and press Enter/Return. Repeat and enter "Texture" in the keyword field.

7. Using the path bar at the top of the Bridge window, navigate back to the chapter_3_exercises folder, Ctrl-click/Command-click to select **bug1.psd** and **CostaRicaProvinces.psd**, and check the Interactive InDesign checkbox.

8. Choose Metadata from the workspace switcher options at the top of the window and note that the keyword appears for both files in the Content pod.

9. Click once on **bug1.psd** to deselect the map, and choose Keywords again from the workspace switcher dropdown. Check the "Fauna" keyword under Photographs to add it to the bug1.psd image.

10. Click the arrow to the right of the chapter_3_exercises folder in the Path Bar at the top of the Bridge interface, and choose **links** to open the folder. If you accidently click on the folder name instead of the arrow, you can get to the folder by typing "links" at the end of the path. Apply the "Flora", "Fauna" and "Texture" keywords to the corresponding images in the folder.

11. Return to InDesign and, if necessary, collapse Mini Bridge.

CHAPTER SUMMARY

This chapter was all about getting acquainted with the InDesign interface, and then customizing both it and the application preferences to support a productive workflow. While getting familiar with the tools that you'll use in designing for interactivity, you also learned a lot about setting up the interface in ways that will serve well for any type of project. Specifically, you learned how to:

- Set up and save a custom workspace that included the:
  - › Animation panel
  - › Bookmarks panel
  - › Buttons panel
  - › Hyperlinks panel
  - › Media panel
  - › Object States panel
  - › Page Transitions panel
  - › Preview panel
  - › Timing panel
  - › Align panel
  - › Effects panel
  - › Object Styles panel
  - › Pathfinder panel
  - › Preflight panel
  - › Links panel
  - › Mini Bridge

- Customize application menus

- Set preferences and defaults

- Create, load, and save document presets

- Customize the Control panel

- Customize the Preflight panel

- Customize the Links panel

- Correct Preflight errors

- Work with Mini Bridge and Bridge to:
  - › Set preferences
  - › Preview your files
  - › Do advanced searches
  - › Save Smart Collections
  - › Navigate your files
  - › Create and apply Keywords

In the process you:

- Set up Drag and Drop text editing

- Set up Dynamic Spelling

- Learned to automate Autocorrect to enter customized text

- Set Units & Increments

- Worked with the New Document dialog

- Set Document Setup and Margins and Columns preferences

- Corrected overset text

- Used the Multiplace cursor to place multiple images

Now that the tools you'll need are handy and everything is in it's place, it's time to get busy exploring the world of possibility that's literally at your fingertips. The next section provides a deep dive into Buttons, the very heart of interactivity in InDesign.

Part 2

BUTTONS

Buttons are at the very heart of interactivity in InDesign, and this section
will teach you all about them. You'll
learn about button appearances, button
states, image-based buttons, multi-
object buttons, button triggering events,
and button Actions. By the time you're
finished, you'll be a button-making
maestro, creating buttons for dropdown
menus, image galleries, popup tooltips,
and more.

• Chapter 4

ABOUT BUTTONS

Just wait until you see what you can do with buttons in InDesign. Not just for navigation, buttons open the door to creation of a rich, interactive user experience. This chapter lays the foundation for all the work you'll be doing with buttons, introducing you to button events, button states and appearances, and button actions. You'll become familiar with the Sample Buttons Library, learn to modify sample buttons, and, in the process, gain experience working with both the improved Layers panel and effects.

Introduction

Converting an object to a button in InDesign magically imbues it with superpowers. All of a sudden, it is transformed from a static graphic object that sits passively on a page, to an object with the ability to initiate and respond to a host of interactions. InDesign buttons can be made to display various appearances; navigate from one page of a document to another; play and stop sounds, video, animations; and more. Converting an object to a button also enables it to be directed by commands from other buttons, dramatically expanding your creative possibilities.

Anatomy of a Button

There are three aspects of a button that combine to create its functionality. First is the button appearance, the aspect of the button actually seen by the viewer. Second is the mouse interaction, or event to which the button is made to respond. Third is the actual function that is initiated through that interaction.

The area of the button that responds to user interaction is called a hotspot. In InDesign, the button hotspot is defined by the rectangular bounding box of the button graphics, and will include whatever empty space is in the rectangle. In the case of a round button, for example, the hotspot will include the empty corners of the rectangle that encloses the button.

The hotspot area of the round button shown above is defined by its rectangular bounding box, indicated by the blue dashed line.

Button Events

Button functionality is triggered by user interaction with the mouse. These interactions are referred to as *events*. InDesign buttons can be made to respond to six different events:

1. **On Release:** The button action is triggered when the mouse is positioned over the button hotspot and released. It's good practice to apply button actions to the release of the mouse rather than the click. This makes it possible for the user to change their mind after pressing, but before releasing the mouse. In such a case, the user can drag the clicked mouse away from the button without triggering an action.

2. **On Click:** The button action is triggered when the mouse is positioned over the button hotspot and clicked. The user needn't release the mouse in order to trigger the action.

3. **On Roll Over:** The button action is triggered when the mouse is moved into the area of the button hotspot.

4. **On Roll Off:** The button action is triggered when the mouse is rolled out of the area of the button hotspot.

5. **On Focus: (PDF only):** The button action is triggered when the cursor is tabbed into the object.

6. **On Blur: (PDF only):** The button action is triggered when the cursor is tabbed out of the object.

Button Appearances

A change of appearance when the user's mouse is dragged onto or off of a button, or when a button is clicked or released, can provide valuable visual feedback and create an enhanced user experience.

Typically, a button will be designed with at least two, and sometimes up to four, visual states:

- **Normal:** The default appearance of the button without interaction.

- **Rollover:** The appearance of the button when the mouse is moved into the button hotspot.

- **Click/Down:** The appearance of the button when the mouse is clicked or held down in the button hotspot.

- **Disabled:** The appearance of the button when the button is unavailable for interaction.

InDesign makes it possible to design buttons with as few as one, and as many as three, different button appearances: Normal, Rollover, and Click.

Button Actions

A button makes certain functions available to the user. In InDesign, these functions are referred to as *actions*. Actions are assigned to the triggering events: On Release, On Click, On Roll Over, On Roll Off, On Focus, and On Blur. Some of the actions available for InDesign buttons translate effectively when published to both SWF and PDF,, while others are specific to the output platform.

We'll be digging more deeply into the intricacies of button actions a little later but first, let's take a look at the Sample Buttons library.

Exploring the Sample Buttons Library

InDesign comes with a Sample Buttons library that contains a collection of pre-made buttons with actions and multiple visual states already defined. To access the Sample Buttons library, with the Interactive workspace selected, go to Window > Sample Buttons.

The Sample Buttons library contains 2 navigation bars and eight button styles in five colors each. You can edit both the appearance and function of the sample buttons, so you're not limited by the preset definitions. If the existing buttons don't meet your needs, you can easily use them as the jumping off point for creating an endless variety of buttons customized to your requirements.

Exercise 4.1: Exploring Sample Buttons

1. Open **ex4_1_start.indd** from the chapter_4_exercises folder.

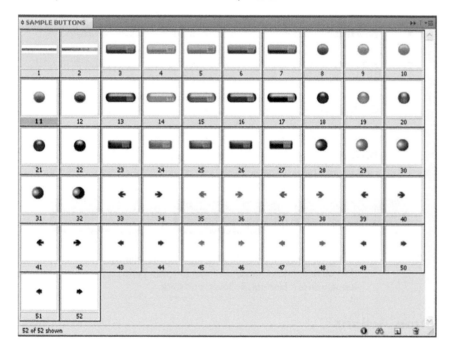

The Sample Buttons Library

Although the exercise file appears to be blank, there are two placed audio files on the pasteboard.

Note: For more information on audio and incorporating it into your InDesign documents, see Part 4, Working with Media In InDesign.

2. Check the Workspace Switcher at the upper right of your screen to ensure that the Interactive workspace is selected (not Interactive PDF).

3. Go to Window > Sample Buttons or click the 🖼 icon in the panel dock to open the Sample Buttons library. Select button 30 from the Sample Buttons library and drag it onto your document. Note that the object is identified as a button by the 🖐 icon at its lower right.

4. Collapse the Sample Buttons library. Go to File > Save As and then save your document as **ex4_1.indd** in the chapter_4_exercises folder.
If you don't save the file to the chapter_4_exercises folder, your sounds will not play when you add the button action.

5. Click 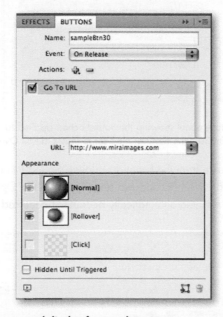 in the panels dock at the right of your screen or go to Window > Interactive > Buttons to open the Buttons panel.

6. With the Selection tool, select and then double-click the button on the document to display the Appearance states in the Buttons panel. Note that sample button 30 has been given a default name. Change the name of the button to "sampleBtn30" in the Name field at the top of the panel and press Enter/Return.

The Buttons panel display for sampleBtn30. You can see that the sample button is built with a Normal and a Rollover state.

7. Click back and forth between the word "[Rollover]" and the word "[Normal]" in the panel, and watch the change in the button on the document. When you've seen both button states, be sure that you end with the Rollover state active and highlighted in the panel.

8. Note that, for this button, the On Release event is selected in the Event dropdown, and it has a Go To URL action applied. To make the action work, enter a complete web address in the URL field. We entered http://www.miraimages.com.

9. Click the Event dropdown and select the On Roll Over event. You can tell there is no action yet associated with this event because the panel displays the message "[No Actions Added]."

10. To the right of the word "Actions", click the Add New Action button (⚡), and select Sound from the popup menu. The Sound action appears in the Buttons panel.

11. Click the Sound dropdown and select **btnOver.mp3**.

12. Note that Play is the default Options selection. Click the Options dropdown to see the other choices, and then ensure that Play is the selected option.

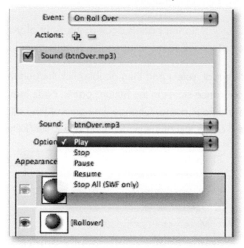

The Buttons panel showing the Sound action applied to sampleBtn30, with btnOver.mp3 set to Play On Roll Over.

13. Choose On Release from the Event dropdown, Sound from the Actions popup, **click.mp3** from the Sound dropdown and Play from the Options dropdown. (Click.mp3 was selected automatically because it occurred first alphabetically.)

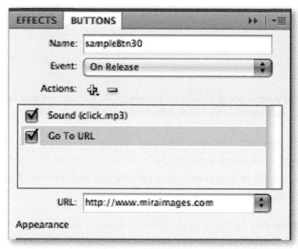

Multiple actions can be applied to a single event, as shown for the On Release Event for sample button 30.

Provided you have speakers or a headset, and an installed browser with an internet connection, you can preview your button, hear the sounds you just added, and follow the added URL.

14. Click the Preview Spread button (⊡) at the bottom left of the Buttons panel, or press Shift+Ctrl+Enter/Command+Shift+Return to open the Preview panel.

15. The button should appear in the Preview panel, but may be too small for you to easily see the rollover changes. To enlarge the Preview panel, mouse over its lower left corner. When the cursor changes to a double-sided diagonal arrow (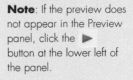),   click and drag down and to the left to expand the panel.

Note: If the preview does not appear in the Preview panel, click the ▶ button at the lower left of the panel.

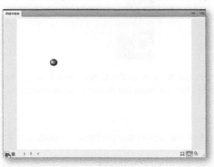

The Preview panel displaying sampleBtn30 in Preview Spread Mode.

16. Rollover the button to hear the sound and see the drop shadow rollover effect. Click the button and note that the sound plays when the mouse is released rather than pressed. Your browser should open to the URL you entered. Close the browser and return to InDesign. Click the double arrows at the upper right of the Preview panel to collapse it.

17. Open the Sample Buttons Library and drag button 1, the first navigation bar, onto your document.

    The navbar is actually a collection of objects. You'll group them to make them easier to manage.

18. With the newly placed objects still selected, press Ctrl+G/Command+G to group them.

    The round button and the first button in the navbar are set to the Rollover state. InDesign provides a convenient menu command to set all your buttons back to the Normal state, all at the same time.

19. Return to the Buttons panel and open the Buttons panel menu. (Click the menu button ( ) at the upper right of the panel.) Watch for the change in the button and navbar on the page while you click Reset All Buttons to Normal State. The buttons should all display the Normal state appearance.

    To better see the appearance of the button states in the Buttons panel, you might want to enlarge the button thumbnails. That too can be done very simply.

20. From the Buttons panel menu, choose Panel Options. Click the radio button for the button thumbnail size that works best for you, and then click OK.

To change the size of the button thumbnails, choose Panel Options from the Buttons panel menu.

Buttons can be converted to objects with just a click. The converted object takes on the appearance of the active button state, and all other states are discarded.

21. On your document, Alt-drag/Option-drag sampleBtn30 with the Selection tool to duplicate it.

22. With the duplicate button selected, click the Convert Button to an Object icon (⬚) at the bottom right of the Buttons panel. Click OK in the warning alert and note that you have just that easily, stripped that button of its superpowers. You've also made the graphic(s) available for inclusion in other buttons.

You can just as easily convert nearly any object to a button.

23. With the button graphic still selected, create a new button by clicking the Convert Object to Button 🖼 icon at the lower right of the Buttons panel.

By default, your new button has a Normal state only, and no actions applied. Next, you'll add a Rollover state, and give it a distinct appearance to make your button more user-friendly.

24. To add a Rollover state, simply click the [Rollover] entry in the Appearance section of the panel.

The new Rollover state duplicated the Normal state appearance. Next, you'll want to make some changes to the Rollover state appearance to provide your audience with visual feedback.

25. With the Selection tool, double-click your new button, and then double-click the Fill swatch on the Control panel to open the Color Picker.

A button acts like an envelope that wraps around the graphic objects that give it its appearance. A double-click takes you into the button envelope to access the objects inside.

26. Choose a new color and note that the Add Swatch button at the right of the panel is set by default to add a CMYK swatch. Since this document is destined for the web, you're working with an RGB palette. To change the Add Swatch mode to RGB, first click the L radio button for Lab color, and then click the R radio button for RGB. The button text changes to read: "Add RGB Swatch." Add the swatch and click OK to close the dialog.

The new color is applied to the Rollover state of the button. Because you saved the new color to a swatch, applying the same color to the Normal state is easy.

27. In the Buttons panel, select the Normal state and double-click the button with the Selection tool to access the Normal state graphic.

28. On the Control panel, click the right-facing arrow next to the Fill swatch to open the Swatches panel ( ).

29. Select the Rollover state swatch color you just saved to apply it to the Normal state of the button.

30. Save and keep the file open for the next exercise.

Editing Button Appearances Using Effects

Effects, which also include blending modes and transparency settings, influence the way an object visually interacts with other objects in a document. A robust set of features, the InDesign effects include many of the same effects found in Photoshop and Illustrator. InDesign enables you to apply effects to an object, the object stroke, the object fill, and/or the text inside the object.

The Control panel features a set of effects tools that are grouped together for easy access. When applying effects from the Control panel, first click the Apply Effects To button and then choose the aspect of the object you would like to affect.

Before applying effects, you can specify the target of the effect from the Control panel.

To apply a Drop Shadow effect that uses preset shadow settings, simply click the Drop Shadow button (▢) on the Control panel. The Drop Shadow button acts as a toggle and displays its on-state (▢) when an object with a drop shadow is selected. To remove a drop shadow without straying from the Control panel, select the aspect of the object from which you want the shadow removed, and then click the Drop Shadow button.

To adjust opacity from the Control panel, either click the right-facing arrow of the Transparency field and drag the slider, or type a value in the text field (▢ 100% ▸).

While you can modify object opacity from several places in InDesign, the setting controls for effects such as Drop Shadow and Outer Glow can only be accessed through the Effects dialog box. Click the *fx.* button (FX for Effects) on the Control panel or at the bottom of the Effects panel to open the Effects options menu. Then, select an option. Alternatively, you can go to Object > Effects and make a selection that will take you to the Effects dialog.

Note: For more information on Blending Modes, see InDesign Help: Using InDesign CS5/ Transparency effects/ Blending colors.

The Effects tool group on the Control Panel.

These controls are visible when the Type tool or the Note tool are *not* selected in the toolbar. If the effects controls are not showing, choose Customize from the Control panel menu and ensure that the Effects checkbox is checked in the Object section of the dialog.

Working with the Effects Dialog Box

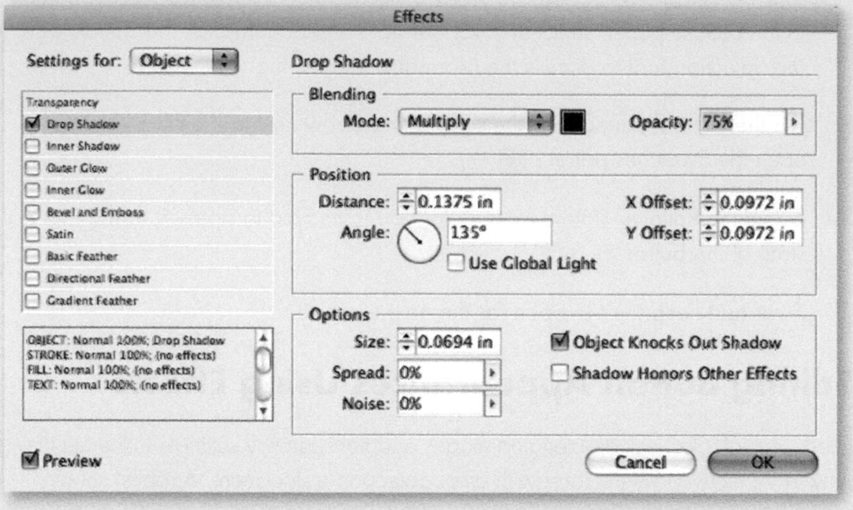

If you're already familiar with Photoshop or Illustrator, this dialog should make you feel right at home. If not, it's really pretty simple to navigate once you get the hang of it. The dialog is essentially split into two sections, with the list on the left providing access to the controls for the different effects. The thing to be aware of is that you must click the effect *name*, rather than its associated checkbox, to make the controls for that effect appear on the right. If you click the checkbox instead, you'll turn on the effect with its default settings, and you won't gain access to the customization settings.

Different from the Effects dialog in Photoshop and Illustrator is the Settings for dropdown at the upper left of the dialog window. The option you select dictates whether the effects you choose will be applied to the object, its stroke, its fill, or its text. To apply different settings to different object attributes, simply choose the first attribute, apply your settings, and then repeat the process accordingly.

The Effects dialog is a place where people have been known to disappear for days without surfacing. The effects you can create are truly endless, so make a point to take some time to explore. The invested time will pay dividends, since you can save the fruit of your efforts as Object styles that you can use over and over again. (More on Object styles later.)

To learn more about working with effects, see InDesign Help: Transparency effects / Adding transparency effects.

While the Effects tools on the Control panel provide quick and easy access, there is also a dedicated Effects panel. The Effects panel offers a more complete visual read of what's actually going on with an object than you can get from the Control panel. It's a particularly useful tool when working with buttons and multistate objects. To access the Effects panel, go to Window > Effects.

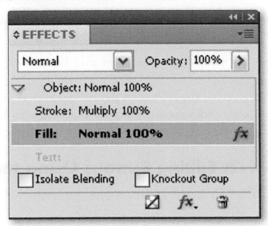

The Effects panel displaying the settings for Sample button 30.

Blending mode and transparency controls are located at the top of the Effects panel and enable you to adjust transparency and blending mode at each object level.

The *fx.* button at the bottom of the panel provides easy access to the Effects dialog. You can access the Effects dialog by double-clicking on any entry in the panel that isn't grayed out.

Blending mode options can be accessed from the dropdown at the top of the Effects panel.

Mousing over the *fx.* icon at the right of the Object, Stroke, Fill, or Text entries in the panel triggers a pop-up tool tip that tells you exactly which effects are applied to a selected object.

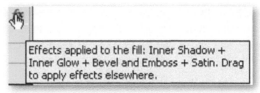

Effects applied to the fill: Inner Shadow +
Inner Glow + Bevel and Emboss + Satin. Drag
to apply effects elsewhere.

When you mouse over the _fx._ icon at the right of the Effects panel entries, a Tool Tip detailing the applied effects appears.

The Effects panel also makes it easy to move an effect from one aspect of an object to another or, just as easy, to copy an effect to another object aspect. For example, to move an effect from the object fill to its stroke, just drag the _fx._ icon at the right of the Fill row up to the Stroke row. If you wanted to duplicate the effect, you would Alt-click/Option-click and drag it to another aspect of the object.

Exercise 4.2: Editing Buttons Using the Effects Panel

1. If you kept the file open from the last exercise, you're good to go. Otherwise, open ex4_2_start.indd and save it as ex4_2.indd. With sampleBtn30 (the green button) selected on the page, go to Window > Effects to open the Effects panel. If you see the word "Group" displayed on the first line in the panel, double-click the button on the page. The panel display should update to reflect characteristics of the object, rather than the group. If necessary, click the arrow to the left of the word "Object" in the panel to display the object details.

2. Examine the effects settings for sampleBtn30 to see that it has a 100% Normal blending mode applied to the object, stroke, and fill. Additional effects are applied to the fill as indicated by the _fx_ on the Fill line of the panel.

3. To edit the effects applied to the fill of the button Normal state, ensure that the Fill line of the panel is highlighted, and click the _fx._ button at the bottom of the panel. Note that the list of effects options appears with check marks next to effects that have been applied.

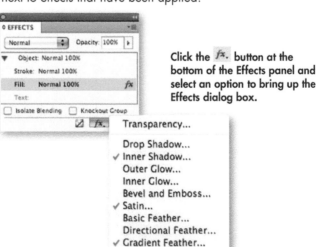

Click the _fx._ button at the bottom of the Effects panel and select an option to bring up the Effects dialog box.

4. Select Bevel and Emboss from the options menu. When the Effects dialog opens, notice that the Bevel and Emboss controls are visible at the right of the dialog and the accompanying checkbox on the left is checked.

5. If necessary, move the Effects dialog box so you can see the button on your document. Change the Style to Emboss and the Direction to Down. Play with adjusting some of the other settings to see what they do, and then click OK to apply your changes.

6. To make changes to the effects on the button Rollover state, select the Rollover state in the Buttons panel and double-click the Fill line in the Effects panel. Remember, if the Effects panel displays a line item entitled Group rather than Object, Fill, and Stroke, double-click the button on the document to access the button graphic before accessing the effects controls. Save and close your file.

Exercise 4.3: Replacing Missing Fonts

Bell Gothic Std, the font used in the first navbar in the Sample Buttons library, is no longer included with the install of InDesign. Since it's possible you may not have the font installed on your system this presents the perfect opportunity to address the topic of missing fonts.

1. Open **ex4_3_start.indd** and save it as ex4_3.indd.

    The **ex4_3_start.indd** file contains two versions of the Sample Button 1 navbar: one as it exists in the Sample Buttons library and the other as an expanded version of the same item showing its component parts.

2. If the Missing Fonts alert appears, click Find Font to open the Find Font dialog. If the Missing Fonts alert does not appear, go to Type > Find Font.

NOTE:

The Missing Fonts alert is not an alert you want to ignore. You may choose to wait and correct the issue later, but missing fonts require your attention. What this alert means is that a font included in your document is not installed on your system. By default, missing fonts are indicated by a pink highlight on the text in the body of your document.

If you choose to dismiss the alert, you can access the Find Font dialog at any time by going to Type > Find Font.

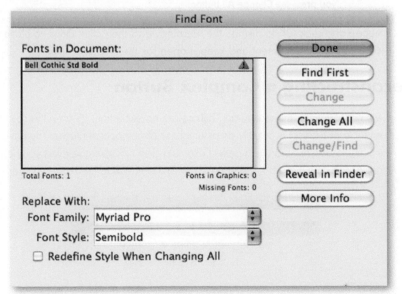

The Find Font dialog

3. Select Bell Gothic Std Bold in the Fonts in Document section of the dialog.

4. From the Font Family dropdown, select Myriad Pro. Choose Semibold from the Font Style dropdown.

5. Click Find First to see where the font occurs in your document.

   The Find Font dialog can locate the font despite the fact that the selected text isn't visible on-screen.

6. Click Change/Find. If the font is missing from your system, the pink highlight will disappear from the word Home. Note also that the name of your newly selected font is added in the Fonts in Document section of the Find Fonts dialog.

7. Now press what we call the "I'm feeling lucky" button, Change All. This replaces every instance of Bell Gothic with Myriad Pro. Note that Bell Gothic Std Bold disappears from the list of document fonts.

8. If a warning alert pops up, it's because you have the Redefine Style When Changing All checkbox checked in the Find Font dialog. No cause for alarm; the alert is just making you aware that the font you've applied to the button text varies from the definition of the [Basic Paragraph] Paragraph style that was applied to the buttons.

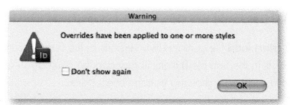

If the Redefine Style When Changing All checkbox is checked in the Find Font dialog, a warning dialog will pop up when you press the Change All button.

9. If necessary, click OK to dismiss the warning, and then click Done to close the dialog. Save the document and keep it open for the next exercise.

Deconstructing a Complex Button

Things are not always as they seem, and buttons are no exception. It's often the case that what looks like one object is actually an assemblage of component pieces. The navbar from the Sample Buttons library is a perfect example. The next exercise takes you behind the scenes to see how it all fits together and how to use effects to customize your results.

The sample button 1 navbar. Below the assembled navbar is an expanded view of its component pieces.

Exercise 4.4: Deconstructing the Sample Button 1 Navbar

1. If you don't already have the file open from the previous lesson, open ex4_4_start.indd from the chapter_4_exercises folder and save it as ex4_4.indd.

2. With the Selection tool, in the expanded view of the navbar, select the black rounded rectangle that serves as the button background. Click the Fill swatch on the Control panel and change the color to dark blue.

    Changing the color of this object will change the background color of the entire navbar when you put its pieces back together.

3. Select the long, highlight rectangle that's directly below the navbar background. Drag it up, onto the background, holding the Shift key as you drag to keep it aligned. Release the mouse when the top of the highlight is positioned a couple pixels from the top of the background. You can use the arrow keys on your keyboard to nudge the highlight into position.

4. With the Fill swatch active in the Tools panel, go to Window > Color > Gradient or click the ▣ icon in the Panels dock to open the Gradient panel.

5. When the Gradient panel opens, note that the object has a linear gradient fill going from white to black. To see the effect more clearly, click the white gradient stop to activate it and then click the Swatches panel icon (▦) in the Panel dock. The Gradient panel will collapse when the Swatches panel opens. Alt-click/Option-click the cyan swatch in the Swatches panel to replace the white color in the gradient.

    If you don't hold the Alt/Option key when you click the color swatch, the gradient in the navbar highlight will be replaced by solid cyan. If this happens, press Ctrl+Z/Command+Z to undo, and then start over by reselecting the white gradient marker in the Gradient panel.

6. Collapse the Swatches panel and note the change of appearance of the object on your document.

7. Click the *fx.* button on the Control panel to expand the list of effects.

8. Note that a check mark appears next to the Gradient Feather option to indicate that the effect is applied to the highlight. Click it to open the Effects dialog to the Gradient Feather controls.

    The Gradient Feather is applied at the object level with a gradient that goes from black to white. Previously a job for Photoshop, with the Gradient Feather effect you can make an object fade out to full transparency. Since the effect is applied to the frame rather than its contents, you can swap out what's in the frame and still retain the transparency effect. This means you can incorporate feathered images in your documents that you can change on the fly. *Very* cool!

9. Click the black gradient stop under the gradient ramp to select it, and note that its opacity is set to 100%.

10. Click the white gradient stop and note that it's opacity is set to 0%. If necessary, check the Preview checkbox. Then, with the stop still selected, click the arrow to the right of the Opacity text field and drag the Opacity slider to the right to increase the opacity percentage. Release the slider when the Opacity percentage is about 15%.

Note: In a linear gradient, the colors or transparency variations are applied sequentially from left to right as they appear on the gradient ramp. When applied to an object, they maintain that sequence from one edge of the object to the other. In a radial gradient, the colors or transparency variations radiate out from a center point in the order of the stops on the gradient ramp. Unless you reverse the gradient, the left edge of the ramp represents the point from which the radial gradient radiates.

The default Effects panel settings for the Gradient Feather applied to the navbar.

Note that the white gradient stop in the dialog changes to darker shades of gray when you increase the Opacity percentage, and the navbar highlight on the document becomes more solid in color.

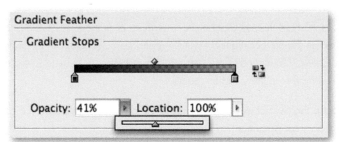

The colors of the gradient stops in this particular dialog represent opacity rather than color. A black swatch in the stop indicates that the selected object is completely opaque, white indicates that it is completely transparent, and shades of gray indicate degrees of opacity.

InDesign provides two options for gradient type: Linear and Radial. Click the Type dropdown in the dialog to choose between them. (For now, leave the Linear gradient selected.)

Note that the angle of the Gradient Feather is -90°, resulting in a gradient transparency effect that goes from opaque to transparent, from the top to the bottom of the object.

11. Drag the Angle pointer until the Angle value reads 90° and observe that the gradient on the object in your document has reversed direction. Type "-90" in the Angle field to return to your original setting.

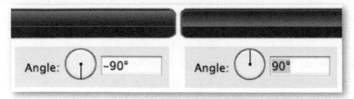

A linear Gradient Feather effect at -90° goes from opaque to transparent; at 90°, it goes from transparent to opaque. You can change the gradient angle by dragging the Angle pointer or entering a value in the text field.

12. Note that there's a summary of applied effects in the box at the lower left of the Effects dialog, and then click OK to close the Effects dialog.

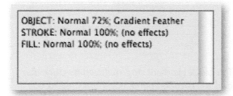

Effects panel summary of the applied effects.

13. Next, you'll modify the button text. With the Selection tool, click and drag a marquee to select the four rectangles and the three vertical lines that you've not yet moved onto the navbar. Shift-drag the selected objects to center them on the navbar, and then use the arrow keys on your keyboard as necessary to nudge them into place.

14. With the Selection tool still active, double-click the word "Blog" to switch to the Type tool. Double-click again to select the text, and change it to "Contact Us."

    Notice that the Control panel displays the Type controls and that the font used for the button text is Myriad Pro Semibold.

15. Press Esc to deselect your text and automatically switch to the Selection tool.

16. Select the button directly below the word "Home" from the row of remaining rectangles that you haven't yet moved to the navbar. Open the Buttons panel and notice that the default button name appears at the top of the panel. Note also that the button has a Go To Page action applied to the On Release event and is currently set to navigate to page 1 of the document.

17. If the Appearance section of the panel is empty, double-click the button on the document to access the button states.

    Note: The button has no fill or stroke, so be sure to click on its edge rather than its interior to select it.

18. Select the Rollover state in the Buttons panel. You can see that there are two objects on the document that combine to create the appearance of this state.

19. Double-click on the object with the gradient fill in the upper half of the button. The gradient should appear in the Fill swatch on the Toolbar and the Control panel.

20. Open the Gradient panel to see the white to black gradient applied to the object. Select the black gradient stop, open the Swatches panel and Alt-click/Option-click the same dark blue you applied to the navbar background.

21. Return to the Gradient panel, select the black diamond above the gradient ramp and enter 45 in the Location percentage field to move the halfway point for the gradient transition. Leave the Angle at -90°.

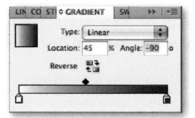

The black gradient stop replaced by dark blue, and the Location percentage changed to 45°.

22. In the Effects panel, note that the opacity of the object is set to 81%. Double-click the Object: Normal item in the panel to open the Effects dialog.

23. Click the black gradient stop at the right of the gradient ramp. Change the opacity percentage to 0 and then click OK to apply your changes and close the dialog.

24. Select the other object comprising the button's Rollover state and change its fill to the same dark blue you used in the gradient.

25. Select the second button with the Selection tool, hold down the Shift key, and click the two remaining buttons to add them to your selection. Press the Delete key on your keyboard to delete all three buttons. You'll duplicate your formatted button to create the other buttons on the navbar.

26. Hold down Alt+Shift/Option+Shift and drag the first button to the right. Release the mouse when you see a green vertical smart guide indicating that the duplicate button is aligned to the center of the Products text on the navbar above.

Alt+Shift+drag/Option+Shift+drag to duplicate the button and constrain its horizontal position as you drag it.

27. Repeat the procedure until you have a total of four buttons, each aligned under their respective text.

28. Drag a marquee selection around all four buttons with the Selection tool. Hold down the Shift key to constrain vertical movement, and drag the buttons straight up to center them on the navbar. If necessary, use your arrow keys to nudge the buttons into place.

29. Preview the Spread in the Preview panel and roll over the buttons on both versions of the navbar. Save the file and keep it open for the next exercise.

The original sample button 1 navbar (top) and the edited result (bottom).

The InDesign CS5 Layers Panel

Prior to the release of InDesign CS5, all the objects on a given layer were represented in the Layers panel by one indivisible layer. It wasn't possible to select individual objects using the Layers panel, and when there were multiple objects stacked above one another, selecting an object on the document at the bottom of the layer stack could be tough to do. But all that has changed, and just in time, since the flexibility provided by the new Layers panel proves essential in designing for interactivity.

The InDesign CS5 Layers panel makes it possible to select individual objects within a layer (we'll call these object layers), change object stacking order and visibility, and lock individual objects to prevent any changes. Layers can be used as an organizational tool, like a containing folder for related objects. Like the objects they contain, the containing layers can be rearranged to change the stacking order of whole groups of objects at a time. When not in use, Layers can be collapsed to hide their object sublayers and de-clutter the panel display.

Understanding Layers and Object Layers

If the concept of layers is foreign to you, think back to an anatomy book you may have encountered in school when learning about the human body. In this book, the skeletal structure appears on a white page, and transparent acetate pages are overlaid for the various systems of the body. There might be one sheet illustrating the internal organs, another showing the musculature, and yet another for the vascular system. Think of each of these acetate sheets as layers, with the uppermost sheet representing the top layer in the stacking order.

To better understand the workings of the Layers panel, and InDesign altogether as an application, it helps to understand that, like Illustrator, InDesign is a vector-based application. For the uninitiated, this means that the objects created in InDesign are mathematically based and are defined by point coordinates, curve and corner

The Layers Panel Deconstructed

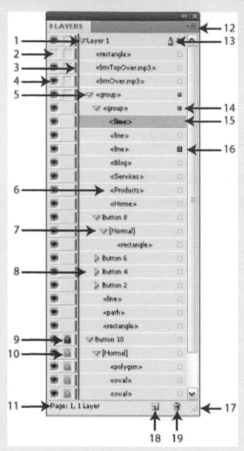

1) The default name (Layer 1) indicates a master layer. Clicking the arrow expands and collapses the layer to display the object layers it contains.

2) The empty square in the visibility column indicates a hidden layer. Click in the square to show the object(s) on the layer.

3) The color bar reflects the color key for the master layer in which the object resides. Object bounding boxes are the color of the layer color key.

4) The eye in the visibility column indicates that layer objects are visible. Click the eye to hide the layer objects.

5) By default, a grouped object is indicated in the Layers panel by the word "<group>".

6) A text frame is indicated in the Layers panel by the text it contains.

7) A button's state is indicated in the Layers panel as a sublayer of the button. The button graphic is a sublayer of the button state.

8) A button is indicated in the Layers panel by its name. Each button has a unique name. The default name for a button is Button N, where "N" is a number.

9) The lock indicates that the layer or object is locked and cannot be moved or modified.

10) The grayed out lock indicates that a parent layer is locked, thereby locking its sublayers.

11) The active document page and the number of layers it contains is indicated at the bottom of the panel.

12) Layers panel menu button.

13) The Pen icon indicates that the current layer is active. New objects created will land on the layer displaying the Pen icon.

14) The small square in the selection column indicates that an object in a layer is selected, but the entire content of the layer is not. You can select an object by clicking in the selection column of the object layer. Shift-click in the selection column to add additional objects to the selection.

15) A dark gray highlight indicates that a layer is active, although the objects it contains may not be selected. A layer must be highlighted in order to reposition it in the stacking order. You can move objects from one layer to another by highlighting and dragging the object layer. Shift-click to select multiple layers.

16) The large square in the selection column indicates that the entire content of the layer is selected.

17) Click and drag the sizing control to change the height and width of the panel.

18) The New Layer button creates a new master layer.

19) The Delete Layer button deletes selected layers.

angles, stroke and fill, etc. Very different from pixel-based artwork, which is resolution dependent, objects created in InDesign can be scaled and transformed nearly without limit and still remain crisp and clear.

There are some caveats to scalability however. While the vector objects created in InDesign are themselves resolution independent, the images placed within them are not. Therefore issues of resolution are still of primary concern when preparing an InDesign document for publishing.

Because of it's vector nature, each object created in InDesign is distinct. Having each object represented individually in the Layers panel makes it easy to select objects wherever they are in the document, regardless of how many objects may be stacked above them.

Selecting Stacked and Grouped Objects

Now that you've explored the inner workings of the component pieces of the deconstructed navbar, let's take a look at how you can select them.

Buttons are essentially grouped objects. One way to select elements of a grouped object is to double-click the object in the group that you wish to select. This can be especially tricky with buttons, since some buttons may have no fill or stroke, and selecting them requires a precisely placed click on the button bounding box. If, as is the case with the navbar buttons, a text field is laid over the button, a double-click could easily activate the textbox rather than the button object. In instances such as these, trying to select the actual button using the Selection tool can become an exercise in futility. Thankfully, there is more than one way to approach the challenge.

The Select container and content tools on the Control panel enable you to access and navigate through stacked objects and objects in a group. The vastly improved Layers panel is also an invaluable tool for locating and selecting any object in your file.

Exercise 4.5: Selecting Stacked and Grouped Objects

This exercise provides an introduction to the improved Layers panel, as well as the Select container and Select content tools. You'll learn to use these tools to select objects that elude selection with the Selection tool.

A   C
B   D

The Select container and Select content tools.
A) Select container   C) Select previous object
B) Select content   D) Select next object

1. If you don't have the file open from the previous exercise, open **ex4_5_start.indd** and save it as ex4_5.indd.

2. Open the Layers panel (Window > Layers) and click the right-facing arrow on Layer 1 to twirl it down and show its object sublayers. Expand the <group> object layer to show its component elements.

3. Expand and drag the Layers panel out of the panel dock.

4. Select the black navbar on the document with the Selection tool, and click the Select content button (⊕) on the Control panel to go inside the group. Note the large blue square at the right of the <group> object layer in the Layers panel that indicates the group is selected.

5. Click the Select next object button (⬚) four times on the Control panel. Watch the blue selection square appear at the right of the <rectangle>, <path>, and <line> object layers, and then end at Button 26.

6. With the blue square to the right of Button 26 notice that the Home button is selected on the document. Expand Button 26 in the Layers panel and then expand its Rollover state.

7. Click the Select content button again and note that, in the Layers panel, the (Rollover) layer is selected with a big blue square indicating that the entire state is selected.

The Rollover state of Button 26 is selected as indicated by the large blue square. One way to select an object is by clicking in its selection column in the Layers panel.

8. Again, click the Select content button, noting that you have selected the path that provides the button highlight. This is also indicated by the appearance of the gradient fill in the Fill swatch on the Control bar and the Toolbar.

9. Click the Select next object button on the Control bar to select the button background object.

   You can also select the button elements directly from the Layers panel by clicking in the selection column of the appropriate sublayer.

10. Save and close the file.

CHAPTER SUMMARY

You've covered a lot of territory in this chapter, learning the fundamentals of buttons, how they work, and how to change their appearance. Specifically you learned about:

- Button appearances
- Button events
- Button states
- Button actions
- The Sample Buttons Library
- The Buttons panel

As part of your exploration, you also become familiar with a number of the wonderful features and tools in InDesign. You got some experience with:

- The Find Font dialog
- Creating a new RGB swatch from the Color Picker
- Using the Control panel to work with effects
- The Effects panel
- The Gradient Feather effect
- Replacing a gradient color
- Selecting objects with the Select container and Select content buttons on the Control panel
- Selecting objects using the Layers panel
- Gradient types, gradient angles
- Transparency

Now that you have a foundation, you're ready to build some buttons of your own. Chapter 5 will introduce you to creating simple buttons, and then you'll build from there.

● Chapter 5

SIMPLE IMAGE-BASED BUTTONS

You can create buttons from any object, and a placed image is an obvious starting point. This chapter will have you creating elegant image-based buttons in no time, adding effects, and then using the buttons to control visibility of other objects in your document. Making objects appear and disappear with user interaction is a fundamental part of the interactive experience you can create with InDesign. So, it's time to put on your top hat and get out your magic wand, and let the fun begin!

Introduction

While it's nice to have a starting point, and the Sample Buttons Library certainly provides that, it's also good to know how to design buttons of your own. The robust drawing tools in InDesign allow you to get as crazy as you like with shapes, highlights, and effects to create an unlimited variety of button appearances.

One simple and easy approach to button making is to create them from placed images. With an effect applied to the Rollover state, image-based buttons can be an elegant solution to adding interactivity.

Exercise 5.1: Creating Simple Image-based Buttons

In this exercise, you will place multiple images, convert them to buttons, and add rollover appearances. You'll then add Show/Hide actions to the buttons to control the visibility of larger versions of the button images.

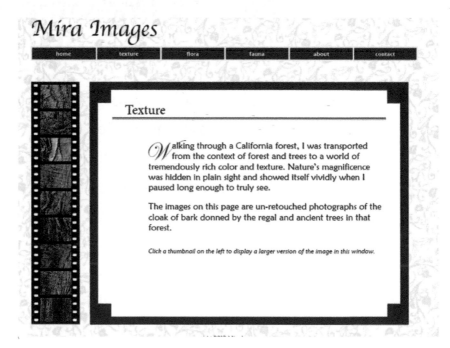

1. Open **ex5_1_end.indd** and press Shift+Ctrl+Enter/Shift+Command+Return to open the Preview panel. (Be patient, this may take 30 seconds to a full minute to preview.) If necessary, click the Play button to generate the preview. Rollover and click each of the filmstrip thumbnails to see how they work.

2. Close the Preview panel and explore the file. Open the Buttons panel and, with the Selection tool, select each of the texture buttons at the left of the page to see the events and actions applied to them.

3. Alt-click/Option-click the texture page 1 layer in the Layers panel to expand the layer and all the object sublayers. When you've finished exploring, keep the file open for reference.

4. Open **ex5_1_start.indd** and save it as ex5_1.indd.

   First you'll zoom in on the filmstrip and then you'll add guides to help in your layout.

5. With the Selection tool selected, hold down Ctrl+Spacebar/Command+Spacebar and note that the cursor changes to the Zoom tool. Position your mouse at the upper left of the filmstrip graphic and, still holding the modifier keys, drag on a diagonal, down, and to the right, as if you were dragging a box around the entire filmstrip. Release the mouse and then release the keys on your keyboard to see the now zoomed-in view of the graphic. This is called a marquee zoom.

6. Place your cursor in the horizontal ruler at the top of the document window, and while holding down the mouse, drag down onto the page to drag a guide. Release the mouse when you see 141 px in the Y coordinate field on the Control panel. The position of the guide updates dynamically as you drag. If you release the guide before getting it properly positioned, you can select it with the Selection tool and enter the correct coordinate value in the Control panel.

The Y coordinate field on the Control panel reflects the position of the guides as they are dragged from the horizontal ruler.

7. Drag a second horizontal guide to 630 px.

8. Drag guides from the vertical ruler to 81 px and 145 px.

   Next, you'll import the thumbnail images you'll use for the buttons.

9. Press Ctrl-D/Command-D or go to File > Place. Navigate to chapter_5_exercises > chapter_5_links. Click to select texture_01.jpg and then hold down the Shift key to select texture_09.jpg. Click Open to load your cursor with all nine images.

   In the upper left of the cursor thumbnail, you'll see a brush and a number representing the number of files loaded and ready to be placed.

   - Use the right and left arrows on your keyboard to navigate through the loaded files.

   - To remove a loaded file from the cursor, when its thumbnail is visible, click Esc on your keyboard.

   If you inadvertently replace the content of a selected frame with a file you've loaded in the cursor, press Ctrl+Z/Command+Z to undo. The loaded file will be removed from the page and loaded back into the cursor.

Note: The lock icon at the upper left of the filmstrip graphic indicates that it is locked and cannot be selected or repositioned.

To lock an object, select it and click Ctrl+L/Command+L or go to Object > Lock.

To unlock the graphic, click the lock icon on the object.

Note: If Rulers are not visible, press Ctrl+R/Command+R or go to View > Show Rulers.

Note: Hold the Ctrl/Command key while you drag a guide to extend it across all pages of a multipage spread. Dragging a guide from the ruler into the pasteboard rather than the page will also make the guide extend across the spread. To switch the direction of a guide between horizontal and vertical, hold down Alt/Option while dragging.

Importable File formats:

InDesign enab,les you to place a wide variety of file formats including native Illustrator, Photoshop, and InDesign files, multipage PDFs, as well as TIFF, JPEG, GIF, EPS, BMP, PNG, DOC, DOCX, TXT, RTF, XLS, XLXS , FLV, F4V, SWF, MP4, and MP3 files.

Note: InDesign's multiplace feature enables you to load the cursor with multiple files of any supported file type. You can place loaded files in a grid by using the arrow keys on your keyboard to add and remove columns and/or rows of frames. When you release the mouse, the loaded files are placed in the grid.

10. Position your cursor at the intersection of the guides at the upper left of the filmstrip. Hold down the mouse and drag down and to the right. Still holding the mouse, press the up arrow on your keyboard and horizontal dividers will appear in the frame.

    Before pressing the up arrow, you may have noticed that, as you dragged, the frame maintained the aspect ratio of the placed file. To override this default behavior, hold the Shift key while dragging, and InDesign will let you drag any size frame you like.

11. While still holding the mouse, press the up arrow a total of eight times to create nine uniformly sized frames. Drag the cursor to the intersection of the guides at the lower right of the filmstrip, and release the mouse. All nine loaded images should be placed and evenly spaced atop the filmstrip graphic.

    Since the aspect ratio of the frames doesn't quite match the images, the images don't quite fill the frames. You'll fix that with InDesign's Fitting options.

12. With the Selection tool, click the first placed graphic, being sure *not* to click the target icon that appears in the center of the image when the mouse is rolled over it.

    Clicking the target selects the object within the frame rather than the frame itself. Once selected, you can scale and transform the placed object without affecting the frame.

When the mouse is rolled over a placed object, a target icon appears in the center of it.

13. Right-click/Ctrl-click the image and select Fitting > Fill Frame Proportionally.

    In order to streamline the process of applying the same fitting option to the other eight objects, you'll store the object settings in an Object style.

14. Go to Window > Styles > Object Styles (Ctrl+F7/Command+F7) to open the Object Styles panel.

15. Alt-click/Option-click the Create New Style button at the bottom of the panel to open the Object Styles dialog.

16. In the Style Name field of the New Object Style dialog, name your new style "ProportionalFit".

    It's good practice to name styles according to their function rather than appearance. This leaves you latitude to make changes in color or effect with the original name remaining an appropriate identifier.

Frame Fitting Options

InDesign offers a variety of options to define the way placed content is scaled to fit in a frame. To access frame fitting options, go to Object > Fitting, or Right-click on a Graphic or Unassigned frame and choose Fitting from the contextual menu. Fitting option buttons also appear on the Control panel.

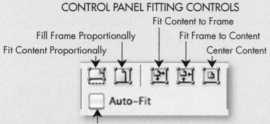

CONTROL PANEL FITTING CONTROLS

Fit Content to Frame
Fill Frame Proportionally   Fit Frame to Content
Fit Content Proportionally   Center Content

Auto-Fit

Windows menu.   Mac menu.

When your content fits in the frame the way you want it and you apply Auto-Fit, the content scales automatically when the frame is scaled.

Fill Frame Proportionally: Proportionally scales the content to match the width or height of the frame, and fills the frame leaving no whitespace. If the aspect ratio of the content does not match the frame, some portion of the content will be cropped.

Fit Content Proportionally: Proportionally scales the content to match the width or height of the frame. If the aspect ratio of the content does not match the frame, there will be whitespace at the top and bottom or left and right of the content.

Fit Frame to Content: Scales the frame to the exact size of the content. This button works for text too, scaling the text box to the perfect size.

Fit Content to Frame: Adjusts the size of the content to fit the proportions of the frame. If the aspect ratio of the content does not match the frame, the content will be disproportionately scaled.

Center Content: Centers the content in the frame.

Clear Frame Fitting Options: Clears all fitting options applied to the frame.

Frame Fitting Options: Opens the Frame Fitting Options dialog box. The Frame Fitting Options dialog offers refined fitting controls, including clipping parameters and a registration alignment proxy. Selecting the upper left point on the proxy aligns the content to the upper left of the frame, the center point aligns the content to its center, etc. You can further refine the content alignment by specifying values in the Crop Amount fields. For example, with the upper left point selected on the proxy, and a Top and Left Crop Amount of 100 px, the upper left corner of the image moves up and left, beyond the frame boundaries by 100 px.

The Frame Fitting Options dialog box.

A value of 100 px entered in the Top and Left Crop Amount fields results in the upper left corner of the image being moved up and to the left by 100 px. You can achieve the same effect by manually repositioning the image in the frame.

Working with Styles

Whether it be a Paragraph, Character, Cell, Table, or Object style, the easiest way to create a new style is to first format an object with the attributes you want to save. Then, have InDesign capture those settings in a style definition.

To create a new style, select your formatted object, hold down the Alt/Option key and click the New button at the bottom of any of the Styles panels. When the style dialog box opens, enter a name for the style. If you forget to click the Alt/Option modifier key, InDesign will generate a new style with a numbered default style name, such as "Paragraph Style 1". If you double-click the style name in the Styles panel, the options dialog will open and you can rename or edit the style.

To apply a style, click the name of the style in the style panel with your object or text selected. Before double-clicking a style definition to open it for editing, be sure to deselect anything to which you don't want that style applied.

WARNING: Be aware that if you edit or select a style with no object or text selected, that style will be applied to every new object you create.

The Object Styles Dialog Box

The Object Styles dialog box.

Object styles can capture an extremely wide range of attributes, ranging from color and fill to effects, Paragraph styles, Frame Fitting options, and more. They are tremendously handy for maintaining consistency in button formatting, and can increase your productivity exponentially.

The Object Styles dialog functions in much the same way as the Effects dialog, with a list of attribute categories on the left and corresponding controls on the right. Checking the attribute checkbox turns on the checked attribute, but you must click directly on the name of the attribute for its controls to appear on the right.

Be sure to pay attention to the Effect for section of the dialog since the selection you make here dictates where your settings are applied. You can apply different settings to the object, fill, stroke and text of the same object by changing the Effect for selection.

17. In the Basic Attributes section of the dialog, check the Frame Fitting Options checkbox in the column at the left. This incorporates your fitting settings in the style definition. Check the Apply Style to Selection checkbox at the lower left of the dialog and click OK to close it.

Note: When a selected object or text has a style applied to it, that style is highlighted in the Styles panel.

18. Select the second placed image, and, holding down the Shift key, click on each of the remaining images to add them to the selection.

19. Click once on ProportionalFit in the Object Styles panel to apply the style.

20. Deselect all the objects on the page by clicking on your pasteboard or pressing Command+Shift+A/Ctrl+Shift+A.

21. Select the first placed image (**texture_01.jpg**) and open the Buttons panel. Click the Convert Object to a Button icon at the bottom right of the panel.

22. Change the name of the button to "texture_1_sm."

23. Still in the Buttons panel, click the word "[Rollover]" to create and activate the rollover button appearance.

24. Open the Effects panel (Window > Effects) and note that the panel displays the word "Group". Double-click the button on your document and the Effects panel changes to display Object, Stroke, and Fill.

25. Select Object in the Effects panel and click the *fx.* button at the bottom of the panel. Select Inner Glow from the Effects options.

26. If necessary, check the Preview checkbox at the lower left of the Effects dialog in order to preview your changes.

27. In the Blending section of the dialog, click the white color swatch to the right of the Mode dropdown. Click on the word "Swatches" in the Effect Color dropdown, and choose RGB. Pick a color for the Inner Glow. We chose an orange color: R=255 G=134 B=0.

28. Adjust the opacity as desired. We chose 42%.

29. Increase the Size setting to 25 px and then click OK to apply the effect and close the dialog.

The Effects panel settings for the button Rollover state with Inner Glow applied.

30. With the button still selected and the Rollover state still active, Alt-click/Option-click the New button at the bottom of the Object Styles panel to create a new Object style. Name the style "textureOver."

31. Convert each of the remaining filmstrip images to buttons and name them consecutively: "texture_2_sm," "texture_3_sm," etc.

32. For each button, create a Rollover state and apply the textureOver Object style.

Button with textureOver Object style applied to the Rollover state

33. Press Ctrl+Shift+Enter/Command+Shift+Return to open the Preview panel and then test your rollovers.

34. After you've styled the Rollover state for all the buttons, and tested that they work, choose Reset All Buttons to Normal State from the Buttons panel menu. The orange highlight will disappear from all the buttons on the document.

35. Open the Layers panel and click the triangle at the left of the texture page 1 layer to expand it. Locate the textureDescription sublayer and click the eye icon to its left to hide the layer (the tool tip will say "Toggles visibility"). Press Ctrl+0/Command+0 to zoom out and fit the page in the window.

36. Save the file and keep it open for the next exercise.

Naming Conventions

If you explored the contents of the Texture Images layer, you saw that the lesson file already contains larger versions of the nine images used to create your buttons. Note that the large images have been converted to buttons too.

In InDesign, for an object to talk to another object in order to send or receive commands, both objects must have unique names. Converting an object to a button enables you to name it. You can either keep the default name provided by InDesign or you can name it yourself, as you did earlier in this lesson.

Setting up reliable naming conventions and adhering to them will save you *lots* of time and aggravation as you develop projects containing potentially hundreds of objects, and numerous layers and styles. Naming objects, layers, and styles consistently also makes a project more decipherable to other designers and developers in a shared workflow. As an example, the large image buttons have names that correspond to the small image buttons to make them easy to pair (texture_1_sm corresponds to texture_1_l).

Because InDesign CS5 files can be exported to Flash Professional for development, we've adhered to the rules for naming Flash variables when suggesting button names.

The standard rules for naming variables are:

- Start your variable name with a lower case letter or an underscore, not a number.
- Use only lowercase letters, numbers, dashes, and underscores in the variable name.
- *Never* use spaces.

If you've chosen a button name that combines multiple words, use a lowercase letter for the first word and either begin the following words with an uppercase letter (myVariableName), or use an underscore or a dash to separate the words (my_variable_name).

Not to worry, you won't break anything if you name your InDesign objects according to a different convention. Whatever convention you decide on, though, be consistent in using it. You'll find yourself spending much less time trouble-shooting and your workflow will move much more smoothly.

Exercise 5.2: Using Buttons to Control Visibility

The buttons you created will show a large version of their thumbnail image when clicked. This behavior is accomplished using the Show/Hide Button action found in the Actions section of the Buttons panel.

1. If you closed the file from the previous lesson, open **ex5_2_start.indd** and save it as ex5_2.indd.

2. Select the texture_1_sm thumbnail button, the first button on the filmstrip, and open the Buttons panel.

3. With the default On Release Event selected, click the plus icon next to the word "Actions" and select Show/Hide Buttons from the list of actions.

4. In the Visibility section that appears in the Buttons panel, you'll notice that all the texture buttons have an X next to them. Click once on the X next to texture_1_lg to make the large image show when the thumbnail button is clicked and the mouse released. An open eye icon replaces the X. Alternatively, you can select the texture_1_lg item in the Visibility section and click the Show icon (👁) below the list.

5. Click twice in the Visibility column for texture_2_lg to hide that image when the texture_1_sm button is released. An eye icon with a red slash through it indicates that the object will be hidden. Another way to set the object visibility would be to select the texture_2_lg item and click the Hide icon (👁) below the list.

> **Note:** For the Show/Hide Action, the X to the left of an object in the Visibility section of the Actions panel indicates that the object will retain its default visibility when the button is clicked. The 👁 icon indicates that the object will show and the 👁 icon indicates that the object will be hidden.

Getting Around in the Preview Panel

The Preview panel provides three modes for previewing your work: Selection, Spread, and Document.

The Preview Selection mode enables you to preview selected objects, such as a specific button or buttons. The preview will display only the objects selected, so if there are internal links to other document pages, or actions controlling other unselected objects, they will not be functional in this mode. Go To URL actions applied to the object will function as expected, however, enabling navigation to external web addresses and sending of email.

The Preview Spread mode previews the entire spread. Actions affecting objects within the spread will work as will Go To URL actions. Any animations in the spread will play as designed. Navigation to other pages in the document will not be active in this mode.

THE PREVIEW PANEL:
1) Play preview (Alt-click/Option-click to replay preview. 2) Clear preview. 3) Go to Previous Page. 4) Document page number (mouse over to see tooltip displaying file name and page number). 5) Go to Next Page. 6) Set Preview Selection Mode. 7) Set Preview Spread Mode. 8) Set Preview Document Mode.

The Preview Document mode generates a preview of the entire document that demonstrates the full functionality and interactivity it contains. All navigation, internal and external, and all animation, will perform as it will in the final project. Navigate through the document pages by clicking the previous and next buttons, or any internal links you've established.

You may find that when the Preview panel first opens, nothing but a blank screen appears. If this is the case, click the Play preview button and then wait while InDesign generates the preview. Depending on the size of your document and the interactivity you've added, this can take a little while. However, it's well worth the wait to see your buttons functioning, links working, and animations playing.

If you've generated a preview in one mode and wish to switch to another, select the preferred preview mode and then click the Play preview button. InDesign will generate a new preview based on your selection.

To replay a preview from its start, hold the Alt/Option key and click the Play preview button.

6. Hide the following buttons:

textureDescription

texture_3_lg

texture_4_lg

texture_5_lg

texture_6_lg

texture_7_lg

texture_8_lg

texture_9_lg

Visibility:	texture_1_lg
	texture_2_lg
	texture_3_lg

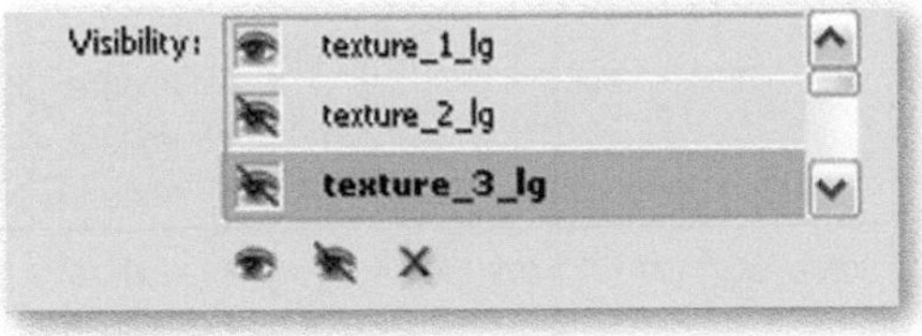

7. Now, when the texture_1_sm button is released, the description and all the large images except texture_1_lg will be hidden, and the texture_1_lg image will show.

8. To test your work, click the Preview Spread icon ( ) at the bottom of the Buttons panel.

9. When the Preview panel opens, if you don't see the preview of your spread, click the Play button at the lower left of the panel. If necessary, enlarge the panel by dragging the lower left corner down and to the left, and then click on the texture_1_sm thumbnail to show the texture_1_lg image.

10. Close the Preview panel and reopen the Buttons panel. For each of the remaining thumbnail buttons, follow steps 2 through 6, naming the buttons and establishing the Show/Hide settings as follows.

Button Name	Show	Hide	
texture_2_sm	texture_2_lg	• textureDescription • texture_1_lg • texture_3_lg • texture_4_lg • texture_5_lg	• texture_6_lg • texture_7_lg • texture_8_lg • texture_9_lg
texture_3_sm	texture_3_lg	• textureDescription • texture_1_lg • texture_2_lg • texture_4_lg • texture_5_lg	• texture_6_lg • texture_7_lg • texture_8_lg • texture_9_lg
texture_4_sm	texture_4_lg	• textureDescription • texture_1_lg • texture_2_lg • texture_3_lg • texture_5_lg	• texture_6_lg • texture_7_lg • texture_8_lg • texture_9_lg
texture_5_sm	texture_5_lg	• textureDescription • texture_1_lg • texture_2_lg • texture_3_lg • texture_4_lg	• texture_6_lg • texture_7_lg • texture_8_lg • texture_9_lg

Button Name	Show	Hide	
texture_6_sm	texture_6_lg	• texture_1_lg • texture_2_lg • texture_3_lg • texture_4_lg • textureDescription	• texture_5_lg • texture_7_lg • texture_8_lg • texture_9_lg
texture_7_sm	texture_7_lg	• texture_1_lg • texture_2_lg • texture_3_lg • texture_4_lg • textureDescription	• texture_5_lg • texture_6_lg • texture_8_lg • texture_9_lg
texture_8_sm	texture_8_lg	• texture_1_lg • texture_2_lg • texture_3_lg • texture_4_lg • textureDescription	• texture_5_lg • texture_6_lg • texture_7_lg • texture_9_lg
texture_9_sm	texture_9_lg	• texture_1_lg • texture_2_lg • texture_3_lg • texture_4_lg • textureDescription	• texture_5_lg • texture_6_lg • texture_7_lg • texture_8_lg

11. Preview your document again to ensure that each button is performing properly.

CHAPTER SUMMARY

This chapter brought you deeper into the world of buttons and the power they have to transform a static document into one filled with life.

On this leg of the journey, you've learned all about:

- Converting objects to buttons
- Creating buttons from placed images
- Working with the Show/Hide action to control visibility
- Modifying effects
- Creating, editing, and applying Object styles
- Frame Fitting options and how to assign them

You became intimately familiar with the Preview panel, an essential tool for testing your interactive work, and also learned about:

- Importable image formats
- Working with naming conventions
- Locking and unlocking objects
- Showing and hiding Rulers
- Dragging a marquee selection
- Creating guides
- InDesign's Multiplace feature
- Placing files into a grid

Chapter 6 moves further into the interactive landscape expanding your available design options with multi-object buttons.

• Chapter 6

MULTI-OBJECT BUTTONS

When it comes to buttons, working with multiple objects multiplies your design options exponentially. In this chapter you'll create buttons from a collection of objects, combining them in order to establish the different button states, and then modifying or removing select objects to define distinctive button state appearances. With multi-object buttons, you can create button effects that would otherwise be impossible to achieve.

Introduction

While you can get lots of mileage from buttons consisting of only one object, your design options expand dramatically when you know how to make buttons from a combination of objects. It's not all that tricky, but there are a few nuances that are good to know.

The first secret to creating a multi-object button is to group the objects you want to include in the button. If you select and convert multiple objects that aren't grouped, InDesign creates buttons from each of the objects individually.

If you want to create a button with different objects in its different states, it's easiest to combine all the objects from all the states and then group them. Create the button, and then create the Rollover state. Next, delete the objects from the state in which you don't want them to appear. While this strategy takes a bit of pre-planning, in the long run you'll find it to be the easiest approach.

Of course, there will be times when you have an existing button to which you want to add another object. This is when the Layers panel proves particularly useful. As mentioned earlier, a button is a group, of sorts, and it appears in the Layers panel as an object sublayer, with a sublayer of its own that reflects the active button state.

To add an object to an existing button state follow the steps below:

1. Select the object you want to add to the existing button.
2. Expand the sublayer for the button (Button 1) in the Layers panel, and then expand the sublayer for the button state [Normal].
3. In the Layers panel, drag the layer for the object you want to add into the sublayer for the button state, and release it when you see a black line appear. (Initially, you may need to drag the new object layer to the bottom of the button state layer. Once the new object is part of the button state, you can rearrange the button object sublayers by dragging them to correct the stacking order.)

The image below illustrates the <oval> layer being dragged into the button [Normal] state. The black line below the <rectangle> object layer indicates the new location of the <oval> layer after the mouse is released. The stacking order of the objects comprising the button can then be changed by dragging the <oval> object layer above the <rectangle> object layer once they are both within the Button 1 sublayer.

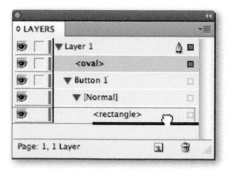

The Layers panel displaying the expanded Button 1 sublayer.

Exercise 6.1: Creating Multi-object Buttons

You can create buttons from multiple objects to achieve
effects such as text appearing on rollover.

1. Open **ex6_1_end.indd** from the chapter_6_exercises folder. Explore the
    slideshowBtn at the lower right of page 3. With the button selected, open the
    Buttons panel to see the action and button appearances.

2. With the Buttons panel still open, open the Pages panel (Window > Pages, or
    click the 📖 icon in the panel dock). Double-click on page one to open it in
    the document window. Click on the tree bark Texture image on the page,
    and look at its button states and the action assigned to it in the Buttons panel.
    Check out each of the remaining image buttons, and when you're finished
    exploring, keep the file open for reference.

3. Open **ex6_1_start.indd** and save it as ex6_1.indd. On page 3 of the
    document, zoom in on the small "see Flora slide show" text and the arrow
    graphic at the lower right corner of the document. Use the Zoom tool (🔍)
    from the Tools panel, or drag a rectangle around the objects while holding
    down the Ctrl+Spacebar/Command+Spacebar keys. Release the mouse
    before releasing the keys to target the zoom.

    see Flora slide show ▶

    **The selected see Flora slide show text and
    arrow graphic before being grouped.**

4. Using the Selection tool, Shift-click to select both the "see Flora slide show"
    text and the arrow graphic. Press Ctrl-G/Command-G to group the objects,
    or choose Group from the Object menu.

5. Open the Buttons panel and click the Convert Object to a Button icon at the
    bottom of the panel. Name the button "slideshowBtn" and click [Rollover] to
    create a button Rollover state.

6. Double-click the text portion of the button on the document with the Selection tool. The active tool should switch automatically to the Type tool.

7. Triple click anywhere in the text object to select the entire line and then open the Swatches panel. Confirm that the Formatting affects text button (T) is selected at the upper left of the panel. Choose one of the dark reds for the text color.

8. Select the arrow graphic with the Selection tool. You may first have to click away from the text and then double-click the arrow to select it.

9. If necessary, reopen the Swatches panel and select the Fill icon. Choose one of the dark reds for your fill color. In the Buttons panel, click [Normal] to reset your button to the Normal appearance.

Note: Hyperlink Destinations are essentially anchors built into a document which can be used as link destinations. For more on Hyperlink Destinations, see Creating Hyperlink Destinations on page 116.

10. Leave the default On Release event setting, click the ⊕ button, and choose Go To Destination from the Actions options.

11. Click the Destination dropdown to see that a destination has been created for each page in the document. Select the flora2 destination and keep the other default settings.

12. Select the button you just created, and at the bottom of the Buttons panel, click the Preview Spread button (⊡).Rollover the button to see the change of appearance and then close the Preview panel. Navigate to page 1 of the document.

    Note that the two images on the top row have already been converted to buttons, while the images on the bottom row have not. You'll convert the bottom images to buttons, and then add and style text for the button Rollover states.

Note: While the Preview Spread mode will enable you to see the button rollover effect, the Go To Destination action will not work. To test the Go To Destination action when the Preview panel opens, first select Preview Document Mode ( ), and then click the Play button to generate the preview.

13. Open the Layers panel, select the home page layer, and twirl down the triangle to expand it.

14. Select the Type tool and draw a small text frame approximately 140 px wide by 40 px tall on top of the bird image. Type the word "Fauna" in the text frame.

15. Double-click the word "Fauna" with the Type tool to select it and change the font face and size. We chose Myriad Pro Bold, 22 px.

16. Select a color for your text. We chose the R=240 G=234 B=227 swatch from the Swatches panel, a light cream color.

17. Click the **TT** button in the Character Formatting section of the Control panel to apply all caps.

18. Choose Paragraph Rules from the Control panel menu. When the dialog appears, apply the following settings:
    - Click Rule Above, choose Rule Below, check Rule On
    - Weight: 5 px
    - Color: Text Color
    - Width: Text (not Column)
    - Offset: 2 px

    Check the Preview checkbox to see your changes and then click OK.

Tips for Setting Font Face and Size

Like Illustrator and Photoshop, InDesign offers an assortment of ways to modify font face and size. The obvious approach, of course, is to select from the dropdown menu options. The font size dropdown provides only a limited number of options, however, and 22 px is not among them.

If you know the name of the font face, or have a particular font size you want to use, you can select the existing text field value on the Control panel and type in a new one. As you type the letters of a font name, InDesign jumps to the first name that matches those letters, so you rarely need to enter the entire font name. For example, if you enter "Ari", InDesign jumps to Arial.

There are also a couple ways to style your text visually, in the context of your page. To change font size, select the text you want to style, and then click in the Font Size field on the Control panel. Press the up and down arrows on your keyboard to increase and decrease the font size.

A similar approach can be used to select a font family. With your text selected on the document, click inside the Font field on the Control panel. Then, press the up or down arrow on your keyboard to move in alphabetical order through the fonts on your system. The text you've selected on the page will change as you cycle through the font list.

Another, and more flexible way to modify font size is to first select either the text with the Type tool, or the text frame with the Selection tool. Then, while holding down the Ctrl+Shift/Command+Shift keys. press the > key on the keyboard to increase font size incrementally, or the < key to decrease it. Adding Alt/ Option to the mix will result in incremental changes five times as large.

The default Preference setting for keyboard increments (the amount of change using the Ctrl+Shift+>/ Command+Shift> or Ctrl+Shift+</Command+Shift+< shortcuts) is 2 px if the ruler units are set to pixels. If you prefer a finer adjustment, you can go to Edit > Preferences > Units and Increments (Windows) / InDesign > Preferences > Units and Increments (Mac) and set the Size/Leading increment to 1. If you set the Preference with *no documents open*, this becomes the preference for all new documents.

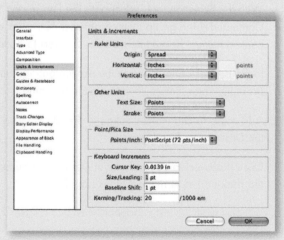

The Units and Increments section of the Preferences pane.

The Paragraph Rule settings for the Rollover state of the button titles.

19. Hold down the Ctrl/Command key to temporarily switch to the most recently selected Selection tool. In this case, it should be the regular Selection tool with the black arrow. Double-click the lower right corner of the text frame, and the text frame will magically snap to the size of your text. If necessary, reposition the text frame on the image while still holding the Ctrl/Command key.

The Rollover state for the image button.

20. Double-click on the word "Fauna" to select it. Open the Paragraph Styles panel and Alt-click/Option-click the Create New Style button at the bottom of the panel. Name the style "homeRollover" and make sure the Apply Style to Selection and Preview checkboxes are checked. Click OK to close the dialog.

21. With the Selection tool, select both the image and the text and press Ctrl+G/ Command+G to group them. Right-click/Ctrl-click on the group, and, from the context menu, choose Interactive > Convert to Button.

22. In the Buttons panel, change the default button name to "faunaImage" and press the Enter/Return key to commit the name.

23. Add a Go To Destination action to the On Release event and select fauna from the Destination dropdown.

24. Click [Rollover] to add a Rollover state to the button and then switch back to the [Normal] state in the Buttons panel.

    You only want the text to appear when you rollover the button, so you'll delete the text from the button's Normal state.

25. Double-click the button text in the document to select it and get inside the button group. Delete the text.

26. Select the Type tool and draw a text field on top of each of the three remaining images and enter the text as follows:
    - Upper-left image: Texture
    - Upper-right image: Flora
    - Lower-right image: About

27. Switch to the Selection tool, Shift-click to select all three text frames, and then click homeRollover in the Paragraph Styles panel to style the text.

28. Click off the text frames to deselect them. Double-click the lower right corner of each text frame to fit the frame to the text, and then reposition the text on the button images as necessary.

29. Group the About text and its image, and then click the Convert Object to a Button icon at the bottom of the Buttons panel. Name the button "aboutImage". For the Go to Destination action, choose about from the Destinations dropdown. Create a Rollover state for the button and delete the text from the Normal state.

    Next, you'll add text to the Rollover state of the existing textureImage button.

30. Select the textureImage button (upper-left) on the document, and then select its Rollover state in the Buttons panel. In the Layers panel, if necessary, expand the home page layer, the textureImage layer, and then the [Rollover] sublayer nested below it.

31. Locate the <TEXTURE> text layer in the Layers panel and drag it into the [Rollover] sublayer of the textureImage button, below <texture6.jpg>. Once it's in the [Rollover] layer, if necessary, drag to reposition it above <texture6.jpg>.

Dragging the <TEXTURE> object layer into the Rollover state of the textureImage button.

If you look in the Buttons panel, you should see the text on the thumbnail of the Rollover state in the Buttons panel.

32. Select the floralImage button on the document and then select its Rollover state in the Buttons panel. In the Layers panel, drag the <FLORA> text layer into the expanded [Rollover] sublayer to complete the buttons on the Home page.

33. Open the Preview panel, click the Preview Document Mode button (the rightmost button at the bottom of the panel [Q]), and click Play.

34. When the preview appears, test your buttons. Use the navigation controls at the bottom of the panel to return to the Home page from the interior pages.

The Preview panel navigation controls.

CHAPTER SUMMARY

In this chapter you took your button-making skills to the next level. You learned to create buttons using multiple objects and to differentiate button states by using different combinations of objects to define them. In the process, you learned to:

- Create buttons from multiple objects
- Add and remove objects from existing button states
- Work with the Layers panel to add objects to existing buttons

You also deepened your experience with text formatting and gained experience with:

- Applying all caps formatting to text
- Formatting paragraph rules
- An assortment of ways to set font face and font size

In addition, you got better acquainted with the Preferences dialog by taking a side trip to set units and increments.

At this point, you've got all the fundamentals of button-making under your belt. The next chapter takes you a bit outside the box to explore some of the less obvious ways you can employ buttons in your interactive projects.

● Chapter 7

BUTTON VARIATIONS

The previous chapters provided you with the foundation skills that you'll use for every button you create. This chapter expands on those skills with variations that will fill in the picture and enrich your repertoire.

You'll learn to create invisible buttons and work with multi-button groups. You'll create a navigation bar with dropdown menus, and then wrap up your deep dive into buttons by learning to create email and web links.

Invisible Buttons

Invisible buttons, also known as hotspots, enable you to add interactivity to a static image. A typical scenario for the use of invisible buttons might be a map where you'd like to have additional information pop up when the user mouses over a particular part of the image. Invisible buttons are also ideal for setting up tooltips that pop up to provide clarification or additional information. For situations that don't lend themselves to the use of traditional buttons, laying an invisible hotspot over existing content can provide an elegant means to add interactivity.

Because InDesign is vector-based, it's possible for an object to exist even without the visible presence that a stroke or fill color provides. The mathematical definition of the object exists despite the fact that you can't see it on the page. When an object with no stroke or fill is converted to a button, it can be used to initiate actions in the same way that other buttons can. As with any button, you can add a rollover appearance to an invisible hotspot button to provide visual feedback to the user when the hotspot is triggered.

Exercise 7.1: Invisible Buttons

In this exercise, you'll create invisible hotspot buttons on a map of Costa Rica. When a button is moused over, its corresponding province on the map will be highlighted in green. To create the highlights, the shape of each province was traced with the pen tool and converted to a button. Each province button is named with the province name appended by the word map; for example, guanacasteMap.

Map of the provinces of Costa Rica with invisible hotspot buttons on the province names and green highlighted buttons on the provinces.

1. Open **ex7_1_end.indd** from the chapter_7_exercises folder. Press Ctrl+Shift+Enter/Command+Shift+Return to preview the file. Mouse over the province names on the map, below the words "Pacific Ocean," to see the provinces highlighted in green. When finished exploring, close the Preview panel and keep the file open for reference.

2. Open **ex7_1_start.indd** and save it as ex7_1.indd. When the file opens, it is zoomed in on the list of Costa Rica provinces on the map. Note the two vertical guides that define the width of the buttons you will create.

3. Select the Rectangle tool and position your cursor on the left guide, just below the first entry on the list. Click and drag up and to the right to draw a rectangle 10 px high that covers the Alajuela text. The dimensions should appear in the smart guides display as you drag. If necessary, after dragging the rectangle, you can change its height in the Control panel. The rectangle should have no fill or stroke but its bounding box should be visible on the page.

You will draw a rectangle with no fill or stroke over each province name and will convert it to an invisible hotspot button.

4. If you need to, reposition the rectangle so its bottom edge is centered between list entries 1 and 2. You can use the arrow keys on your keyboard to nudge it into place.

5. Switch to the Selection tool, hold down the Alt/Option key, and drag a duplicate rectangle straight down until its top edge meets the bottom edge of the original rectangle.Both rectangles should be vertically aligned.

    You need a total of seven buttons, and you could easily repeat the above process a total of five more times. However, InDesign provides a set of wonderful commands that enable you to repeat a transformation on single or multiple objects. Go to: Object > Transform Again to see these commands.

    It's debatable as to whether it's more efficient in this specific case to manually duplicate the buttons, or to repeatedly select the menu command. Instead, you'll streamline the process by creating a custom keyboard shortcut to automate the task.

6. Go to Edit > Keyboard shortcuts, and choose Object Menu from the Product Area dropdown.

7. Scroll through the list of Commands to find Transform Again: Transform Again and select it. Note that there is no shortcut currently assigned to the command.

8. Place your cursor in the New Shortcut field at the bottom left of the window and press Shift+Ctrl+D/Shift+Command+D on your keyboard.

    You will see a notation saying that the shortcut is currently assigned to Links. You could try other key combinations to arrive at one that's not already in use; however, in this case, you'll overwrite the existing shortcut instead.

Note: While the buttons you are creating will eventually be invisible, it's OK for now to leave the default color and stroke.

![Keyboard Shortcuts dialog box]

Keyboard Shortcuts

Set:
[Default]   New Set...   Delete Set

Product Area: Save   Show Set...
Object Menu

Commands:

Text Frame Options...
Transform Again: Transform Again
Transform Again: Transform Again Individually
Transform Again: Transform Sequence Again
Transform Again: Transform Sequence Again Individually
Transform: Flip Horizontal
Transform: Flip Vertical
Transform: Move Guides...
Transform: Move...
Transform: Rotate 180°

Current Shortcuts:

Remove

New Shortcut: Context:
Shift+Cmd+D   Default   Assign

Currently Assigned to:
Links

Cancel   OK

Go to Edit > Keyboard Shortcuts to add a keyboard shortcut to the Transform Again: Transform Again command found under the Object Menu.

Note: If you are migrating to InDesign from Quark or PageMaker, the set of Quark or PageMaker keyboard shortcuts may have some appeal. It's in your best interests to resist the temptation to use them, however. Many of the shortcuts used in InDesign carry over to other Adobe applications, and learning them will likely translate to greater efficiency throughout the Creative Suite environment.

Tip: The shortcut you created will enable you to repeat any transformation: scale skew, rotate, size, duplicate, and position. Transform Sequence Again is another command worth exploring, allowing you to repeat a series of transformations with just one click.

9. Click Assign to accept the new shortcut and click Yes on the alert that reads: "Cannot modify the default set. Create a new set based on the Default set?"

10. Name the new set "Interactive" and click OK.

11. Click the Set dropdown to see that you now have four sets of shortcuts to choose from: InDesign's default, Shortcuts for PageMaker 7.0, Shortcuts for QuarkXPress 4.0 and the Interactive set you just created. Click OK to exit the Keyboard Shortcuts dialog.

12. With your new keyboard shortcut set up and ready to go, hold down the Shift+Ctrl/Shift+Command keys and press D, five times to automatically duplicate and position the required buttons.

13. With the Selection tool, click and drag through all seven rectangles to select them. If the rectangles have a fill and/or stroke color, press the / key on your keyboard, press the X key to swap focus between the stroke and fill, and then press / again to remove the color.

Your rectangles should now be invisible, save for the bounding boxes that appear in InDesign's Normal view mode.

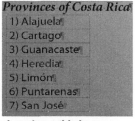

Provinces of Costa Rica
1) Alajuela
2) Cartago
3) Guanacaste
4) Heredia
5) Limón
6) Puntarenas
7) San José

Selected invisible hotspot rectangles with no stroke or fill color.

14. Open the Buttons panel, select the first rectangle, and convert it to a button. Name the button "alajuelaBtn," press Enter/Return, and add a Rollover state.

15. With the Rollover state active, click the arrow to the right of the Fill swatch on the Control panel to open the Swatches panel. Choose the R=232 G=232 B=232 color swatch, a very light gray color.

16. Double-click the button with the Selection tool to access the button rectangle, and click the *fx.* icon on the Control panel. Choose Transparency from the Effects options.

17. Select Overlay from the Mode dropdown in the Effects dialog and click OK.

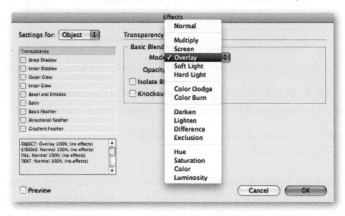

Add an Overlay Transparency effect to the Rollover state of the hotspot.

18. Open the Object Styles panel, create a new Object style, and name it "provincesOver." Be sure to apply the style to your button.

19. Return to the Buttons panel and change the Event to On Roll Over.

20. Add a Show/Hide Buttons action and show the alajuelaMap button.

21. Change the Event to On Roll Off and add a Show/Hide Buttons action to hide the alajuelaMap button.

    When you preview your button in the next step, you'll note that, while your button works properly, the alajuelaMap button is visible when the page first loads, and only disappears when you roll off the alajuelaBtn hotspot. You'll need to set the province buttons to be hidden until they are triggered by the hotspots.

22. Preview your page in the Preview panel, roll over and roll off the alajuelaMap button, and then close the Preview panel.

23. In the Layers panel, expand the flora page 1 layer, and then expand the provinces sublayer.

24. Click in the selection column to the right of the alajuelaMap sublayer to select the button. Then, in the Buttons panel, check the Hidden Until Triggered checkbox at the lower left of the panel.

25. Set each of the remaining six province buttons to Hidden Until Triggered so they aren't visible when the page first loads.

26. Convert each of the remaining hotspot rectangles to buttons, add a Rollover state, and then apply the provincesOver object style. Name the buttons and target their actions as follows:

Button Name	Show/Hide Target
cartagoBtn	cartagoMap
guanacasteBtn	guanacateMap
herediaBtn	herediaMap
limonBtn	limonMap
puntarenasBtn	puntarenasMap
sanjoseBtn	sanjoseMap

27. Preview the page to check that each of your buttons is functioning properly.

28. Select all seven buttons and group them (Ctrl+G/Command+G). You may find it easiest to select them in the Layers panel rather than on the page.

By grouping the buttons, you create a sublayer in the Layers panel that helps to keep things organized.

29. Note that the button group appears as a sublayer in the Layers panel with the default name of <group>. Click once on the sublayer name, pause very briefly, and click again to activate the name field. Rename the sublayer "provinces hotspots."

Notice that the province buttons appear in the Layers panel in the order in which they were created, with alejuelaBtn at the bottom of the stack. You may find navigating the layers in the panel easier if they reflect the position of the buttons on the document. Rearranging the object stacking order is quite simple, just select and drag each object layer to a new position.

30. Select the alajuelaBtn object layer and drag it to the top of the provinces hotspots group in the Layers panel.

31. Rearrange the remaining province buttons accordingly to reflect the sequence of provinces on the document.

The province buttons in the Layers panel arranged to reflect their order in the document.

32. Save and close the file.

Compound Multi-button Groups

The fact that buttons continue to function when part of a group is particularly useful in situations where you need an object with richer functionality than one simple button can provide. In such cases, it is possible to create a grouped object that contains multiple buttons, each with their own functionality.

Exercise 7.2: Compound Multi-button Groups

In this exercise, you'll create pop-up buttons from text objects that contain information about the active volcanoes in Costa Rica. The buttons will be hidden when the page loads, and will appear when you release the mouse after clicking a hotspot on the corresponding volcano name. You will also add a Close button to each volcano pop-up to create a compound button group that appears as a single object.

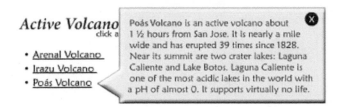

The volcano pop-up is triggered when a hotspot over the volcano name is clicked and released. The Close button and the volcano popup are separate buttons that have been grouped to appear as a single object.

1. Open **ex7_2_end.indd** and press Ctrl+Shift+Enter/Command+Shift+Return to preview the file. Click each volcano name to display the corresponding volcano pop-up. If necessary, use the Close button to hide the pop-up. Close the Preview panel and, if you like, leave the file open for reference.

2. Open **ex7_2_start.indd** and save it as ex7_2.indd.

3. Go to View > Entire Pasteboard to see the collection of objects placed to the left of the spread. Press and hold Ctrl+Spacebar/Command+Spacebar and, when the Zoom icon appears on the cursor, drag a rectangular marquee around the objects to zoom in on them.

4. Open the Buttons panel, select the object containing the Arenal Volcano text, and convert it to a button. Name the button "popupAV" and check the Hidden until Triggered checkbox at the bottom of the panel.

5. Convert each of the remaining text objects to buttons and check the Hidden until Triggered checkbox for each of them. Name the buttons as follows:
   - Irazu Volcano text object: popupIV
   - Poás Volcano text object: popupPB
   - Turrialba Volcano text object: popupTV
   - Rincón de la Vieja Volcano text object: popupRVV

InDesign Libraries and Snippets

The .indl extension stands for "InDesign library." A library is a standalone file that enables you to store page elements for later use. Library items can include text, graphics, grids and guides; anything you can include on a document page. Identical in format and function to the Sample Buttons Library, you can add elements from a page or spread, even an entire page layout, to an InDesign library. In fact, anything you can add to an .indl file, you can add to the Sample Buttons Library as well. There is nothing in the structure of the Sample Buttons Library that restricts it to containing only buttons.

To create a library, go to File > New > Library, name your library file, and save it in a location of your choosing. The new library will open in InDesign, and a panel displaying its contents will appear in the panel dock. All libraries, including the Sample Buttons Library, display the same panel icon, and libraries you create display the .indl file name at the top of the panel. You can open as many libraries as your computer memory can handle at any given time.

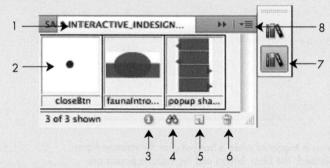

Object Library

1. Library file name. **2.** Object thumbnail and name. **3.** Library Item Information button. **4.** Show Library Subset button. **5.** New Library Item button. **6.** Delete Library Item button. **7.** Library panel icon. **8.** Library panel menu.

Library items travel with all their formatting including Character, Paragraph, Object, Cell and Table styles, as well as swatches for each of their colors.

So, if you were to save a formatted table to a library, not only would the table maintain its styling when placed from the library into your document, it would actually populate the Style panels with the definitions for all the styles applied to it. And, while you can drag library items to any position on a page, if you use the Place Item(s) command from the Library panel menu instead, the library item will be automatically positioned at the original x,y page coordinates.

There are a number of ways to add items to a library:

- Select and drag the items from your document into the Library panel.
- Select the items and click the New Library Item button at the bottom of the panel.
- Add selected items using any of the Add options in the panel menu.

With each of these methods, the item is added to the library with a default name of "Untitled." This can become problematic as the number of items in your library grows.

The Library panel menu.

The library's Show Subset feature enables you to filter library items based on item name, creation date, object type, and description. Of course, you must enter a name and description in order to take advantage of this organizational feature. Holding the Alt/Option key while clicking the New button will add your new item to the library, and also open the Item Information dialog where you can enter a name and description. For an existing library item, double click the item to access the dialog. Note that the Creation Date and Object Type are entered automatically.

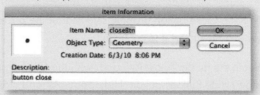

Alt-click/Option-click the New Library Item button or double-click
an existing library item to access the Item Information dialog.

To filter the objects appearing in your library, click the Show Library Subset button at the bottom of the panel. The Show Subset dialog provides the option to search the entire library, or only the items that are currently visible in the panel. You can choose any combination of search parameters to create any level of granularity for your search. When you press OK, only the items conforming to your search criteria appear in the panel. To restore the view of the complete library collection, choose Show All from the panel menu. You can also sort the visible items based on name, description, type, and creation date from the panel menu.

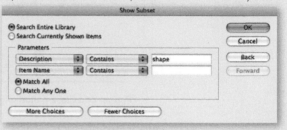

Select search parameters in the Show Subset dialog to
display only the library items that match your criteria.

Snippets

Snippets are essentially library items without the Library panel. Just like library items, Snippets can include any item or collection of items on a page or spread. To create a Snippet, select the objects you want to include and go to File > Export. Choose InDesign Snippet from the Save As Type (Windows) or Format (Mac) menu dropdown in the Export dialog. Save the file to your preferred location.

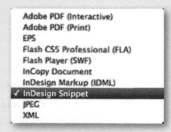

Format dropdown from
the Export dialog.

You place a Snippet just as you would place any other file; go to File > Place (Ctrl+D/Command+D) and browse to the desired file. Like library items, Snippets can remember their original page coordinates. If you go to Preferences > File Handling, you can set the behavior for placed Snippets to be positioned at either the cursor location or their original page coordinates. Regardless of the default, you can override it and invoke the opposite behavior on a case-by-case basis by holding down the Alt/Option key when you click to place a Snippet on the page.

The file extension for InDesign CS5 Snippets is now .idms, but was .inds in previous versions of the application. InDesign CS5 Snippets are backward compatible to InDesign CS4 only, and cannot be opened in earlier versions of the program.

The buttons you just created will act as pop-ups, so you won't be adding any functionality to them directly. Instead, you'll create an additional button that will be grouped with the pop-up and that will serve to close it.

6. Go to File > Open and open **lib7.indl** from the chapter_7_exercises folder.

7. Select the popupAV button on the pasteboard, and then drag the Close button graphic from the Library panel onto its upper right corner, as shown below.

8. With the Close button graphic selected on the pasteboard, open the Buttons panel and convert it to a button.

9. Name the button "closeAV" and, with the On Release event selected, add a Show/Hide Buttons action. Hide popupAV and closeAV and check the Hidden Until Triggered checkbox at the bottom left of the panel.

10. Select both pop-upAV and the closeAV button with the Selection tool. On the Control panel, click the [icon] button and choose Align to Selection. Click the Align top edges and Align right edges buttons to align the Close button to the upper right of the pop-up.

Pop-up and Close button aligned with the Control panel alignment tools.

11. Alt+Shift+drag/Option-Shift+drag the closeAV button onto the popupIV button to create a duplicate and keep the duplicate button vertically aligned. (Be sure to release the mouse before releasing the keys on your keyboard.)

Don't rename the duplicate button just yet. You'll do that after you've created the close buttons for the other pop-ups.

12. To repeat the transform using the keyboard shortcut you set up in steps 6-11 of the previous exercise (page 105), hold down the Shift+Ctrl/ Shift+Command keys and click the D key three times. You should now have four duplicates of the closeAV button, all vertically aligned.

13. Select popupIV and its Close button, and click the Align top edges icon on the Control panel.

14. Select each remaining pop-up and its Close button, and align their top edges.

15. Select the closeAV button and position your cursor after the text in the X coordinate field at the far left of the Control panel. Type "-6" and press Enter on your keyboard. InDesign does the math for you and subtracts 6 from the X coordinate to reposition the button on the document.

16. Tab to the Y text field and type "+5" after the Y coordinate to move the close button down 5 px on the page.

17. Select the Close button on popupIV and Shift-click to select the Close buttons on popupPV, popupTV, and popupRVV.

18. Go to Object > Transform > Transform Sequence Again Individually. Ta-da! Like magic, all the Close buttons are precisely and uniformly positioned atop their respective pop-ups.

19. Select the Close button for popupIV and rename it "closeIV". Change the Show/Hide action to hide popupIV and closeIV. InDesign may already "know" which Close button you want to hide, but you will still need to manually hide the pop-up.

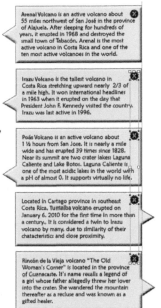

The **Transform Sequence Again Individually** command enables you to position all the selected buttons uniformly with one click.

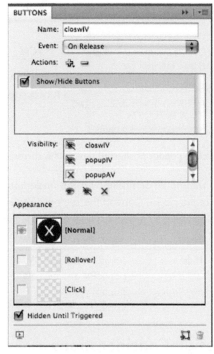

20. Select the Close button for popupPV and rename it "closePV." Change the Show/Hide action to hide popupPV and closePV.

21. Select the Close button for popupTV and rename it "closeTV." Change the Show/Hide action to hide popupTV and closeTV.

22. Select the Close button for popupRVV and rename it "closeRVV." Change the Show/Hide action to hide popupRVV and closeRVV.

23. Group each of the pop-ups with their respective Close buttons.

24. Select and rename each pop-up group in the Layers panel with the volcano name appended by the word "popup." ("Arenal popup," "Irazu popup," etc.)

25. Position the first three pop-ups on the document so their arrows point to the appropriate volcano names. Use the arrow keys on your keyboard to nudge them into place as necessary.

26. When you're happy with the placement of the volcano pop-ups in the first column, hide them in the Layers panel and position the remaining two pop-ups.

27. Show the hidden pop-ups in the Layers panel, select all five pop-ups, and group them. Rename the group sublayer "volcano popups" and hide it in the Layers panel.

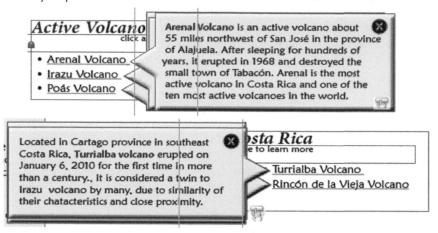

The two columns of volcano popups positioned next to the corresponding volcano name.

28. Draw a rectangle with no fill or stroke over the underlined Arenal Volcano text at the lower right of the page. Convert the rectangle to a button and name it "btnAV." Add the following to a Show/Hide action on the On Release event:

Show:	popupAV and closeAV
Hide:	popupIV and closeIV
	popupPV and closePV
	popupTV and close TV
	popupRVV and closeRVV

Interactive Design Considerations

There is almost always more than one way to approach the functional aspects of an interactive project. In thinking about the volcano pop-ups, an alternative approach might be to use On Roll Over and On Roll Off events to trigger the Show/Hide actions instead of the On Release event. Rollover buttons would eliminate the need for the Close buttons on the pop-ups, and would make the Show/Hide events less complex.

Without the Close buttons, if the pop-ups were triggered to show by a rollover event, they would require an On Roll Off event rather than an On Release event to close. Otherwise, dragging the mouse over an open pop-up could inadvertently trigger the rollover event on one of the hotspot buttons hidden below.

If a pop-up provides information that a user might want to note, such as a phone number or contact information, having it "stick," as the volcano pop-ups do, would most likely provide a more user-friendly experience. An On Release event could easily have been added to the pop-ups themselves, however, the Close buttons provide a visual cue that enhances usablity.

An alternative to grouping the pop-ups with the Close buttons would be to group the Close graphic and the pop-up text before converting to a button. In such a case, the entire button would act as a hotspot for the triggering event.

You'll want the hotspot buttons that trigger the popups to both show their associated pop-up and close buttons, as well as hide the other pop-up groups. This will make it possible for a user to open one pop-up after another without having to manually close each pop-up.

29. Make four duplicates of btnArenal and position a button over each of the remaining volcano names. Name each button and add a Show/Hide action as follows:

Button Name	Show	Hide
btnIV	popupIV and closeIV	popupAV and closeAV popupPV and closePV popupTV and close TV popupRVV and closeRVV
btnPV	popupPV and closePV	popupAV and closeAV popupIV and closeIV popupTV and close TV popupRVV and closeRVV
btnTV	popupTV and closeTV	popupAV and closeAV popupIV and closeIV popupPV and closePV popupRVV and closeRVV
btnRVV	popupRVV and closeRVV	popupAV and closeAV popupIV and closeIV popupPV and closePV popupTV and closeTV

30. Select the five invisible hotspot buttons and group them. Name the group "volcano buttons" in the Layers panel.

31. Show the volcano pop-ups sublayer and preview the spread to check your work. If you don't show the pop-ups in the Layers panel, they won't appear when you preview.

32. Save and close the file.

Creating a Navigation Bar with Dropdown Menus

An obvious and fundamental part of any website is its persistent navigational structure, often referred to as the navbar. For the sake of usability, it's important that navigation to the primary destinations within the site be consistent from page to page. InDesign master pages are designed to contain objects that appear on multiple document pages, making them the perfect repository for navigational elements. To learn more about working with master pages, see Working with Master Pages starting on page 302.

Creating Hyperlink Destinations

As you know, it's possible to publish interactive InDesign documents to both SWF and PDF. As mentioned previously, some actions are available for both output formats, while others are format-specific. In instances when there are multiple ways to accomplish a particular behavior, it makes sense to focus on using as many cross-functional features as possible, to minimize development time, ensure the greatest possible scope and provide uniformity in performance.

While SWFs support a Go To Page action, interactive PDFs do not. Hyperlink destinations work when output to both SWF and PDF, however, and make it possible to create navigation targeted to specific document pages. With hyperlink destinations, you can design one InDesign document with navigation that functions uniformly for both PDF and SWF.

To create a hyperlink destination, go to Window > Interactive > Hyperlinks, and then select the New Hyperlink Destination option from the Hyperlinks panel menu.

Hyperlink destinations can target a page, a text anchor, or a URL. To target a page, In the New Hyperlink Destination dialog, select Page as the destination Type, and enter a name for the destination (or you can enable the Name with Page Number checkbox). Then, select the document page you wish to target. The Zoom setting determines the magnification at which the targeted page will display, based on the dimensions of the page and the display window.

✓ Fixed
Fit View
Fit in Window
Fit Width
Fit Height
Fit Visible
Inherit Zoom

Zoom options for hyperlink destinations targeted to a specific page.

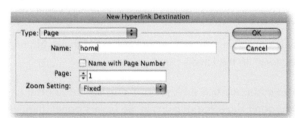

Hyperlink destinations make it possible to create page navigation that works in both exported SWFs and PDFs.

To create a hyperlink destination that targets a text anchor, select the target text and open the New Hyperlink Destination dialog. In the dialog, choose Text Anchor as the destination Type, and enter an anchor name.

For a URL target, in the New Hyperlink Destination dialog, choose URL as the destination Type, enter a name for the destination, and then enter the full URL. You can use any valid protocol: http, mailto, file, or ftp. If you want the actual URL to display on the page, type the URL address where you want it to appear, and select it. Then go to Window > Interactive > Hyperlinks and choose New Hyperlink from URL from the Hyperlinks panel menu. In order for this to work, you must include the protocol in the hyperlink text. While http://www.miraimages.com will work, www.miraimages.com will not.

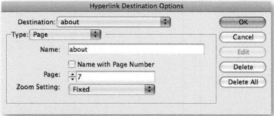

To edit a hyperlink destination, choose Hyperlink Destination Options from the Hyperlink panel menu, select a destination, and then click Edit. Enter the necessary changes and click OK.

Exercise 7.3: Creating Hyperlink Destinations

1. Open **ex7_3_end.indd** and open the Preview panel. If necessary, select Set Preview Document Mode (![icon]) at the bottom right of the panel and then press Play. (If you have either of the other two modes selected, the navbar won't work.) Test the links on the side navbar and note that it appears identically on every page. Keep the file open for reference or close it as you desire.

2. Open **ex7_3_start.indd** and save it as ex7_3.indd. If necessary, navigate to page 1.

3. Go to Window > Interactive > Hyperlinks to open the Hyperlinks panel or click the ![icon] icon in the Panel dock.

4. From the Hyperlinks panel menu, choose New Hyperlink Destination.

5. Ensure that Page is selected from the Type dropdown and that Name with Page number is unchecked. Enter "home" in the Name field, and click OK.

6. Create destinations for each of the remaining site pages as follows:

Destination	Page #
texture	2
flora1	3
flora2	4
fauna1	5
fauna2	6
about	7
contact	8

7. Save the file and keep it open for the next exercise.

Exercise 7.4: Creating a Navbar

1. If the file from the last exercise isn't still open, open **ex7_4_start.indd** and save it as ex7_4.indd. Click the down arrow in the page navigation controls at the bottom left of the document window. Select A-Master to navigate to the Master page that will contain the navbar.

The page navigation controls at the bottom left of the document window.

The master page contains two elements that you will use in constructing the navbar: a rectangular graphic that will serve as its background, and a text box with the word "home" that will be the foundation for the buttons.

2. If necessary, switch to the Selection tool and select the text frame containing the word "home." Right-click/Ctrl-click the text frame and choose Interactive > Convert to Button from the contextual menu.

3. When the Button panel opens, name the button "homeNav" and click [Rollover] to add a Rollover state. Leave the Rollover state active.

4. Select the button text with the Type tool and then choose Paragraph Rules from the Control panel menu. Choose Rule Below and check the Rule On checkbox. Set the Weight to 5 px, the Width to Text, and the Offset to 4 px. Leave the default Text Color setting and click OK.

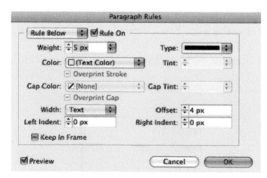

Paragraph Rule settings for the Rollover state homeNav button text.

5. With the text still selected, create a new Paragraph style and name it "navOver". Be sure to check the Apply Style to Selection checkbox.

6. Switch to the Selection tool and, with the On Release event active in the Buttons panel, add a Go To Destination action. Choose home from the Destination dropdown and ensure that the selected document is ex7_4.indd.

Note: You can target a Go to Destination action to a hyperlink destination in an external document. Select an open document from the Document dropdown or click the folder icon to browse for the document containing the hyperlink destination you want to target.

The Buttons panel with a Go to Destination action targeted to a Named Destination called "home."

7. Select the upper left point in the Control panel Reference Point proxy. With the Selection tool, Shift+Alt+drag/Shift+Option+drag the button to the right to duplicate it. Release the mouse when the smart guide X coordinate reads 184 px.

8. Go to Object > Transform Again and repeat four times to create a total of six buttons on the navbar. (Or you can use the Shift+Ctrl+D/Shift+Command+D keyboard shortcut you set up in Exercise 7.1.)

9. Select the Type tool and replace the text of the button Rollover states for the duplicated buttons, as shown in the navbar image below.

Note: Double-click in a word to select it. Triple-click to select a line. Click four times to select a paragraph. Five clicks selects all (but may wear out your pointing finger). With the Type tool active in a text frame, press the Esc key to select the object rather than the text, and automatically switch to the Selection tool.

| home | texture | flora | fauna | about | contact |

The Rollover state of the navbar buttons. The text on the buttons should appear in the following sequence: home, texture, flora, fauna, about, contact.

10. From the Buttons panel menu, choose Reset All Buttons to Normal State and correct the normal state button text for each duplicated button.

11. With the Selection tool, select each duplicated button and change its name and destination in the Buttons panel as follows:

Button Text	Button Name	Destination
texture	textureNav	texture1
flora	floraNav	flora1
fauna	faunaNav	fauna
about	aboutNav	about
contact	contactNav	contact

12. Click the ▣ icon in the panel dock or click Shift+Ctrl+Enter/ Shift+Command+Return to open the Preview panel. Click the Preview Document Mode (▣) button at the bottom of the panel and then click Play.

13. When the preview appears, test each of your buttons to ensure that they navigate to the appropriate page. Close the Preview panel.

Although not really complicated, the behavior of the navbar submenu warrants some thinking through.

- You want the submenu buttons to appear when the user rolls over the texture and flora buttons on the navbar, and disappear when the mouse is rolled off. This will require adding a Show/Hide action to the On Roll Over and On Roll Off events of the textureNav and floraNav buttons.

- The two buttons for each of the submenus will need to be hidden until triggered.

- In addition to a Go To Destination action, the On Release event for each submenu button will require a Show/Hide Action that hides its submenu button pair.

- Each submenu button will require a Show/Hide action on its On Roll Over and On Roll Off events to show and hide its submenu button pair.

Now to create the submenu buttons...

The texture and flora navbar buttons with their submenus.

14. Still on the Master page, with the Selection tool, Shift+Alt+drag/ Shift+Option+drag the floraNav button straight down until the smart guides Y coordinate reads 94.5 px. Go to Object > Transform > Transform again.

15. Select the first duplicated button, and set the object fill to R=128 G=29 B=17 for both its Normal and Rollover states. Repeat for the second button.

16. Change the name of the first dropdown button to "floraAboutBtn" and change the button text to "about" for both button states. Leave the flora1 Destination setting and check the Hidden Until Triggered checkbox.

17. Change the name of the bottom button to "floraSlideshowBtn" and change the button text to "slide show" for both button states. Change the Destination to flora2 and check the Hidden Until Triggered checkbox.

18. Select both submenu buttons with the Selection tool and Shift+Alt+drag/ Shift+Option+drag to the right until the smart guides X coordinate reads 451 px.

19. Change the name of the first fauna submenu button to "faunaScrapbooktBtn" and change the button text to "scrapbook" for both button states. Change the Destination to "fauna1."

20. Change the name of the bottom fauna submenu button to "faunaFilmstripBtn" and change the button text to "filmstrip" for both button states. Change the Destination to "fauna2."

Now it's time to add the actions. You'll start with the actions on the main navbar buttons that show and hide the submenus.

21. Select the floraNav button with the Selection tool and, in the Buttons panel, change Event to On Roll Over. Add a Show/Hide action and show floraAboutBtn and floraSlideshowBtn.

22. With the floraNav button still selected, change Event to On Roll Off and add a Show/Hide action. Hide the two flora buttons.

23. Select the faunaNav button and add a Show/Hide action to the On Roll Over event. Show faunaScrapbookBtn and faunaFilmstripBtn.

24. With the faunaNav button still selected, add a Show/Hide action to the On Roll Off event. Hide the two fauna buttons.

Next, you'll add Go to Destination actions to the submenu buttons, and actions to show and hide them accordingly.

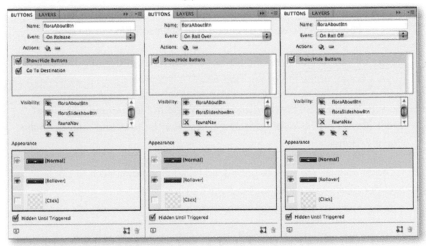

Actions settings for floraAboutBtn. Each submenu button requires actions on three separate events.

25. Select floraAboutBtn and, in the Buttons panel:
    - With the On Release event still selected, add a Show/Hide action. Hide floraAboutBtn and floraSlideshowBtn.
    - Select the On Roll Over event and add a Show/Hide action. Show floraAboutBtn and floraSlideshowBtn.
    - Select the On Roll Off event and add a Show/Hide action. Hide floraAboutBtn and floraSlideshowBtn.

26. Select floraSlideshowBtn and in the Buttons panel:

    - With the On Release event still selected, add a Show/Hide action. Hide floraAboutBtn and floraSlideshowBtn.

    - Select the On Roll Over event and add a Show/Hide action. Show floraAboutBtn and floraSlideshowBtn.

    - Select the On Roll Off event and add a Show/Hide action. Hide floraAboutBtn and floraSlideshowBtn.

27. Select faunaScrapbookBtn and in the Buttons panel:

    - With the On Release event still selected, add a Show/Hide action. Hide faunaScrapbookBtn and faunaFilmstripBtn.

    - Select the On Roll Over event and add a Show/Hide action. Show faunaScrapbookBtn and faunaFilmstripBtn.

    - Select the On Roll Off event and add a Show/Hide action. Hide faunaScrapbookBtn and faunaFilmstripBtn.

28. Select faunaFilmstripBtn and in the Buttons panel:

    - With the On Release event still selected, add a Show/Hide action. Hide faunaScrapbookBtn and faunaFilmstripBtn.

    - Select the On Roll Over event and add a Show/Hide action. Show faunaScrapbookBtn and faunaFilmstripBtn.

    - Select the On Roll Off event and add a Show/Hide action. Hide faunaScrapbookBtn and faunaFilmstripBtn.

29. Select all your buttons and the navbar background and group them. In the Layers panel, name the group "top nav."

30. Be sure to select Set Preview Document Mode in the Preview panel and press Play to preview your document. Test your buttons and then close the Preview panel.

    Congratulations! You've now got a solid foundation from which to create robust and persistent site navigation. Next you'll save this navbar as a library item so you can use it as the basis for future navbars.

31. With the top nav group selected, open the Sample Buttons Library from the Buttons panel menu. Alt-click/Option-click the New Library Item button at the bottom of the panel and name the item "dropdown navbar". Enter a description. We entered: "6 button navbar with submenus."

32. Save and close your file.

Creating Email and Web Links

So far, all the action in the document has taken place internally; however, creating external links is as simple as adding a Go To URL action. For links to external web pages, it's important to enter the full URL: http://www.mywebsite.com. Email links are equally easy, with the email address preceded by "mailto:"

Exercise 7.5: Creating Email and Web Links

emailBtn button.

1. Open **ex7_5_start.indd** and save it as ex7_5.indd. Select the email button with the Selection tool.

2. Add a Go To URL action to the On Release event and enter mailto:info@miraimages.com?subject=Interactive InDesign in the URL field.

Go To URL settings for emailBtn.

Go To URL settings for webURL button.

The "**?subject=Interactive InDesign**" portion of the email address populates the Subject line of the email.

3. Select the webURL button and, in the Buttons panel, add a Go To URL action to the On Release event. Enter "**http://www.miraimages.com**" in the URL field.

webURL button.

4. Save the file and preview the page. (Choose Set Preview Spread Mode at the bottom of the Preview panel.) Test your buttons to see that the email button opens the mail client resident on the system and the web button opens the default browser.

5. Close out of the email client and the browser, and then save and close the InDesign file.

CHAPTER SUMMARY

You really covered a lot of territory in this chapter! Starting with invisible button hotspots that triggered pop-up highlights on a map, you then moved on to groups of multiple buttons designed to appear as one object. From there you created a navbar with dropdown menus, using hyperlink destinations to establish multiple internal links. You wrapped up the chapter, and your exploration of buttons, by creating an email link with a subject line, and a link to an external web page.

In addition to working through the technical details of creating complex buttons, you thought about how best to design the interactivity of the interface to create an optimal user experience.

As part of your explorations, you became familiar with InDesign libraries and snippets and learned how to:

- Create library items and snippets
- Add items to a library
- Add library items and snippets to a page
- Filter library items

You made additional refinements to the InDesign environment by establishing a custom keyboard shortcut and became familiar with two powerfully useful commands:

- Object > Transform > Transform Again
- Object > Transform > Transform Sequence Again

With your deep dive into buttons complete, the next leg of the journey takes you into the world of animation! No longer are you limited by the static object on the printed page; InDesign CS5 lets you bring your designs to life. Part 3 gives you all the tools you need to master the magic of motion in InDesign. So, fasten your seat belt because you're in for a wild ride!

Part 3

ANIMATION

The introduction of animation to InDesign is nothing short of revolutionary. With the ability to make objects fly, InDesign takes off to a new dimension, becoming a vehicle that's perfect for creating presentations and engaging interactive projects.

In this portion of the book, you'll learn to animate objects on a path called a motion path; extend existing animation presets; and set duration, sequence, timing delays, and triggering events. You'll learn a host of ways to take the magic of animation outside the box and create masterful illusions of objects moving through space. In short, you'll learn everything there is to learn about creating animation in InDesign CS5.

● Chapter 8

INTRODUCING: ANIMATION IN INDESIGN!

Animation is a natural, if not absolutely essential, factor in creating an engaging user experience. After all, what better way to bring a document to life than with objects that perform mobile antics on a page?

In this chapter, you'll learn to combine rotation, scale, and opacity animation with existing animation presets, as well as set triggering events, duration, sequence, and timing delays. You'll learn to animate objects on a path called a motion path, and then apply all these skills to captivating your audience with the compelling experience of a document in motion.

Introduction

InDesign makes it extremely easy to animate any object, including placed files, text boxes, graphics, and even buttons. The Animation panel and the Timing panel provide all the controls you'll need to create and manage your animations. The Animation panel is where you'll set all the animation parameters, and the Timing panel is where you'll control the sequence of play and any timing delays. Of course, the Preview panel is where you'll test and view your creations.

The Animation Panel

The Animation panel is chock full of controls, all in one neat little package. You can find it with all the other interactive panels at Window > Interactive > Animation.

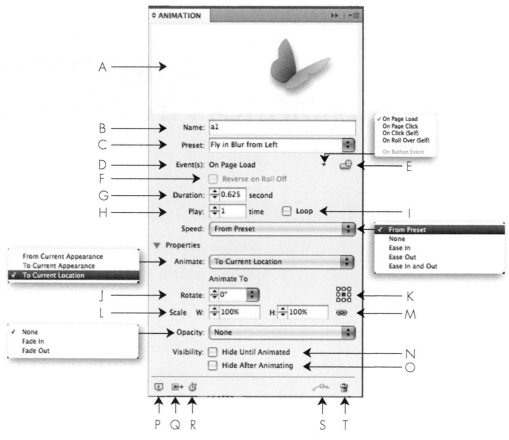

The Animation panel: A) Animation Preset preview. B) Name field. C) Preset dropdown. D) Events triggering animation. E) Create Button Trigger. F) Reverse on Roll Off: available when Roll Over Self event is applied; reverses animation. G) Duration of animation. H) Number of times to play animation. I) Loop animation. J) Degrees of rotation to animate. K) Anchor point for rotation and scale. L) Width and height scale percentages to animate. M) Lock to scale proportionately or unlock to scale disproportionately. N) Hide object until animated. O) Hide object after animating. P) Preview Spread Q) Show Animation proxy. R) Open Timing panel. S) Convert path to Motion Path. T) Remove animation.

Motion presets provide a starting point for most of the animations you'll create in InDesign. In fact, they are the very same presets you'll find in Flash Professional. At the very top of the Animation panel is a proxy display of the selected motion preset. That little pink butterfly takes the guesswork out of choosing a preset by demonstrating the animation for you right in the preview window. Be aware, however, that the butterfly is for presets only. Once you make a change to the preset parameters, the butterfly disappears.

The first field on the panel is the Name field. As you learned with buttons, objects need a name in order to be controlled by actions and events. Since the document is communicating programmatically with the animations, they, like buttons, need to be named. InDesign obliges by providing a default name for each animation. If you have multiple animations in your document, you'll find it useful to replace the default names with names more relevant to the animation. This will make it much easier to identify which animation is which, should you need to change timing or sequencing.

The best way to understand the Animation panel is to put it through it's paces so, let's just dive right in.

Working with Motion Presets

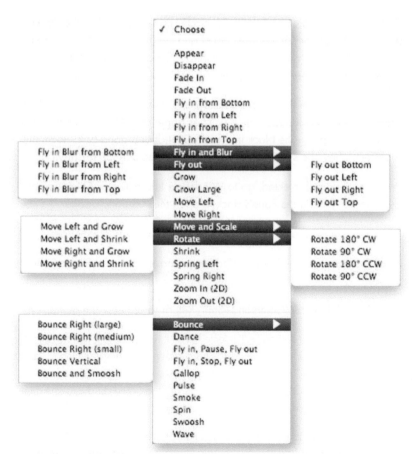

Animation presets are accessed from the Presets dropdown in the Animation panel.

The easiest way to get started with animation in InDesign is to select an object you want to animate, open the Animation panel, and choose a motion preset. InDesign does the rest. Of the 47 motion presets that ship with InDesign, more than a quarter of them animate changes in scale, rotation, opacity, and/or speed. The controls on the Animation panel make it possible to create these sorts of animations from scratch, or to modify existing presets. The remaining motion presets are complex animations that go beyond what can be created directly in InDesign.

Exercise 8.1: Easing, Duration, and Motion Presets

As "Hello world!" is to programmers, the bouncing ball is to animators. Animating a bouncing ball has long been the traditional initiation into the world of animation. In homage to this hallowed tradition, naturally, your first InDesign animation has to be a bouncing ball.

Note: The Ellipse tool is hidden under the Rectangle tool (not the Rectangle Frame tool). Click and hold the Rectangle tool to expose the Ellipse tool so you can select it.

1. Go to File > New and, in the New Document window, choose Web as the Intent. Leave the other settings at the defaults and click OK.

2. Select the Ellipse tool (L). Hold down the Shift key and drag to create a small, perfect circle. Release the mouse before releasing the Shift key.

3. Switch to the Selection tool. With the circle still selected, click the Stroke swatch at the bottom of the Tools panel and set the color to None. Then, select the Fill swatch at the bottom of the Tools panel to ensure that it's active, and open the Gradient panel (Window > Color > Gradient).

4. Choose Radial from the Type dropdown and then click the black gradient color stop to select it. Open the Swatches panel and Alt-click/Option-click any color to replace the black in the gradient. If you don't hold down the Alt/Option key, the swatch color you click will replace the gradient.

5. With the circle still selected, go to Window > Interactive > Animation or click the ✴ icon in the Panels dock to open the Animation panel.

6. Type "ball" in the Name field to replace the default name of "circle."

7. Near the bottom of the Preset dropdown, choose Bounce > Bounce and Smoosh.

8. Press Ctrl+Shift+Enter/Command+Shift+Return to preview the animation.

Easing:

Transitions in animation speed are referred to as *easing*. InDesign has six easing options:

From Preset: Inherits easing from Preset.

None: No easing.

Ease In: Starts slowly and increases in speed to give the impression of acceleration.

Ease Out: Starts fast and slows down to give the impression of deceleration.

Ease In and Out: Starts fast, slows in the middle, and speeds up at the end.

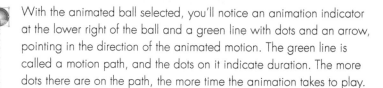

With the animated ball selected, you'll notice an animation indicator at the lower right of the ball and a green line with dots and an arrow, pointing in the direction of the animated motion. The green line is called a motion path, and the dots on it indicate duration. The more dots there are on the path, the more time the animation takes to play.

In the image to the left, the duration of the first ball animation is the Bounce and Smoosh preset default of 3.125 seconds. The second instance of the animation was set to a duration of 1 second. As you can see, the shorter animation has fewer dots. Notice, too, that the dots are not spaced evenly on the motion path; the way these dots are spaced indicates easing. The closer the dots, the less distance is traveled, the slower the motion. The farther apart they are, the more distance is traveled, the faster the motion. For this particular preset, you can see that the velocity of the ball is variable, starting out slow, accelerating, then alternately slowing and accelerating with the bounce. This preset incorporates a sequence of transformations in scale and easing that are beyond what you can create in InDesign. You can, however, make modifications to the preset to incorporate changes of rotation, scale, and opacity.

9. Alt-drag/Option-drag the ball with the Selection tool to duplicate it. Rename the duplicated animation "ball2."

10. With ball2 selected on the document, from the Interactive workspace, drag the Preview panel to a column of its own in the Panel dock. Open the panel and drag the lower left corner to enlarge it.

11. Open the Animation panel. If necessary, twirl down the Properties arrow to display additional controls. Both the Preview panel and the Animation panel should be visible and accessible, with the Animation panel overlapping the Preview panel.

12. Preview the animation again to see that the first animation plays through before the second animation begins. By default, InDesign animations play in the order in which they were created.

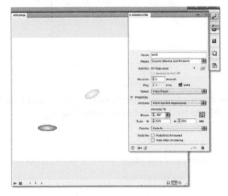

With the Preview panel open, you can change the animation properties of a selected object in the Animation panel, and then click the Play button in the Preview panel to refresh the animation.

13. With both panels still open, change the Duration of the ball2 animation to 1 second. Set Opacity to Fade Out. Make sure the Constrain the Scale Value link icon is linked (🔗) (to the right of Scale Height), and enter "50" in the W field. Tab to populate the H field with the same value.

14. Click the Play button on the Preview panel to refresh the animation preview.

Easing can give your animation a more realistic feel, conveying a sense of momentum or deceleration. While sometimes subtle, appropriate use of the Speed options can lend authenticity to your work.

15. Delete the second ball. With the remaining ball selected, choose Fly in From Top from the Preset dropdown in the Animation panel. Change the Duration to 3 seconds.

16. Alt-drag/Option-drag to duplicate until you have a total of five balls. In the Animation pane, name each of the ball animations: "ball1", "ball2", "ball3", "ball4", "ball5."

17. Position one ball near the left margin and another near the right margin, with the other three balls in between. Select all five balls and go to Window > Object and Layout > Align to open the Align panel.

While there are Align controls on the Control panel, the Distribute Spacing commands are only available through the Align panel.

18. From the Align panel menu, choose Show Options to display the Distribute Spacing commands. Confirm that Align to Selection is chosen and then click the Distribute Horizontal Space button.

The Align panel with panel options displayed and the Distribute Horizontal Space button highlighted.

19. Choose Align to Page from the Align to dropdown and then click the ![icon] button to align the vertical centers of the objects to the vertical center of the page. This will enable you to see the entire animation.

20. Select the first ball and ensure that the Speed option in the Animation panel is set to From Preset. Select the second ball and set the Speed to None, the third to Ease In, the fourth to Ease Out, and the fifth to Ease In and Out.

21. At the bottom of the Animation panel, press the ![icon] button to open the Timing panel.

22. Select the first item in the list, hold the Shift key, and select the last. With all the items selected, click the Play Together button (![icon]) at the bottom of the panel.

23. Click the Preview Spread button at the bottom of the panel. In the preview, note the differences in the Ease settings. Save the file as **ex8_1.indd** in the chapter_8_exercises folder and then close your document.

Working with the Pen Tool

The Pen tool in InDesign is the same tool found in Illustrator and Photoshop. It's a tool that people just love to hate. If you're one of those folks who want to tear their hair out at the mere mention of the Pen tool, take heart. With a few simple pointers and a little bit of practice, you'll be on your way to mastery.

Working efficiently with the Pen tool entails use of several keyboard shortcuts. The first of these shortcuts is the Ctrl/Command key. While you hold down this key, the active tool switches temporarily to the Direct Selection tool. When you release the key, the original tool returns. You'll be placing points as you draw with the Pen tool, and there will be times when you'll need the Direct Selection tool to select and manipulate those points.

The next thing you'll want to be aware of is the Corner Options controls at the far right of the Control panel. These controls are available when any tool other than the Type tool or the Note tool is selected. In order for the Pen tool to function as intended, *ensure that the Corner Options control is set to None* before you start drawing with the Pen tool.

Ensure that the Corner Options are set to None on the Control panel before drawing with the Pen tool.

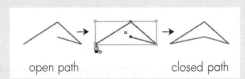

open path   closed path

You can hold down the Ctrl/Command key and click off a path to deselect it. To close an active, open path, mouse over the first point on the path, and click when the Pen tool cursor displays a little circle.

Drawing straight lines with the Pen tool is simple. Just click where you want to place a point, and then release. When you click and release a second point, you will have a straight path joining the two points. Holding the Shift key when you click and release constrains placement of a point to an angle that's a multiple of 45° from the previous point. So, to draw a path that is perfectly horizontal or perfectly vertical, hold the Shift key when you click, and then release the mouse without dragging, before you release the Shift key..

Straight lines drawn at angles in multiples of 45° by holding the Shift key when clicking with the Pen tool.

When you've finished drawing an open path, hold the Ctrl/Command key and click off the path to deselect it, or press P on your keyboard. P is the shortcut for the Pen tool, and when you press it while drawing a path, it gets ready to draw a new one, as indicated by a small X at the lower right of the Pen tool cursor.

To draw curves with the Pen tool, it helps to think of a rubber band that you're stretching in the direction you want the curve to go. When you click and hold with the Pen tool to place an anchor point, and then drag, direction lines appear that enable you to shape the curve. The trick is to drag the direction line in the direction you want the curve to go. Drag up when you want the curve to move upward, and drag down when you want the curve to flow down.

When drawing curves with the Pen tool, drag the direction handles in the direction you want the curve to flow.

You want to place as few anchor points as possible in order to keep your curves smooth. When you wish to sharply change the direction that a curve is flowing, you need to convert the anchor point of the curve to a corner point. The Convert Direction Point tool is made for this very purpose. While dragging a direction line with the Pen tool, hold the Alt/Option key to temporarily switch to the Convert Direction Point tool. Then drag the handle in the new direction.

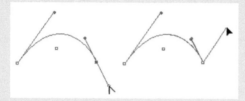

Hold the Alt/Option key to switch to the Convert Direction Point tool and then drag the direction handle to change the trajectory of a curve.

The Convert Direction Point cursor of the Pen tool.

When you mouse over a newly placed anchor point with the Pen tool, the cursor changes to display the icon for the Convert Direction Point tool. Click the anchor point to remove the second direction line in order to make a corner for a straight path.

The Pen tool provides feedback by changing the appearance of the cursor. When it's ready to draw a new path, it displays an X at the lower right. When it's engaged in drawing a path, the cursor displays only the pen. The most common stumbling block when using the Pen tool is forgetting to Ctrl-click/Command-click off (or Press P) when you've completed drawing a path. The changes in the Pen tool cursor are a useful reminder of whether a path is or is not in process.

When hovering over an existing and active path, but not over an anchor point, the Pen tool displays the Add Anchor Point cursor. If you click when this cursor is visible, you'll add an anchor point to the path. Similarly, if you hover over an existing point on an active path, you will see the Delete Anchor Point cursor. If you click, you'll remove the anchor point from the path.

The many faces of the Pen tool cursor: A) Ready to draw a new path. B) A path is being drawn. C) Click an endpoint on an existing path to pick up and continue drawing. D) Click to close the path. E) Click to snap to guide—only available when Snap to Guides is turned on. F) Add anchor point. G) Delete anchor point. H) Convert direction point.

Exercise 8.2: The Pen Tool

Mastery of the Pen tool takes a bit of practice, but it's worth the investment of time. Once you have it down, you'll be able to modify any vector graphic, create perfect tracings, and, in the case of animation, make motion paths that bend and twist in any way you desire.

This exercise provides an introduction to the basic skills you'll need in order to develop your Pen tool chops.

1. From the chapter_8_exercises folder, open **ex8_2_start.indd** and save it as ex8_2.indd.

2. Choose a stroke color from the Tools panel and set the fill color to None.

3. Select the Pen tool (P).

4. With the Pen tool, click the center of the first red target (⊕) on path A1, and then release.

5. Hold down the Shift key, and click once on each of the red targets on the path, releasing after each click without dragging. (The Shift key constrains the path to angles that are a multiple of 45°. After you click the last target, release the Shift key, hold the Ctrl/Command key, and click off the path to deselect it (or press P).

6. For the second path in A, click and release each of the targets consecutively, starting with 1. This time, don't hold down the Shift key. After you click target 7, position the Pen tool over point 1. When you see the close path cursor for the Pen tool (✍₀), click to close the path.

7. For B, click the first red target and, still holding down the mouse, drag a direction line up to the red dot and release. Always drag direction lines in the direction you want the curve to go.

8. For each of the remaining targets in B, click and drag the direction line to follow the curve, and then release the mouse at the red dot.

9. After dragging the direction line for the last target, press the P key on your keyboard to end the path.

10. For C, click the first target and drag the direction line up to the first red dot. Click the second target and drag down to the second red dot. *Keep holding the mouse!* Press the Alt/Option key and drag the direction line up to the first yellow dot. Be sure to release the mouse before releasing the Alt/Option key.

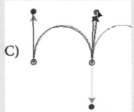

Changing the direction of the curve using the Convert Direction Point tool to create a corner point. Drag the adjustment handle to follow the trajectory of the new curve.

11. After dragging the direction line for the last target, hold the Ctrl/Command key and click off the path to deselect it.

12. For D, click the first target, drag up to the red dot, and release the mouse. Click the next target and drag down to complete the curve. Then, release the mouse and position your cursor over the point you just placed. When you see the Convert Direction Point cursor of the Pen tool (🖋), click and release to create a corner point. This will automatically remove the second direction line.

13. Hold down the Shift key, click the next target, and release the mouse. By holding the Shift key, you keep the points in horizontal alignment.

14. Position your cursor over the point you just placed, and when the Convert Direction Point cursor appears (an upside down V), click and drag down to the red dot to start the next curve.

15. Continue the process outlined above, dragging the direction lines to create curves and Shift-clicking to draw straight lines. For each point you place, convert the anchor point by clicking with the Convert Direction Point cursor of the Pen tool.

16. After placing the last point, hold the Ctrl/Command key and click off the path to deselect it.

17. Save and close the file.

Working with Motion Paths

As seen in the last exercise, motion paths determine the path travelled by an animated object. You can edit the paths in Motion Presets and you can create Motion Paths of your own. The motion path is actually distinct from the object being animated and must be manipulated independently. The simplest way to modify a motion path is with the Selection tool and the Transform tools. For changes in the actual shape of a path, you'll need the Pen and Direct Selection tool.

Exercise 8.3: Modifying Motion Preset Motion Paths

1. Open **ex8_3_end.indd** from the chapter_8_exercises folder and preview the document (Ctrl+Shift+Enter/Command+Shift+Enter). Note the text frames flying in from the left sequentially. Click the purple polygon at the left of the first row to watch it trace the motion path to the center. Click the purple polygon at the right of the second row to see it travel to the center as well. Click the purple polygon in the middle of the last row to see it travel to the right, away from the center. Close the Preview panel.

   The polygon animations demonstrate the three destination options available through the Animate dropdown in the Animation panel. The animation for all the objects, including the text, started with the same motion preset: Fly in From Left. For the text frames, the motion paths were scaled to cover a greater distance, and for the polygons, the contour of the paths was changed.

2. With the Selection tool, select each object on the page in turn, and inspect the settings in the Animation panel. When you're done exploring, keep the file open for reference.

3. Open **ex8_3_start.indd** and save it as ex8_3.indd.

4. Select the Polygon tool (nested under the Rectangle tool) and click once on the document. When the Polygon dialog opens, enter 61 px for Width, 53 px for Height, 8 for the Number of Sides, and ensure that the Star Inset is set to 0. Click OK to create the polygon and then position it on top of the yellow polygon in the top row of the background image.

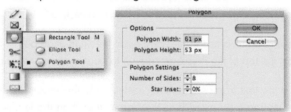

The Polygon tool and Polygon Settings dialog box. The Polygon tool is hidden with the Ellipse tool under the Rectangle tool. Click and hold the visible tool to display the other shape tools. Click once on the document with the Polygon tool selected to open the Polygon dialog.

Note: The most recently used shape tool icon will show in the Tools panel so it's a good idea to get familiar with each of the possible icons.

---

5. Select the polygon with the Selection tool and, if necessary, give it a fill. We chose purple. Open the Animation panel and choose Fly in From Left from the Preset dropdown. Click the Show animation proxy button () at the bottom of the panel. This displays a ghost of the starting point of the animation.

6. Alt-drag/Option–drag the polygon you created straight down to copy it, and align it on top of the middle polygon in the background image. Copy it again and position it on the bottom polygon.

7. Shift-click to select all the text frames and apply the Fly in From Left motion preset from the Animation panel.

8. Save and preview your document. Note that the animations play sequentially. Note also that the order in which the text frames play is incorrect.

   The text frame animations originate directly on the page. You will edit them so their animations begin from outside the boundaries of the page.

9. Zoom in on the left edge of the text frames, go to View > Grids and Guides, and confirm that Snap to Guides is checked. Switch to the Selection tool.

10. Click once on the first text frame to select it. Note the green line of the motion path running through the text, with a dot at either end.

Note: When the cursor changes to a double-sided arrow, click and drag to the left to lengthen the motion path.

• A number of the InDesign Animatio

Selected text frame with motion path applied.

11. Mouse over the motion path until you see a tooltip saying "Motion Path, click to edit." Click the motion path to select it.

12. Mouse over the left edge of the motion path. When the cursor changes to a double-sided arrow, drag left to the vertical guide located on the pasteboard.

13. Preview the spread and note the apparent acceleration of the first text frame as it travels along the motion path. Confirm that the animation is selected rather than just the motion path, and open the Animation panel. Note that Duration is still set at 1.

14. From the Animation panel menu, select Save. When the Animation Preset dialog appears, enter "Fly In Text" in the Name field and click OK.

15. Select the remaining text frames and open the Animation panel. Select Fly In Text from the top of the Preset dropdown to apply your new motion preset.

16. Deselect the text frames and then reselect only the second text frame. Notice that the motion path extends to the right rather than the left. A peek at the Animation panel reveals that the selected Animate option is set to From Current Appearance.

17. Reselect the text frames and choose To Current Location from the Animate dropdown. Preview and save the file.

Next, edit the motion paths for the polygons.

18. With the Selection tool, click once on the top-most polygon to select it, and then select its motion path.

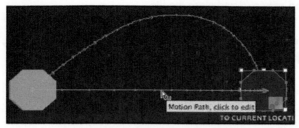

Editing a motion path with the Pen tool.

19. With the motion path selected, press P to switch to the Pen tool. Mouse over the point in the middle of the path, and, when you see the plus sign at the lower right of the Pen tool cursor, click on it once.

20. Hold down the Ctrl/Command key (to switch temporarily to the Direct Selection tool), and drag the point to the apex of the curve, as shown below. Release the mouse and then release the Ctrl/Command key.

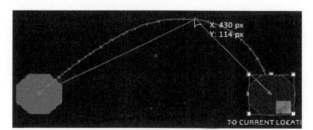

Repositioning a point added to a motion path with the Pen tool.

21. Holding down the Alt/Option key (to switch temporarily to the Convert Direction Point tool), click the point and drag down and to the right, extending the direction line in order to round out the curve.

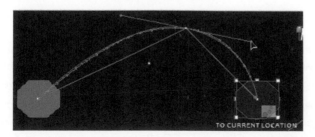

Converting a corner point to a curve with the Convert Direction Point tool.

22. Select the polygon, and, from the Animation panel menu, choose Save. Name the preset "Arch". Select the remaining two polygons and apply the Arch preset.

23. Select the second polygon with the Selection tool and, in the Animation panel, choose To Current Appearance from the Animate dropdown to change the direction of the animation.

24. Save, and preview, and close the file.

Working with Timing, Triggering Events, and Buttons

As mentioned, by default, animations are triggered by the On Page Load event and play in the order they were created. In addition to On Page Load, there are four other events you can select in the Animation panel to trigger animation. Each of them rely on user interaction: On Page Click, On Click (Self), On Roll Over (Self), and On Button Event. The On Button Event is only available from the Animation panel Event dropdown if there is already a button in the document with an action targeted to an existing animation. You can use the On Button Event option to have a button trigger an animation using any of the four button events: On Click, On Release, On Roll Over, and On Roll Off.

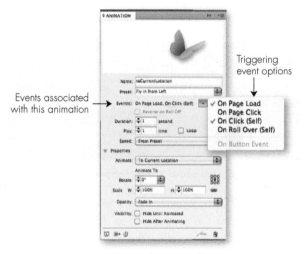

The events associated with the selected animation are listed in the Events section of the Animation panel.

Just below the Preset dropdown on the Animation panel, you'll find the list of events associated with the selected animation. To add or remove events, press the little arrow (⬚) to the right of the listed events, and select or deselect the desired event.

Events can be applied to multiple animations at the same time, and any animation can be triggered by multiple events. When multiple animations are set to play On Page Load, On Page Click, and/or On Button Event, you can use the Timing panel to change the order in which the animations play.

In the Timing panel (Window > Interactive > Timing), changing the animation sequence is as simple as dragging the animation name to the proper position in the play list. You can group animations to have them play simultaneously, and you can add delays to customize the timing.

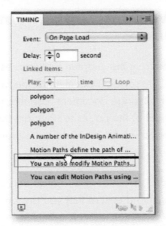

**In the Timing panel, drag animation names up or down
in the stack to change the order in which they play.**

To set animations to play together, Shift-click on each animation you want to group, and click the ⬚ button at the bottom of the panel. To remove an animation from the group, select it and click the Play separately button (⬚).

**To play animations together, select them in the Timing
panel and click the link button at the bottom of the panel.**

The events available from the Timing panel Event dropdown are determined by the triggering events established for each animation in the Animation panel. To adjust the timing for animations associated with a particular event, you must first select the event in the Timing panel. To show animations triggered by the On Page Click event, first select On Page Click from the Event dropdown. All the animations associated with that event will appear in the panel, and you can set their timing. For the Timing panel to show animations triggered by button events, the triggering button must be selected on the document. If a button has multiple events that trigger animations, such as On Roll Over and On Roll Off you can choose the triggering event from the Timing panel Event dropdown when the button is selected on the document.

You can apply a Play Animation action to an existing button right from the Animation panel. Select the animation on your document and then click the Create button trigger button (⬚) in the Event section of the panel. Next, just click the button to add the action. The Button panel opens, allowing you to make any changes. The default button event is On Release, but you can, of course, add actions to other events.

Exercise 8.4: Working with Timing, Triggering Events, and Buttons

1. Open **ex8_4_end.indd** from the chapter_8_exercises folder and preview the file. Be sure to select Set Preview Document Mode at the bottom of the Preview panel, since this is a multi-page document. Use the next and previous arrow buttons at the lower right of the pages to navigate through the document. When you're done exploring, you can close the Preview panel and keep the file open for reference.

2. Open **ex8_4_start.indd**, save it as ex8_4.indd and preview the file as above. Close the Preview panel and ensure that you are on page 1 of the document.

   As you saw in the preview, the text animations on the first and second pages need to be reordered.

3. Go to Window > Interactive > Timing or click the ⏱ icon in the Panel dock to open the Timing panel. Since the text animations are automatically named with the text they contain, they are easy to identify. Select the animation that starts with "A number…" and drag it to the top of the stack of text animations.

4. Select the text animation that starts with "You can also…" and drag it to the bottom of the stack.

The text animations ordered in the proper sequence in the Timing panel.

   For a little variety and more interactivity, you'll set the polygon animations on page 1 to be triggered when clicked rather than by the On Page Load event. You'll want to let the user know that they can click to activate the buttons, so you'll add text to the polygon objects to clue them in.

5. With the Type tool selected, type the words "click to play" in the second and third polygons on page 1. Don't worry about formatting the text just yet; although, if necessary, you can make it smaller to fit in the shape.

6. With the Type tool active in one of the polygons, press Ctrl+B/Command+B (Object > Text Frame Options) to open the Text Frame Options dialog. Choose Center from the Vertical Justification Align dropdown and click OK.

7. Press Ctrl+A/Ctrl+C to select the text and then press Shift+Ctrl+C/ Shift+Command+C to center it. Choose a typeface and font size. We chose Myriad Pro and set the size to 10 px.

8. When you're satisfied with the appearance of the text, select the Eyedropper tool and click the text to capture its formatting. You'll see that the Eyedropper fills with black ink. Click and drag the loaded Eyedropper across the text in the other two polygons to apply the formatting.

Note: With your text or text frame selected, hold down the Shift+Ctrl/ Shift+Command keys and click the > key to increase font size, or the < key to decrease it.

The Eyedropper captures the formatting of the text but not of the text frame. We've created an Object style to handle the vertical centering of the text in the text frame, to save you a few steps.

9. Select all three polygons. From the Object Styles panel, click the buttonText style to apply it.

Note: A triple click in the middle of the text with the Eyedropper tool will apply the new formatting to the entire line.

There's no reason to apply the Object style to the first polygon other than to keep the objects uniform. This puts you in a good position later, should you decide that you want to make a universal change in appearance.

10. With the polygons still selected, open the Animation panel. Click the button to access the trigger events and deselect On Page Load to stop the animation from playing automatically when the page is displayed. Click the button again and choose On Click (Self). Notice that the On Click (Self) event appears in the panel next to the word "Event(s)."

The On Click (Self) event applied to multiple animations. Notice that the Name field is empty.

11. Save the document and preview the spread. Notice that the text flies in in the proper order, and the buttons don't play until clicked. Close the Preview panel.

12. Navigate to page 2 of the document and open the Timing panel. Rearrange the text animations to reflect their order on the document.

13. Select all three polygons and apply the Fly in from Left motion preset. Choose From Current Appearance from the Animate dropdown.

14. Click off to deselect and then reselect the first polygon. In the Animation panel, set the Duration to 1.5 seconds, and set the Rotate value to 90°.

15. Select the second polygon and set the Duration to 2 seconds. Set both W and

H to 175%.

16. Select the last polygon, leave the default duration of 1 second, and choose Fade Out from the Opacity dropdown.

Note that there are three text buttons sitting just within the left page margin, one for each of the polygons. You can add a Play Animation action to each of the buttons from the Buttons panel, but it's easier to use the Create Button Trigger button on the Animation panel.

Note: When you click the Create Button Trigger button, the cursor changes to a target until you click the button that you want to trigger the animation.

17. Select the polygon with the rotate animation, and, in the Animation panel, click the Create Button Trigger button to the right of "Event(s)". Then, click on the click to play button to the left of the animation. The Buttons panel pops open to display the Animation action and the default On Release event. Note that each of the buttons have been named with reference to the animations they will trigger.

18. Drag the button onto the rotate polygon, select both objects, and press Ctrl+G/Command+G to group them.

19. Repeat steps 17 and 18 for the two remaining polygons. Save and preview the spread. Leave the Preview panel open.

20. Navigate to page 3 of the document and preview the spread. Note that all the animations on the page are triggered by the On Page Load event and that they all play sequentially. Close the Preview panel.

21. Select all six polygons on page 3. In the Animation panel, remove the On Page Load triggering event.

22. Deselect, and then reselect the first large polygon. In the Animation panel, click the Create Button Trigger button, and then click the playDelay1 button (the button to the left of the first set of polygons).

23. Select the two remaining large polygons and, once again, click the Create Button Trigger button and then click the playDelay1 button.

24. Note that clicking on a button with the Create Button Trigger button selects the button. With the playDelay1 button thus selected, open the Timing panel. Note that only the animations associated with the button appear in the panel, and the event displayed is the On Release event. Note also that the animations have been named to make them easier to identify.

25. Select delay1b in the Timing panel and set the Delay to 1 second.

26. Select delay1c in the Timing panel and set the Delay to 2 seconds. Preview your animation and close the Preview panel.

27. Select the three small polygons, open the Animation panel, and click the Create Button Trigger button. Then click the button to the left of the small polygon group (the playDelay2 button) to set it as the trigger button.

28. With the button still selected, open the Timing panel and Shift-click on each of the animations to select all three. Click the up arrow next to the Delay field to set the delay to .25 seconds.

The up and down arrows of the Delay field initially increment the delay value by .25 seconds. However, if you hold an arrow down for several seconds worth of increments, the values begin to shift by whole seconds. If you prefer, you can instead click in the Delay field and type in a value.

29. Select the playDelay1 button and drag it on top of the first large polygon. Drag through the polygon with the Selection tool to select both the polygon and the button, and press Ctrl+G/Command+G to group them.

30. Select the playDelay2 button and drag it on top of the first small polygon. Drag through the polygon and the button with the Selection tool to select both objects, and press Ctrl+G/Command+G to group them as well. Click off the group to deselect.

31. In the Timing panel, Shift-click to select all the text animations and click the ⟲ button at the bottom of the panel to set them to play at the same time.

32. Save and preview the file to check the timing of your animations.

33. Close the Preview panel and return to the Timing panel. Select the first text animation in the list and set its delay to 1 second. Set the delay for the second text animation to 2 seconds, the third to 3, and the fourth to 4.

34. Save and preview the document, paying particular attention to the effect of the timing settings you established. Close the Preview panel, and then save and close the file.

CHAPTER SUMMARY

This chapter laid the foundation for every animation you'll create in InDesign. Starting with the Animation panel, you explored the provided motion presets and then proceeded to customize them by modifying their parameters. In making adjustments to the default settings, you gained an understanding of:

- How to interpret the markings on a motion path
- The differences between the Animate options:
  » From Current Appearance
  » To Current Appearance
  » From Current Location
- How to set the duration of an animation
- Using the easing options to control the appearance of acceleration and deceleration:
  » Ease In
  » Ease Out
  » Ease In and Out
  » From Preset
- How to save and apply a custom motion preset
- How to set triggering events for your animations including:
  » Choosing a trigger event from the Event dropdown options
  » Creating a button trigger
  » Using the On Click (Self) event

With multiple animations in your document, you then explored the Timing panel and learned how to:

- Set the sequence of your animations
- Set animations to play together
- Set animation delays

Peripheral to your animation work, you gained a solid foundation in use of the Pen tool and learned to draw straight and curved paths, streamlining the process with the use of modifier keys. You got an in-depth view of the Corner Options controls, set parameters for the Polygon tool and used the Distribute Spacing feature of the Align panel. You also employed the Eyedropper tool to capture and apply formatting.

With the essentials of InDesign animation solidly in place, you're ready to innovate. The next chapter takes you well beyond the basics to create advanced animation effects that will make you proud.

● Chapter 9

....

GETTING FANCY WITH ANIMATION

Now that you've got the fundamentals down, let's start looking at what kinds of effects you can achieve with a little bit of creativity and some inspired sleight of hand. This chapter opens up whole new vistas for what's possible with animation in InDesign, and then takes that knowledge to another dimension, literally, to create the illusion of objects moving through 3-D space. You'll animate multiple objects on open and closed paths and learn techniques to create transitions, animated buttons, and continuous, looping animations.

Introduction

Now for the fun part! You've got all the building blocks, now it's time for a taste of the really cool effects you can create. In addition to what you can do with individual motion presets and the Animation panel, you can take the possibilities further still by assembling multiple motion presets to appear as one seamless sequence.

One of the most obvious opportunities to employ this type of technique is with text. Title text offers an open invitation for animation, providing the first exposure to a page. This chapter will give you some ideas for playing with text and expanding on work with motion paths. So, without further ado, let's get started.

Exercise 9.1: Animating Letters

ANIMATION

While this animation example is a bit over the top, it does show you how you can sequence multiple animations to create a greater whole.

1. Open **ex9_1_end.indd** and preview the file. After previewing, dig around a bit in the Layers panel and note that each letter appears twice. There are actually two animations for each letter that play one after the other to give the appearance of a single effect. Keep the file open for reference.

2. Go to File > New, set the Intent to Web, leave the Page Size at 800 x 600, and click OK. Save the file as **ex9_1.indd** in the chapter_9_exercises folder.

3. Select the Type tool and draw a text box that stretches across most of the page. Type the word "ANIMATION" and press Ctrl+A/Command A to select it. Choose a typeface and enlarge the text to fill the text frame by holding Shift+Ctrl+>/Shift+Command+> until the font is the desired size. Hold Alt+right arrow/Option+right arrow to increase the tracking and add a little breathing room for the letters. (Use the left arrow to decrease tracking.)

   For this animation, you'll need to animate the letters individually. Because there's no need for the letters to remain editable text, rather than drawing each letter separately and manually aligning them, you can just enter the text and then let InDesign do the work of separating the letters for you. The obvious approach would be to convert the text to outlines, but this results in a complex path that you would then have to tediously divide. An ingenious approach (found in an article by Mike Rankin at InDesignSecrets.com: http://indesignsecrets.com/a-cs5-treat-the-animation-sandwich.php) neatly separates each letter into a self-contained path. The trick is to alternate the letter colors before converting the text to outlines. InDesign turns each letter into its own separate path. Simple and elegant. Thanks, Mike!

4. With the Type tool selected, select the first "N" in "ANIMATION" and change its color. Change the color of every other letter in the rest of the word.

ANIMATION

To break the letters of a word into individual shapes, alternate the colors of the letters, switch to the Selection tool, and then go to Type > Create Outlines.

5. Press Esc to switch to the Selection tool. This selects the text frame. If you don't select the text frame, each letter will become an anchored object in the text frame when you convert the text to outlines.

6. Go to Type > Create Outlines to convert the letters to a grouped collection of individual letter shapes. While the group of shapes is still selected, change the fill to a solid color to color the shapes uniformly.

7. Go to Object > Ungroup or press Shift+Ctrl+G/Shift+Command+G to ungroup the shapes. With the selection still active, apply the Fly in and Blur from Left motion preset in the Animation panel.

    Since each of the animated shapes will appear in the Animation panel with a default name of either path or compound path, naming them according to the letter they represent will be essential in keeping track of them. Since several of the letters occur multiple times in the word, you'll want to name them in a way that helps you distinguish which one belongs where.

8. With the Selection tool, click outside the letter shapes to deselect them, and then select the first "A." In the Animation panel. Name the shape "a1". Name the second "A" "a2." Follow the same convention for the other letter shapes, naming them according to the letter they represent and their placement in the word.

9. Save and preview the file. Note that the order of the animation sequence is backwards, with the letter shapes appearing in the order the letters of the word were typed, rather than from the last letter to the first. The animation is also very slow and, depending on where you placed the original text frame on the document, you may see the initial blur of the animated letters on the page.

10. Select the letter shapes with the Selection tool and change Duration to .125 seconds in the Animation panel.

11. Open the Timing panel and rearrange the letter shapes so they animate from the last letter to the first.

    Next, you'll extend the motion path for each letter shape so it begins outside of the page.

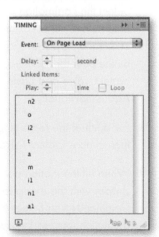

The letter shapes reordered to fly in from the last letter to the first.

Although it may be subtle, if the motion paths are different lengths, the animated objects will appear to travel at different speeds. Unfortunately, there is no way to adjust the length of multiple motion paths at the same time; you need to scale them individually.

You'll use the controls on the Control panel to scale the motion paths precisely, but this will change the position of the letter shapes. You'll set up a guide to help in positioning the letter shapes once the motion paths have been adjusted.

12. Drag a guide from the Vertical Ruler to the left edge of the a1 animation (the first "A" in "ANIMATION").

13. Select n2 (the last letter in "ANIMATION") with the Selection tool and then select its motion path. Mouse over the left edge of the path and when the cursor changes to a double-sided arrow, drag to extend it at least the width of one of the letter shapes beyond the left edge of the page.

14. With the motion path still selected, look on the Control panel to find the L value that indicates the length of the motion path. Select the value and press Ctrl+C/Command+C to copy it.

When a motion path is selected, the path length can be controlled through the L field on the Control panel.

15. With the Selection tool, select the n2 object rather than the path, and go to Object > Lock (Ctrl+L/Command+L) to lock it.

16. Select the o2 animation and then select its motion path. Select the entire L value in the Control panel and press Ctrl+V/Command+V to paste the value copied from n2. Click Enter/Return to commit your change and note that the o2 object jumps to the right.

17. Select the i animation and then select its motion path. If you set up the Shift+Ctrl+D/Shift+Command+D keyboard shortcut for the Transform command on page 105, use that now to scale the path to the same length as the path for n2. If you didn't set up the shortcut, either select the Control panel L value and paste, or go to Object > Transform and select Transform Again Individually.

18. For each of the remaining letters, one by one, click the motion path and then choose Object > Transform > Transform Again (or use your shortcut).

19. When all the motion paths are modified, the position of all the letter shapes with the exception of n2 will be skewed to the right. Press Ctrl+A/Command+A to Select All. Holding the Shift key, drag them left until the a1 animation touches the guide you placed at the beginning of the exercise.

20. The first leg of the animation is now complete. Save and preview the file.

Now to add the jiggle to each of the letter shapes. While you can only accomplish so much by editing motion presets, you *can* sequence one preset after another to create the impression of continuous animation.

21. Click the lock on the n2 object to unlock it and then select all the letter shapes with the Selection tool.

22. Press Ctrl+C/Command+C to copy and then lock the layer in the Layers panel by clicking the Toggles Lock column to the left of Layer 1. Click the New Layer button at the bottom of the panel and go to Edit > Paste in Place (Alt+Shift+Ctrl+V/Option+Shift+Command+V) to paste the copied letters directly over the originals into the new layer.

23. With the letter shapes still selected, open the Animation panel, change the motion preset to Dance, set Duration to .5 seconds and check the Loop checkbox.

    You want the Dance preset to play after the Fly in and Blur animation. In order to make the animation appear continuous, you don't want the letter shapes for the second leg of the animation to show until the first letter shapes fly in and reach their final position.

24. Still in the Animation panel, with the shapes still selected, check the Hide Until Animated checkbox at the bottom of the panel. Deselect the letter shapes.

25. Select and rename each of the Dance preset animations in the Animation panel by appending the word "Dance" to the existing name.

    Just as you want the Dance animations to be hidden until ready to play, you want the Fly in and Blur animations to be hidden once their animations are complete.

26. Change the name of Layer 2 to "Dance" and lock the layer. Rename Layer 1 "Fly in" and unlock it if it's locked. Click in the Layers panel selection column to select all the objects on the layer.

27. With the Fly in animations selected, check the Hide After Animating checkbox in the Animation panel.

    The last thing to do is set the animation sequence so the jiggle of the letters directly follows the arrival of the letter shapes on the page.

28. Open the Timing panel and drag each of the Dance animations to just below its corresponding Fly in animation, as pictured in the screenshot to the right.

29. Save and preview the file and then close it. You've completed the lesson and learned to sequence multiple animations on multiple objects.

Position The Dance animations directly below the corresponding Fly in animations.

Custom Motion Paths, Transitions, and Cool Effects

Once the creative juices start flowing, you'll likely surprise yourself with all the animation ideas that will fill your head. Animation doesn't have to be complicated to enrich the texture of a project or page. Just a little bit of motion can go a long way. One caution about interactive design and animation that demands careful consideration is this: before you fill your pages with gratuitous motion of all shapes and sizes, remember—just because you can, doesn't mean you should. If a little is good, more is not necessarily better. A simple transition, maybe some title animation, possibly text that flies in or buttons that animate on rollover: all good. The truth of the matter is, animation such as the jiggling letters gets old pretty quickly. Better to go for simple elegance over bells and whistles that jangle and clang. If your animation serves to engage and enhance, great. If it's there simply because you thought it was cool, it may be best to think again.

That said, this section of the chapter is all about more cool stuff you can do. And while the actual examples may not necessarily represent the pinnacle of elegance, they should serve to stimulate some ideas and prime that creative pump. With new tools in your toolbox, it'll be up to you to find elegant ways to employ your expanded skills.

An area that opens lots of room for exploration and creativity is transitions, where you can achieve elegant effects, often very simply. InDesign has a panel dedicated expressly to built-in page transitions (which we'll be exploring later), but the same type of animation can often be used effectively for page elements as well.

While you've been working with the motion paths built into the motion presets, you can also make motion paths of your own. You can even combine motion presets with custom motion paths to take your animations to the next level. You can nest animations one inside another, animate buttons... the list goes on and on.

It's all about creating a convincing illusion, so pull out your magic wand and let's get started.

Exercise 9.2: Intro to Custom Motion Paths

They say the quickest way to get from point A to point B is a straight line. The same idea carries over to motion paths. There's a lot you can do with just a straight line of motion when it comes to animation, beyond objects flying onto and off of a page. Whether a straight line or an elaborate path with twists and turns, the process of connecting that path to an object in order to set it in motion remains the same.

The simplest motion path is merely a straight line connecting two points. InDesign's Line tool does the job quite nicely with just a click and drag. You can apply the Fly in presets to animate on a straight path with the click of a button. However, if you'd rather do it yourself, animating on a custom motion path is accomplished in three basic steps: 1) Create the object you want to animate. 2) Create the path. 3) Connect them. It's that simple.

1. Open and preview **ex9_2_end.indd_** Click the button and try to figure out how it was done. After previewing, open the Layers panel and expand the Transition1 layer to show its object sublayers. Hold down Alt/Option and click the Toggles Visibility eye to the left of the playTransition1 object layer in the Layers panel. This turns off the visibility for all the other object layers. Starting at the bottom of the stack, turn the layers back on one by one to see how the file is built. When you're done exploring, keep the file open for reference.

2. Open **ex9_2_start.indd** and save it as ex9_2.indd. In the Layers panel, expand the Layer1 layer and note that two instances of flower5.jpg and one instance of flower4.jpg are placed on the page.

   To create the illusion of the image splitting in two, you will actually create two frames that combine to appear as one whole image. You will then animate the pieces to move off of, and away from, the image placed below.

3. Click with the Selection tool to select the flower image that's visible on the page. In the Control panel, ensure that the link constraining the width and height values is unlinked, so you can scale the width and height of the graphic frame separately. Confirm that the upper left corner is selected in the Reference Point proxy. In the H field, click after the existing text and type "/2" (forward slash and then 2), and then press Enter/Return. This will result in a graphic frame that's half the original height.

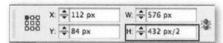

InDesign will add, subtract, multiply, and divide for you when you enter the function in the properties fields. Use + and – to add and subtract and use * and / to multiply and divide.

4. Select the adjusted image frame with the Selection tool, hold the Alt/Option key, and then click and drag the frame down to duplicate it. Align it so its upper edge is aligned to the lower edge of the now scaled original.

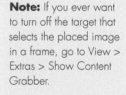

Note: If you ever want to turn off the target that selects the placed image in a frame, go to View > Extras > Show Content Grabber.

5. Mouse into the duplicated frame, and then click the target in the center (the Content Grabber) to access the placed image. Click the center reference point on the Control panel proxy and set the Y value to 0 to precisely align the bottom image with the top.

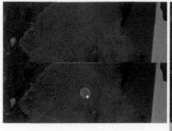

Click the target to access the placed file and then reposition it to create the illusion of one continuous image.

6. Click off the image to deselect, and confirm that there's a color assigned to the stroke. Select the Line tool (\). Click close to the center of the upper frame, hold the Shift key, and drag the mouse straight up and off the page to the gray area surrounding the pasteboard. The motion path you are drawing must be long enough to move the animated frame completely off the image beneath it that will be revealed by the animation.

7. With the line still selected, press V on the keyboard to switch to the Selection tool. Shift-click the upper frame so both the line and the frame are selected. Open the Animation panel and click the Convert to motion path button ( ) at the bottom of the panel. Name the animation "goUp". That's all there is to it. You've created your first custom motion path.

8. Drag a line with the Line tool from the center of the bottom image, down and outside the page, to the gray area around the pasteboard. Select the line and the image, and click the Convert to motion path button. Name the animation "goDown."

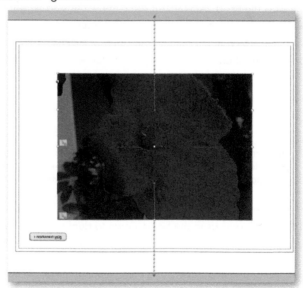

Drag the motion paths into the gray area beyond the boundary of the page, so they are long enough to move the animated image entirely off of the image being revealed.

As you remember, by default, animations are triggered to play by the On Page Load event, in the sequence in which they were created. You need to set the two transition animations you just created to play at the same time.

9. Open the Timing panel, Shift-click on each animation to select it, and then click the Play together link at the bottom of the panel to link their timing.

10. Preview the file.

The animation works but the animated objects remain visible as they travel outside the boundaries of the original image frame. You'll create a faux mask to correct this.

The Pathfinder Panel

The Pathfinder panel (Window > Object & Layout > Pathfinder) bundles a slew of useful commands into one nice, neat package. Although not identical, it bears a number of similarities to the Pathfinder panel in Illustrator. All the commands available through InDesign's Pathfinder panel can be found under the Object menu, but having them together on one panel can save you multiple trips to the Menu bar.

The Paths section of the panel makes it easy to connect points, open and close paths, and reverse path direction. The buttons in the Pathfinder section are great for slicing and dicing shapes. You can use them to create shapes that would be nearly impossible to draw by hand. The Convert Shape options enable you to change one shape into another, and provide a convenient visual reference. The Convert Point tools can be helpful when making adjustments to paths.

The Pathfinder panel.

A. **Join Path:** Connects two endpoints.

B. **Open Path:** Opens a closed path.

C. **Close Path:** Closes an open path.

D. **Reverse Path:** Reverses the direction of a path.

E. **Add:** Combines selected objects into one shape.

F. **Subtract:** Subtracts the frontmost objects from the backmost object.

G. **Intersect:** Creates a shape from the intersecting shape areas and deletes the rest.

H. **Exclude Overlap:** Creates a shape from all but the overlapping areas and deletes the rest.

I. **Minus Back:** Subtracts the backmost objects from the front object.

J. **Rectangle:** Converts the current shape to a rectangle.

K. **Rounded Rectangle:** Converts the selected shape to a rounded rectangle based on the current Corner Options radius size.

L. **Beveled Rectangle:** Converts the current shape to a beveled rectangle based on the current Corner Options radius size.

M. **Inverse Rounded Rectangle:** Converts the current shape to an inverse rounded rectangle based on the current Corner Options radius size.

N. **Ellipse:** Converts the current shape to an ellipse.

O. **Triangle:** Converts the current shape to a triangle.

P. **Polygon:** Converts the current shape to a polygon based on the current Polygon tool settings.

Q. **Line:** Converts the selected shape to a line.

R. **Orthogonal Line:** Converts the selected shape to a horizontal or vertical line.

S. **Plain:** Changes the selected point to have no direction handles.

T. **Corner:** Changes the selected point to have independent direction handles.

U. **Smooth:** Changes the selected point to be a smooth curve with connected adjustment handles.

V. **Symmetrical:** Changes the selected point to be a smooth curve with direction handles of equal length.

11. With the Transition1 layer expanded in the Layers panel, lock goUp, goDown, and playBtn.

12. Zoom out so the entire page is in view (Ctrl+0/Command+0), and select the Rectangle tool (M). Set the fill to [Paper], InDesign's name for white, and set the stroke to None. Draw a rectangle that extends just beyond the boundaries of the page in all directions.

13. In the Layers panel, drag the white rectangle below the two animation layers.

14. Deselect the rectangle you just drew, change the fill color to something other than white, and ensure that smart guides are turned on. (Go to View > Grids & Guides and there should be a checkbox next to Smart Guides. If not, click the Smart Guides option to activate them. The shortcut is Ctrl+U/Command+U.) Draw one rectangle that covers the animated flower images, matching their combined size exactly.

15. Press V to switch to the Selection tool and drag through the large and the small rectangles to select them. Go to Window > Object & Layout and open the Pathfinder panel (the ▦ icon on the Panel dock). Click the Subtract button (▭) to delete the small rectangle from the large one.

16. In the Layers panel, drag the compound path layer to the top of the stack and lock it.

    While there may be occasions where you would like to play a transition such as the one you just built On Page Load, there will be times where a user-triggered action is preferable. Next you'll create a button for such a circumstance.

17. Select the Type tool and draw a small text frame that will become a button. For the button text, enter "play transition 1." Format the text and press Shift+Ctrl+C/Shift+Command+C to center it.

18. Open the Swatches panel, and, if necessary, click the rectangular button next to the T (▭T) at the top of the panel to select the text frame rather than the text. Select a color for the background of your button and adjust the Tint as necessary. We chose 10% black.

19. Press Ctrl+B/Command+B and choose Center from the Vertical Justification Align dropdown.

20. Select the button shape with the Selection tool and then click the yellow square at its upper right to activate Live Corners. Drag any one of the yellow diamonds to reshape the corners to your liking.

Note: Click the yellow square at the upper right of a shape to activate Corner Options. To affect an individual corner. Hold the Shift key and click and drag. To change the corner style, hold the Alt/Option key while you click a yellow diamond.

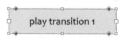

After clicking the yellow square to activate the Corner Options, drag the yellow diamonds to round the object corners.

21. Unlock and select the top and bottom of the flower animation with the Selection tool, and open the Animation panel. Click the Events down arrow and remove the On Page Load event. Click the Create Button Trigger button. Then click the play transition button text to convert it to a button and add Play Animation actions for both animations.

22. When the Buttons panel opens, change the button name to "playTransition1."

23. With the playTransition1 button still selected, open the Timing panel, select both animations, and click the Play together link. Save and preview the finished effect.

The linked animations in the Timing panel.

With just a few changes, you can create a very different effect.

24. Go to File > Save As and change the file name to **ex9_2_b.indd**.

25. Switch to the Direct Selection tool (A) and click once on the goUp animation (the top flower) to select the image inside the frame. Copy the image and go to Edit > Paste in Place (Alt+Shift+Ctrl+V/Option+Shift+Command+V). Hide the new flower5.jpg object layer in the Layers panel.

26. If necessary, select the goUp animation image with the Direct Selection tool again and delete it, leaving the empty frame on the document. The frame will display a big X, indicating that it is a graphic frame. Select the frame with the Selection tool, go to Object > Content, and select Unassigned to remove the X from the frame. Give the frame a [Paper] fill.

> **Note:** The X in the graphic frame won't show when the project is exported, but removing it gives you a better view when building the project.

27. Repeat step 26 for the goDown animation frame.

When the user clicks the button, you want the top flower image to disappear and the white reveal animation to play. Because the flower image has to have a name in order for you to tell it to disappear, you will convert it to a button.

28. In the Layers panel, make the flower image at the top of the stack visible, click in its selection column to select it, and open the Buttons panel. Convert the image to a button and name it "flower1."

29. Leave the Buttons panel open and select the playTransition1 button. Add a Show/Hide Action to its On Release event and hide flower1.

30. Delete the white mask compound path, and then save and preview the file. When you're finished, close the file.

More Transitions

The possible variations for transitions are virtually endless. To add to your lexicon and provide you with some additional great InDesign tricks, we'll explore a few more transition ideas.

Exercise 9.3: More Transitions

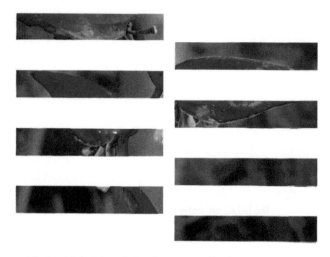

1. Open **ex9_3_end.indd** and check it out. In the Preview panel, be sure to choose Set Preview Document Mode and then play with the transitions on every page. After previewing, take a look at the layer structure, the animations, and the buttons. Note the way things are organized and named.

2. When you've finished exploring, open **ex9_3_start.indd** and save it as ex9_3.indd. Ensure that you're on page 1 and open the Layers panel. Expand the Transition 1 layer to see that there are three sublayers: flower6.jpg, flower5.jpg, and playBtn.

3. Draw a rectangle the same size as the frame of the flower image, directly on top of it. Fill it with a color and give it no stroke.

4. With the rectangle still selected, click the center square in the Reference Point proxy on the Control panel. Ensure that Constrain Proportions for width & height is on (it appears linked) and select the text in the H field. Enter "103%", and press Enter/Return to scale the rectangle from the center.

Note: You're making the rectangle larger than the image to ensure that the image will be completely covered.

5. Click the upper left proxy point and unlock the Constrain Proportions link. Place your cursor after the text in the H field, type "/8" and press Enter/Return. This will resize the rectangle to one-eighth the original height, and position it at the top of the image. Note the height of the rectangle. We had 55.62 px.

In order to ensure that none of the image peeks through the transition blinds before they're opened, we'll allow for a bit of overlap between the slats on either side of the reveal transition.

6. Change the height of the rectangle to 58 px and go to Edit > Step and Repeat (Alt+Ctrl+U/Option+Command+U). In the Step and Repeat dialog, check the Preview checkbox and enter 7 for count. Enter 55 for Vertical offset and 0 for Horizontal. Click OK.

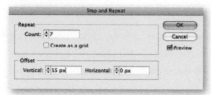

The Step and Repeat dialog makes it possible to duplicate and precisely place multiple objects in uniform increments.

You now have eight slats for the blinds reveal; four for each side. Now, you'll combine each group of four into a compound path with the Pathfinder tool.

7. Click off to deselect. With the Selection tool, click the first rectangle, hold the Shift key, and then click to select the third, the fifth and seventh rectangles. If necessary, go to Window > Object & Layout, open the Pathfinder panel, and click the Add button ( ) in the Pathfinder section of the panel.

8. To make it easier to see where things are, temporarily change the fill color of the compound path you just created so you can see the difference between it and what will become the side of the blinds. You'll change the fill to white when you're finished.

9. With the Line tool, hold the Shift key and click on the horizontal center of the slats. Drag right and beyond the edge of the page to create what will become your motion path. The length will be close to 800 px.

10. With the line selected, hold down the Ctrl/Command key to temporarily switch to the Selection tool, add the Shift key, and click the compound path to add it to the selection. Release the keys and click the Convert to motion path button In the Animation panel. Name the animation "goRight."

11. Switch back to the Selection tool and deselect the animation. Shift-click to select the remaining slats and click the Add button in the Pathfinder panel. With the Line tool, drag left from the horizontal center of the new compound path to a length of roughly 800 px. Select both the compound shape and the line and click the Convert to a motion path button in the Animation panel. Name the animation "goLeft."

    As with the transition in the previous lesson, you'll set both animations to be triggered by the On Release event of the button below the image at the bottom of the page. The button is already named but has no actions yet applied.

12. Select both animations and remove the On Page Load event in the Animation panel. Click the Create Button Trigger button and then click the playBtn button with the target cursor. When the Buttons panel opens, confirm that a Play Animation action for each animation has been added.

13. With the button still selected, open the Timing panel and select goRight and goLeft. Click the Play together button at the bottom of the panel.

14. Select both animation objects and change the fill to Paper. Save and preview your document.

    This animation works because both the blinds and the page color are the same. As with the previous exercise, if you were to fill the blinds with an image, and wanted to restrict the transition to the edges of the original image frame, you would have to add an object to hide the animated image as it moved out of view. Otherwise, the blinds containing the image would be visible as they expanded past the boundaries of the image and off the page.

15. In the Pages panel, drag page 1 to the New button at the bottom of the panel to duplicate it. Note that the new page appears at the bottom of the Pages panel after the existing pages. Drag the page up and to the right of page 1. When you see a black line appear, release the mouse to reposition the page as page 2 of your document. Save your file.

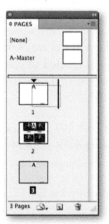

You can rearrange pages in the Pages panel by dragging them to their new position.

Note: Be careful when attempting to rearrange pages with threaded text frames on them, or you could end up with a rat's nest something like this.

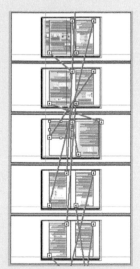

You'll learn about working with text fromes and how to prevent such calamities in Threaded Text Frames starting on page 284.

16. Confirm that you're on page 2 of the document. In the Layers panel, hold the Alt/Option key and click the Transition 1 layer arrow to expand all the object sublayers. Click in the selection column for flower5.jpg to select the image. Press Ctrl+C/Command+C to copy the image and then hide the flower5.jpg sublayer.

17. Select one side of the blinds and go to Edit > Paste Into (Alt+Ctrl+V/ Option+Command+V) to paste the image into the compound path for the blinds.

18. Select the other side of the blinds and go to Edit > Paste Into.

    The white fill that was in the shapes before you added the image extends beyond the image edges and needs to be removed to achieve the full effect.

19. Select both sides of the blinds and set the fill to None. Save your file and preview the completed transition.

Page 3 of the file has an assortment of transitions that, with one exception, are extremely easy to achieve. The buttons and layers are already set up for you. All you need to do is add the animation and the button triggers.

Four Transitions: 1) Shrink. 2) Rotate and Shrink. 3) Fly Up. 4) Fade.

20. Navigate to page 3. Select the image on the upper left and open the Animation panel. Note that the object is already named "shrink", to reflect the nature of the animation it will become.

21. In the W field in the Scale section of the Animation panel, enter "0" and press Tab. If it doesn't populate automatically, enter "0" in the H field as well. Select From Current Appearance from the Animate dropdown and click the Create Button Trigger button. Click the button under the image on the document to assign the Play Animation action to it. When the Buttons panel opens, you will see that the button has already been named "playShrink."

22. Preview the spread to see the animation play when the page loads, and then test the button.

    The animation for the next transition combines change of scale, rotation, and speed.

23. Select the second image (rotateGrow) on the top row of the page. In the Animation panel, set Rotate to 180° and set Play to 2 times in order to animate the image one complete rotation.

    Setting the Rotate property first will activate the other property controls.

24. Set Speed to Ease Out, and both the width and height to 0%. Choose To Current Appearance from the Animate dropdown, click the Create Button

---

Trigger button, and then assign the Play Animation action to the button beneath the image on the page.

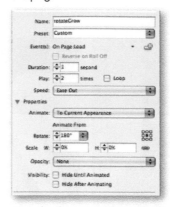

The settings for the rotateGrow animation, incorporating speed, rotation, and scale.

25. Preview the animation and pay particular attention to the effect of the easing setting you applied.

   Adding easing to the animation makes it feel like the image accelerates to snap into place as it completes its rotation. You may wonder why the animation starts out slowly and then speeds up with an Ease Out setting applied. InDesign's default Animation setting is From Current Appearance. In this particular case, we've chosen to animate To Current Appearance instead. Apparently, this turns InDesign's sense of direction upside down and backwards, at least when it comes to Speed and Opacity options. When animating To Current Appearance, Ease In eases out and Ease Out eases in. Opacity also gets turned around, with Fade In fading out and Fade Out fading in.

26. With the Selection tool, select the cyan shape at the left of the page and open the Layers panel. The shape will serve to mask the animation as it moves beyond the boundaries of the original frame. Hide the flyUp and flower2.jpg object layers and note the window cut into the mask that allows the animations to show. Change the compound object fill to white and make both flower layers visible again. Select the flyUp object and open the Animation panel.

27. Select Fly Out > Fly Out Top from the Preset dropdown and then change the Opacity setting to None. Click the Create Button Trigger button and tie the animation to the button beneath the image on the page. Preview the spread.

   The last transition is the easiest of all and potentially the one that you will use most often.

28. Select the last image. In the Animation panel, set Opacity to Fade In and connect the button to the animation. That's it. Couldn't be more simple, right?

29. In the Pages panel, drag A Master from the top of the panel onto the icon for page 2 to add a next button to the page. Save, preview, and then close your finished file.

Multiple Objects and Open Paths

Now that you're getting warmed up a bit, let's give those animator muscles a bit more of a workout. With just a little ingenuity, you can create some very interesting results.

Making multiple objects appear to travel along the same path requires that each object be placed on its own instance of the path, and that the paths be aligned and stacked. The exercise at the beginning of this chapter had the word "ANIMATION" form itself letter by letter with each letter appearing to be connected to the others. As you know, each letter travelled a separate path that was aligned with the paths of the other letters. The only difference between the paths was the points at which they started and ended. Of course, this same technique works with lines that aren't straight, enabling you to flow movement of multiple objects along any open path you choose.

Exercise 9.4: Multiple Objects and Open Paths

In this exercise, you'll create the illusion of multiple objects flowing onto the page to position themselves along a shared curved path.

The exercise example.

Note: Objects on hidden layers are not visible when you preview the document.

1. Open **ex9_4_end.indd** and preview the file. Note that the thumbnail images all appear to travel along the same path. Click each of the thumbnails to see a larger version of the image, and then click the large image to hide it.

2. After previewing the file, open the Layers panel, expand the fauna page layer, and hide the faunaImg1 through faunaImg8 object layers to see what's going on underneath. Select each of the animated objects and take a look at their motion paths. When you're done checking out the file, you can keep it open for reference.

3. Open **ex9_4_start.indd** and save it as ex9_4.indd.

4. Zoom out to find the eight image thumbnails on the pasteboard to the left of the document page. Each thumbnail has already been turned into a button. Each button has already been named and styled, and each has a Show/Hide action assigned that will show the large version of its thumbnail image. On the

document itself is the path you'll use as the foundation for the motion paths to animate the thumbnails. Take a look in the Layers panel to see that the object layers containing the buttons with the large versions of the thumbnails are hidden, and that the path you will use for the motion paths is at the top of the Layer stack.

The easiest way to approach the task at hand is to first scale and position the images as you want them to appear on the path. The buttons are named faunaBtnN, where N is a number from 1 to 8. They are ordered on the pasteboard by number, with the top row containing buttons 1-4 and the bottom row containing buttons 5-8.

You'll notice that the path is above the thumbnail layers in the Layers panel. If you want to convert a path to a motion path, it must be above the object to which you're connecting it in the layer stacking order. This will also make it easier to position the images on the path.

5. Starting with faunaBtn8 (bottom row, furthest to the right), drag the thumbnails one at a time onto the page, and center them on the path. Initially, they'll need to overlap slightly so they all fit.

Note: If you use the Selection tool instead of the Free Transform tool to scale the thumbnail, you'll scale the frame rather than the image inside.

6. To scale and rotate the thumbnails, first select a thumbnail and then select the Free Transform tool (E) (![icon]). Mouse over a corner of a thumbnail; when the cursor changes to a double-sided straight arrow, hold the Shift key to constrain the proportions and drag the image corner. Drag away from the image to enlarge it; or toward its center to shrink both the frame and the image it contains. When all is said and done, you don't want the images to overlap.

7. With the Free Transform tool still selected, position the cursor a bit outside one of the corners. When it changes to a curved double-sided arrow, drag it to rotate to whatever angle you like. In order for the animation to appear as if all the thumbnail images are travelling the same path, it's essential that each thumbnail be centered on the path.

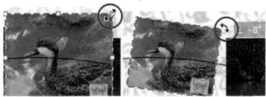

The straight double-sided arrow indicates that dragging will scale the object. A curved double-sided arrow indicates that dragging will rotate the object.

Note: When exporting to SWF and Interactive PDF, buttons may break when they come in contact with transparency. Initially, the arched text frame on the page had a Bevel and Emboss effect, but it broke the buttons whose corners overlapped it. Removing the effect fixed the buttons. Good to remember!

After transforming each of the thumbnails, and positioning them to your satisfaction, the next thing you'll do is duplicate the path.

8. Select the path and press Ctrl+C/Command+C to copy it. Open the Layers panel and expand the fauna page layer. Then go to Edit > Paste in Place (Alt+Shift+Ctrl+V/Option+Shift+Command+V). Repeat a total of six times for a total of seven copies of the path, one for each image except the first.

You'll see a new layer appear in the Layers panel each time you repeat this shortcut.

The Control Panel Transform Controls

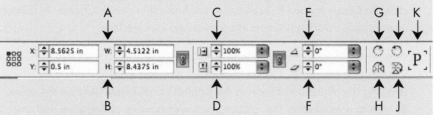

A & B) Width and height controls.

C & D) Scale X scales horizontal percentage, Scale Y scales vertical percentage.

E) Rotation angle.

F) Shear X angle.

G) Rotate 90° clockwise.

H) Flip horizontal.

I) Rotate 90° counter-clockwise.

J) Flip vertical.

K) Transform proxy: The P rotates and flips to reflect the object transform.

To rotate or scale an object by a specific amount, you can use the Control panel Transform controls. If you click directly in the field, you can use the up and down arrows to the left of the field or on your keyboard to incrementally increase and decrease the values. The up and down arrow trick works in 85% of the fields (in dialogs and panels) in Adobe programs. You can also manually enter a value in the text field. If you want to enter a value in a unit of measure other than the document default, type the abbreviation after the value: i or " = inches, px = pixels, pt = points, p = picas, mm = millimeters, c = centimeters. When using the "p" for picas and points, the placement of the letter determines the way the value is interpreted:

> 5p1 = 5 picas and 1 pt
>
> p5 = 5 pts
>
> 5p = 5 picas

9. Drag one of the paths you duplicated to just above each of the faunaBtn thumbnails in the Layers panel, except faunaBtn1. This is just to help you keep track of which path goes with which thumbnail. Hide all the paths except the last one. You may find it less distracting to hide the adjacent button (faunaBtn7) on the page as well.

The setup in the Layers panel for the thumbnail buttons and their respective paths.

---

10. Confirm that faunaBtn8 is positioned so the end of the path intersects with its center. Select faunaBtn8 and the path above it in the Layers panel, and then click the Create Motion Path button in the Animation panel. Choose To Current Appearance from the Animate dropdown and lock the layer.

11. If you'd like to animate the change in rotation, you can also set that parameter in the Animation panel. Find out how much you rotated each object by selecting the object and checking the Control panel Rotate field for the value. Be sure to note whether the rotation value was positive or negative and enter it appropriately in the Rotate field of the Animation panel.

    When you cut the path and convert it to a motion path in the next step, if necessary, the path will reposition itself to center its endpoint on the thumbnail. If the thumbnail motion paths are repositioned by too much, the misalignment will destroy the illusion of each thumbnail travelling the same path. Therefore, before you cut the path, be sure it intersects with the center of the thumbnail.

12. Hide faunaBtn8. Show faunaBtn7 and the path above it. Select the path and then select the Scissors tool (C). Position your cursor over the path, as close as possible to where it intersects the center of the thumbnail, and click with the Scissors tool to cut it.

13. Switch to the Selection tool (V), and the portion of the path that you want to use as your motion path is selected. Shift-click the thumbnail to add it to the selection, and then click the Convert to motion path button at the bottom of the Animation panel. Choose To Current Appearance from the Animate dropdown. Optionally, adjust the Rotate setting to match the rotation on the thumbnail.

14. Select the portion of the path that remains on the page, and delete it.

15. Hide faunaBtn7, and show faunaBtn6 and the path above it. Select the path and switch to the Scissors tool (C). Click to cut the path where it intersects the center of the thumbnail. Press V to switch to the Selection tool, and Shift-click the thumbnail to add it to the selection. In the Animation panel, click Convert to motion path and choose To Current Appearance from the Animate dropdown. Optionally, adjust the Rotate setting to match the thumbnail rotation. Select the remaining portion of the path and delete it.

16. Repeat the process in step 15 for each of the remaining thumbnails, cutting the path at the appropriate point, converting it to a motion path, and deleting the remainder of the path.

17. There is no path associated with faunaBtn1, but you can still animate its rotation if you like.

18. When all the animations have been set, show all the layers in the Layers panel, and then open the Timing panel. If necessary, adjust the animation order, and then, select all the animations and click the Play together button at the bottom of the panel.

19. Turn on the visibility for the large image buttons, and then save and preview the file.

You may need to nudge the position of some of the paths to make the animation flow more smoothly. A little nudge here or there won't hurt the impression that the objects are following the same path. And, there you have it: multiple objects on open paths.

Multiple Objects and Closed Paths

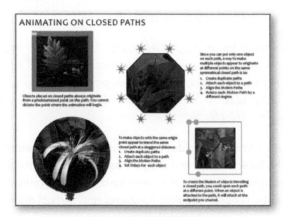

Closed paths can also be used as motion paths. They don't, however, provide the opportunity to dictate where on the path the animation begins. To achieve the effect of multiple objects originating from different points on a closed symmetrical path, you can attach your objects to their respective closed paths, and then rotate the paths to create the illusion of different starting points. If you don't mind the objects originating from the same point, an alternate approach is to align and stack your paths and set an incremental delay for each instance of the animation. A third alternative would be to maintain the illusion of a closed path, but to actually cut the paths at the points at which you'd like the animation to originate.

Exercise 9.5: Multiple Objects and Closed Paths

This exercise will give you a chance to experiment with the three techniques outlined above and make multiple objects appear to travel the perimeter of the same closed shape.

Note: Since each of the multi-object animations is actually *nested* inside another animation, you may find it easiest to use the Layers panel to select the individual objects.

You read that right: the animations are nested. Another door to expanded possibilities!

1. Open **ex9_5_end.indd** and preview the file. Note that on the third animation, two of the triangles travel in one direction and two in the other. After previewing, select each of the stars on the second animation to see how they are arranged on the motion paths. Next, select each of the triangles on the third animation and check out the delay settings in the Timing panel. Lastly, note the placement of the circles on the fourth animation. Each circle is placed at a break in the motion path. When you're done exploring, you can keep the file open for reference.

2. Open **ex9_5_start.indd** and save it as ex9_5.indd.

3. Select the rectangle tool (M) and click once on the document to open the Rectangle dialog. Enter 172 for Width, press Tab, and enter 172 for height.

If you're entering values in a dialog box in increments matching the document preference settings, you need only enter the value. InDesign will add the unit of measure for you.

4. Your square should have a stroke color but no fill.

   Here are some tips for adjusting stroke and fill. If the rectangle has a stroke and the fill color is set to None, press Shift+X to swap the colors. If it has both a stroke and a fill, and the stroke is active in the Tools panel, press X to switch the focus, and then press / to apply None as the fill color. If both the stroke and the fill have no color, select a color for the stroke.

5. Go to View > Grids and Guides and confirm that Smart Guides is checked. Switch to the Selection tool and drag the square over the first flower image. Release the square when you see green horizontal and vertical smart guides centered on the image, indicating horizontal and vertical alignment.

**Smart Guides indicating alignment with the
horizontal and vertical centers of the image.**

6. Hold the Shift key and click the gradient shape at the upper left to add it to the selection. In the Animation panel, click the Convert to motion path button to link the object to the path and create the animation. Check the Loop checkbox.

7. Save and preview your animation.

   For the next animation, you'll create a total of eight stars, each originating from a different corner of an octagonal path.

**Rotate a symmetrical motion path to create the illusion
that objects originate at different points on the path.**

8. Select the star and the outer octagonal path, Right-click/Ctrl-click to access the context menu, and then choose Copy. Right-click/Ctrl-click again and choose Paste in Place a total of six more times to end up with a total of eight stars and eight octagons.

The octagons and stars will be paired in the Layers panel, which will make it easy to select and convert them to animations.

9. Hold the Shift key and click the selection column in the Layers panel to select both the topmost polygon and path. Click the Convert to motion path button at the bottom of the Animation panel, and name the animation star1. Hide the star1 object layer in the Layers panel.

10. Repeat step 9 for the next six star/path pairs, naming each animation sequentially. Select the last octagon and star on the document page with the Selection tool. Click Convert to motion path in the Animation panel and name the animation "star8". Locate the star8 object layer in the Layers panel and drag it up in the stack so it is directly below star7. Lock the layer.

The star8 animation will stay in its position and you will rotate each of the other animations to position a star at each corner of the octagon.

11. Show star7 in the Layers panel and select it. With the Selection tool, mouse over the motion path until you see the tooltip telling you to click to edit. Click to select the motion path, and then position your cursor just outside a corner of the bounding box for the path. The blue resize handles are your indicator that the path is still selected. When you see the Rotate cursor, click and drag the octagon around to the right. As you near the next corner on the octagon, hold the Shift key, and the angle will pop to precisely 45° to match the rotation angle to the angle of the path. Lock the star7 object layer.

12. Repeat step 7 for the remaining stars, rotating each path to position a star at a different corner of the octagon. If you like, add opacity and rotation changes to some of the stars to add some visual interest. If you'd prefer to enter precise values in the Control panel rather than manually rotate the octagons, use the following rotation angles: 45°, 90°, 135°, 180°. -135°, -90°, -45°.

13. In the Timing panel, Shift–click to select all the star animations and click the Play together button at the bottom of the panel. Save and preview the file.

Note: In the last exercise, you learned that motion paths snap to the center of the object to which they are connected. To maintain the illusion of multiple objects on a path, with paths for each object aligned, move the objects to be animated to the origin of the path. This way, when the object snaps to the motion path, the path will maintain its original position. The multiple paths will retain their alignment and the illusion will be preserved.

You can apply timing delays to stagger the spacing of objects on a closed path.

For the circle animation, you will employ delays to stagger the triangles along the path. You will also reverse the direction of two of the motion paths to make the triangles travel in the opposite direction.

14. With the Selection tool, select the circle path around the third image. Copy and Paste In Place three times so you have a total of four circles. Hide three of them in the Layers panel (the sublayer name will be <path>) and then select the visible circle and the red triangle. Press Ctrl+/Command+ to zoom in and then click the Convert to motion path button in the Animation panel. Note that the animation takes on the name of the object attached to the motion path (redTriangle). Choose Ease In from the Speed dropdown and hide the redTriangle object layer in the Layers panel.

15. Show the next triangle layer and then repeat step 14 for each of the remaining three triangles. Choose a different easing option for each animation.

16. If necessary, show the green and the blue triangles in the Layers panel. Select the greenTriangle animation, then click to edit the motion path. Open the Pathfinder panel (Window > Objects and Layout > Pathfinder). and click the Reverse Path button to make the triangle travel in the opposite direction. Repeat for the blueTriangle.

17. Open the Timing panel and group the triangle animations. Assign a delay to each of them. Experiment by first setting a uniform delay and then vary the delays for each animation, previewing your file in between to see your results. Save the file.

The last in this series of closed path animations relies completely on illusion to achieve the effect. You will simply slice the motion paths at the point where you want each animation to originate.

You can achieve precise placement of objects on a "closed" path by cutting the path where you want the animation to originate.

18. Zoom in on the fourth image at the lower right of the page. Select the square path and the dot, and then Copy and Paste In Place three times. Shift-click the dot to deselect it (To avoid the transform handles, click the part of the dot that's inside the corner of the rectangle.) Then select the Scissors tool (C).

19. To make the ball in one of the four animations originate in the corner, position the Scissors tool at the upper left corner of the rectangle and click to cut the path. Switch to the Selection tool and Shift-click the dot to add it to the selection. In the Animation panel, select Convert to motion path and name the animation "circle1." Change Duration to 5 seconds and check the Loop checkbox. Close the Animation panel and lock the layer in the Layers panel.

20. Select the next path, switch to the Scissors tool (C), and click just about halfway down on the left side to cut the path. Switch to the Selection tool and drag a dot over the cut you made in the path. (You may need to deselect the path before you can select the dot.) Hold the Shift key and click the path to add it to the selection, and then click the Convert to motion path button in the Animation panel. Name the animation "circle2," set Duration to 5 seconds, and check the Loop checkbox. Depending on where you cut the path, the animation may shift position. Just drag it back, visually positioning the motion path over the other rectangle. Lock the object layer in the Layers panel.

21. Repeat the process for the remaining two dots, positioning a cut in each path. For each dot/path pair, choose Convert to motion path in the Animation panel. Set the Duration to 5 seconds and check the Loop checkbox.

22. Unlock all the locked layers. Take some time to play with the timing and other animation parameters and observe the effect of different duration settings on each of the dots.

    To wrap it up, you'll make each animation example fly onto the page with the multi-path animations nested inside.

23. Click and drag a selection marquee with the Selection tool to select all the elements of the first example, including the text. Press Ctrl+G/Command+G to group them and then choose Fly in From Left from the Preset dropdown in the Animation panel. Repeat for each of the remaining examples and then save and preview your file.

Well, that's it for multiple objects on a path. Take a second to catch your breath, and then we'll move on to making objects appear to move through 3D space.

Moving through 3D Space...But Not Really

By now you should be getting the idea that this animation thing relies completely on illusion. Add a little extra smoke and mirrors to the techniques you already know and you can make it seem like objects are moving through 3D space. You're not going to believe how easy this really is.

Pure and simple, the trick is to hide the animated object as it travels certain portions of the motion path. The objects masking the animated object just need to be above it in the Layer stacking order. In many cases, the most challenging part will be to create a convincing path.

Note: To see the effect in action and to get a good look behind the curtain, open **ex9_6_end.indd** and preview the file.

Exercise 9.6: Simulating 3D Motion

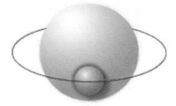

A portion of the motion path is hidden to create the illusion of 3D motion.

In this exercise you'll make a "sphere" appear to orbit another sphere.

1. Go to File > New and choose Web from the Intent dropdown. Keep the default page size and click OK.

2. Select the Ellipse tool (L) and, holding down the Shift key to constrain the horizontal and vertical proportions, drag to draw a circle. Set the stroke to None, press X to swap focus and press the Period key to fill with a gradient.

3. Open the Gradient panel (Window > Color > Gradient) and click the gradient ramp to activate the controls. Choose Radial from the Type dropdown, and, if you wish to change a color, click a gradient marker (the roof on the little house turns black when selected), then open the Swatches panel. Alt-click/ Option-click a color swatch to assign that color to the marker. If you wish to change the origin or angle of the gradient, select the Gradient tool (▣) (G) in the Tools panel. Click anywhere on the circle to place the center point of the radial gradient and drag. The gradient will stretch from the point where you clicked to the point where you release. Experiment with dragging the gradient beyond the edges of the circle and also with drawing a short gradient angle, stopping inside the circle. The longer the gradient line, the more gradual the transition between colors.

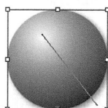

Click and drag the Gradient tool to refine the direction of the gradient coloring the object. A shorter line will condense the gradient colors, a longer line will distribute them more widely along the gradient path.

4. When you're done experimenting with the gradient, draw a substantially smaller circle and fill it with a gradient as well. If you'd rather, you can Alt-drag/Option-drag your existing circle and scale it down.

5. To create the orbit path, copy the larger circle and go to Edit > Paste in Place. Set the fill to None and choose a stroke color. In the Control panel, confirm that the center point is chosen in the Reference Point proxy and that

the Constrain proportions for scaling link is unlocked. Enter 30 in the Scale Y Percentage text field (⬒) and press Enter/Return. Enter 150 in the Scale X Percentage text field (⬓).

6. Select the smaller circle and the orbit ellipse you just made and click the Convert to motion path button in the Animation panel. Name the animation "orbit."

7. Press Ctrl+A/Command+A to Select All and go to Window > Object & Layout > Align. In the Align panel, choose Align to Page from the Align To dropdown. Press Align horizontal centers and then Align vertical centers.

8. Stop at this point to preview the animation, just to see what it does.

    The motion path is visible and is positioned above the large circle.

9. Hide the orbit layer in the Layers panel.

10. Copy the large circle and paste it in place.

11. Select the Rectangle tool (M), and draw a rectangle that is a bit wider than the diameter of the circle and at least half as tall.

12. Position the rectangle so it completely covers the bottom half of the circle.

13. Select both the circle and the rectangle and click the Subtract button on the Pathfinder panel (Window > Object & Layout > Pathfinder). You should now have a half circle that is identical to the large sphere already aligned with the motion path.

The half circle you just created will hide the top half of the motion path to create the illusion that the small circle is transiting behind the large one.

14. Show the hidden layer and preview your animation. The half circle hides the transit of the small sphere around a portion of the motion path, making it appear that the small sphere is orbiting behind the large one.

15. Save the file as **ex9_6.indd** and close it.

You can elaborate on the principle from the previous example to create the illusion of one object spiralling around another.

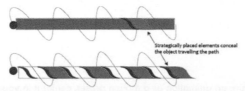

Strategically placed elements conceal the object travelling the path

By strategically placing masking objects over portions of the motion path, you can make one object appear to spiral around another.

16. Choose File > New, set the Intent to Web, and click OK. Select the Ellipse tool (L) and, holding down the Shift key, draw a small circle about 20 px in diameter. Give it a fill and no stroke.

17. Switch to the Selection tool, deselect your circle, and Press Ctrl+D/ Command+D. Open the chapter_9_exercises folder. Select **candy_cane.idms** and then hold down the Ctrl/Command key and click **red_green_stripe.idms** to add it to the selection. Click OK to load your cursor.

18. Click twice anywhere on the page to place the Snippets.

    You will load a motion preset that was exported from InDesign and use it to make the ball appear to revolve around the candy cane. You'll use the red and green stripes to hide the ball as it travels portions of the path.

19. Choose Manage Presets from the Animation panel menu. When the Manage Presets dialog opens, click the Load button and navigate to the chapter_9_exercises folder. Select **horizontal_spiral.xml** and click Open. Click Done in the Manage Presets dialog to load the motion preset and close the dialog.

Custom Motion Paths and Motion Path Previews

To create a custom motion preset, select the animation you want to capture and then choose Save from the Animation panel menu. Enter a name for your preset and click OK.

With the completed animation on your page, go to File > Export and browse to the animation panel's custom preset folder in order to create a preview for your motion preset. In Windows, the path to the folder is
C:\Users\<username>\AppData\Roaming\Adobe\InDesign\Version 7.0\en_US\Motion Presets

On a Mac, the path is
Mac/Users/[username]/Library/Preferences/Adobe InDesign/Version 7.0/en_US/Motion Presets

In the Save dialog, set the Format dropdown to Flash Player (SWF) and click OK.

In order for the preview to show properly in the preview section of the Animation panel, it works best to scale the motion path and the object so their total dimensions do not exceed a width of 250 px and a height of 100 px. Center the animation on the page and then export it. Anything in the 250 px x 100 px window will show in the Preset preview.

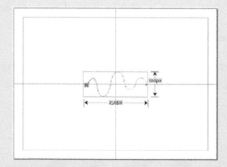

To capture an animation as a motion preset, center it in your document window in an area no more than 250 px wide by 100 px high.

20. Select the circle on your page. In the Animation panel, choose horizontal-spiral from the custom presets in the top section of the Presets dropdown.

21. Position the animation on top of the candy cane with the ball just outside its left edge and the path vertically centered over it. The lines of the motion path should fall halfway between the candy cane stripes. You can use your arrow keys to nudge the circle animation into place if necessary.

22. Preview the animation and note that the ball is traveling either entirely behind or entirely in front of the candy cane, depending on the layer stacking order. If the motion path and ball are behind the candy cane, Right-click/Ctrl-click on the ball and choose Arrange > Bring to Front to bring the animation to the top of the stack.

23. Drag the stripe pair onto the candy cane and align its red stripe with the first red stripe on the candy cane. With the stripe pair still selected, hold down the Alt/Option key and drag to the left to duplicate them. Skipping one red stripe on the candy cane, align the red stripe from the stripe pair with the next red stripe. Nudge the stripe pair into place with your arrow keys if necessary. Repeat to fill the candy cane with alternating stripes and a total of 5 stripe pairs. The last pair of stripes will cover the ball.

Alt-drag/Option-drag to duplicate the stripe on the candy cane.

24. Hold down the Shift key and click each pair of stripes you placed on the candy cane. Then, Right-click/Ctrl-click, and, from the context menu, choose Arrange > Bring to Front to ensure that the stripes are positioned above the candy cane in the stacking order.

25. Preview your file again and pat yourself on the back! You've created an effective illusion of an object looping through space.

Continuous Loops

While a number of the ideas you've played with in this chapter are cool, this next section involves a project that is also elegant and practical. The idea is pretty straightforward. Start with a bar or banner that loops from one side of a page to the other, and then put things on the banner like buttons, animation, text, etc. In the next example, there are image thumbnail buttons on the banner that show a larger image when clicked. You could use the same idea to create navigation for an entire site if you were to put the button banner on a Master page. There are *lots* of exciting possibilities to play with, so let's show you how.

You have nearly all the pieces you need already. You know how to make buttons, how to animate with motion presets and custom motion paths, and you know how to make an animation loop. You know how to add Show/Hide actions, and how to set the animation timing to make all your animations play together. The only piece that's missing, and this is the piece that makes or breaks the entire effect, is how to get the animation to loop seamlessly. Now that, dear reader, is the secret!

When you add a motion path to animate an object From Current Appearance, the path attaches to the center of the object. The object moves the distance of the motion path; so, in order for an animation to appear to loop, the appearance of the object at both ends of the path needs to match. You can see how this works in the diagrams below. Look at the green squares in the first example and the yellow squares in the second; in each case, the motion path starts halfway into one square and ends halfway through the other. If you were to paste together the ends of the graphic spanning the motion path, you would have the seamless loop that we're looking for. But that's literally only half the story. The motion path pulls the animated object to the right a distance equal to its length. The remainder of the object its dragging needs to be at least the length of the path, or a portion of the viewing window will be empty. In other words, the animated object must be at least twice the length of the path. Again, in order to make it seamless, the end of the animation must match up with the beginning. Therefore, the pattern in the graphic defined by the motion path must be repeated to complete the loop.

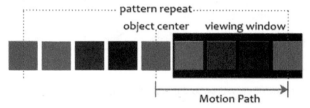

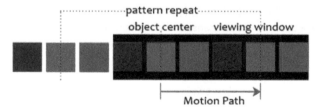

To create a continuous loop, the animated object must be at least twice the length of the motion path.

There's no better way to learn than by doing. The next exercise gives you a chance to put all the pieces together to see how it works.

Exercise 9.7: Continuous Scroller

1. Open **ex9_7_end.indd** and preview the file. Be sure to select Set Preview Document Mode. You'll want to be able to take a look at the second page to see an example of the technique in action. Keep the file open for reference.

2. Open **ex9_7_start.indd** and save it as ex9_7.indd. Navigate to page 2 of the file.

3. Go to File > Place (Ctrl+D/Command+D) and select all six flower files in the links folder in the chapter_9_exercises folder. Click Open to load the cursor.

Scrolling navbar created using a continuous loop animation.

4. Position the loaded cursor at the upper left corner of the large, red rectangle and click six times to place the six flower images at their full size.

5. Select the topmost image. In the Buttons panel, click Convert Object to a Button. Change the button name to "f1Big." Hide the button in the Layers panel.

6. Repeat step 5 for the remaining flower images, using the same naming convention and naming them consecutively (f2Big, f3Big, f4Big, f5Big, f6Big). When all the images are converted to buttons, you can turn their visibility back on in the Layers panel.

7. Press Ctrl–/Command– to zoom out until you see the placement guide at the lower right of the pasteboard. Press and hold Ctrl+Spacebar/ Command+Spacebar and click and drag a rectangle around the placement guide to zoom in on it. Release the mouse, and then release the keys to center the guide in view.

8. Again, load all six flower files for placement. You'll use a keyboard shortcut to place all the images into a one-row, six-column grid. Position the loaded cursor at the upper left corner of the guide, click, and begin dragging slightly down and to the right. Still holding down the mouse, press the right arrow key five times to divide the frame into a total of six individual frames on the horizontal axis. Continue dragging to match the contours of the placement guide, and then release the mouse. The six placed thumbnail images are of uniform size and distance from one another.

9. Select the first thumbnail image and convert it to a button in the Buttons panel. Name the button "f1Btn," click the ⬇ button, and add a Show/Hide action to the On Release event. Show f1Big and hide f2Big through f6Big.

10. Repeat step 9 for each of the remaining thumbnails. Name each button consecutively (f2Btn, f3Btn, etc.), and then add a Show/Hide action. Show the corresponding Big button and hide the remaining five Big buttons.

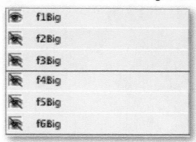

For each button, show its corresponding Big button and hide the others.

11. Zoom out far enough that you can see all the buttons you just created, as well as the entire page. Select all six small buttons with the Selection tool and group them. Hold down the Alt+Shift/Option+Shift keys and drag to the left to position the duplicate buttons to the left of the originals. Don't worry about the spacing; you'll fix that in a minute. Hold down Alt+Shift/Option+Shift and drag to the left again to make a third set of buttons, again placing them to the left of the existing buttons.

12. Zoom in closely enough on the buttons to visually adjust the space between the button groups, holding the Shift key to constrain movement to the horizontal if you need to drag a group to the left or right. You can also use the arrow keys on your keyboard to nudge the groups into place.

13. Press Ctrl+0/Command+0 to fit the spread in the window. Select all the buttons and press Shift+Ctrl+G/Shift+Command+G to ungroup them.

14. With the buttons still selected, go to Window > Object & Layout > Align. If necessary, choose Show Options from the Align panel menu to display the Distribute Spacing controls.

To access the Distribute Spacing controls on the Align panel, choose Show Options from the panel menu.

15. Select Align to Selection from the Align To dropdown and then press the second button on the last row (Distribute Horizontal Space) to space the buttons evenly across the bar. Press Ctrl+G/Command+G (Object > Group) to group the buttons.

Copying the buttons as you just did had the effect of properly naming and ordering the duplicate buttons in the Layers panel. Unfortunately, the Show/Hide Actions are not copied with the buttons. For this example, due to the width of the viewing window, the scrolling bar needs to be at least 15 thumbnails wide. You wouldn't actually know that from the beginning, though, so let's go through the process of figuring it out. You'll want to determine how many thumbnails you need before spending the time adding Show/Hide actions to buttons you might end up deleting.

16. Select the Line tool and position your cursor over the center of the rightmost button. Holding down the Shift key, click and drag left across the first six button images. Release the mouse at the center of the first button image that matches the one where you started the path and then release the Shift key. The path you just created will become your motion path.

17. Switch to the Selection tool (V) and Shift-click to select the thumbnail group. Click the Convert to motion path button at the bottom of the Animation panel and name the animation "scroller". Check the Loop checkbox and, for now, leave the Duration set to 1 second, so you don't have to wait too long to see whether or not the motion path needs to be adjusted.

The line for the motion path was drawn from the center of an image at the right to the center of the first matching image to its left. Because the path was drawn from right to left, the default flow of the animation is right to left as well.

Because you drew the path from right to left, you need to reverse the direction of the motion path to get the animation to travel in the proper direction.

18. Select the motion path with the Selection tool and click when you see the tooltip that says Click to Edit. In the Pathfinder panel (Window > Object & Layout > Pathfinder), click the Reverse Path button ( ).

Reversing the path automatically repositions the animation.

19. Align the right edge of the button group with the right edge of the large, solid black rectangle on the page.

Before previewing the file, take note of the placement of the motion path on the graphic. Remember, the path always connects to the middle of the animated object when it is set to animate From Current Appearance. You know the path is the right length since it goes from the center of a thumbnail to the center of its first duplicate. Now it's just a matter of, first, seeing if the animation works, and second, determining if the scroller length can be shortened.

20. Preview your file to see if the scroller scrolls continuously.

Congratulations! You've got that part handled. Now let's eliminate some of the buttons. In shortening the scroller, you need to ensure that you include at least three duplicates of the same thumbnail; one for the beginning, one for the middle, and one for the end of the loop. You also need to ensure that the length of the graphic to the left of the origin of the motion path is at least the length of the Path. The last thing to keep in mind is that, as you change the length of the scroller, the attachment point for the motion path shifts to the new center of the object. InDesign does this automatically. Taking one of the thumbnails from the left will shift the motion path to the right.

21. With the Selection tool, double-click on and then delete the last three thumbnails at the left of the scroller. Test your animation again to see that it still works.

Awesome, right?! At this point, you've accomplished the main intention of the exercise. There are just a few things to do to wrap up the project.

22. For each of the remaining button thumbnails, add a Show/Hide action. Hide all the large image buttons except the one associated with the thumbnail and show the large version of the thumbnail image.

23. Save and test your file, pat yourself on the back, and close it when you're done.

Animated Buttons

As you've seen, you can animate buttons as easily as you can animate anything else. The On Roll Over (Self) event makes it possible to mimic the rollover behavior that you would otherwise create in the Buttons panel. When you assign the On Roll Over (Self) Event to an animation, the Reverse on Roll Off checkbox becomes available. Applying the On Roll Over (Self) and Reverse on Roll Off events to an animation results in an effect similar to a multistate button created in the Buttons panel, with the benefit of the rollover state being animated.

Clearly, not all the animation presets lend themselves to button rollover states. After all, it might be a bit disconcerting for a user to roll over a button and have it disappear or fly away. There are a few presets, however, that are obvious candidates for button animation: Grow, Pulse, Rotate, and possibly even Dance. But there are ways to use animation with buttons that are less obvious too. This section explores some of those possibilities.

Exercise 9.8: Animated Buttons

In this exercise, you'll apply a variety of techniques to combine buttons with animation. First you'll draw and animate an object for the purposes of testing your buttons.

Note: To see the exercise examples in action, open **ex9_8_end.indd** in the chapter_9_exercises folder and explore.

1. Go to File > New, choose Web from the Intent dropdown and click OK.

2. Select the Polygon tool from the Tools panel and click once on the document. In the Polygon dialog, set width and height to 100, Number of Sides to 5, and Star Inset to 65%. Click OK to create your star.

3. Set the stroke to None and the fill to RGB Red. In the Animation panel,

choose Rotate > Rotate 180° CW. Name the Animation "rotateStar," set the Play value to 2 times, and change the other default settings any way you like. Click the Event down arrow and deselect On Page Load.

Next you'll create a circle that you'll convert to a button. You'll then add animation to the button that will be triggered by the On Roll Over (self) Event.

4. Select the Ellipse tool (L).Hold the Alt+Shift/Option+Shift keys and drag, drawing a circle from the center outward. (Not that you have to in this case, but it's a good thing to know how to do.)

5. Give the circle any color stroke and no fill, and select the Type tool.

6. Hover over the circle with the Type tool and click to convert the object to a text object.

The Type tool displays parentheses on either side of the I-beam cursor to indicate that InDesign recognizes a closed path. When you click, the closed path is converted to a text frame, with text flowing into the contours of the path, regardless of the shape.

7. Type the word "play" in the button shape and center the text (Shift +Ctrl+C/ Shift+Command+C). Press Ctrl+B/Command+B to open the Frame Options dialog and choose Center from the Vertical Alignment dropdown. Click OK to close the dialog.

8. Press Esc to return to the Selection tool, Right-click/Ctrl-click the circle, and choose Interactive > Convert to Button from the contextual menu. When the Buttons panel opens, name the button "growBtn". With the On Release event active, choose Animation from the Actions dropdown. Choose rotateStar from the Animation options and leave Option set to Play.

9. With the growBtn selected, open the Animation panel and select the Grow preset. Remove the On Page Load event and add On Roll Over (Self). Check the Reverse on Roll Off checkbox. Check the Loop checkbox and set both width and height to 75%.

The Animation panel settings for the animated button named "growBtn."

10. Save the file as **ex9_8.indd** in the chapter_9_exercises folder, and preview to test your button.

    The button you just made was a button nested inside an animation. The next button will combine an animated object with a separate button object.

11. Draw a circle and a square, and make the square slightly bigger than the circle. Hold the Shift key as you draw to constrain the proportions of the shapes, and then give them each a different fill color with no stroke.

12. Convert the circle to a button and name it "circleSquareBtn." Select the rotateStar animation on the page, and click the Create Button Trigger button in the Animation panel. Click the circleSquareBtn button to set the button to trigger animation of the star.

13. Select the square and type the word "play" into it. Center-align the word and then set the vertical alignment to Center in the Frame Options dialog (Ctrl+B/ Command+B).

14. Press Esc to switch to the Selection tool. With the square selected, choose the Shrink preset in the Animation panel. Remove the On Page Load event and add On Roll Over (Self). Check the Reverse on Roll Off checkbox and set Duration to .25 seconds. Select 180° from the Rotate options; for Scale, set width and height to 10%. Name the animation "squareShrink."

15. On the Control panel, ensure that Align to Selection ( ) is active. (If you don't see the Align controls on the panel, go instead to Window > Object & Layout > Align.) Select both the circle and the square and align their vertical and horizontal centers. Group them together (Ctrl+G/Command+G) and preview to see the effect.

The initial button appearance and the button On Roll Over appearance, with the square spinning away into oblivion.

Although two separate objects, the circle and square appear as though they are one, and the combination creates an interesting result. The only reason this button solution is actually functional is that the animated square becomes so small, so quickly that it's unlikely the user will be able to click on it when clicking the button. If by some chance the shrunken square is clicked directly, the button action won't work. You can set the scale percentage to 0 to preclude that possibility.

The next button combines a graphic and a button with a Fade In animation, creating a more subtle transition than can be achieved with a traditional rollover.

16. With the Rectangle tool (M), drag a rectangle approximately 105 px wide by 21 px high. Give the rectangle a black fill and no stroke. At the top of the Swatches panel, drag the tint percentage to 25 to change the black to gray.

17. Switch to the Type tool and type "button normal" into the button shape. Center the text horizontally and vertically and then make it black.

18. Press Esc to switch to the Selection tool. Click the gray button shape and then click the yellow square at its upper right corner to activate Live Corners mode. Drag one of the diamonds at any corner to round the corners as desired.

19. Copy the button shape and paste it in place (Alt+Shift+Ctrl+V/ Option+Shift+Command+V).

20. Change the fill color of the duplicate button shape to 100% black and the text color to 100% [Paper].

21. Convert the duplicate shape to a button and name it "fadeBtn". Select the rotateStar animation and open the Animation panel. Click the Create Button Trigger button and then click fadeBtn to add a Play Animation Action for rotateStar.

22. Still in the Animation panel, select fadeBtn and apply the Fade In Preset. Set Duration to .5 seconds and remove the On Page Load event. Assign the On Roll Over (Self) event and check the Reverse on Roll Off checkbox.

23. Select both the button shape and the button, and then align and group them. Save the file and preview to test the button.

That last button was strictly illusion. The shape that provided the initial button appearance wasn't a button at all. The actual button faded in from nothing when the animation detected an On Roll Over event. Ah, the webs we weave....

The next example is a less obvious use of animation with a button, and employs the Fly in from Left animation preset.

24. Draw a rectangle about 166 px wide and about 16 px high, and round the corners if you like. Fill the rectangle with black and give it a 10% black stroke.

25. Draw a small circle, about 8 px x 8 px and fill it with 10% black. Position it on top of the black rectangle, near its left edge.

26. Zoom in on the button and select the Line tool (\). Holding the Shift key, drag a line from the center of the circle to the right edge of the black rectangle. Select both the circle and the line with the Selection tool and click the Convert to motion path button in the Animation panel. Name the animation "circleFlyIn" and remove the On Page Load event.

The circle with a motion path attached, positioned atop the rectangle.

27. Draw another rectangle on top of the first and give it no stroke and no fill. With the Type tool, add text to serve as button text. We added the words "Button Text." Set the text color to 10% black.

Note: When you center text vertically using Text Frame options, it doesn't look exactly centered. You can correct this by adding a baseline shift of -1 or -2 px to optically center the type and compensate for the descenders in the typeface.

Note: While the Paste in Place shortcut may seem a little daunting, it's one that will save you a lot of time, particularly when working with the interactive aspects of InDesign.

28. In the Buttons panel, convert the rectangle to a button and name it "circleFlyInBtn." Choose On Roll Over from the Event dropdown and add a Play Animation action. Choose circleFlyIn from the Animation dropdown.

29. Still in the Buttons panel, choose the On Roll Out event and add a Stop Animation action to stop the circleFlyIn animation.

30. Last but not least, choose the On Release event in the Buttons panel and add a Play Animation action to play the rotateStar animation.

31. Position the circleFlyInBtn on top of the original rectangle, Shift-click to select the other two objects, align their horizontal and vertical centers, and then group them.

32. Save and preview the button.

The next and last example of ways to mix and match buttons with animation actually uses the On Roll Over and On Roll Off events in the Animation panel, as well as a button Rollover state. We found it particularly interesting because it enables you to change the actual color in the animation.

33. Draw a circle with whatever fill and stroke you like and open the Animation panel.

34. Choose Pulse from the bottom of the Preset dropdown and name the animation "pulse". Remove the On Page Load event and add an On Roll Over (Self) event. Leave the Reverse on Roll Off checkbox unchecked and check the Loop checkbox.

35. In the Buttons panel, select Convert Object to a Button at the bottom of the Buttons panel and name the button "pulseBtn." Click [Rollover] to add a rollover state and change the button fill and/or stroke color. Add a Play Animation action to the On Release event to play the rotateStar animation.

36. Save your file and test the button. When finished, close the file.

That wraps up the combination button-animation examples, but there are still a few more animation tricks to pull out of the hat before we wrap up this section.

Off-center Animation

One of the seeming limitations of animation in InDesign is that the animation always flows toward or away from object center. There may be occasions, however, where you need an object to appear to animate from one side or the other, rather than from its middle: for example, if you wanted to scale an object to the left or the right.

Note: If you nest an animation in a button, and then add a rollover state, both the normal and rollover states will have the same animation. Changing the animation for one state changes it for the other.

Also, if you convert a group that contains an animated object to a button, the animation will not play. You can, however, convert a single animated object to a button and the animation will still work.

Note: To view the examples in this exercise, open ex9_8.indd.

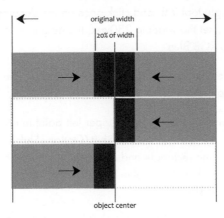

You can create the illusion of an object animating from a point other than center by using background-colored elements to manipulate the object's graphical appearance.

Since you can't manipulate placement of the motion path, the next best thing is to manipulate the appearance of the object itself in order to achieve the desired effect.

It's all about illusion. The image above illustrates three rectangular objects that stretch from one of the gold vertical bars to the other. The actual width of the objects is the same, but by filling half with the background color of the page and the other with color, the illusion is that only the colored portion of the object exists. The other half effectively disappears.

The purple in the image above represents the objects you'd see on the page before animation. The dark purple represents the appearance of the object after it's been animated to a scale of 20%. The dotted lines on the bottom two objects indicate the portion of those objects filled with the white background color. By using the background color of the page, when the bottom objects in this particular example scale to center, the illusion is that the object is instead scaling toward its right or left edge.

The best way to understand this is to actually see it in action. The next exercise walks you through the steps so you can get a hands-on understanding of how it works.

Exercise 9.9: Off-center Animation

1. To see where this is headed, open **ex9_9_end.indd** from the chapter_9_exercises folder. Preview the file and then explore the InDesign file. Keep it open for reference.

2. Now it's time to do it yourself. Go to File > New, select Web from the Intent dropdown, and click OK.

    You're going to create three animated rectangles. Two of them will actually be composed of two grouped rectangles. For the rectangle groups, one half of the group will have a fill color, and the other half will be filled with the color of the page background, making the object appear to be only half its actual width.

3. Select the Rectangle tool (M), and click once on the document page. In the Rectangle dialog, set the width to 230vpx, the height to 50 px, and then click OK. Set the fill to RGB Blue.

4. Switch to the Selection tool and center the rectangle on the page with its top aligned to the top margin of the page.

5. In the Control panel, confirm that the upper left point in the Reference Point proxy is selected. Hold down the Alt+Shift/Option+Shift keys and drag down to duplicate the rectangle and constrain its alignment with the original. Release the mouse when the Y value in the Smart Cursor is 100 px, and then release the modifier keys.

6. Select the duplicated rectangle and copy it. Go to Edit > Paste in Place (Alt+Shift+Ctrl+V/Option+Shift+Command+V) to paste a copy of the rectangle directly on top of the rectangle you copied.

7. Change the fill color of the duplicated rectangle to cyan. In the Control panel, select the upper right square on the Reference Point proxy to define the point from which you want the object to scale (⧉).

8. Ensure that the Constrain proportions for scaling link is unlocked. Enter "50" in the Scale X text field and press Enter/Return.

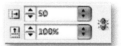

The Control panel X and Y Scale controls, set to scale only the X Scale to 50%.

9. The rectangle will scale to fill the right half of the original. Select the blue rectangle below it that was exposed when you scaled, and change its fill to [Paper].

10. Shift-click to add the scaled cyan rectangle to the selection and Alt-drag/ Option-drag a copy of the cyan and [Paper] colored rectangles down to align it below the other stacked rectangles. Release the mouse when the Smart Spacing guides appear, showing that the rectangles are evenly distributed.

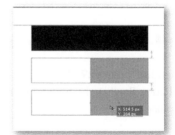

Duplicate the cyan/[Paper] rectangle pair by Alt/Option dragging down.

11. With the two duplicated rectangles still selected, click the Align Left Edges button in the Align section of the Control panel. (Alternatively, use the Align panel buttons: Window > Object & Layout > Align.) Group the two rectangles (Ctrl+G/Command+G).

12. Select the two middle rectangles and group them as well.

13. Select all three stacked rectangle groups (Ctr+A/Command+A) and, in the Animation panel, choose the Shrink preset. Unlock the Constrain the scale value link and set the width percentage to 20%. Press Tab and set the height percentage at 100%. Press Enter/Return to commit your changes.

14. In the Timing panel, select all three animations and press the Play together button at the bottom of the panel. Press Shift+Ctrl+Enter/Shift+Command+Return to preview your animation.

15. Save your file as **ex9_9.indd** and close it.

Knowing how to work around the default animate-from-center behavior with InDesign will open the door to many effects that would otherwise be impossible. It's all about experimentation from here. You've learned the fundamentals of animation in InDesign and gone beyond, to learn some techniques that should provide a solid foundation for further exploration and discovery. An introduction to animation in InDesign wouldn't be complete, however, without discussion of multi-state objects, so be sure to check out the next chapter.

CHAPTER SUMMARY

This chapter had you apply your animation knowledge to the creation of a wide range of advanced animation effects. You learned how to:

- Animate text
- Sequence multiple animation presets
- Create a variety of animated transition effects
- Animate objects on customized motion paths
- Create the illusion of multiple objects traveling the same closed path
- Create the illusion of multiple objects traveling the same open path
- Stagger the timing of animations on a closed path
- Create the illusion of objects moving through 3D space
- Animate a continuous scroller with interactive buttons
- Create a variety of animated buttons
- Create the illusion of off-center animation

You also broadened your animation skills by:

- Creating custom motion paths
- Connecting objects to custom motion paths
- Reversing path direction to reverse the direction of your animation
- Loading and exporting motion presets
- Creating a motion path preview

In addition to strengthening your animation skills, you gained experience with more of InDesign's powerful tools including:

- The Pathfinder panel
- The Free Transform tool
- The Control panel Transform controls

You also learned a number of useful techniques including:

- How to convert text to outlines
- How to create compound shapes
- How to rearrange pages in the Pages panel
- How to use the Control panel controls to calculate values

Animation in InDesign doesn't stop with motion paths and timing. The next chapter introduces multi-state objects. Ideal for slideshows but robust enough to create fully interactive and animated presentations, multi-state objects provide yet another powerful option for incorporating motion in your projects.

Chapter 10

MULTI-STATE OBJECTS

Perfect for a slideshow but rich in other possibilities, multi-state objects allow you to create one object with an unlimited number of states, each of which can contain anything you can put on a page. A multi-state object is almost like having an interactive document within your interactive document. You can use multi-state objects to create a complete interactive presentation that can be placed as a single object and then shared between documents. With a little imagination, multi-state objects can serve as a powerful presentation tool, bringing multiple elements together in a single container.

Introduction

Note: Don't be disheartened by the fact that multi-state objects export only to SWF. Check out Adding Animation to an Interactive PDF on page 352 for a workaround that extends their use to PDFs.

Multi-state objects lend themselves to slide show creation, but they can be employed for so much more. With a multi-state object, you can essentially package multiple pages into one object that can then be placed on any page of any document. You can create buttons to navigate to specific states, or move backward and forward through the previous and next object states. The only downside of multi-state objects is that they only work when exported to SWF. If you export a document that contains a multi-state object to PDF, only the state that was active at export appears on the page, and the buttons that navigate through the states don't function. In other words, multi-state objects are a SWF-only option—but what an option they are.

There is no limit to the number of states a multi-state object can have. So, in considering the slide show idea, you could place any number of images in your document, select them all, align them, and then convert the collection of images into one multi-state object. The actual conversion requires no more than the click of a button. With the content for each of the states selected, simply click the Convert selection to multi-state object button at the bottom of the Object States panel. To access the panel, go to Window > Interactive > Object States or click the 🔲 icon on in the Panel dock.

If you choose to create a multi-state object slide show from a collection of images with different dimensions, it will look best if you align the vertical and horizontal centers of the images before converting them. The multi-state object will take on the horizontal and vertical dimensions of the widest and tallest images in the collection.

For the most part, anything you can put on a page, you can also put in a multi-state object (with the exception of another multi-state object). This includes text, graphics, images, PDFs, and even video and sound. When you include animation and buttons in a multi-state object, you can go beyond the simple slide show paradigm to create something more on the order of an animated PowerPoint presentation. As with so much of what has already been discussed, within certain constraints, the sky's the limit.

Once you've created a multi-state object, you can still add and remove states, and you can add and remove objects from existing states as well.

Work through the next couple exercises to get more familiar with the ins and outs of multi-state objects and the broad range of things they can do.

Exercise 10.1: Multi-state Object Slide Show

1. Open **ex10_1_end.indd** and preview the spread. Use the previous and next buttons to view all the images in the slide show. When done previewing, look in the Layers panel to see that the flora page 2 layer contains only three objects: a previous and a next button, and the multi-state object named floralmages1. With the Selection tool, select floralmages1 on your document, and then open the Object States panel (Window > Interactive > Object States). Click through the various states to see their appearance on the page. When finished exploring, keep the file open for reference.

2. Open **ex10_1_start.indd** and save it as ex10_1.indd.

3. Press Ctrl+D/Command+D and browse to the **links** folder inside the chapter_10_exercises folder. Click on **flower1.jpg** and Shift-click **flower7.jpg** to select all but the last flower image. Click Open to load the cursor.

4. Click seven times at the upper left corner of the red rectangular guide to place all seven images between the previous and next buttons.

5. Once placed, the left edge of the images should be flush with the right edge of the previous button. If necessary, select all the images by dragging onto them with the Selection tool, and adjust their placement.

6. With all the images selected, switch to the Free Transform tool (E). Hold down the Shift key and drag the lower right corner of the images until their bottom edge meets the bottom edge of the rectangle guide. There will be a white gap at the right of the images, which you'll correct in the next step.

7. Switch to the Selection tool (V). Drag the middle adjustment handle on the right side of the images to meet the left edge of the next button. Since you only want to change the width of the frame, don't hold the Shift key, as that would scale both the width and height of the frame.

When you drag a frame adjustment handle with the Selection tool, you resize the frame and not the content it contains. Use the Fitting options to scale the contents to fill the frame proportionally.

The image frames are the right size but the images don't fill them. You'll use the Fitting options to correct the issue.

8. Right-click/Ctrl-click the image stack and choose Fitting > Fill Frame Proportionally from the contextual menu. (Alt+Shift+Ctrl+C/ Option+Shift+Command+C). All the images should be filling the area between the two slide show buttons.

Well, that was the hard part. As for creating the multi-state object from the images, there's really nothing to it.

9. With the images still selected, go to Window > Interactive > Object States to open the panel. Click the Convert selection to multi-state object button at the bottom of the panel.

Note: The Object States panel is something of a cross between the Layers panel and the Buttons panel. Its menu options allow you to add and remove entire states, add and remove objects from states, change state sequence, and release states to their component objects. Similar to button states in the Buttons panel, the active state in the panel is the state that is visible on the document.

Transform multiple selected objects to one multi-state object by clicking the Convert selection to multi-state object button at the bottom of the Object States panel.

10. Click through the panel states to see each image appear on the document and to ensure that each is appropriately scaled. At the top of the panel, name the object "floralmages1."

Note that the order of the images in the object reflect the order they appeared on the page, but the sequence is the reverse of the image file names. You'll reorder and rename the object states to accurately reflect the intended image sequence.

11. Drag State 7 up to the top of the stack and then reorder the remaining states in descending order according to the State name. Rename each of the states "flower1" through "flower7" from the top down. To rename, click once in the existing state name, pause for just a moment, click again to activate the name field, and then type in the new name. When finished, you will have reversed the order of the original states and renamed the states to match the image file names.

The floralmages1 multi-state object with each state reordered and renamed to match its image file name.

Next, you'll add another image to the multi-state object.

12. Click outside the images to deselect. Press Ctrl+D/Command+D (File > Place) and browse to the **links folder inside the chapter_10_exercises folder again. Select** flower8.jpg and click Open. Position your loaded cursor at the upper left corner of the multi-state object and click once to place the image. This image has already been scaled to the right proportions.

13. Select both the placed image and floralmages1. From the Object States panel menu, choose New State to convert the placed image to a new object state. Rename the new state "flower8."

14. Select the big black arrow on the left side of the page (the previousFloral button). In the Buttons panel, add a Go To Previous State action to the On Release event.

15. Select the nextFloral button (the big black arrow on the right side of the page). In the Buttons panel, add a Go To Next State action to the On Release event.

16. From the Object States panel menu, choose Reset All Multi-state Objects to First State.

17. Save your file and preview the spread. When you've finished your preview, close the file.

Now that you've created a simple slide show, let's get more of a feel for what you can really do with multi-state objects. The next exercise incorporates animation and buttons into the object states for a robust, PowerPoint-style presentation.

Exercise 10.2: Creating Presentations Using Multi-state Objects

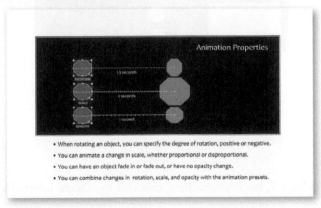

1. Open **ex10_2_end.indd** and preview the document. Play the animations and use all the buttons to navigate through the object states. When you're finished previewing, dig around a bit in the Layers panel, check out the Object States and Buttons panels, and then keep the file open for reference.

2. Open **ex10_2_start.indd** and save it as ex10_2.indd.

3. Press Ctrl+A/Command+A to Select All. If necessary, open the Object States panel. Hold the Alt/Option key and click the New button at the bottom of the panel.

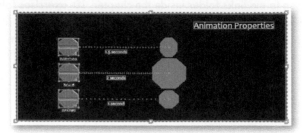

State 1

Note: To add an object to a multi-state object as its own state, select the object and the multi-state object, and then click the New button at the bottom of the Object States panel.

Holding the Alt/Option key when you click the New button on the Object States panel adds all the selected objects to a single state. Without the Alt/Option key, clicking the New button would convert each object to its own state.

Because a multi-state object must have more than one state, you'll notice that InDesign creates two copies of the new state in the Object States panel. You'll remove the duplicate once you've added another state.

4. In the Layers panel, make the Motion Path Animation layer visible and press Ctrl+A/Command+A to Select All.

Note: To duplicate a state, select the state and either choose New State from the panel menu or click the New button at the bottom of the panel.

5. Alt-click/Option-click the New button at the bottom of the Object States panel to add a new state to the existing multi-state object. To confirm that the new state was created correctly, click on State 3 in the Object States panel.

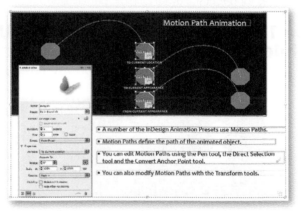

State 2.

6. Select State 2, the duplicate state, and click the Delete selected state button at the bottom of the panel. An alert saying "Deleting the state also deletes the content associated with it. Delete the state anyway?" will pop up. Click OK to dismiss the alert.

7. Turn on the visibility for the Delays layer in the Layers panel. Press Ctrl+A/Command+A to Select All once again.

8. Alt-click/Option-click the New button at the bottom of the panel to add the third and final state to the object.

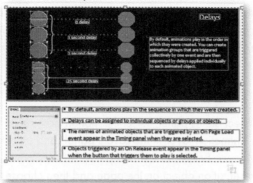

State 3.

9. At the top of the panel, rename your multi-state object "presentation". Name the object states as follows:
   - State 1: properties
   - State 2: motion paths
   - State 3: delays

   To rename the states, click once on the existing state name, pause for just a moment, and click again to activate the Name field. Type in the new state name and press Enter/Return to commit the change.

Note: To convert a multi-state object back to individual objects, select a state in the Object States panel and choose Release State To Object from the panel menu.

10. Make the Buttons layer visible in the Layers panel and twirl down the triangle at its left to expand it. Select the next button by clicking in its Selection column in the Layers panel. Open the Buttons panel (Window > Interactive > Buttons) and click the ✦ next to Actions. Select Go to Next State from the list of actions and confirm that Event is set to On Release.

11. Select the previous button and add a Go to Previous State Action to its On Release event. Save your file.

Note: Set up navigation buttons before previewing a multi-state object. When you preview a multi-state object, the first state displays first, regardless of the active state in the Object States panel.

12. Preview the spread and check each object state using the previous and next buttons to move from state to state. Click the yellow polygon buttons to test the animations, and make particular note that the sequence of the text animations on the Delays page is incorrect. Close the Preview panel.

   When converting to a multi-state object, InDesign occasionally rearranges the play sequence for animations included in a state. That's what happened with the delays state and you're going to correct it now.

13. With the Selection tool, select the presentation object on the page. If necessary, select the delays state in the Object States panel to show it on the page. Open the Timing panel and rearrange the text animations to match their order on the page.

   When working with object states, there may be times when you need to add content to an existing object state. The next several steps show you how.

Note: For a quick way to set your multi-state objects back to their initial state, choose Reset All Multi-State Objects To First State from the Object States panel menu.

14. Select the properties state in the Object States panel; then, in the Layers panel, expand the Animation Properties layer. Show and unlock the bullet text object layer and click in its selection column to select it. Hold the Shift key and click the selection column for the presentation object layer to add it to the selection. Return to the Object States panel and choose Add Objects to State from the panel menu.

   You can also paste objects into an existing state. You'll give that a try next.

15. Still in the Object States panel, select the motion paths state. Expand the Motion Path Animation layer in the Layers panel, and unlock and show the bullet text sublayer. Select the text and press Ctrl+X/Command+X to cut it. Select the presentation object on the page and then choose Paste Into State from the Object States panel menu to add the animated text to the state.

16. With the motion paths state still active, open the Timing panel and drag to rearrange the text animations to match their order on the page.

17. Select the properties state in the Object States panel and go back to the Timing panel. Rearrange the text animations to match their order on the page.

   Last, you'll add actions to each of the navigation buttons at the bottom of the page.

18. Select the animation properties button (apBtn) and open the Buttons panel. Add a Go to State action to the On Release event and choose properties from the State dropdown.

The Go to State action settings for apBtn.

19. Select the motion path button (mpBtn) and add a Go to State action to the On Release event. Choose properties from the State dropdown.

20. Select the delay button (dBtn) and add a Go to State Action to the On Release Event. Choose delays from the State dropdown.

21. Save and preview the spread and make any necessary corrections. When finished, you can close the completed file.

CHAPTER SUMMARY

In this chapter you learned all about multi-state objects. In the process of working with the Object States panel and creating multi-state objects, you learned how to:

- Combine multiple images to create a multi-state object slide show
- Add states to an existing multi-state object
- Duplicate an existing object state
- Remove states from a multi-state object
- Add objects to an existing object state
- Reorder object states
- Rename object states
- Work with Go To State actions
- Reset a multi-state object to its first state
- Create a multi-state object presentation
- Include animation and buttons in a multi-state object

By now you've learned nearly all there is to know about animating in InDesign. The next chapter adds one more piece and gives you a practical opportunity to apply your skills by creating a banner ad.

Chapter 11

BANNER ADS

The Web is riddled with them. Love 'em or hate 'em, they're here to stay. While InDesign can't generate banner ads that meet commercial file size guidelines, don't let that stop you from creating banners for your own site and possibly for other non-commercial venues. Whether or not you use them in creating banner ads, the technique you'll learn in this chapter—for sequencing animations and controlling timing— can be carried forward into any project you do.

Introduction

Web banners, like any advertising medium, are governed by specific guidelines. In Exercise 3.3: Document Presets and Application Preferences starting on page 34, you loaded a collection of document presets that represent a number of standard banner dimensions. File size is another significant factor in commercial web banners, with a standard range between 10k and 40k. As a point of reference, and to clearly illustrate why InDesign is not yet web-banner worthy, we'll share the results of a simple test. An InDesign document that was 234 px x 60 px, with no animation, and only a rectangle on the page, resulted in a file that was 112K when exported to SWF at the highest compression. OUCH! Not ready for prime time, at least not for commercial advertising. As we said earlier though, you may have occasion to create banners for sites without such rigorous file size restrictions.

If you want to learn more about commercial banner ad specifications, by far the best resource is the IAB (Interactive Advertising Bureau) website. Founded in 1996, the IAB is a group of over 460 media and technology companies that together sell somewhere in the neighborhood of 86% of all U.S. online advertising. The IAB is an advocate for, and provides education about, the interactive advertising marketplace. Together with its member companies, the IAB makes recommendations for standards and practices for interactive advertising. You can find a comprehensive chart for banner dimension and size guidelines on the IAB website at:
http://www.iab.net/iab_products_and_industry_services/508676/508767/Ad_Unit.

Exercise 11.1: Creating a Banner Ad

1. Open **ex11_1_end.indd** from the chapter_11_exercises folder and preview the file. Take a look at the animations on the objects and check out the Timing panel to see how things are put together. When you're finished, keep the file open for reference, open **ex11_1_start.indd,** and save it as ex11_1.indd.

    The animation takes place in two parts. The first part is composed of three lines of text that fly onto the page in sequence. The second part is one three-line message, as well as a triangle and text that fly in from the corner.

2. If necessary, open the Layers panel (Window > Layers) and expand the Layer1 layer. The four hidden layers contain the objects for the second phase of the animation. Click the triangle at the left of the messagesGroup layer to show the individual text object layers. Click in the Selection column to the right of <Learn Photography>. Hold down the Shift key and click in the Selection column for both <A Rewarding Hobby> and <A Colorful Career>.

Note: You can animate a group separately from the objects in the group.

It's important to select the individual messageGroup sublayers in the Layers panel rather than the group itself.

By selecting the objects separately, when you apply an animation, it applies to each of the selected objects individually, with only one click.

3. If necessary, open the Animation panel (Window > Interactive > Animation) and select Fly in from Right from the Preset dropdown. Choose None from the Opacity dropdown at the bottom of the panel, and keep the other default settings.

4. Open the Timing panel (Window > Interactive > Timing) and drag Learn Photography to the top of the stack, followed by A Rewarding Hobby. Select A Rewarding Hobby and give it a Delay of .5 seconds. Do the same for A Colorful Career.

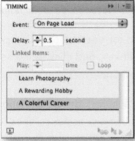

The text objects properly ordered in the Timing panel with a .5 second Delay applied.

5. With the Selection tool, click off to deselect and then click the text on the document to select the messagesGroup object. Open the Animation panel and choose Fade Out from the Preset dropdown. Set the Duration to .5 seconds.

    You want the viewer to have time to read the animated text before the next part of the message appears. Since you've already set a delay of a half-second for the second and third lines of text, another 2 seconds before the message fades out should provide ample time for your audience to read it.

6. Go to the Timing panel, select messagesGroup, and set the Delay to 2 seconds.

7. Hide the messagesGroup layer in the Layers panel and show the motion path, <Click now to enroll...>, corner, and <Register Now> layers.

8. Select <Click now to enroll...> from the Layers panel selection column and return to the Animation panel. Choose Fade In from the Preset dropdown and set the Duration to .5 seconds.

    You're going to animate the corner graphic and the Register Now text separately, but you want both animations to fly in at the same angle. Before converting the path to an actual motion path, you'll duplicate it so you can be assured that the animation angle of the two objects will match.

9. In the Layers panel, click and drag the motion path layer down onto the Create new layer button at the bottom of the panel. When you see the plus sign on the cursor, release the mouse to duplicate the layer.

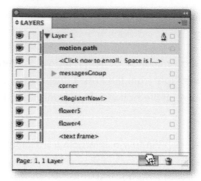

You can duplicate a layer in the Layers panel by dragging it
onto the Create new layer button at the bottom of the panel.

10. Click the selection column for one of the motion path layers in the Layers panel, hold down the Shift key, and click in the selection column for the corner layer to add it to the selection.

11. In the Animation panel, click the Convert to motion path button at the bottom of the panel. From the Animate dropdown, choose To Current Location and set the Duration to .5 seconds.

12. Return to the Layers panel and select the second motion path and the Register Now text object.

13. Return to the Animation panel and click the Convert to motion path button at the bottom of the panel. Select To Current Location from the Animate dropdown and set the Duration to .5 seconds.

14. Open the Timing panel, select corner, and set its delay to .5 seconds. Hold down the Shift key and click Register Now and Click Now to Enroll. Click the Play together button at the bottom right of the panel.

The point of a banner ad is to get the viewer to take action, to click the banner for more information . For that to happen, you need something to click. You'll wrap up the exercise and the banner by creating an invisible button that effectively converts the entire banner into a link.

15. Switch to the Rectangle tool (M) and drag a rectangle from the upper left corner of the banner all the way down to its lower right corner. Set both the fill and the stroke to None. Go to the Buttons panel (Window > Interactive > Buttons), and press the Convert Object to a Button icon at the bottom of the panel. Name the button "registerBtn," and add a Go to URL Action to its On Release event. Enter "http://www.interactive-indesign.com" in the URL field.

16. Turn on the visibility of the messagesGroup layer in the Layers panel and press Shift+Ctrl+Enter/Shift+Command+Return to open the Preview panel and preview the spread.

17. Feel free to play with the timing to see how it can change the feel of the animation. Then, save and close your file to complete the lesson.

CHAPTER SUMMARY

Congratulations! You can now consider yourself an InDesign animation pro. Just add your imagination to the host of animation tricks and techniques up your sleeve to make the magic happen. There's virtually no limit to the possibilities.

Before your exploration of animation in InDesign is complete, you'll want to become familiar with page transitions and the interactive page curl effect. With just a few clicks, page transitions can take your multi-page documents from lackluster to lively. Check out the next chapter to see how simple it can be.

● Chapter 12

PAGE TRANSITIONS

Page transitions are a quick and easy way to add visual interest to a project. With a few simple clicks, you can make your document pages flip, fade, wipe, or dissolve, and put an otherwise static document into motion.

This chapter discusses best practices for using transitions, how to apply and remove them, and how to publish them to SWF and PDF. You'll also take a quick trip to Acrobat to experience the chapter project in full screen mode.

Introduction

Adding page transitions is the easiest way to add animation to a multipage document. Supported in both SWF and Interactive PDF, a fade or wipe from one page to the next can add just the right amount of spice to your project. Everything in moderation, though—and page transitions are no exception to this rule. Used sparingly, they can help to bring your project to life. Too many different transitions, however, like too many different fonts on a page, create a visual cacophony that cheapens even the most beautifully designed document.

Transitions can be applied on a page-by-page basis or document-wide, and there is a dedicated panel to manage them. Go to Window > Interactive > Page Transitions to get to it. With 12 categories, and variations in direction and speed available for most of them, there is an abundance of transitions from which to choose. This is both a blessing and a curse; a blessing in that you have so many choices, a curse in that you might feel compelled to choose too many of them. The likelihood is that you'll play for a while, and then choose a couple of favorites upon which you'll come to rely.

With that notion in mind, the next exercise lets you get some of that playing out of your system. At the same time, it's designed to get you familiar with the available page transition options. So for now, throw caution (and good design principles) to the wind, and for the next little bit, just use this opportunity to experiment and enjoy.

Exercise 12.1: Working with Page Transitions

1.   Open **ex12_1_end.indd** from the chapter_12_exercises folder and preview the file to get familiar with how it works. When you're done previewing, check out the Pages panel and note the transitions icon next to each of the pages. When you're done exploring, you can keep the document open for reference.

   So you have a feel for how the document was set up, here's a little overview. Hyperlink destinations were established for each of the document pages and named with the associated page number. The images on the first page are buttons. Each button has a Go to Destination action targeted to the page that displays a larger version of the button image. The document master for these pages has an invisible button laid over the photo in the center of the page, with a Go to Destination action targeted to page 1.

2. Open **ex12_1_start.indd** from the chapter_12_exercises folder and save it as ex12_1.indd.

   The document has nine pages so you've got a lot of opportunity to play with the different transition options.

3. Go to Window > Interactive > Page Transitions or click the  button in the Panel dock to open the Page Transitions panel. Ensure that page 1 is highlighted in the Pages panel.

4. To get an experience of all the transitions you can choose from, select Choose... from the Page Transitions panel menu.

The Page Transitions dialog lets you preview 12 different page transitions all in the same place. From this dialog, you can apply a transition to only the page that is active in the Pages panel, or to all the spreads in your document.

5. Mouse over each transition to get a feel for how it works. Ensure that the Apply to All Spreads checkbox at the lower left of the dialog is unchecked. Then, select the Blinds radio button and click OK to assign the transition to page 1.

6. When the Page Transitions dialog closes, the default settings for the Blinds transition are active in the Page Transitions panel. Mouse over the preview at the top of the panel to play the animation. Select Vertical from the Direction dropdown and preview the transition again. Try each of the speed settings and choose the settings you prefer.

   Be aware that page transitions are applied to the highlighted page in the Pages panel, regardless of the page showing in the document window. For this reason, be sure to first select a page in the Pages panel before applying your transition.

7. In the Pages panel, mouse over the page transition icon next to page 1. A tooltip pops up that says "Page Transition Applied."

An ⧗ icon next to a page in the Pages panel indicates that a page transition has been applied to it.

8. Select page 2 in the Pages panel and choose Box from the Transition dropdown in the Page Transitions panel. Choose a direction and speed.

9. Assign a different transition to each page, exploring the options for each transition along the way. Skip the Page Curl for now; you can apply that document-wide when you export to SWF.

10. Open the Preview panel and choose Edit Preview Settings from the panel menu. From the General tab of the Preview Settings dialog, confirm that the All Pages radio button is selected. If necessary, check the Generate HTML file and View SWF after Exporting checkboxes. Leave the other default settings and check the Include Interactive Page Curl checkbox at the bottom of the dialog. Click Save Settings to close the dialog.

Note: The Interactive Page Curl is definitely cool, but, unfortunately, it doesn't work when you export to PDF.

The Preview Settings dialog is identical in content to the Export SWF dialog which you'll learn more about in Chapter 20: Output, starting on page 331. The settings you enter in this dialog are applied to both the movie displayed in the Preview panel and the file that's generated when you choose the Test in Browser option from the Preview panel menu.

11. In the Preview panel, click the Preview Document Mode button ( ) and then click the Play Preview button. When the preview appears, click each button on the home page to jump to the enlarged version of the button image. Then click the large image to return to the home page.

12. To check out the page curl, mouse over a page corner. As long as it's not the first or last page in the document, the page corner will automatically curl, just a little bit. When you see the curl, click and drag to begin turning the page. If you drag so that just over half the height of the page is curled, and then release, the page will flip as if you were turning a page in a book.

You only have to drag the interactive page curl
a little bit, and then release it to turn the page.

When previewing the document, you saw that, rather than enhancing the presentation, the many transitions served to overpower and distract from the content.

13. In the Page Transitions panel, select Fade from the Transition dropdown and make a selection from the Speed dropdown. Click the Apply to All Spreads button (🔲) at the bottom right of the panel and preview the file again.

Note: To clear all the page transitions from a document at once, choose Clear All from the Page Transitions panel menu.

14. From the Preview panel menu, choose Test in Browser. When the file opens, note the position of the movie on the page, and then test the buttons and the page curl.

15. Return to InDesign and open the Edit Preview Settings dialog again to remove the page curl. Test the movie in the browser again to see that the movie is now located in its normal position at the upper left corner of the page. Close the browser and return to InDesign.

Next, you'll take a look at the file when published to Interactive PDF.

16. Go to File > Export and choose Adobe PDF (Interactive) from the Format dropdown. Click Save. If necessary, check the View After Exporting checkbox and the Open in Full Screen Mode checkbox. Confirm that Include All is selected from the Buttons and Media section of the dialog and leave the other default settings. Click OK to export the PDF.

Note: The change in the position of the movie on the page resulting from the page curl transition isn't something you can control when publishing from InDesign. You can, however, alter the HTML that contains the exported SWF. To learn how, see Adjusting a SWF HTML Page, starting on page 358.

The Export to Interactive PDF dialog.

17. When the export is complete, Acrobat should open. Click Yes to put the document in full screen mode.

Note: To get the latest version of the Free Adobe Reader, go to http://get.adobe.com/reader/.

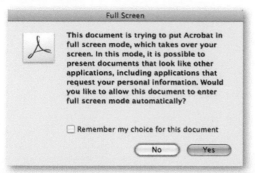

Interactive PDF page transitions can only be viewed in full screen mode

Note: If you check the Remember my choice for this document checkbox, you won't need to deal with the Full Screen alert again for this file, as long as you don't change the file name.

18. Click through the pages. When you've finished viewing the document, press Escape to exit full screen mode. (Ctrl+L/Command+L will also toggle in and out of full screen mode.) Close the document and quit Acrobat (or Reader).

If you have Adobe Reader configured as your default application for viewing PDFs, you will see the same alert that appears in Acrobat, and the same keys apply to control full screen mode. If you use a different application to view PDFs, the features you add to your Interactive PDF files most likely won't work.

Note: If you add, remove or rearrange pages in a document containing page transitions, InDesign will present you with the following alert:.

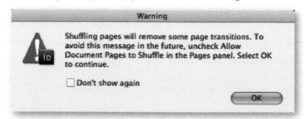

Unless you specify otherwise, pages in your document will rearrange, or shuffle, from one spread to another when pages are added or removed from within a document. This causes any page transitions applied to the spreads affected by the shuffling the of pages to be removed.

You can pretty much disregard this message entirely if your document doesn't use facing pages or manual spreads. Transitions are applied to an entire spread rather than individual pages, so, for documents with facing page spreads, shuffling pages from one spread to another results in page transitions being lost.

CHAPTER SUMMARY

Page transitions are an incredibly easy way to add sparkle to a multi-page document. In this chapter you learned how to apply one page transition uniformly to the pages of an entire document in the Export dialog, and to add different transitions to individual pages using the Page Transitions panel. You also used the panel to customize the default page transition settings by changing transition direction and speed.

In order to see your page transitions in action, you made modifications to the Preview panel settings and previewed your SWF document in a browser. You also took a trip to Acrobat or Adobe Reader and viewed the Interactive PDF version of your document in full screen mode to see the impact of your efforts.

This chapter completed your explorations of animation in InDesign. Congratulations! You can now consider yourself an InDesign animation pro. Just add your imagination to the host of animation tricks and techniques you've learned and make the magic happen.

The next portion of the book is dedicated to video and audio. You'll learn how it works, how to compress it, and how to include it in your projects. There's all kinds of great technical information on video and audio compression in Chapter 12, if you enjoy that stuff. If not, you can skip right over to Chapter 13 and learn how easy it is to add media to your InDesign documents.

Part 4

LIGHTS, CAMERA, ACTION!

WORKING WITH MEDIA IN INDESIGN

How exciting is it to be able to add movies and sound to a print document and preview the result right inside InDesign?! Really!

Learn how easy it is to add audio, video, and Flash SWF media files to your projects, and to make them look great. As a bonus, you'll learn your way around the Adobe Media Encoder and be handed the keys to decoding its mysteries.

• Chapter 13

ADOBE MEDIA ENCODER

The hardest part of working with media in your interactive projects isn't getting it in there, it's getting the right compression settings to make it look and sound great. Adobe Media Encoder holds the secret, and this chapter provides the key.

Video Basics

For starters, video, like animation, is nothing more than the illusion of motion over time. This illusion is achieved by a showing a sequence of still images in fast enough succession to give the appearance of smooth and continuous motion. At one time or another you've likely had occasion to play with a flip book, a booklet with a slightly different drawing from page to page. When you flip through the book fast enough, the drawing looks like it's moving on the page. If you can imagine each page of that booklet as a still frame of a film, the rate at which you flip the pages equates to the frame rate of the movie. Frame rate is measured in frames per second (fps). The higher the frame rate, the more pages get flipped per second, and, consequently, the more of them you need to fill up any given amount of time. A video with a frame rate of 30 fps will require twice as many frames to fill one minute as a video with a frame rate of 15 fps. Usually, the more frames you have, the bigger the size of the video file, and the more bandwidth you need to deliver that file smoothly and quickly. The size of a video file is also influenced, of course, by the physical dimensions of each of its frames. A video with dimensions of 640 px x 480 px is going to be dramatically larger than the same video, with the same compression, at half the size (320 px x 240 px).

Note: Bitrate refers to the amount of encoded video or audio data as it relates to time. Bitrate is measured in kbps (kilobits per second), mbps (megabits per second), and sometimes MBps (megabytes per second). For internet transmission, you want to keep the bitrate as low as possible to enable the fastest delivery of your file, but high enough to maintain picture quality.

Because video files can be so huge, compression is essential for storage, transmission, and playback. Compression considerations for video and audio are similar to those for JPEG compression of still images. With JPEG compression, the goal is to find the optimal balance between image quality and file size. For audio and video, the goal is to find the optimal balance of quality, file size, and bitrate. In each case, when preparing files for the web and devices, compression is a lossy process, meaning that, in order to make the file smaller, data is actually discarded each time compression is performed. Multiple compressions result in a degradation of quality, and can introduce artifacts that distort the appearance or sound of the file. For this reason, whether for still images, audio, or video, or if you need multiple variations of a file, it's always preferable to start with an uncompressed original and compress it specifically to meet your needs.

The intricacies of video compression algorithms and codecs can get pretty complicated. Fortunately, Adobe Media Encoder does a pretty good job of checking out the details of your imported file and automatically populating the appropriate conversion settings when you load a file into the queue. If you never have to mess with these settings, all the better. If there should come a time, however, when you need to further reduce file size or change the dimensions of your movie, for example, it's good to have a rudimentary understanding of what's at work behind the scenes.

Note: There are eight bits in a byte. When abbreviating measures related to bits, a lowercase b is used: kb. For measures relating to bytes, an uppercase B is used: MB.

Interlaced and Progressive Video

If the term *interlaced* is a mystery to you, here's a brief explanation. When frames of a video or film are displayed on a television, each frame is divided into two fields that are shown in rapid succession to create the impression of a complete image. Each field is divided into two sets of horizontal lines: the odd field, or top field, and the even field, or bottom field.

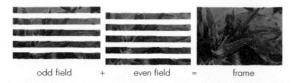

odd field   +   even field   =   frame

Illustration of the interlaced fields comprising one video frame. The odd field (upper field) plus the even field (lower field) combine to create one full frame.

Display of these interlaced fields is alternated at a rate of 50 interlaced fields/second (25 frames/second) or 59.94 interlaced fields/second (29.97 frames/second), depending on the standard used.

Devices like computer media players, iPods, iPads, Android Slates, and other media devices rely on progressive noninterlaced display, rather than interlaced display. In contrast to interlaced display, progressive renders the lines of the image sequentially, in one progressive scan. One of the huge benefits of progressive is that it eliminates the headache of timings and field inherent in working with interlaced video. For creating interactive video and media player video, you'll be relying on progressive rather than interlaced video.

Frame Rates and Standards

Now for the technical mumbo jumbo. Don't get too crazy with it; it's really just to provide some background. As long as you get the fundamental concepts, you'll be fine. Here goes…. It used to be that there were three main broadcast standards used throughout the world: NTSC, PAL, and SECAM. All of these standards are analog systems for color television that are being replaced throughout the world with emergent ATSC[1] digital standards.

NTSC stands for *National Television Systems Committee,* and it was the color video standard employed in the US until the majority of over-the-air transmissions were replaced by ATSC on June 12, 2009. Lines were scanned across the NTSC TV screen at about 60 Hz (59.94 interlaced fields/second), resulting in a frame rate of almost 30 fps.

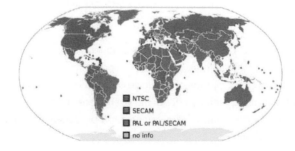

NTSC, SECAM, and PAL distribution worldwide as of March 2010

---

1   ATSC stands for *Advanced Television Systems Committee* and is a set of standards for digital television transmission that support Hi-Def TV and Dolby Surround Sound. ATSC uses MPEG-2 video compression and Dolby Digital audio compression. It encompasses a wide range of screen resolutions and frame rates, as well as interlaced and progressive noninterlaced formats.

PAL stands for *phase alternating line*. It produces better color and image fidelity than NTSC at a slightly lower frame rate of 25 fps with fifty interlaced fields. SECAM, or SÉCAM, stands for *séquentiel couleur à mémoire*: sequential color with nemory. SECAM transmits only one color at a time, and is therefore not prone to the color artifacts that occur in both NTSC and PAL. Like PAL, SECAM updates the display at a rate of 50 fields/second. 35mm film, the motion picture standard, records at a rate of 24 fps.

Compression Basics

Generally, one way to reduce the size of a video file is to reduce the frame rate. Fewer fps equates to less data, which equates to a smaller file. Video plays best at its native frame rate, so, if you need to change frame rate when modifying a file, it's best to change it by a factor of the original rate. For example, if the original frame rate were 24 fps, the video would play most smoothly if the reduced frame rate were 12, 8, 6, 4, 3, or 2 fps.

The amount of compression you can apply to video is greatly affected by how much the visual content changes from one frame to the next. Footage with lots of motion, where a good portion of the image changes dramatically from frame to frame, will not compress as well as footage of a talking head, for example, where movement is minimal. The reason for this is the algorithms used in the compression process.

There are three primary compression algorithms, also referred to as picture types or frame types: I, P, and B. An I-frame or intra-coded picture, can be compared to a free-standing, static image; it's compressed without reference to any other frame. This type of compression is called *intra-frame* or *spacial* compression. Of the three frame types, I-frames can be compressed the least, and typically require more bits to encode than other picture types. I-frames are also called key frames: whole frames that are coded at consistent intervals throughout the video. Key frame distance is the interval at which key frames are recorded when encoding the video. The smaller the key frame distance, the shorter the interva; the more key frames, the bigger the file. Flash player can only seek and pause from key frame to key frame, so if you want your audience to be able to skip around your video, consider using a lower value for key frame distance.

A P-frame, or *predicted picture*, contains only data that is different from the preceding frame, and therefore requires less file space than an I-frame. A B-frame, or *bi-predictive picture*, comprises an average of the changed data from both the previous and next frames, thereby conserving even more space. Compression that compares frames to other frames in the compression process is called *temporal* or *inter-frame* compression.

H264/MPEG4 AVC is the latest international standard, and is the video codec generally used in the F4V format (Flash Video), along with the AAC audio codec. Of all the codecs, it is the most commonly used. In fact, a great number of everyday devices play H264, including YouTube, Vimeo, TiVo, Apple TV, iPods, iPads, iPhones, Android phones and devices, etc.

Note: When you reduce key frame distance, you're reducing the space between keyframes, thereby increasing their number. Reducing keyframe distance may require that you raise the bitrate. More key frames mean more data to transfer. An increase in bitrate balances the decreased key frame distance to maintain comparable image quality. Keep in mind that this will require more processing power from the user's machine in order to decode the compressed data.

Note: The word codec is derived from a combination of the words "compressor" and "decompressor," or, more commonly, "coder-decoder." Codecs encode data that is then decoded and interpreted for playback at its destination.

Note: AAC stands for *advanced audio compression*.

H264 applies variations of I, P, and B compression, augmented by additional algorithms, to slices of the frame, rather than to the frame as a whole. This enables even more precisely targeted compression that results in a higher quality image, while maintaining the same compression ratio.

H-264 enables you to make adjustments in data rate, which introduces a second set of balances for consideration. An increase in data rate can increase perceived quality, but greater processing power is required to decode the data. This could result in degraded or potentially stalled playback. With too low a data rate, the video will be indecipherable.

Note: With so many compression options, it's important to keep in mind the file extension the destination device requires. For example, Apple devices like iPad and iPhone want M4v files and will not play files with an MP4 extension.

Video Compression Tips

There are a lot of variables when it comes to compressing video, so here are a few guidelines to help you get the best results.

- If possible, keep rapid movement to a minimum when filming. Remember, the more change there is from frame to frame, the more key frames will be required to capture it, and the larger your file will be.

- Keep your video as short as possible, cropping as necessary, and trimming any extraneous material from its beginning and end. Edit out any superfluous content.

- Keep your video in its native format until the final output. Use raw, uncompressed footage to avoid incremental degradation of quality.

- Reduce noise and grain. You can use Gaussian Blur in Adobe Media Encoder to do this, but it will compromise image quality. You'd be better off using Premiere, After Effects, or another video editing application instead.

- Optimize your compression settings. The idea is to get the maximum amount of compression while maintaining acceptable quality. If you're happy with the appearance of your video, increase the compression in increments until you get a result that you absolutely can't use. Then use your last acceptable, most highly compressed result.

- Use the smallest dimensions, lowest frame rate, and highest key frame distance you can get away with.

Note: Adobe Premiere Pro edits most RAW (or native) formats from AVCHD and DSLR cameras that shoot video, as well as Flip Cameras and most pocket cameras with a USB port, also known as tapeless cameras. By editing native camera files, you're able to maintain the highest possible quality all the way to export.

Note: If your video doesn't have a lot of fast moving action shots, you can often export at 15 or 12 fps to get small files that still appear to play at 30 fps. This is especially common for screen capture needs.

Audio Compression

The objective when compressing audio is pretty much the same as for video. You want to end up with the smallest possible file of acceptable quality. As with video, you want to work with original raw files for as long as possible. If your original file was recorded in mono, your final file should be in mono too. If you can't transfer your content to Adobe Media Encoder digitally, you'll want to use the best available sound card to avoid introduction of the distortion and artifacts that can occur with analog transfer.

Note:
1000 Hertz = 1 KiloHertz

When compressing Flash Video in Adobe Media Encoder, the audio compression options are, thankfully, less numerous than those for video. A short overview should help to make some sense of them.

When it comes to audio compression, the two main terms to understand are *frequency* and *bitrate*. Bitrate in audio compression is conceptually the same as bitrate in video. Frequency is used interchangeably with *sampling rate* and equates pretty closely to the concept behind key frame distance. The shorter the distance between key frames, the more key frames will be encoded in the video, the larger the file size. With sampling rate, the number represents the number of times per second an audio sample is taken. You can think of samples as similar to key frames; the higher the sample rate, the more samples are taken, and the larger the file size.

Sound audible to the human ear ranges, at best, between 20 Hz and 20,000 Hz. The sampling rate for CDs is 44.1 kHz, meaning that the sound is sampled 44,100 times every second. A sampling rate of 44.1 kHz records a maximum frequency of 22,000 Hz, which is outside the human hearing range; the result is that all audible sound is recorded.

In addition to a frequency setting of 44.1 kHz, Adobe Media Encoder also provides frequency options of 22.05 kHz and 11.025 kHz. While either of these two options will reduce your file size, they will also reduce the quality of the recording, causing the sound to flatten out and dull the higher notes.

When compression is a priority over quality, you can get away with a sampling rate of 22.05 kHz for speech recordings and AM radio. A frequency of 11.025 kHz results in a very poor quality recording all the way around.

Adobe Media Encoder

The version of Adobe Media Encoder that installs with Flash Professional exports only to the two Flash video formats: FLV and F4V. Versions that install with Premiere Pro, After Effects, Production Premium, and Master Collection can export to a wider range of formats depending on the codecs installed on the system.

For purposes of this discussion, we'll concentrate on settings relevant to Flash Video compression, since both FLV and F4V are supported when exporting from InDesign to SWF, interactive PDF, and FLA.

Import & Export File Formats

Some file extensions actually represent container formats rather than data formats. The MOV, AVI, FLV, and F4V extensions fall under this category. The data in the containers may employ different compression and encoding schemes. Depending on the installed codecs, Adobe Media Encoder may be able to import the container, but not the data inside it.

First, let's take a look at the two flavors of Flash Video. FLV is an older format that generally contains video encoded using the On2 VP6 or Sorenson Spark codec

Note: For all kinds of tutorials and truly awesome resources, check out Adobe TV. at http://tv.adobe.com/.

For video content, don't miss http://tv.adobe.com/show/davtechtable/ presented by David Helmly. Besides being a wealth of information, David graciously contributed to this chapter to ensure that we got the technical details straight.

Also for video, you might want to check out Adobe Beginner classes (ABCs) at:

http://tv.adobe.com/channel/video-and-audio/video-production/.

Note: If you haven't installed Flash Professional and are running InDesign as a standalone application, or as part of Design Standard, you probably don't have Adobe Media Encoder on your system.

If this is the case, or if you don't want to take the time to go through the encoding steps in the exercise, you'll find a copy of each of the exercise output files in the chapter_13_exercises folder to use for comparison.

*Unfortunately, Adobe Media Encoder is not available for download or purchase as a standalone application.

and MP3 encoded audio. Both versions of FLV play on Flash Player 8 and later. Files encoded using On2 VP6 support an 8-bit alpha channel that can be used for video compositing. Adobe Media Encoder cannot import Sorenson Spark encoded files.

F4V files generally contain H.264 encoded video files (also known as MPEG-4 AVC) and audio files using the AAC audio codec. H.264 encoding provides a higher quality image with a lower bitrate than On2 VP6 encoded video can achieve. F4V video can be played in Flash Player 9.0.115.0 and later.

Note: AAC stands for *advanced audio coding*. AVC stands for *advanced video coding*.

You can extend the number of file formats Adobe Media Encoder can import by adding assorted codecs onto your system. Installing QuickTime is one way to extend the capabilities of Adobe Media Encoder. For a comprehensive list of supported formats, see Adobe Media Encoder Help.

Working with Adobe Media Encoder

Using Adobe Media Encoder is actually quite straightforward and easy; it's the settings that can get complicated. But now that you have some understanding of the terminology and the concepts, you should be able to find your way around, even if you do have to deviate from the presets at some point.

Exercise 13.1: Working with Adobe Media Encoder

1. If you haven't already, locate Adobe Media Encoder CS5 on your hard drive and open it. On the Mac, it should be in your Applications folder. On Windows, it should be in the Program Files folder in either the Adobe or Adobe Creative Suite Design Premium, Web Premium, Production Premium, or Master Collection folder.

Note: Adobe Media Encoder CS5 incorporates the 64 bit Mercury Engine, which adds software and hardware acceleration (select NVIDIA cards) for much faster exporting. For more information on which cards add hardware acceleration, check **Adobe.com/premiere**.

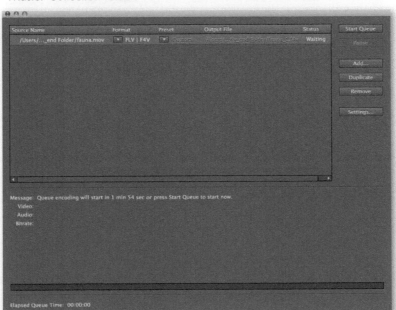

Adobe Media Encoder with a file having customized settings added to the conversion queue.

2. Click the Add button at the right of the panel, browse to the chapter_13_exercises folder, and select **fauna.mov**. Click Open to load the file into the queue.

3. Click the down arrow in the Format column and select FLV/F4V. Click the down arrow in the Preset column, and, if necessary, select the F4V– Match Source Attributes (High Quality) preset.

F4V – Match Source Attributes (High Quality)
F4V – Match Source Attributes (Medium Quality)
FLV – Match Source Attributes (High Quality)
FLV – Match Source Attributes (Medium Quality)
F4V – 1080p Source, Quarter Size (Flash 9.0.r115 and Higher)
F4V – 720p Source, Half Size (Flash 9.0.r115 and Higher)
F4V – HD 1080p (Flash 9.0.r115 and Higher)
F4V – HD 720p (Flash 9.0.r115 and Higher)
F4V – Web Large, NTSC Source (Flash 9.0.r115 and Higher)
F4V – Web Large, PAL Source (Flash 9.0.r115 and Higher)
F4V – Web Large, Widescreen Source (Flash 9.0.r115 and Higher)
F4V – Web Medium (Flash 9.0.r115 and Higher)
F4V – Web Medium, Widescreen Source (Flash 9.0.r115 and Higher)
FLV – 1080p Source, Quarter Size (Flash 8 and Higher)
FLV – 720p Source, Half Size (Flash 8 and Higher)
FLV – Web Large, NTSC Source (Flash 8 and Higher)
FLV – Web Large, PAL Source (Flash 8 and Higher)
FLV – Web Large, Widescreen Source (Flash 8 and Higher)
FLV – Web Medium (Flash 8 and Higher)
FLV – Web Medium, Widescreen Source (Flash 8 and Higher)

Edit Export Settings...

The Adobe Media Encoder presets.

4. Click the Settings button on the right of the dialog. If it isn't available, select the file name in the Media Encoder dialog. When the dialog opens, if you don't see the details below, twirl down the arrow for Export Settings, and then the arrow for Summary, to display the Output and Source information.

This is the place to see all the details for your source file, as well as the preset settings.

Note: The numbers at the lower right of the Source Clip information in the screenshot to the right represent a time code:

00;02;01;02

00 - Hours
02 - Minutes
01 - Seconds
02 - Frames

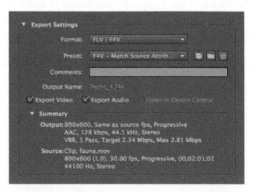

The Export Settings dialog auto-populates with information gleaned from the source file. The Summary section under Export Settings tells you everything you need to know about both the source and the output settings for the selected file in the queue.

Notice that the source video dimensions are 800 px x 600 px, the frame rate is 24 fps, it is progressive rather than interlaced, it's just over 2 minutes in length, and it includes high quality stereo sound. The output is set to match the video dimensions and frame rate; like the source, it will also be progressive. It will encode the audio as high quality stereo using an AAC audio codec with a bitrate of 128 kbps. The video will be encoded using one pass with a variable bitrate targeted to 2.34 Mbps, and a maximum of 2.81 Mbps.

What's pretty cool is that most of what you just read should actually sound somewhat familiar from what you read at the beginning of the chapter. There are a couple things that may require clarification but, for the most part, all that mumbo jumbo should be starting to make some sense. You know that *bitrate* refers to the amount of data transmitted over a measure of time. VBR stands for *variable bitrate*, meaning that the data stream gets more or less dense depending on the requirements of the file. The target and max values set the range for the variation in the bitrate.

There are two flavors of variable bitrate encoding: *variable constrained* and *variable unconstrained*. With variable constrained encoding, you get to set a range for the data rate. Depending on the maximum bitrate you choose, it is likely that, in order to fit within your specified constraint, more complex frames will be more compressed than less complex frames. Variable unconstrained encodes each frame with whatever amount of data it requires, without limit. The variable unconstrained option in Adobe Media Encoder enables you to target an average bitrate.

An alternative to vriable bitrate (VBR) is *constant bitrate* (CBR) encoding where each frame is compressed at the same fixed data rate. As with variable constrained encoding, this means that more complex frames get compressed more than those that are less complex. An advantage to CBR encoding is that, when streaming over a network, you can rely on consistent bandwidth usage. The downside of CBR encoding is that a higher bitrate than necessary may be allocated to simple frames, while more complex frames may be over-compressed. The result will likely be a file of less than optimal quality, that is also larger than it needs to be.

1 Pass encoding means that the encoder makes a single pass through the file from beginning to end to encode it. Adobe Media Encoder provides a total of three bitrate encoding options: CBR; VBR,1 Pass; and VBR, 2 Pass. While single-pass encoding is faster, the dual-pass encoding produces superior quality and superior compression, resulting in a smaller file.

Note: You can add any number of files to the encoding queue and Adobe Media Encoder will process them automatically. Each file can have unique compression settings, and, by default, Adobe Media Encoder will increment the file name with an appended number; for example, fauna_1.f4v.

For longer movies especially, with larger dimensions (*big* files), you might elect to add them to the queue and let Adobe Media Encoder run overnight. Large/long movies can take hours and hours to encode.

The Export Settings window controls.

Note: Conversion time can vary widely based on system resources (processor and RAM). If Adobe Media Encoder is running slow, you might consider doing your encoding at a time when you have no other applications running and you're not working on the computer.

5. In the tabbed section of the window, below the Export Settings, ensure that the Video tab is selected and, if necessary, twirl down the arrows for each of the settings subsections. Mouse over each of the settings options for two seconds to see its explanatory tool tip. Then make note of the Estimated File Size at the very bottom of the window: 37 MB, just above the Metadata button. The starting file was 92+ MB!

6. In the Export Settings section of the window, click the Output Name (**fauna.f4v**) to open the Save As dialog. Rename the file **fauna_default.f4v** and note that the default file location is the containing folder for the source file. Click Save to exit the dialog.

7. At the bottom right of the Export Settings window, click OK to return to the encoding queue. Note the countdown timer below the file list that will, if you do nothing, begin encoding after two minutes. Click Start Queue.

8. Watch the preview and note the dynamic display of Elapsed Time and Estimated Remaining as the compression progresses. When the conversion is complete, note the Elapsed Queue Time. (Our conversion took 49 seconds.)

9. Locate the compressed F4V file in the chapter_13_exercises folder and check its file size. (Our file was 26.8 MB.)

10. Return to Adobe Media Encoder and load the **fauna.mov** file into the queue again. Click on the path below Output File and rename the file "**fauna_1pass_high_24fps.f4v**." click OK, then click the Settings button.

    800 px x 600 px is *really* large for video delivered electronically. It would be better to make the movie dimensions smaller (smaller file size), and choose the lowest bitrate that achieves an acceptable result (less demand on the system decoding the video, and less bandwidth requirement for delivery).

Note: To export a preset, Alt-click/Option-click the Save Preset button (☐) and browse to where you'd like to save the file. Name your preset in the Export Preset dialog and then click Save to exit.

11. With Format set to FLV/F4V, choose the first option from the Preset dropdown: F4V - Match Source Attributes (High Quality). Note the Estimated File Size at the bottom of the dialog, toward the middle, just above the Metadata button. If necessary, switch to the Video tab (below the Export and Summary sections of the dialog) and check the Resize Video checkbox. Confirm that the link to maintain the frame aspect ratio while resizing is linked (☐), click the Frame Width value to activate the field, and enter "400." Then press Tab to automatically populate Frame Height with the correct value (300).

12. Note that the Frame Rate (fps) dropdown just below the Width and Height fields (you may need to scroll) is automatically set to Same as source (24 fps in this case). Scroll down to the Bitrate Settings to see that the default setting for Bitrate Encoding is VBR, 1 Pass (Variable Bit Rate, one pass through the file to encode it). Note also that the default Bitrate Level is set to High. Look again at the Estimated File Size to see that it has reduced to 10 MB.

13. Click OK to exit the Export Settings window and click Start Queue to start encoding.

---

14. Make note of the Elapsed Queue Time. (It took us 40 seconds.) Locate the file to check the file size. Our file was 8.8 MB.

15. Add **fauna.mov** one more time into the compression queue and click on its Output File Name. In the Save As dialog, rename the file fauna_2pass_low_12fps.f4v and click the Settings button.

16. Click the Import Preset button (▣) to the right of the Preset dropdown and browse to the chapter_13_exercises folder. Select **low_2p_400x300_12fps.epr**, click Open, and then click OK in the Choose Name dialog to load the preset.

You can load and rename custom Adobe Media Encoder presets.

17. Look through the settings to see that the Frame dimensions have been set to 400 px x 300 px, Frame Rate to 12 fps, Bitrate Encoding to VBR 2 Pass, and Bitrate Level to Low. Check the Use Maximum Render Quality checkbox.

    Hold that button! To spare you unnecessary frustration, you should be aware that there's a known issue with Adobe Media Encoder CS5 that can cause dual-pass encoding to fail. From what we've been able to discover, it seems to result from the 5.01 Adobe Media Encoder (AME) CS5 update. Apparently, Adobe has issued a patch to correct the problem for Windows, but at the time of this writing, Mac users are not so fortunate. So, if you've not updated to 5.01, you might want to wait until 5.02 comes out. If you have updated, and AME fails in compressing the dual-pass file, don't despair: we actually found a fix. It might be as simple as uninstalling AME 5.01 and reinstalling AME 5.0. Then, BEWARE of updates! (Beware of updates to Adobe Media Encoder that is. Normally, we recommend checking for updates regularly; this case is a rare exception.) If you do have a problem with this, *please don't* call us about it. This is everything we know. Honest! Now that you've been duly informed....

18. Click OK to return to the queue and click Start Queue.

    Our resulting file was 7.6 MB, reflecting nearly a 24% reduction in size, due to the combination of dual-pass encoding, reduced frame rate, and reduced bitrate. The question is whether the resulting file passes the quality test. You'll be the judge.

19. Launch InDesign and open **ex13_1_start.indd** from the chapter_13_exercises folder. Open the Preview panel, and, from the panel menu, choose Test in Browser. When the browser opens, mouse over each video and click the stop button on the controller that pops up. Click the ▣ button on each controller to turn off the audio, and then click both play buttons. As the movies play, compare the quality of the images but, most importantly, pay close attention to

the transitions from one image to another. Close the browser and close the file in InDesign. Keep Adobe Media Player open for the next exercise.

The movie that was compressed at 12 fps flickered more noticeably than the one at 24 fps. The question is, "Is this something you could live with if you were to post it on the web?" Within a relatively narrow threshold, the tipping point of what's acceptable and what's not is ultimately a choice based on your personal aesthetic.

Admittedly, fauna.mov is most likely not typical of the video you'll be working with, so please don't construe the compression settings in the exercise as recommendations for your videos. An unfortunate fact: compression choices that work for one movie won't necessarily work for another. There is no magic formula, as much as we would have loved to provide one.

Hoping to offer a more specific recommendation for optimizing your files, we performed a number of experiments with the fauna movie. In the process, we came across some rather surprising and counterintuitive results. If nothing else, our findings should bring home the fact that video compression is as much art as science.

The truly surprising thing we found is that a reduction of frame rate did not reliably result in a reduction of file size. Haven't figured that one out yet. Predictably, lower bitrate did have some impact on file size, but the most consistent result was the reduction in file size achieved through dual-pass encoding. So, if you're one of the unfortunates experiencing AME dual-pass encoding failure, knowing this should be an incentive to get it straightened out.

Bitrate Level	Bitrate Range	Passes	24 FPS	12 FPS
High	0.50 Mbps -	1 Pass	9,933 bytes	9,962 bytes
High	0.70 Mbps	2 Pass	8,897 bytes	9,944 bytes
Medium	0.50 Mbps -	1 Pass	9,932 bytes	9,307 bytes
Medium	0.60 Mbps	2 Pass	8,583 bytes	8,854 bytes
Low	0.40 Mbps -	1 Pass	9,858 bytes	8,082 bytes
Low	0.48 Mbps	2 Pass	8,530 bytes	7,566 bytes

File size comparison of the same movie compressed with variations in bitrate level, number of passes and frames per second.

The intention of this exercise was to introduce you to some of the Adobe Media Encoder settings. Next, you'll take a few minutes to trim the fauna video and reduce size even further.

Trimming and Cropping

The birds in the last several images in the fauna.mov file are a little hard to find, and the movie will likely read better without them. The image area can also be cropped a bit to better emphasize the birds in the other photos. You can take care of such edits right inside Adobe Media Encoder, using its trim and crop capabilities.

Exercise 13.2: Trimming and Cropping

1. From the queue window of Adobe Media Encoder, click the Add button and browse to the chapter_13_exercises folder. Select **fauna2.mov** to add it to the compression queue, and click the Settings button to open the Export Settings window.

2. Mouse over the center of the vertical divider that separates the window in two. When your cursor changes to a double-sided arrow, click to expand the editing pane to fill the entire window. (To view the export controls again, mouse over the right edge of the window and click when you see the double-sided arrow.)

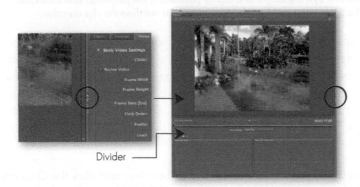

Divider

The Editing pane of the Export Settings window can expand to fill the entire window.

3. Click the dropdown arrow next to the word "Fit" in the center of the screen, and choose 100% from the list of magnification options. Scale the window so the width of the video fits without scrolling. If you still need to scroll to see the full height of the video, mouse over the divider below Source Range and above the Cue Point settings. When your cursor changes to a double-sided arrow, click and drag down until the entire video frame is visible in the window.

4. Scrub the timeline (the yellow line) by dragging the playhead (⬛) to the right. Notice that the yellow time code at the left changes as you drag, reflecting the elapsed time at the position of the playhead. Notice also that the duration of the entire clip appears in white at the right of the timeline.

   The video is simply a series of still images fading from one into the next. As you scrub the timeline, you'll be able to identify the precise frame at which each transition begins and ends.

5. Drag the playhead through the clip to see each of the images and to identify the transition points.

---

6. Position the playhead at the beginning of the transition after the image of the black bird with the red and yellow beak and legs. Use the next and previous arrow keys on your keyboard to move the playhead frame-by-frame for greater precision. We came up with a time code of 00;01;40;04 for the frame preceding the start of the transition. With the playhead at that point on the timeline, click the Set Out Point button ( ) just to the left of the Fit dropdown. The white duration time code changes when you set the new out point, indicating that the video will be trimmed to the new duration when it's encoded.

You can trim the length of a clip by positioning the playhead and then clicking the Set In Point and Set Out Point buttons to redefine the clip duration.

Cropping the image area is equally easy with the crop controls at the upper left of the preview window. You have the option of typing in specific values, dragging over the crop values to adjust them, or dragging a cropbox that you can size and position on the image area as desired. You also have the option to constrain your crop to particular proportions. Because this video will be played using Flash Player, you can select any display dimensions you like without having to maintain particular proportions.

7. Drag the playhead to the first frame of the movie and click the Crop tool ( ) at the upper left of the preview window. Click and drag the sizing handle at the lower right to scale the crop window. If you want to maintain the image proportions, hold Shift while you drag. We aligned the upper left corner of the cropbox to the upper left corner of the image, and set the cropbox dimensions to 759 x 527 pixels. The measurements for the crop parameters were as follows: Left: 0, Top: 0, Right: 41, and bottom 73. You can enter the values manually at the upper left of the window.

You can crop the image area by dragging the sizing handles or edges of the cropbox, by dragging left or right through the crop values at the upper left of the window to increment them, or by entering values manually.

8. Click the Output tab at the upper left of the preview window to see the result of your crop. Be sure to set the magnification percentage to 100% to properly evaluate the result. Then scrub through the timeline to see that your crop settings work for all images in the clip.

9. Because the last couple peacock images are portrait rather than landscape images, the black border on the left and the right are now uneven. Click the Source tab at the upper left of the window, and enter 41 for the Left value, to match the crop amount on the right. Scrub the timeline from either the Source or Output window to confirm that the crop is good, and then click Enter or Return to register your edits and return to the conversion queue.

10. Click Start Queue to process the movie.

Working with Cue Points

Note: Cue point information is stored differently in F4V and FLV files. If you're adding cue points with the intention of working with them in Flash, you can learn more about them in the Programming ActionScript 3.0 reference guide.

Cue points are named anchors that you can add to your video during the encoding process. There are two kinds of cue points: *event* cue points and *navigation* cue points. You can use either type of cue point in conjunction with ActionScript in Flash to trigger additional events in the movie. For example, with cue points in the movie of the birds, you could use ActionScript to cause a blurb to pop up about each type of bird when it appears in the movie. Event cue points are hidden from the video navigation controls, but can be coded with ActionScript to trigger events. Navigation cue points insert a key frame in the timeline, enabling a user to navigate to that place in the video. You can also add navigation cue points to your video directly in InDesign. The good news is that navigation cue points inserted in Adobe Media Player show up in InDesign, and can be targeted by InDesign button actions to jump to specific points in the video. The bad news is that InDesign codes its cue points by hundredths of a second rather than frame-by-frame, like AME. The result is that there can be a timing discrepancy when you bring AME cue points into InDesign. We'll talk more about that in the next chapter when we discuss adding video to InDesign. In Adobe Media Encoder, you add cue points from the Edit pane of the Export Settings window.

Cue Point Guidelines

Since navigation cue points define a point that Flash Player can seek, they are most useful for video content containing scenes or discrete informational segments. Add navigation cue points to enable a viewer to jump to a scene, a topic, or even a particular increment of time (every minute, for example). Used in this way, cue points typically won't be required in videos shorter than five minutes long. Of course, if you're using cue points to trigger play of synchronized enhancements, such as captions or complementary graphics, the content will dictate where you insert them in your movie.

Adding Cue Points

You can add cue points in Adobe Media Encoder from either the default or edit view of the Export Settings window, but only the default view has a dropdown that lets you specify the cue point type. To add a cue point, simply position the playhead at

the desired location in the video timeline, and click the Add Cue Point button. ()
You can then name the cue point, adjust the time code (if necessary) and select a
cue point type from the Type dropdown.

**Adding cue points in Adobe Media Encoder is as simple as positioning
the playhead and pressing the Add Cue Point button.**

Exercise 13.3: Adding Cue Points

To see how easy it is, you'll take a few minutes to add a few navigation cue points
to the fauna video.

1. Add **fauna.mov** to the Adobe Media Encoder queue and click the Settings
    button to open the Export Settings window.

2. In the left side of the window, with the playhead at the very beginning of
    the video, click the Add Cue Point button. Choose Navigation from the Type
    dropdown, and then click the words "Cue Point" to activate the name field.
    Name the cue point "flamingos."

3. Drag the playhead to the first duck photo, just after the transition is
    complete. You can use the next and previous arrows on your keyboard to
    nudge the playhead into precise position. Alternatively, you can select the
    time elapsed time code and type in "00;00;21;10." Add a cue point, name
    it "ducks," and set the cue point Type to Navigation.

4. Position the playhead at the beginning of the peacock photos, just after the
    transition (00;01;08;01). Add a cue point and name it "peacock." Set the
    cue point Type to Navigation.

5. Select the time code and enter 00;01;59;10 for the last cue point. Name
    the cue point commonMoorhen and set the Type to Navigation.

6. Select low_400x300_12fps from the Preset dropdown. Click to the
    right of Output Name and change the name of the file you're saving to
    low_400x300_12fps_cue_points.f4v.

7. Click OK to exit the Export Settings and then start the queue.

Note: You can export
cue point settings in the
same way you export
presets. From the group
of cue point controls, click
the Save Cue Points button
( ), browse to a location,
then name and save your
file. To load saved cue
points, click the Import
Cue Points button ( ) and
browse to the cue points
XML file. (Try it with the
fauna_cue_points.xml file
in the chapter_13_exercises
folder).

Note: If you're
experiencing issues with
the dual pass encoding,
we've provided a single
pass preset that you can
try instead. Choose Import
Preset at the right of the
Preset dropdown in the
Export Settings dialog and
navigate to the chapter_13_
exercises folder. Load
low_1p_400x300_12fps.epr.

Queue Clean Up

If you leave compressed movies in the queue after conversion, you can use them as a template of sorts for additional conversions. Simply select a converted movie and click the Duplicate button. All the settings in the duplicated movie are copied into the new instance and can be used as is, or modified through the Export Settings window.

To clear the queue at any time, select any number of items, whether complete or waiting, and click the Remove button. Click Yes in response to the alert asking if you're sure you want to remove the selected items, and the items will be removed.

Metadata Export

Before wrapping up discussion of Adobe Media Encoder, we'll make brief mention of the metadata options it provides. Technically, metadata is information about information. In AME, there are a multitude of options for adding descriptive and technical identifiers. At the bottom of the Export Settings window is a Metadata button that gives you access to templates in which to enter a wide selection of metadata information, well beyond author and copyright notices. You can customize and save templates, and then embed the metadata in your video and/or generate a metadata sidecar file that travels with the movie.

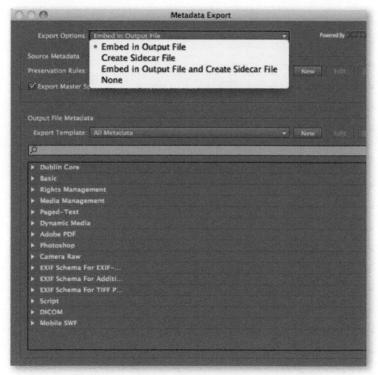

The Adobe Media Encoder Metadata Export pane, with extensive metadata options. Metadata can be embedded in the compressed video file, saved in a sidecar file, or both.

To learn more about including metadata in your media compression workflow, check out Adobe Media Encoder Help and search for Metadata.

CHAPTER SUMMARY

In this chapter you've gotten a head full of media encoding acronyms and a solid footing in the principles guiding video compression. Although you might not remember every detail, you can always go back to review as you have the need.

In addition to gaining a foundation in working with video, you became familiar with Adobe Media Encoder, and, in the process, learned how to:

- Add media to the Adobe Media Encoder queue
- Customize encoding settings
- Load encoding presets
- Export encoding presets
- Use existing movies as compression templates
- Crop and trim your video
- Add navigation cue points
- Export navigation cue points
- Clear the queue

Along the way, you learned a number of video compression terms, including:

- FPS: frames per second
- Interlaced and progressive video
- VBR: variable bitrate, CBR: constant bitrate
- Codec: coder-decoder/compressor-decompressor
- NTSC: National Television Systems Committee; PAL: phase alternating line; SECAM: *séquentiel couleur à mémoire* (sequential color with memory)
- ATSC: Advanced Television Systems Committee
- AAC: advanced audio compression
- AVC: advanced video coding
- I-Frame: intra-coded picture; P-frame: predicted picture; B-frame: bi-predictive picture
- H264/MPEG4AVC
- Key frame distance
- Frequency/sampling rate
- FLV/F4V
- Metadata

Now that you've gotten the technical details out of the way, it's time for the fun part. In the next chapter, you'll learn to add audio and video to your projects in InDesign. You'll be surprised at how easy it is!

• Chapter 14

ADDING MEDIA IN INDESIGN

The Media panel is command central for adding video and other media to your InDesign projects. Use this panel to set play preferences, select controllers, and preview your media directly in InDesign. This chapter covers the Media panel and more, to ensure that your media performs to rave reviews.

Introduction

Regardless of the type of media you're working with, the import process is pretty much the same. You can place media the same way you would place any other file. First, load the multi-place gun in one of three ways: Ctrl+D/Command+D, File > Place, or click the Place a Media File button (▶︎▦) at the bottom of the Media Panel. With the cursor loaded, just click to place the media in the same way you would any other file. Unlike other files, however, we recommend that you don't drag to define a custom size for the containing media frame; instead, click once to place. Dragging can cause undesirable display anomalies and possibly scale your movie disproportionately. You can scale, transform, and position your movie after it has been placed.

While the import process is pretty routine, the export process presents its own set of considerations. Although supported for import, MOV, AVI, and MPEG media files will play only when exported to interactive PDF, and not if exported to SWF or FLA. For video and audio that will play in all three, stick with Flash Video (either FLV or F4V) or H.264 encoded files such as MP4. For audio, use MP3. These formats will play universally in Acrobat 9, Adobe Reader 9, and Flash Player 10 and later.

About Media Export

Media placed in an InDesign document exports to SWF and Interactive PDF. If you export to FLA (Flash Professional), the media files are replaced by representative images only, and you will have to re-import the media files in Flash. When exporting to interactive PDF, if both the horizontal and vertical centers of a movie are positioned outside the boundaries of the page, the movie will not export with the file. While we can't imagine why you'd want to have less than a quarter of your movie showing in your final output, if you do, you may encounter this strange behavior.

The Media panel enables you to set media to play on page load, to loop it, and, in the case of movies, to choose a representative poster and controller. Additionally, you can set navigation points throughout a movie. As mentioned in the previous chapter, the InDesign movie controls are not nearly as finely tuned as those in Adobe Media Encoder (AME). Also, InDesign counts time based on hundredths of a second rather than by frames, so the carry over of navigation cue points from AME to InDesign is less than perfect. That aside, the awesome thing is that you can add button actions in InDesign that will navigate to and play your movie from the navigation points set in either application.

Before launching your multimedia project for general consumption, you'll want to do extensive testing, particularly focused on the performance of the project in various browsers and on various systems. As challenging as testing may be, it will save you endless issues and unpleasant surprises on the back end. Testing is not always fun, but it's one of those often neglected precautions that pays itself back in spades.

Exercise 14.1: Adding Media

To start, you'll get familiar with the Media panel in order to import and set the parameters for your media files. You'll then test a couple versions of your movie in a browser to see how well they perform.

1. Go to File > New and choose Web from the Intent dropdown. Then choose 1024 x 768 from the Page Size dropdown and click OK. Open the Media panel (Window > Interactive > Media, or click the (▣) icon in the panel dock).

2. Click the Place a video or audio file button at the bottom right corner of the Media panel and locate **fauna_default.f4v** in the chapter_14_exercises folder. Select **fauna_default.f4v**, click Open in the Place Media window, and then click once near the upper left corner of the document. (You'll center the video on the page in just a moment.) Save your file as **ex14_1_indd** in the chapter_14_exercises folder.

3. The first frame of the movie should be visible in the Preview pane of the Media panel. Click the play button (▶) at the left of the panel, just below the preview. When the movie starts, the sound is a bit loud (provided you have speakers, of course). While you can't moderate it from the Media panel, you do have the option to mute it completely. The sound button acts as an on/off toggle (🔊 🔇), so, if you prefer, click it to mute the audio.

   InDesign may have automatically created a poster from the first frame of the video as a visual placeholder. You can choose any frame of the video you like to populate the poster.

4. Scrub the playhead through the timeline or play the movie until you find a frame you would like to use as the poster representing the video on the page. (We chose the peacock image at 01:26.71.) Choose From Current Frame from the Poster dropdown and, if necessary, click the Refresh button to make the poster appear on the page.

Note: In contrast to Adobe Media Encoder, the InDesign Media panel measures time in minutes and seconds at intervals of 1/100th of a second.

Note: Looping works in exported SWF files only, not in PDF files.

The Media panel allows you to preview your media, set Play options, and assign controls when appropriate.

5. Click the Controller dropdown and choose SkinOverAllNoFullNoCaption from the options list.

The Controllers are compiled Flash SWF files called *skins*. All the skin options in InDesign display on top of the video, rather than beneath it. The skin you've selected includes all possible controls, with the exception of the full screen option and captions. The controls the skin contains are Play, Stop, Rewind, Seek, Mute and Volume. It also allows you to scrub the playhead through the video timeline.

6. Check the Play on Page Load and Show Controller on Rollover checkboxes.

7. Select the video on the page with the Selection tool. At the upper right of the Control panel, select Align to Page from the Align to dropdown. Then, click the Align Horizontal Centers and Align Vertical Centers buttons. Now with your movie centered on the page, you're all set to take it for a spin.

8. Press Shift+Ctrl+Enter/Shift+Command+Return to view the spread in the Preview panel. You may want to enlarge the panel for a better view, but even if you're viewing it at a very reduced size, all the video controls are fully functional.

While the Preview panel can give you a good idea of the way your project will appear in terms of sequencing, it's not going to provide an accurate picture of how the project will perform when delivered over the internet and rendered in a browser. There are several factors outside of your control that can impact the experience of your audience. First, the user's internet connection speed will determine how quickly they are able to receive the project data. Second, the amount of traffic on the server hosting your project can affect how quickly the data can be delivered. Third, the capabilities of the user's system to process the data it receives can affect how smoothly the project will play.

While viewing your movie in a browser will present a slightly more realistic scenario, it's important to know that viewing your project file on your local machine does not take into account the factors discussed in the previous paragraph. One thing is certain, though; if you experience performance problems testing locally, it's a good guess that it isn't going to get any better when you try to deliver the file over the web.

9. From the Preview panel menu, choose Test in Browser. It may take a moment for the movie to show up on the page.

10. Again, you may want to turn down the volume, but for purposes of the test, you want to be able to hear the sound. Watch and listen to the entire video. It's likely that the performance will be choppy, with skips in the music and possibly the images as well. It may start out playing smoothly, and then skip as it reaches closer to the end. The bottom line is that the file is simply too big.

11. You can leave the browser open, but close the page, and then return to InDesign. Select the movie on the page and open the Links panel (Window > Links). Notice that since the video is selected on the page, fauna_default.f4v is selected and highlighted in the Links panel. Click the Relink button (🔗) and select **fauna400x300_12fps.f4v** from the chapter_14_exercises folder. Click Open to relink the file and close the dialog.

12. In the Control panel, ensure that the center point is selected in the Reference Point proxy, and that the Constrain proportions for width and height link is linked. Enter 400 px in the width text field and click Tab to populate the height value.

13. Right-click/Ctrl+click on the movie, and, from the context menu, choose Fitting > Fit Content Proportionally. If you'd like, choose a poster for the movie and once again, choose Test in Browser from the Preview panel menu.

14. Play the movie through with the music. Hopefully, you'll find that the skips have disappeared and the file plays smoothly. Save and close the file.

    You'll want to further your tests once your file is posted on a remote server. You'll also want to test on other systems—but by testing in a browser, you've made a good start. Before you get involved in serious testing, you'll want to read the section on Output to pick up some tips on how you can optimize your file.

Working with Cue Point Navigation

In the Adobe Media Encoder section, you learned all about adding cue points to your document for use as navigational aids. The InDesign button options include a video action that enables you to target the cue points you've added to your movie. In the next exercise, you will place your movie, add a controller, and target buttons to jump to the navigation points in the video.

Exercise 14.2: Working with Cue Point Navigation

1. Navigate to the chapter_14_exercises folder, open **ex14_2_start.indd**, and save it as ex14_2.indd.

2. Press Ctrl+D/Command+D to place, and navigate to the chapter_14_exercises folder. Select **fauna.f4v** and click Open to load your cursor. If necessary,

---

select the Video layer in the Layers panel to ensure the movie will be properly placed. (The Interface layer should be locked. If it is not, when you click to place the video, it will be placed inside the rectangle on the Interface layer.) Click once inside the white-stroked rectangle to place the video.

3. With the Selection tool selected, drag the video until you see both vertical and horizontal smart guides, indicating alignment to the center of the white-stroked rectangle.

Note: If you don't see the green smart guides, go to View > Grids & Guides > Smart Guides (Ctrl+U/ Command+U).

Smart Guides indicating horizontal and vertical alignment.

As discussed in the Animation section, you can animate nearly anything; and media is no exception.

4. If necessary, select the video with the Selection tool and open the Animation panel. Choose Grow from the Preset dropdown. If necessary, twirl down the Properties arrow to show the Properties options. Set the Scale to 20% for both width and height, and, from the Animate dropdown, choose To Current Appearance. Choose -180° from the Rotate dropdown and set the Speed to Ease Out. Leave the On Page Load event and the other defaults, and then save and preview the file.

Note: Caution: animating the video could present some performance issues. Be sure to test extensively before deciding to include animated video in your final project.

The settings for animating the video.

5. Open the Media panel. If you don't see a poster preview on the document, choose From Current Frame from the Poster dropdown and click the Refresh button ( ) to update the page.

6. Check the Play on Page Load checkbox and choose a controller with volume controls. Then click the Show Controller on Rollover checkbox.

   Note that the cue points inserted in the video with Adobe Media Encoder appear in the Navigation Points section of the panel.

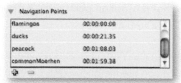

Navigation cue points established in Adobe Media Encoder carry over to InDesign.

7. Select the playFlamingosV button on the page () and open the Buttons panel. Add a Video action to the button On Release event. Since there is only one video in the document, InDesign chooses fauna.f4v automatically. From the Options dropdown, choose Play from Navigation Point and ensure that flamingos is selected from the Point dropdown.

The Play from Navigation Point button action.

8. Select the playDucksV button and add a Play from Navigation Point Video action to the button On Release event. From the Point dropdown, choose the ducks navigation point.

9. Repeat step 7 for the playPeacockV and playCommonMoorhenV buttons, choosing the peacock and commonMoorhen navigation points respectively.

10. Save your document and, from the Preview panel menu, choose Test in Browser. When the browser opens, click each of the buttons to jump to the different navigation points in the video. When you've finished viewing your file, close the browser window and leave the browser open. Return to InDesign.

   You'll find the timing of the cue points to be off somewhat from what you set in AME. This is due to the fact that InDesign measures time in hundredths of a second rather than by frame. Unfortunately, InDesign doesn't allow you to edit cue points imported from AME. You can, however, correct the issue by removing the cue points established in AME and replacing them with new navigation cue points using InDesign's Media panel.

11. Select the video with the Selection tool and open the Media panel.

12. In the Navigation Points section of the panel, select the first point and click the minus sign at the lower left of the panel to delete it. Delete the remaining cue points.

13. With the playhead at the first frame of the movie, click the plus sign at the bottom left of the panel to add a navigation point. Name the navigation point "flamingos."

14. Drag the playhead to the right until you get to the beginning of the duck images and add another navigation point named "ducks." (We added the navigation point at 00:00:21.42.)

    Control of the playhead in the Media panel is nowhere near as precise as AME. Unfortunately, while you can use the arrow keys on your keyboard to nudge the playhead into position, the preview window doesn't update to show an accurate preview. Neither can you type in a specific time code. With a little patience and perseverance, however, you can get the playhead close enough to where it needs to be.

15. Drag the playhead further to the right until you get to the beginning of the peacock images. Add a third navigation point named "peacock." (We positioned the navigation point at 00:01:08.08.)

16. Drag the playhead to the right one last time, until you get to the beginning of the images of the common moorhen. Add the fourth and final navigation point and name it "commonMoorhen." (The time code for our navigation point was 00:01:59.46.)

    Because you removed the cue points that were the target of the button actions, you now need to update each of the buttons.

17. Select the playFlamingosV button and open the Buttons panel. Choose flamingos from the Point dropdown on the panel to properly target the button.

18. With the Buttons panel still open, select the playDucksV button and choose ducks from the Point dropdown.

19. For the playPeacockV and playMoorhenV buttons, change the Point selection to peacock and commonMoorhen, respectively.

flamingos	00:00:00.08
ducks	00:00:21.42
peacock	00:01:08.08
commonMoorhen	00:01:59.46

Approximate time codes for each of the InDesign navigation points.

20. Save the file and test it in your browser. Click each of the buttons to see that they now navigate to the appropriate spots in the video. When finished, close the browser, return to InDesign, and close the file.

Adding Sound for Export to SWF and PDF

Adding sound to your document is quite similar to adding video, but with fewer controls to manage. While you have an option in the Media panel to add a poster as a visual indicator of sound, the poster will show only in an exported Interactive PDF, and not in an exported SWF. To optimize the development cycle, you'll want to conserve your time and focus your efforts on a workflow that serves multiple platforms as effectively as possible. With that objective in mind, you can use a placed image in lieu of the sound poster, and leave the built-in poster associated with the sound file blank.

When designing for output to Interactive PDF, there's a somewhat strange and seemingly unavoidable behavior Acrobat and Adobe Reader have when it comes to playing sounds. As mentioned, when you place a sound in InDesign, the Media panel provides you with the option to choose a poster as a visual placeholder. You can choose the standard poster (🔊), a poster using an image you select, or no poster at all. You would think that if you were to choose no poster, the sound would play without visual representation on the screen. While this is indeed how it works in an exported SWF, with an Interactive PDF, you're not so lucky. When the sound is activated, a controller on a background that matches the dimensions of the sound placeholder in the document pops up, regardless of whether you assigned a visible poster to that sound or not.

To make things still more interesting, the controller pops up above all other content, regardless of where the sound, with or without a visible poster, was located in the stacking order in InDesign. It seems that there's no way to turn off this "feature" with media exported from InDesign to Interactive PDF, so you should plan accordingly when creating your layout.

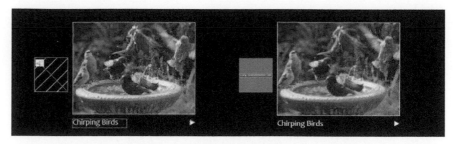

On the left, the "invisible" placeholder poster for the sound placed in InDesign; on the right, the controller on a gray background that pops up when the audio is activated in Acrobat or Adobe Reader.

Unfortunately, there are a few more quirks to navigate with Interactive PDFs when it comes to multiple sounds on the same page. Regardless of whether you have established buttons to control your sound, when you mouse over the sound poster in Acrobat, even if the poster is invisible, a tooltip pops up with an instruction to click to activate the audio. When you click, that's when you get the controller.

Even if the controller is very small, its controls are actually functional. One way to contend with the controller issue is to eliminate any other Play buttons and just use some kind of visual indicator that the user can click to activate the sound. Once they click to activate, the controller appears and takes the place of the initial graphic. The downside of using just the controllers and no buttons is that the user will have to turn the sounds off manually. With buttons, you can add actions to stop other sounds at the same time that you play the sound for the button that is clicked. However, this results in another strange behavior; in Acrobat or Adobe Reader, if buttons playing a sound include Stop actions for other sounds, the first button clicked activates all the sounds at once, resulting in quite a cacophony. After this initial, potentially problematic outpouring of sound, the buttons seem to work as intended.

What it boils down to is that there are some trade-offs if you're expecting to have multiple sounds on a single page in an Interactive PDF exported from InDesign. You have a choice of no Play button at all, a dummy Play button placed where the controller will appear, an actual Play button with only a Play action, which duplicates the controller function, or a Play button with Play and Stop actions that results in an initial din when first clicked. Your call. For the next exercise, we've actually opted for the initial din, given that there are only three sounds and they're all birds, but feel free to play with the options as you see fit.

Exercise 14.3: Adding Sound for Export to SWF and PDF

1. Open **ex14_3_start.indd** from the chapter_14_exercises folder and save it as ex14_3.indd.

2. Take a look at the Layers panel to explore how the file is structured. Expand the Audio layer and click the eye column to show the pdf sound proxy and play buttons sublayers. Click on the Audio layer to highlight it.

    The objects on these layers are grouped to make it easier to hide and show them. If the group is hidden at the time of export, the objects won't appear in the final output. Separating them in this way lets you experiment more easily with the various options for handling the interactive PDF button and controller issues.

    The image used in the pdf sound proxy layer (pdf_sound_proxy.psd) is a screenshot of the PDF controller. Each instance of the image was positioned and sized to match the position and size of the sound poster you will place for the sounds.

3. Press Ctr+D/Command+D and navigate to chapter_14_exercises > sounds. Ctrl-click/Command-click to select the following files: **bird_sings_in_the_morning.mp3**, **gobbler.mp3**, and **loon.mp3**. If you selected the files in the order listed, click the bird images on the page in order, from the top down, to place the sounds. You'll see a green placeholder appear for each sound that you place.

4. Select the placeholder for the Chirping Birds sound (the one at the top), and confirm in the Layers panel that bird_sings_in_the_morning.mp3 is selected. Check the other two sounds to be sure that they're each positioned atop the appropriate image.

5. Select the bird_sings_in_the_morning.mp3 sound again, and open the Media panel. Confirm that None is chosen from the Poster dropdown, and then check the Stop on Page Turn checkbox. Click the Play button in the Panel to hear the sound.

6. Using the Selection tool, align the bottom and the left edge of the first sound placeholder with the bottom and left edge of the corresponding controller proxy. On the Control panel, ensure that the Constrain proportions for width and height link is unlinked, and that the lower left square of the Reference Point proxy is selected (⬚). Enter 114 in the width field and press Enter/Return to update the field.

7. Click the target in the center of the poster to select the graphic inside the poster frame. Once again, enter 114 in the width field on the Control panel. Press Tab and then enter 12 for the height. Select the containing frame for the poster and set the height field on the Control panel to 12.

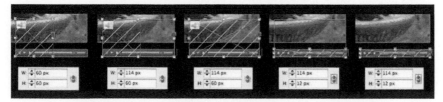

From left to right, the steps to scale the sound poster to match the position and dimensions of the controller when it opens in Acrobat or Adobe Reader.

8. Repeat step 7 for the other two sound posters and save the document.

    Next, you'll set up the button to activate the sound and to get around the Click to Activate pop-up mentioned earlier.

9. Mouse over the white triangular play button below the first bird photo, to the right of the controller image. You should see a green bounding box for the three grouped triangle buttons. Double-click to get through the group to select the top triangle. In the Buttons panel, add a Sound action to the On Release event. From the Sound dropdown, choose **gobbler.mp3** and choose Stop from the Options dropdown. Add a second Sound action to stop **loon.mp3**. Add a final Sound action to play **birds_sings_in_the_morning.mp3**.

10. Select the triangular play button associated with the image of the Turkeys. Add Sound actions to stop **birds_sings_in_the_morning.mp3** and **loon.mp3**. Add a third Sound action to play **gobbler.mp3**.

11. Select the button for the Loon image. Add Sound actions to stop **gobbler.mp3** and **birds_sings_in_the_morning.mp3**. Add a third Sound action to play **loon.mp3**.

12. In the Layers panel, hide the pdf sound proxy object layer, save the file, and test it in a browser. Play each of the sounds and note that when you play a new sound, the previous sound stops playing. (The video runs independently

of the sounds, but you could add a Stop Video action to the buttons to control the video as well.)

13. Quit the browser and return to InDesign. In the Layers panel, show the pdf sound proxy object layer, and then go to File > Export. Choose Adobe PDF (Interactive) from the Format dropdown, and navigate to the chapter_14_exercises folder. Save the file as **ex14_3.pdf**.

14. Since the document is only one page, some of the export options are irrelevant. Do check the View After Exporting checkbox, though, and set the View to Fit Page. For Image Handling, set Compression to JPEG2000 and leave the Resolution at 72 ppi. Confirm that the Include All radio button is selected in the Buttons and Media section of the dialog, and then click OK to export the file.

    With the View set to Fit Page, the full document page will display regardless of the window size in Acrobat or Adobe Reader.

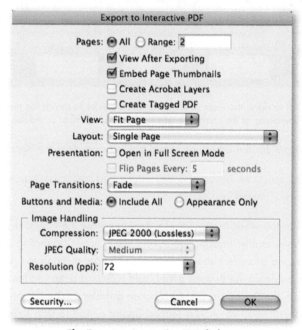

The Export to Interactive PDF dialog.

15. When the document opens in Acrobat or Reader, mouse over one of the controller proxy images. A Click to activate tooltip should pop up. Instead of clicking the proxy image, click one of the white triangular buttons to hear all three bird clips in concert, and to see all the controllers appear. Click the white buttons in turn to note that each button turns off the other bird sounds when its sound starts to play. When you've finished exploring, close the file, quit Acrobat or Reader and return to InDesign.

16. In the Layers panel, drag each of the sounds into its corresponding bird sublayer, and then save and close the file.

CHAPTER SUMMARY

Now that you know how easy it is to add media to your InDesign documents, there will be no stopping you. In this chapter you put the Media panel through its paces to add audio and video, customize a video controller, and select posters to represent your media on the page.

Additionally, you worked with cue point navigation, targeting buttons to jump to predefined points in your video. You discovered:

- The differences between cue points established in AME and navigation points created in InDesign
- How to add and remove navigation points in the Media panel
- How to work with Play from Navigation Point button actions

You also learned to navigate the somewhat quirky behaviors of Acrobat and Adobe Reader when audio is included in an Interactive PDF. Particularly, you:

- Discovered how to take control of the popup PDF audio controller
- Learned how different button actions influence the activation of sound in an Interactive PDF

With the media section of the book under your belt, the next leg of the journey shows you how to use bookmarks, hyperlinks and cross-references in unexpected ways to enhance your interactive projects.

Part 5

BOOKMARKS, HYPERLINKS, AND CROSS-REFERENCES

You may be familiar with bookmarks, and cross-references through your work with long print documents. But, did you know that they have a solid place in the development of interactive projects as well? In this portion of the book, you'll learn to use these tools as well as hyperlinks and hyperlink destinations to extend the ways you can use InDesign to create a dynamic interactive experience for your audience.

● Chapter 15

BOOKMARKS

Bookmarks are exclusively a PDF feature. While traditionally used to navigate long print documents exported to PDF, they can be effectively employed in navigating Interactive PDFs as well. Bookmarks can be generated automatically by InDesign when you create a table of contents, or you can add them manually through the Bookmarks panel. The skills you'll learn in this chapter for creating bookmarks efficiently and effectively will translate equally well to your print and interactive projects.

Why Bookmarks?

Before InDesign was even a glimmer in Adobe's eye, bookmarks were a well-established feature in Acrobat and what was then Acrobat Reader. Particularly useful for navigating long documents, bookmarks can be created directly inside Acrobat Standard or Professional. Residing in a dedicated panel, PDF bookmarks are similar in function to hyperlinks in that they jump to a specific document location. When created in Acrobat, they can hone in on a particular area of a page at a specified magnification. Bookmarks created in Acrobat can also be tied to actions in much the same way as buttons in InDesign, and they possess similar functionality. They can be used to play sounds and video, open files and web links, reset forms, and more.

As far as we can tell Acrobat is one of the most widely adopted and most under-used applications on the market. Few people are really aware of what it can do, but, with the exception of creating animation, the interactive features in InDesign have been part of Acrobat for years. While the design capabilities in InDesign are exceedingly more robust than anything you can accomplish with Acrobat, Acrobat possesses some interactivity features that are notably absent in InDesign. We're speaking particularly of the electronic form creation tools that were first introduced in Acrobat 3.0. (The current version is Acrobat 9.) Forms creation is just one of the many impressive things you can do with Acrobat. Do yourself a favor and take a serious look at the feature set in this truly under-utilized treasure trove of an application. You'll be amazed at what you can do with it. There are currently three flavors of Acrobat to choose from; you can check them out at this link: http://www.adobe.com/products/acrobat/matrix.html.

Enough about Acrobat, let's get back to InDesign! There is a dedicated panel in InDesign just for bookmarks. The panel allows you to create and manage your bookmarks, and also provides the convenience of being able to test them right in the InDesign environment.

The bookmarks you create manually in InDesign can be targeted to a page, selected text, or a selected object. InDesign can also automatically generate PDF bookmarks for entries in a table of contents. Whether created manually or through a TOC, bookmarks can be structured hierarchically to reflect multiple levels. By default, TOC-generated bookmarks are appended to those you create manually. Once created, you can rearrange your bookmarks by dragging them in the panel.

While the bookmarks you create in InDesign export with navigational capabilities only, you can modify them in Acrobat to add actions, set zoom levels and apply limited formatting.

Adding Bookmarks and a Table of Contents

If you can create a table of contents for your document, InDesign will automatically do the tedious work of creating bookmarks for you. Though you might not imagine using bookmarks in an interactive PDF project similar to those in this book, and almost certainly wouldn't expect to use a table of contents for such a project, bookmarks—and therefore the TOC that generates them—can actually be useful interactive tools.

InDesign builds a table of contents based on Paragraph styles. If you use them consistently for the headers in your document, you've already laid the foundation that InDesign needs to build your TOC. Once your content is appropriately styled, to define your TOC, you just need to select the Paragraph styles that are applied to the content you want as your TOC entries. InDesign does the rest, creating the bookmarks you'll use to navigate the document.

For a more site-oriented interactive document, you can use styled interface elements such as page titles to have InDesign generate a TOC, which creates bookmarks as its by-product. Since you really want just the bookmarks, the trick is to put the TOC on the last page of the document. Then, just omit the last page when you export the document as an Interactive PDF, and you have bookmarks for navigation without the TOC in your final document. Pretty nifty, right?

The first thing you'll need to do is style the content that will eventually end up as bookmarks. For a website-type document, you'll add page titles to each page, which will let your audience know where they are in the site. With a little bit of maneuvering, you'll be able to use these page titles to generate a hierarchical list of bookmarks.

Exercise 15.1: Adding Bookmarks and a Table of Contents

1. Launch Acrobat or Adobe Reader and go to File > Open. Browse to the chapter_15_exercises folder and open **ex15_1.pdf**. If necessary, scale the document window so the entire page is in view. The Bookmarks panel should be visible at the left of the window with the bookmarks for each page listed in sequence and appropriately nested to reflect the hierarchy of pages in the document.

   You can also use the buttons in the document to get around, of course. As you explore, you'll note that a number of changes have been made from the version of the document exported to SWF. We'll go into detail about all the changes in Part 7: Output, starting on page 331. But for now, note that the only animation brought over from InDesign was the multi-state object on page 4 of the document. Since InDesign animation does not translate to PDF, we did a little bit of fancy footwork to include the multi-state object in the project. First, we selected the multi-state object, and then we exported it to SWF. The SWF file was then placed back in InDesign. Since interactive PDF supports SWF files, the end result is a PDF page that includes a seamless rendering of the animation, all generated directly from InDesign.

   > **Note:** In Acrobat or Adobe Reader, you can go directly to a page by typing its page number in the text field on the second row of toolbars, just left of where it says "(5 of 10)", for example (5 refers to the page you're currently viewing, and 10 refers to the number of pages in the document).

2. When you've finished exploring, close Acrobat or Reader and return to InDesign. Open **ex15_1_end. indd** from the chapter_15_exercises folder. Use the navigation controls at the bottom left of the document window to browse through the document pages. Go to page 4, select the SWF (**multistate.swf**) with the Selection tool, and open the Media Panel (Window > Interactive > Media). Note that the Play on Page Load option is selected with the Poster dropdown set to None.

Note: While you can zoom in and out of a PDF document, SWF content included in the PDF will not scale, however, its containing frame will. The consequence of this behavior is that portions of the SWF movie may be obscured if the PDF page is displayed at reduced magnification. In the exercise example, if the PDF is displayed at less than 100% magnification, the previous and next buttons for the multi-state object SWF may disappear and make it impossible to navigate the slideshow.

The effect is that, when the page is opened in Acrobat or Reader, the animation plays and the flower image grows to nearly fill the page. The previous and next buttons in the SWF move you through the object states. Export of InDesign animation to SWF and subsequent placement of the SWF back in InDesign is a workaround that enables you to create a more consistent user experience of PDF and SWF output.

3. Go to page 10 of the document. (Press Ctrl+J/Command+J, enter the page number you want to jump to, and click OK.) This is where you'll find the phantom TOC that generated the bookmarks. You may recall that the PDF you explored had only nine pages. When the file was exported to PDF, the last page was simply excluded.

4. Open the Bookmarks panel (Window > Interactive > Bookmarks, or click the 📖 icon in the Panel dock). If necessary, twirl down the arrows next to the Flora and Fauna bookmarks to see the bookmarks nested below. Notice how the bookmarks follow the same hierarchical structure reflected in the TOC. Select any one of the bookmarks and choose Go to Selected Bookmark from the panel menu.

The Bookmarks panel displaying bookmarks for each of the main site pages and their sub-pages.

Note: Master page elements appear on every page where the master is applied. To learn more, check out Working with Master Pages, starting on page 302.

5. When you've finished exploring, keep the file open for reference and open **ex15_1_start.indd.** Save it as ex15_1.indd.

6. At the top of the Pages panel, double-click on A-Master to display the master page in the document window. Go to View > Show Rulers (Ctrl+R/Command R). With the Selection tool, drag a guide from the horizontal ruler to the baseline of the Mira Images text.

Note: The baseline is the bottom of the main body of the character, not including Descenders (the bottom of g, y, or p, for example).

7. Switch to the Type tool. Click above the midpoint of the fauna button (fourth button from the left in the red navbar), and drag a text frame to the right edge of the navbar contact button.

8. Type "page title" in the text frame as placeholder text. Set the font to Lucida Calligraphy (or Myriad Pro) and set the size to 18 pt. Right-align the text (Shift+Ctrl+R/Shift+Command+R).

9. Open the Paragraph Styles panel (Window > Styles > Paragraph Styles). With your cursor active in the formatted text, Alt-click/Option-click the Create New Style button at the bottom of the panel. When the Paragraph Style Options dialog pops up, name the style "section," check Apply Style to Selection, and click OK.

10. Press the Esc key to exit Text mode and switch to the Selection tool. Position the title text box so the baseline is on the guide you created. At the far right of the Control panel, click the Align Bottom button ( ).

Note: Alternatively, to align the text to the bottom of the text frame, go to Object > Text Frame Options and choose Bottom from the Vertical Justification Align dropdown.

By adding the page title to the master, you've added it to each of the document pages, and saved yourself a bunch of time positioning the text precisely or copying and pasting. However, you want the text to read differently on each of the pages. No problem. The cool thing about master page items is that you can unlock them and change the content, and they still maintain their connection to the master (unless you edit the content and then move the object). This means that you can still format the text (or object) on the master page and the items on the document pages will update globally. Gotta love it!

11. Double-click on page 1 in the Pages panel to fit the page in the window. On the document, Shift+Ctrl+click/Shift+Command+click on the page title text to unlock it, then double-click on the middle of the text to select it and switch to the Type tool. Replace the text with the word "Home."

12. Double-click on page 2 in the Pages panel, and Shift+Ctrl+click/ Shift+Command+click to unlock the master page item. Double-click on the text to select it, and then change the page title text to "Texture."

13. Change the titles of the remaining pages as follows:

Page #	Page Title
3	Flora: About
4	Flora: Slide Show
5	Fauna: Scrapbook
6	Fauna: Slide Show
7	Fauna: Movie
8	About
9	Contact

14. With page 9 active in the document window, click the New Page button at the bottom of the Pages panel. A new page should be added at the end of the document, and you should now be looking at it in the document window.

Now that your text is added and styled with a Paragraph style, it's time for the TOC.

15. Go to Layout > Table of Contents to open the Table of Contents dialog. Click the More Options button at the right of the window.

All the Paragraph styles contained in the document are listed on the right of the Table of Contents dialog. The styles you choose to include in your TOC will be listed on the left.

16. The first thing you need to do is remove the [Basic Paragraph Style] from the Include Paragraph Styles section of the dialog. Click to highlight it, and then click the Remove button so you can start with a clean slate.

17. Click the Entry Style dropdown in the Style section of the dialog, and choose New Paragraph Style from the very bottom of the list. When the New Paragraph Style dialog opens, name the new style TOC Section. Choose [No Paragraph Style] from the Based On dropdown, and click OK. This style will define the formatting for the Level 1 TOC entries. You'll edit it later to update the appearance of your TOC.

18. From the list of available Paragraph styles in the Other Styles section of the dialog, choose section, and then click the Add button. Check both the Create PDF Bookmarks and Include Text on Hidden Layers checkboxes in the Options section of the panel.

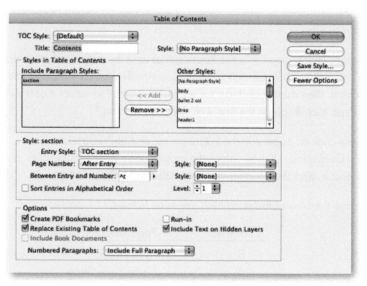

The Table of Contents dialog. Select Paragraph Styles on the right to define the TOC hierarchy on the left. Be sure to check the Create PDF Bookmarks checkbox.

19. Click OK to close the dialog and load the cursor with the TOC. Click once in the document window and you should see the first version of your TOC neatly displayed on the page.

Building a table of contents in InDesign is generally an iterative process. First, you make sure you're getting the right information in the TOC. Then you format its appearance. Because you most likely will want to use different styling for your TOC than you've used elsewhere in your document, it's often easiest to develop the styles that will govern its appearance by formatting the first generation TOC and then saving the styles from there. You can get pretty granular in the process if you're so inclined, with the option of assigning separate Paragraph styles to each level of TOC entries. You can also assign separate Character styles to the TOC page numbers and leaders.

While the appearance of the TOC is irrelevant for this particular application, since we're here, we'll take a short side trip to show you how it all works. Before we do so, however, let's first finish up with the bookmarks.

20. Open the Bookmarks panel and notice that the TOC entries are all there. However, like the TOC entries, they are all on the same level. It might be preferable to have the bookmarks for the Flora and Fauna pages grouped together under their section name.

    There are two ways to accomplish this objective, and determining which is best will depend on the specific requirements of your project and your workflow. The first option, and the one that might initially seem most obvious, would be to manually add the top level bookmarks to the Bookmarks panel. You could then drag the nested bookmarks to their appropriate location. The only problem with this approach arises if you then need to update the TOC. If you add or remove pages and then regenerate the TOC, the bookmarks will get updated too. All the manual ordering you did gets lost and you'll need to start over from scratch.

    An alternate approach involves tricking InDesign into auto-generating the nested bookmarks for you. By taking advantage of the TOC option to include hidden text, you can create invisible text frames that still populate the TOC. In this particular example, you'll add title text to the first Flora page and the first Fauna page, style the titles with the section Paragraph style and hide them. This will generate the top level bookmarks (Flora and Fauna). Then you'll duplicate the section Paragraph style (keeping the same style definition), and apply it to the page titles you want nested. If you add the duplicate style to level 2 of your TOC definition, InDesign will do the work of nesting your bookmarks.

    It sounds more complicated than it actually is. It'll all make sense, though, as you work through the rest of the exercise. While it may take a little more planning up front to get InDesign to generate your bookmarks, it's worth the effort if you're working a large document or you expect the TOC to change routinely.

    You'll first experiment with the manual approach to nesting the bookmarks.

21. Navigate to page 3 of the document and select the Flora: About page title with the Selection tool. Open the Bookmarks panel. Click the new Bookmark button at the bottom of the panel. Enter "Flora" as the bookmark text and press Enter/Return.

22. Navigate to page 5. With the Type tool, select just the word Fauna from the page title. Click the New Bookmark button and note that the bookmark takes on the selected text as its name. Note also that the icon for the bookmark is an anchor symbol (⚓) indicating that the bookmark is tied to the selected text. What's cool about this is that if the text flows to another page, the bookmark destination flows with it.

    Note: When you create bookmarks from selected text, the text becomes the bookmark text and InDesign captures its location in the document.

23. In the Bookmarks panel, drag the Flora bookmark above Flora: About and release the mouse when you see a black line under Texture that extends to the left edge of the bookmark icon.

You can drag to rearrange and nest bookmarks in the Bookmarks panel.

24. Drag the Fauna bookmark above Fauna: Scrapbook.

25. Mouse over the two new bookmarks, and you should see tooltips displaying the destination page number and the bookmark name. Double-click the Flora bookmark to jump to its page in the document.

26. Still in the Bookmarks panel, select Flora: About, and drag it onto the Flora bookmark. When the word Flora is highlighted, release the mouse to nest Flora: About under it.

Nesting a bookmark.

27. Twirl down the arrow to the left of the Flora bookmark and select Flora: Slide Show. Drag it up and to the right, under Flora: About, until a black line extending to the left edge of the Flora: About icon appears. Note that the line is indented compared to the line that appeared under Flora.

More rearranging of bookmarks

28. Use the same technique to nest the three Fauna bookmarks under Fauna.

Now that you've spent all that time rearranging the bookmarks, let's see what happens when you update the TOC.

29. Navigate to page 10 and select the text frame containing the TOC. Go to Layout > Update Table of Contents, and you should get a message confirming that it has been updated successfully. Now take a look at the Bookmarks panel. You're pretty much back to where you started, with all the bookmarks at the same level, and all your nesting gone. Shift+click to select both the Flora and Fauna bookmarks and click the Delete button at the bottom of the panel. Now you're truly back at square one.

Now you'll make changes to the document that will be reflected in the TOC and that will be retained in the bookmark hierarchy when the TOC is updated.

30. Switch to the Selection tool and go to page 3 of the document. Click once on the Flora: About title text box to select it, and then press Ctrl+C/ Command+C to copy it. Double-click the text to activate the Type tool, and delete the colon and the word About. Hide the <Flora> layer in the Layers panel and then go to Edit > Paste In Place.

31. In the Paragraph Styles panel, drag the section style to the New button at the bottom of the panel to duplicate it. Double-click on the section copy style name, change the name to "section2," and apply it to Flora: About.

32. Go to page 4, triple-click in the middle of the Flora: Slide Show text and apply the section2 Paragraph style.

33. Switch to the Selection tool and go to page 5. Copy the Fauna: Scrapbook page title, double-click the text to switch back to the Type tool, and then delete the colon and the word Scrapbook. Hide the <Fauna> layer in the Layers panel. Paste the copied layer in place, triple-click to select it, and then style it with the section2 style.

34. Format the remaining Fauna page titles with the section2 style.

Now you get to see where all this was heading.

35. Navigate back to page 10 and go to Layout > Table of Contents to bring up the TOC definition dialog. Select the section2 Paragraph Style on the right and click the Add button. Notice that the section2 style is automatically positioned in a second tier position in the TOC. Choose TOC Section from the entry dropdown and click OK. The TOC updates automatically.

36. Check out the Bookmarks panel again to see the bookmarks neatly nested. Save the file and then go to File > Export. In the Export dialog, choose Adobe PDF (Interactive) from the Format dropdown and navigate to the chapter_15_exercises folder. Click Save, and, in the Export dialog, choose the Range radio button and type "1-9" in the text field. Set the View dropdown to Actual Size and check the View After Exporting checkbox. Leave the other default settings, and click OK to export the file.

37. Before the export begins, you'll get two alerts. You can safely dismiss them both and proceed. The export will take a little while, so this is probably a good time to take a break and stretch your legs.

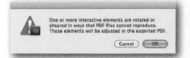
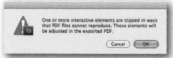

For this particular file, you can safely dismiss the alerts. Be aware that when you encounter these alerts, you may find your PDF file exhibiting all sorts of strange behaviors. (More on that in PDF Peculiarities, starting on page 355.)

Note: The reason for copying and pasting the page titles is that InDesign establishes the order of the TOC entries and the bookmarks based first on the order of the pages, and second on the order objects were placed on the page. Since both titles reside on the same page, the text frame placed first appears first in the TOC. This is the case regardless of the layer stacking order or the position of the text frame on the document page.

Note: By setting the export page range from 1-9 you are omitting the last page that contains the TOC. Even though the TOC is not included, the bookmarks will carry over to the PDF.

While your document contains the bookmark structure you built, the bookmarks will not show automatically unless you explicitly set the PDF to display them. Unfortunately, this is something you need to do directly in the full version of Acrobat.

Note: You must have a full version of Acrobat in order to set the Initial View. Adobe Reader doesn't support this level of modification to a document.

38. To ensure that your audience can take advantage of the bookmark navigation you've established, when Acrobat opens, go to File > Properties and choose the Initial View tab in the Document Properties dialog.

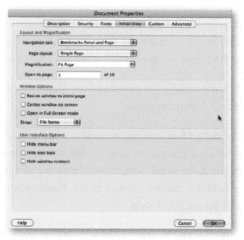

The Adobe Acrobat Document Properties window.

39. From the Navigation tab dropdown, choose Bookmarks Panel and Page. Page layout should be set to Single Page and Magnification to Fit Page. Be sure to deselect the Open in Full Screen mode checkbox. Click OK and then save and close the file.

40. Still in Acrobat, go to File > Open Recent File and select **ex15_1.pdf** from the file list. This time when the PDF opens, the Navigation panel should be open to the Bookmarks pane. Click each bookmark to take them for a test drive and when you're finished, you can quit out of Acrobat and return to InDesign to format your TOC. Keep your file open for the next exercise.

Formatting a Table of Contents

Just in case you might at some time need to create a table of contents that people actually see, we'll wrap up the chapter by taking you through the formatting process.

When formatting a TOC, it's best to build separate styles specific to each level of the TOC. At the very least, you'll want the TOC title and the first level entries to be styled distinctly. If you approach the process of defining your styles somewhat strategically, you can create one overarching TOC style that permits you to change the font throughout the TOC by changing just one Paragraph style definition. What makes this possible is that, when defining styles, you have an option to build one style based on another. This is true for any style, not just as they apply to a TOC. An update to the foundation style flows down to all the other styles based on it.

Note: If you don't want to go through all the formatting steps, you can open **ex15_2_end.indd** and go to Layout > Table of Contents to explore the setup. Then take a look at the Paragraph and Character style definitions to see how it all fits together.

For a TOC, the likely candidate for the base style would be the level 1 entry. Knowing this, you can define it first, and then define the TOC title and subsequent entry level styles using the level 1 entry as a jumping-off point. As mentioned earlier, you also have the option to include special styling for the page numbers and leaders. You do this by creating Character styles that you can then apply in the TOC definition dialog.

The truth is, if you're designing your TOC visually, you can expect to go back and forth a number of times until you arrive at something you like. This can take some time, which is why it's good to know that you can save TOC styles!

A TOC style is saved with the document from which it was generated. You can import a TOC style into another document; in addition to the TOC style, all the Paragraph and Character styles from the originating document are imported with it. The next exercise will show you one way to go about setting up a TOC, and will then show you how you can save your formatting as a TOC style. You'll also learn how to repurpose your efforts by importing that TOC style into a new document and then changing it to meet your needs.

Exercise 15.2: Formatting a Table of Contents

1. The ex15_1.indd file should still be open from the last lesson. If it's not, open **ex15_2_start.indd** from the chapter_15_exercises folder and save it as ex15_1.indd.

2. If necessary, navigate to page 10. With the Type tool, select the word Home and format the font the way you'd like it to appear in the TOC. We chose Lucida Calligraphy Italic, 20 px. You can change the color, the leading or any other character formatting at this point.

   Next, you'll set up the paragraph parameters. By default, the TOC formatting uses the same Paragraph styles that were selected to define the TOC entries. In this case, you created a new style called TOC Section instead. You'll make your formatting changes and then capture them by updating the style definition.

3. Both the section and section2 styles used for the page titles were right-aligned. So, with the Type cursor active in the text frame, press Ctrl+A/Command+A to Select All, and then click the Align Left button (▤) on the Control panel.

   Changing the alignment creates a pretty dramatic change in the appearance of the text, but don't panic: you just need to set up your tabs. Before you do that, though, you'll set up your indents. Let's presume that you want the text frame to stretch the width of the page. The TOC title will be indented slightly, and then the first level entries can be centered on the page.

4. In the Control panel, set both the Left and the Right Indents to 70 px. Now, press Ctrl+0/Command+0 to fit the entire page in the document window. Make sure there is some space above the text frame, and then go to Type > Tabs (Shift+Ctrl+T/Shift+Command+T) to fit the Tab panel to the top of your text frame.

Note: If the Tab panel gets misaligned with your text frame, as long as there's room for it to fit above the active text box, you can click the magnet icon (🧲) at its right to snap the Tab panel back to the top of the text frame.

There are four options for the type of tabs you can create: left-justified, Ccenter-justified, right-justified, and a tab that's aligned to a particular character (the default is a decimal point or period). You can manually position a tab marker by selecting the type of tab you want to create, and then clicking in the white space above the ruler divisions to place it. You can drag the tab indicator to reposition the tab, or you can enter a value in the X text field to position it more precisely.

Click above the ruler markers in the Tabs panel to place a tab that you can drag into position.

5. Select the Right-Justified Tab and enter 830 in the X text field. In the Leader field, type a period and then a space to create the leader pattern. Press Enter/ Return to set your tab and see the dot leaders.

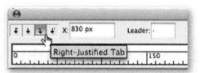

The tab setup for the first level entry in the TOC.

To determine the position for the tab, we first decided that we wanted the page number to be flush with the right paragraph margin. We know that the page is 900 px wide and that the right indent is 70 px. 900 less 70 gives us the 830 px position for the right-justified tab.

6. With your text cursor positioned in the paragraph you just styled, open the Paragraph Styles panel. The TOC Section style should be highlighted, since it's already applied to the text. Choose Redefine Style from the panel menu to capture your changes. You should see all the entries update on the page.

7. To refine the appearance of the entry, select the leader by double-clicking in the line of dots after the word "Home." Make the font size for the dots on the Home entry 14 px and select the R=115 G=35 B=22 swatch in the Swatches panel.

8. Open the Character Styles panel (Window > Styles > Character Styles) and Alt-click/Option-click the New Style button at the bottom of the panel. Name the new Character style "TOC leader." Check both the Apply Style to Selection and Preview checkboxes, and click OK.

9. Select the page number and change the font to Minion Pro, Regular 20 px. If you like, change the size and/or the color and Alt-click/Option-click the New Style button in the Character Styles panel. Name the style "TOC pageNum1" and click OK.

   Now that you've laid the groundwork, the next step is to refine the TOC style definition.

10. Go to Layout > Table of Contents and select section from the Include Paragraph Styles pane. Just below, from the Style dropdown to the right of the

Page Number dropdown, choose TOC pageNum1. Choose TOC leader for the Style applied Between Entry and Number. Note that you are defining the parameters for Level 1 of the TOC and click OK.

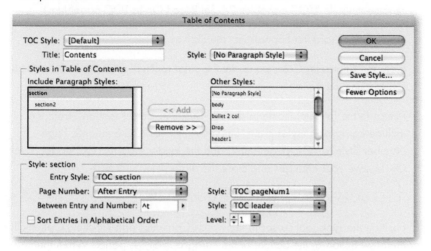

Settings for level 1 of the TOC incorporating styles for the entry, page number, and leader.

11. Go to the Paragraph styles panel, and drag TOC body to the New button at the bottom of the panel to duplicate it. Name the new style "TOC section2." Place the Type tool cursor in the Flora: About text. Double-click TOC section2 in the Paragraph Styles panel to apply the style and open the Paragraph Style Options dialog.

12. From the default view of the dialog, with General highlighted on the left, choose TOC section from the Based On dropdown to the right.

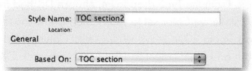

By basing the TOC section2 Paragraph style on TOC section, TOC section2 will update automatically when TOC section is updated.

> **Note:** In any Adobe application dialog, if Preview is checked, pressing the Tab key enables you to see your changes without exiting the dialog. Shift-Tab returns to the previous field.

13. Choose the Basic Character Formats category on the left, and set Size to 16 px.

14. From the Indents and Spacing category, set both the Left and Right indents to 115 px.

15. In the Tabs category, select the right-justified tab and set the X value to 785. Type a period and then a space in the Leader field, and select the tab to the right of the right margin. Drag it far up or down, and off the Tab ruler.

16. Select Character Color on the left of the dialog and set the color to R=115 G=35 B=22. Click OK to commit the style changes and close the dialog.

17. In the TOC, select the Flora: About page number and open the Character Styles panel. Drag the TOC pageNum1 style to the New button to duplicate it. Double-click TOC pageNum1 copy to open the Character Style Options dialog, and rename the style "TOC pageNum2." Set Based On to TOC pageNum1.

18. From Basic Character Formats, set the Size to 18 px.

19. From the Character Color pane, set the color to R=115 G=35 B=22 and click OK to close the dialog.

20. Return to the Table of Contents dialog. This time, select section2 from the Include Paragraph Styles pane. Set Entry Style to TOC Section2, Page Number Style to TOC pageNum2, and the leader style to TOC leader. Click OK to save your changes and close the dialog.

    The second level TOC entries should all update. The last thing to style is the TOC title.

21. Position the Type tool cursor in the word "Contents" and Alt-click/Option-click the New button at the bottom of the Paragraph Styles panel. When the Paragraph Style Options dialog opens, name the style "TOC Title." Set Based On to TOC section and ensure that the Apply Style to Selection checkbox is checked.

22. From Basic Character Formats, set Size to 24 px.

23. From the Indents and Spacing section, set Alignment to Left, Left Indent to 15 px and Right Indent to 0. Set Space After to 16 px.

24. Select Paragraph Rules from the left, then select Rule Below from the Paragraph Rules dropdown. Check the Rule On checkbox and set the stroke Weight to 2 px. From the Type dropdown, choose Dashed from the very bottom of the list. Leave Color set to (Text Color) and choose Black for the Gap Color. Set Gap Tint to 20%. Leave Width set to Column and set Offset to 6 px. Set both the Left and Right Indent to 15 px and then click OK to save your settings and close the dialog.

Note: To visually adjust the Paragraph Rule Offset, click in the Offset field and use the up and down arrows on your keyboard to shift the field value incrementally.

This method of adjusting values works in 90% of the dialog fields in Adobe applications.

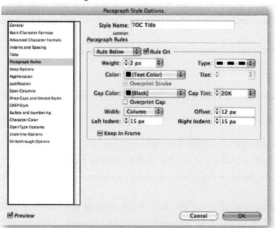

The Paragraph Rules settings for the TOC Title Paragraph style.

25. For one last time, return to the Table of Contents dialog and replace the word "Contents" at the upper left of the dialog with the words "Table of Contents." Pres Tab and choose TOC Title for the Title style. Now that you've invested the time to perfect your TOC, click Save Style to capture your formatting. Name the style **ex15_1_TOC** in the Save Style dialog and click OK. Click OK again to exit the Table of Contents dialog.

26. Check out your formatted TOC, press Esc to switch to the Selection tool, and click off the text to deselect. Open the Paragraph Styles panel and change the font face for the TOC Section Paragraph style to Minion Pro. Note that the formatting for all the text updates automatically.

27. Save the file.

28. Go to File > New and choose Web as the Intent. Choose 900 x 700 for page size and click OK. Even though there is nothing yet in the document, you can still import the Table of Contents style saved in the ex_15_1_toc.indd file. Go to Layout > Table of Contents Styles and click Load. Locate **ex15_1_toc.indd** and click Open.

29. To verify that the Table of Contents style has been added to your new, yet empty, file, go to Layout > Table of Contents and from the TOC Style dropdown, choose **ex15_1.indd** Note that the whole TOC setup, as well as all the Paragraph styles in the original document, carry over with the style. Close the TOC dialog.

30. Open the Character Styles panel and note that the Character styles are also imported, including those not used in the TOC.

Well, that wraps up the side trip into TOC formatting.

CHAPTER SUMMARY

This chapter showed you how to use a table of contents, a feature traditionally employed in long print documents, to create bookmark navigation in your interactive PDFs. As a bonus, you learned how to set up, format, and update a TOC, and then save your work as a Table of Contents style for future use.

In your creation of bookmarks, you employed the Bookmarks panel to:

- Manually add bookmarks targeted to specific text
- Reorder existing bookmarks in the panel
- Create a hierarchical structure of nested bookmarks

In the process of styling the table of contents, you also delved more deeply into the intricacies of text formatting and became familiar with the Tabs panel along the way. Additionally, you learned how to set up your PDF in Acrobat to ensure that your audience can easily access your bookmark navigation structure.

The next chapter shows you how to use hyperlinks, hyperlink destinations, and cross-references to build a navigational structure for an interactive interface.

• Chapter 16

HYPERLINKS AND CROSS-REFERENCES

For both SWF and PDF, hyperlinks and cross-references provide an alternative to buttons for interactive navigation. Internal links, external links, links to text anchors or specific document pages: hyperlinks and cross-references can do it all.

Introduction

InDesign hyperlinks and cross-references bring to your published SWFs and PDFs the familiar functionality you expect from hyperlinks on the web. You can create internal document links and links to related files and web pages, or trigger the opening of an email client to send a message. Not only can you create these links in InDesign, but you can test them, too, without venturing outside the interface. To explore hyperlinks and cross-references, choose Window > Interactive > Hyperlinks.

All the magic happens right from the Hyperlinks panel. Use it to define the source and destination for both hyperlinks and cross-references. The top half of the panel displays the hyperlinks you've set up in your document, and the bottom half displays cross-references.

The Hyperlinks panel is command central for creating and managing hyperlinks and cross-references.

Hyperlinks and cross-references have more in common than just the panel they share. Both have similar appearance options and, when exported to PDF, both can target content in other PDFs.

About Hyperlinks

While cross-references specialize in internal links and links between PDFs, hyperlinks have a broader reach, linking through any valid protocol (http, ftp, mailto, file). From the Hyperlinks dialog, you can create six different types of links: to a URL, file, email, page, text anchor, or shared hyperlink destination. You can select text to serve as the link text or you can let InDesign scour your document for URLs, which it will then happily convert to hyperlinks for you.

To manually create a hyperlink, select the text you want to use as the hyperlink source and click the New Hyperlink button ( ) at the bottom of the Hyperlinks panel. Choose a hyperlink type from the Link To dropdown and then complete the Destination information as required.

Note: To ensure that the hyperlinks you create are included in your exported files, be sure to select the Include All Interactivity and Media option when exporting to SWF and All Buttons and Media when exporting to PDF.

Note: Hyperlinked files open in their native application. EX: a file with a .doc extension will open in MS Word.

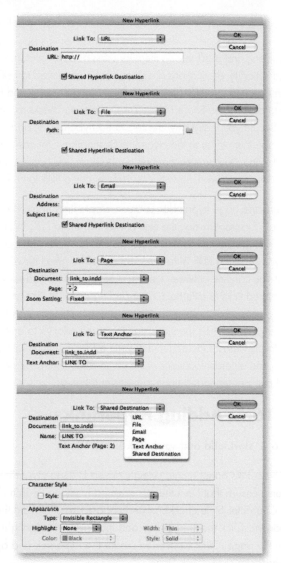

There are six types of hyperlinks you can create through the Hyperlinks panel.

You'll notice that when you create a hyperlink to a text anchor, URL, or file, the Shared Hyperlink Destination checkbox is checked by default. An interesting feature, shared hyperlink destinations demand some discussion, if only to caution you on their use.

When you create a text anchor in a document, that anchor is saved with the file and is accessible for other documents to link to. In fact, that's how cross-references work to link across multiple documents in a book. The same principle applies to saved hyperlink destinations; they are essentially named anchors that can be referenced multiple times within the same file, or accessed between documents. In fact, saved hyperlink destinations can exist in a file even if the document itself doesn't include any actual links. You can think of them as a sort of resource cache for storing information. Theoretically, you could create one document with a complete list of links you often use, and then reference that document to ensure that the paths for your links are always correct. The unfortunate truth is that shared hyperlink destinations can result in quirky and

Note: You learned a bit about hyperlink destinations in Creating Hyperlink Destinations on page 116.

unpredictable document behavior and are, for the most part, best avoided. The general rule is this: only use shared hyperlink destinations for links that will be used frequently in the same document, and don't rely on them for cross-document reference. Cross-document shared hyperlink destinations are sketchy when exported to PDF, and don't work at all when exported to SWF. The bottom line is, since it's checked by default, you want to be sure to deselect the Shared Hyperlink Destination checkbox when you create your hyperlinks. Should you mistakenly create shared hyperlink destinations, you can access and manage them through the Hyperlink Destination Options command in the Hyperlinks panel menu. Your text anchors reside there as well, and you'll be working with them extensively when working with cross-references a little later in this chapter.

Using text anchors and page hyperlinks, you can create links from one InDesign file to another that remain functional when the files are converted to PDF. In order for this to work, you must keep the file names and locations the same, so that the only thing that changes when you export to PDF is the file extension. The good news about cross-file hyperlinks is that you can link between files on a network. The bad news is, at this time, all InDesign-generated links to external files, including non-PDF files, are absolute rather than relative. This means that moving the files to a different location will break the links between them, even if their locations stay the same relative to one another. This is true even if the linked files are located in the same folder. Fortunately, linking to URLs, email addresses, and different locations in the same document pose none of the same challenges, and can be depended upon to perform reliably.

Exercise 16.1: Adding Hyperlinks

1. Open **ex16_1_start.indd** and save it as ex16_1.indd.

2. From the Hyperlinks panel menu, select Convert URLs to Hyperlinks. When the dialog opens, ensure that Document is selected from the Search dropdown. Check the Character Style checkbox and choose crossRef from the Character Style dropdown. Click the Find button and InDesign will highlight the web address on the page. Click Convert to create the hyperlink and apply the crossRef Character style. Click Done.

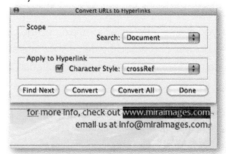

InDesign will locate and convert document URLs to Shared Hyperlink Destinations, and will style them with a Character style of your choosing.

While it's convenient to have InDesign do the heavy lifting for you, the downside of this approach is that the links it creates are saved as—yep, you guessed it—shared hyperlink destinations. So, now that you've got one, it's a good opportunity to show you how to delete it.

3. Choose Hyperlink Destination Options from the Hyperlinks panel menu. When the dialog opens, since it's the only hyperlink destination in the document, your URL will appear in the Destination dropdown. Click the Delete button to delete the destination, and then click OK to close the dialog.

   When the destination is deleted, the icon appearing to the right of the link in the Hyperlinks panel changes from ⊕ to ⬛, indicating that the link destination is missing.

4. In the Hyperlinks panel, select the broken link and click the Delete button at the bottom of the panel. Click OK to dismiss the alert and convert the link back to text.

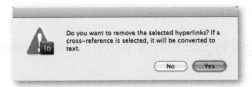

When a hyperlink is deleted, the hyperlink source text is converted to text and keeps the formatting that was applied to the hyperlink.

5. Select the already-formatted link text, and click the New Hyperlink button at the bottom of the panel. From the Link To dropdown, select URL and type a web address in the URL field. Deselect the Shared Hyperlink Destination checkbox. Although it's already formatted, there's no harm in checking the Style checkbox and choosing crossRef as the Character style to apply. Click OK to create the hyperlink and close the dialog.

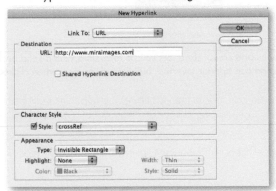

Settings for a URL hyperlink.

Note: When you create a link to a URL, email address, or text anchor, the destination is recorded in InDesign as a named destination. You can modify the destination in the Hyperlink Destination Options dialog accessed through the Hyperlinks panel menu. The name of the destination is distinct from the destination definition, however, so changing one has no effect on the other. To change the name of a hyperlink destination, choose Rename Hyperlink from the Hyperlinks panel menu, enter a new name, and then click OK.

6. Open the Hyperlinks panel menu. Note that the Hyperlink Destination Options menu item is unavailable, since the hyperlink you created wasn't saved as a shared hyperlink destination.

7. Select the email address on the page. Be sure not to highlight the space before it and the comma after. Copy the email address and click the New Hyperlink button at the bottom of the Hyperlinks panel. In the New Hyperlink dialog, choose Email from the Link To dropdown and paste the address into the Address field. For the Subject Line, type "Curious?" Deselect the Shared Hyperlink Destination checkbox and style the link with the crossRef Character style. Click OK to create the email link and close the dialog.

While you could certainly go to the Preview panel to test your links, you can also test them directly from the Hyperlinks panel.

Note: If your link doesn't work, check the text carefully for extra spaces and typos.

8. Select the URL link in the Hyperlinks panel and click the Go To Destination button (⇨) at the bottom of the panel. Your default browser should open and display the URL target. Pretty nifty, yes? Close the browser and return to InDesign.

9. Select the email link in the Hyperlinks panel and click the Go To Destination button. Your default email client should open with the subject line "Curious?" Close the email client and return to InDesign.

10. Save and close the file.

Formatting Hyperlinks and Cross-references

By applying the crossRefs character style to your links, you provided a visual cue that distinguished them from the rest of the content on the page. As an alternative or complement to Character style formatting, InDesign gives you the option of outlining your hyperlinks with a thin, medium, or thick line that is solid or dashed. Additionally, you can choose an option for changing the link appearance when it is clicked. It can appear inverted, highlighted, inset, or, of course, it can display no change at all.

Hyperlinks and cross-references can be formatted with a solid or dashed outline and can appear inverted, highlighted, or inset when clicked.

Within InDesign, you can toggle the visibility of the hyperlink outlines by going to View > Extras > Show (or Hide) Hyperlinks. If multiple hyperlinks share the same appearance, you can change them all at once. Select the links you want to change in the Hyperlinks panel, choose Hyperlink Options from the panel menu, and make the desired changes.

About Cross-references

The real difference between a hyperlink and a cross-reference is that the link text for a cross-reference is dynamically generated. Cross-references capture and display text from a targeted paragraph, or from a predefined text anchor, and change when the referenced text changes.

When exported to SWF and interactive PDF, cross-references become hyperlinks that are actually quite versatile. Traditionally, cross-references provide a means to locate related information in a document. Taken a step further, in the context of interactive design, cross-references can provide an excellent option for site navigation, and, in many cases, offer an attractive alternative to buttons.

Similar to bookmarks, cross-references can be defined based on the Paragraph style they're styled with. Styled page titles in your document, like those used to create the TOC and bookmarks in the previous chapter, can also serve as the foundation for cross-reference-based site navigation.

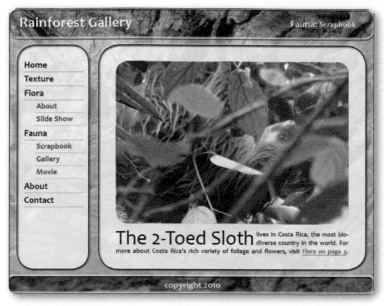

The sidebar navigation pictured above is built using cross-references rather than buttons.

Adding Cross-references

Like any other link, cross-references comprise two parts: the source cross-reference and the destination. The source cross-reference is the text that's populated by the destination content. The destination content Is either a targeted paragraph or a predefined text anchor saved as a hyperlink destination.

In addition to the pre-built cross-reference format options, InDesign lets you create and save custom formats as well. With a tiny little bit of really easy code, you can make your cross-references conform to your wishes.

Exercise 16.2: Adding Cross-References

This exercise will show you how to use cross-references to build site navigation. You'll also learn how to use cross-references in a more traditional manner, linking body content to related information elsewhere in the document.

1. Launch Acrobat or Adobe Reader, and open **ex16_2_end.pdf** from the chapter_16_exercises folder. The sidebar navigation on the left of the pages is constructed using cross-references rather than buttons. Click the Fauna: Scrapbook link and locate the cross-reference to Flora in the body of the page text. Note that the cross-reference includes the page number for the referenced content. Click the link to navigate to page 3. Check out the other nav links, if you like, and then close the PDF and return to InDesign.

Note: The content on most of the pages in the **ex16_2_end.pdf** file is the same lorem ipsum filler text, but each page has a different tile. If you choose to test the links, keep your eye on the titles at the upper right so you know the links are actually working.

2. Open **ex16_2_start.indd** and save it as ex16_2.indd.

    Your initial objective is to create a cross-reference to direct the reader to the first Flora page in the site. In order to set up the cross-reference, you first need to establish a hyperlink destination that will serve as a text anchor.

3. Navigate to page 3 of the document and, with the Type tool, select the word "Flora" in the title text at the upper right of the page.

4. Go to Window > Interactive > Hyperlinks or click the  icon in the Panel dock to open the Hyperlinks panel. From the panel menu, choose New Hyperlink Destination. Note that the destination name auto-populates with the text you selected, and that Text Anchor is the pre-populated destination Type. Click OK to create the text anchor and close the dialog.

    The new hyperlink destination Name and Type are auto-populated when text is selected in the document.

    Before you set up the cross-reference, you'll create a Character style to format it.

5. Navigate to page 5 of the document and, with the Type tool, select flora, the last word in the body text. Go to Window > Styles > Character Styles and Alt-click/Command-click the New Style button at the bottom of the panel.

6. Name the new style "crossRef" and check both the Apply Style to Selection and Preview checkboxes. Select Character Color on the left of the dialog and choose the R=68 G=52 B=56 swatch. From the Underline section, check the Underline On checkbox and set the Weight to 1 px. Set Offset to 5 px and choose the R=68 G=52 B=56 swatch from the Color dropdown. Click OK to save the style and close out of the dialog.

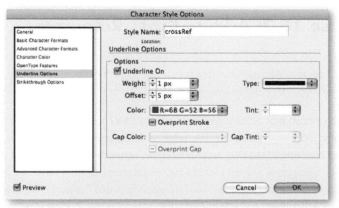

The Underline setting for the crossRef Character style.

7. With flora still selected, if necessary, open the Hyperlinks panel and click the New Cross-reference button at the bottom of the panel (✖※).

8. In the New Cross-Reference dialog, ensure that Text Anchor is selected from the Link To dropdown and that the Destination file is **ex16_2.indd**. From the Cross-Reference Format dropdown, choose Text Anchor Name and Page Number.

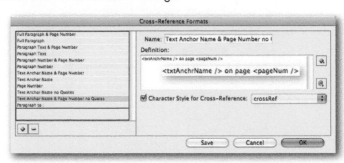

The settings for the cross-reference that links to the text anchor on the first Flora page.

You should see the cross-reference update automatically on the page. The cross-reference will look better styled with the crossRef Character style and without the quotes around the destination.

9. With the dialog still open, click the ✏ button to the right of the Format dropdown to open the Cross-Reference Formats dialog. Select Text Anchor Name & Page Number on the Left, and click the 🗐 button below the list (not the one on the far right). Change the format name to "Text Anchor Name & Page Number no Quotes."

10. Delete the quotation marks on either side of the text "<txtAnchrName />" in the Definition pane, check the Character Style for Cross-Reference checkbox, and choose crossRef from the Character style dropdown. Click Save and then click OK to close out of the dialog and apply your new format. Click OK again to close the New Cross-Reference dialog.

InDesign let's you customize and save cross-reference formats.

Note: Choose Load Cross-Reference Formats from the Hyperlinks panel menu to import formats from other documents.

Note: Don't choose button text as hyperlink destinations; it won't work as a destination when exported to SWF or interactive PDF.

Note: Even though it technically requires that you work with "code," InDesign makes the process of customizing cross-reference formats as painless as possible with a slew of built-in hints to help you craft your code correctly.

Just adding that one cross-reference should've given you a taste of what can be done with them but, as the saying goes, "You ain't seen nothin' yet!" Before really putting cross-references through their paces, though, you'll take a few minutes to pretty things up and make the navbar look respectable.

11. In top section of the Pages panel, double-click on A-Master to select and display it. Select the word "Home" on the document and open the Paragraph Styles panel. Alt-click/Option-click the New Style button at the bottom of the panel. In the New Paragraph Style dialog, name the new style "sideNav." Ensure that the Apply Style to Selection and Preview checkboxes are checked.

12. In the Basic Character Formats section of the dialog, set the font face to Candara, the font style to Bold, and the size to 22 px. If you don't have Candara, choose Myriad Pro. For Character Color, choose R=30 G=14 B=16. In the Indents and Spacing category, for Space After, add 8 px.

   The appearance of dividers between the links is achieved using Paragraph Rules.

13. Still in the Paragraph Styles dialog, select Paragraph Rules from the left and check the Rule On checkbox for Rule Below. Set Weight to 1 px, Type to Solid, and Color to R=30 G=14 B-16. Set Tint to 50%. Ensure that Width is set to Column, and then set Offset to 10 px. Click OK to save your style and close the dialog.

14. Select all the text in the side nav and apply your new Paragraph Style.

15. Deselect the text in the sidebar nav and reselect About and Slide Show. In the Paragraph Styles panel, drag the sideNav style to the New Style button at the bottom of the panel. Double-click the sideNav Copy style, and, when the Paragraph Style Options dialog opens, rename the style "sideNav2." From the Based On dropdown, choose sideNav.

16. Set the Font Size to 19 px, and from the Character Color section of the dialog, choose R=68 G=52 B=56. For Indents and Spacing, set Left Indent to 30 px and Space After to 9 px. For Paragraph Rules, choose Rule Below and check the Rule On checkbox. Set Weight to 1 px, Type to Solid, Color to R=68 G=52 B=56 with Tint of 50%. Set the Rule Width to Column, Offset to 10 px and Left Indent to 26 px. Click OK to save your style and close the dialog.

The Paragraph Rule settings for the sideNav2 Paragraph style.

17. Select the Scrapbook, Gallery, and Movie text and apply the sideNav2 Paragraph Style. Save the file.

Now that you've got your styles set and everything is gorgeous, you're ready to add the cross-reference navigation.

18. Still on the master page, select the word "Home" with the Type tool and open the Hyperlinks panel. Click the New Cross Reference button at the bottom of the panel, and, when the dialog opens, choose Paragraph from the Link To dropdown. Ensure that the Destination Document is **ex16_2.indd** and choose pageTitle from the list of Paragraph styles in the left pane of the dialog. From the right pane, choose the Home paragraph as the cross-reference destination. Ensure that Paragraph Text is chosen from the Cross-Reference Format dropdown. Click OK to create the cross-reference.

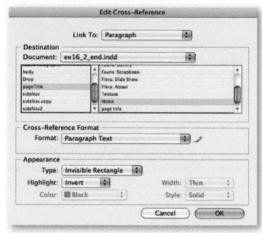

When a cross-reference is defined based on Paragraph Style, you get to choose its text from all the paragraphs in the document that are formatted with the selected style.

19. Select the word "Texture" from the side nav and create a new cross-reference that links to the Texture paragraph. Format it with the pageTitle Paragraph style. Repeat the process to create cross-references for About and Contact, linking them to the About and Contact paragraphs, respectively.

Next, you'll create text anchors for the subnav links.

20. Navigate to page 3 of the document and select the word "About" in the page title at the upper right of the page. Open the Hyperlinks panel, and, from the panel menu, choose New Hyperlink Destination. Text Anchor should appear as the Type, and the Name field should be auto-populated with the word "About". Accept the default settings and click OK.

21. Navigate to page 4 and select the words "Slide Show." Again, create a new hyperlink destination, keeping the default Text Anchor and Name settings.

22. Create additional text anchor hyperlink destinations for the words "Scrapbook," "Gallery," and "Movie" on pages 5, 6, and 7 respectively.

23. Return to the master page and select About in the sidebar. From the bottom of the Hyperlinks panel, click the New Cross-Reference button. When the dialog opens, choose Text Anchor from the Link To dropdown and ensure that **ex16_2.indd** is chosen as the Destination Document. Select About from the Text Anchor dropdown and then select Text Anchor Name from the Format dropdown.

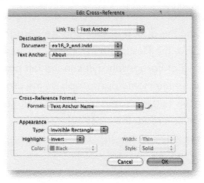

**The cross-reference settings for the Flora: About
text anchor before applying the edited format.**

Here's another case of those pesky quotation marks, but you already know how to remove them.

24. With the dialog still open, click the Edit button (✎). When the Cross-Reference Formats window opens, duplicate the Text Anchor Name format and rename it "Text Anchor Name no Quotes." Delete the quotes in the Definition window, click Save, and then click OK twice to finish creating and formatting your cross-reference.

25. Repeat step 23 for each of the subnav items: Slide Show, Scrapbook, Gallery, and Movie. Since you've already edited the format definition, you can just choose the modified format from the Cross-Reference Format dropdown.

You're nearly there. The last thing to do is format the cross-references for the Flora and Fauna section headers. While you could create text anchors for these headers in the same way that you did for the subnav items, instead, we'll take this opportunity to explore the format customization options a little more deeply.

26. With the master page still active, select the Flora placeholder text in the sidebar. Click the New Cross-Reference button at the bottom of the Hyperlinks panel, and, when the dialog opens, select Paragraph from the Link To dropdown. Check to be sure **ex16_2.indd** is selected for the Destination Document, and choose pageTitle from the Paragraph Styles pane at the left of the window. From the right pane, choose Flora: About. Choose Full Paragraph from the Format dropdown, and click the Edit button to open the Cross-Reference Formats dialog. Select and duplicate the Full Paragraph format and rename the format "Paragraph to :" In the Definition pane, within the opening and closing tag markers and after the **fullPara** text, type **delim=":"** Be sure to leave a space between the closing quotation mark and the forward slash (/). The final Format Definition should read: **<fullPara delim=":" />**.

The code you've just written tells InDesign to include text in the designated paragraph up to the colon and not beyond; in other words, to include a partial paragraph. If you wanted the cross-reference to include the colon as well, inside the tag after the closing quotation mark around **delim=":"**, you would add the following: **includeDelim="true"**. The whole tag would then appear thus: **<fullPara delim=":" includeDelim="true" />**.

If you've had any experience with XHTML or HTML, this markup should look pretty familiar. **fullPara** would equate to an HTML tag selector. **delim** would equate to an attribute, as would **includeDelim,** and the attribute values **:** and **true** are enclosed in quotes, just as they would be with HTML. This structure adheres directly to the rules governing XHTML. The point is, although this is indeed code of a sort, it's actually pretty simple and straightforward when you break it down.

In any case, the end result is that only the section name populates the cross-reference on the page, rather than the entire text of the paragraph. Since you've saved the format, you can apply it to the Fauna section header as well. And *voilà*! You've created dynamically update-able site navigation. But don't take our word for it. Test it out for yourself.

27. Navigate to the last page of the document and change the page title from "Contact" to "Contact Us". You'll notice that the cross-reference doesn't update right away. If you open the Hyperlinks panel, however, you'll see a hazard symbol next to the Contact cross-reference. Click the Update button at the bottom of the panel (⟳). The link text in the side nav updates to reflect your change.

The Hyperlinks panel displays a hazard sign when a cross-reference has changed.

Changing the text anchors requires an extra step. The sidebar link text is generated from the text anchor name, rather than the destination text. You'll need to update the text anchor name and then update the cross-reference. Since the anchor name and the actual destination are separate, you'll also need to update the page title text.

28. With nothing selected, from the Hyperlinks panel menu, choose Hyperlink Destination Options. When the dialog pops up, choose Movie from the Destination dropdown and click the Edit button. In the Name field, replace the word "Movie" with "Video," and then click OK.

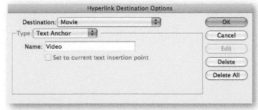

Choose Hyperlink Destination Options from the Hyperlinks panel menu to edit existing hyperlink destinations.

29. To update the sidebar with the change you just made, click the Update Cross-Reference button at the bottom of the Hyperlinks panel.

30. Navigate to page 7 of the document and change the word "Movie" in the page title to "Video."

Hopefully, this chapter has helped to get you thinking outside the box a bit in relation to hyperlinks and cross-references. To top off the topic, here's a key to deciphering the symbols that might show up in the Hyperlinks panel.

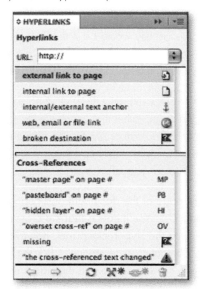

The Hyperlinks panel gives you clues to help manage your hyperlinks and cross-references. MP means the destination is on a master page, PB means it's on the pasteboard, HT means it's on a hidden layer, and OV means the destination is in text that's overset.

CHAPTER SUMMARY

In this chapter you expanded the reach of your documents using hyperlinks and cross-references. You learned to employ hyperlinks to link to:

- URLs
- Files
- Email
- Document pages
- Text anchors

Importantly, you learned about absolute and relative paths and how to maintain the integrity of your links to external files. You created hyperlink destinations, and made use of InDesign's ability to locate hyperlink text in a document and convert it to working links. In the process, you learned about shared hyperlink destinations: what they are, why they can be problematic, and how you can work around them when necessary.

You took an innovative approach to working with cross-references and used them to create a site navigation structure. In the process, you learned to modify and update existing cross-references. You worked with cross-reference formats and customized them to change the content of the link on the page, learned to save your customized formats, and to load formats from an external file.

You topped off the chapter, and Part 5 of the book, with a key to the cryptic icons you might encounter in the Hyperlinks panel.

With an expanded repertoire for creating document interactivity, Part 6 of the book shifts the focus to skills equally important to print and interactive design. The next few chapters are all about working with text, multi-page documents, graphics creation, and color. They're filled with great tips and techniques that are sure to enhance your use of InDesign with any project you undertake.

Part 6

LAYOUT

You'll find the tips and techniques in the next portion of the book to be equally valuable in both your print and interactive work. You'll flow and format text, work with master pages and multi-page documents, learn all about InDesign's vast color resources, and employ its robust graphics tools to create compound shapes. The power-user tips in the next few chapters will take your InDesign skills to a whole new level.

● Chapter 17

WORKING WITH TEXT

Managing text flow, spanning and splitting columns, flowing type on a path: these topics represent just a start to the goodies filling this chapter You'll work with text wrap, create nested styles, convert print documents for on-screen display, and there's still more. Count on it, the time you spend working through this chapter will return dividends.

Threaded Text Frames

Note: When you place text, InDesign automatically creates the text frame that contains it.

In the section on buttons, you were introduced to adding text to your InDesign document, and discovered that all InDesign text resides in a text frame. To create a text frame, you can place text,draw a frame on your document using the Type tool, or convert an existing shape to a text frame by clicking it with the Type tool. Isolated text frames have their place, but there will no doubt be times when you want your text to flow across multiple text frames, and multiple pages as well. You can easily connect any number of text frames and flow text through them. In InDesign, these threaded text frames are referred to as a story.

Note: Turn text threads on with no document open to set it as an application default: View > Extras > Show Text Threads.

Each text frame has an in and an out port that serve as the connection point to other text frames. Text threads connect the ports from one frame to another, and are a visual indicator of the flow of text through a document. You can toggle text thread visibility by going to View > Extras > Show (Hide) Text Threads (Alt+Ctrl+Y/Option+Command+Y). Even with text thread visibility turned on, you need to have a text frame selected with the Selection tool in order to see them.

> The photos in this section of the gallery were taken in Costa Rica, a country known for its biodiversity. Costa Rica's name means Rich Coast and indeed the country is rich in beauty and variety.

> Less than half the size of New York state, Costa Rica is actually more biologically diverse than all of Europe combined. One reason for the great abundance and variety of flora and fauna is Costa Rica's geographic diversity evidenced by 5 mountain ranges, 14 major river systems and at least 60 volcanos, 5 of which are active.

In order to see text threads, you need to select one of the text frames in a story with the Selection or Direct Selection tool. When a text frame is selected, it displays its in and out ports and its sizing handles. (In the image above, the frame on the left is selected.) When sizing a text frame, you need to be careful not to mistakenly click and drag a port instead of a sizing handle.

Threading text frames is easy, but there's one little trick to remember. You need to use the Selection tool rather than the Type tool to thread them. It makes sense if you think of the text frames as objects that are independent until you connect them. To select objects, you need the Selection tool. However, you're most likely to be using the Type tool when the need to thread text frames arises. You may recall that the Ctrl/Command key shortcut temporarily switches to the Selection tool. This shortcut comes in quite handy for threading your text frames without the interruption of a trip to the Tools panel.

Exercise 17.1: Threading Text Frames

In this exercise you'll see how easy it is to create threaded text frames.

1. Open **ex17_1_start.indd** and save it as ex17_1.indd.

    Note that the text in the paragraph starting with the words Costa Rica is overset, as indicated by the red plus sign (⊞) at the lower right of the text frame.

2. With the Selection tool, click on the plus sign, and the cursor should change to a loaded text cursor that displays the start of the actual text in the story.

    If the cursor doesn't load the first time, try again. You want to be sure to single-click. A double-click in the text frame will switch you back to the Selection tool.

The loaded text cursor displays the text from the beginning of your story.

3.   With the loaded cursor, mouse over the empty text frame, below the title and above the Costa Rica map. When the symbol at the upper left of the cursor changes to a link ( ), click once to flow the text into the second frame.

You'll notice that the second frame is also overset.

4.   Click the red plus sign at the lower right of the second text frame to load the cursor once again. Mouse over the text frame to the right of the map, and click once when the link appears on the loaded cursor to flow the text into the frame.

It would look better if the article title were separate from the body of the text. While you could have created a separate un-threaded text frame to hold the title, in this case you'll keep it connected to the story.

5.   Position your cursor after the closing parenthesis in the title, and double-click with the Selection tool to activate the blinking Type tool cursor. Right-click/ Ctrl-click, and, from the contextual menu, choose Insert Break Character > Frame Break to jump the text that's after the title into the next text frame.

The text should now be flowing through all three text frames with the title text in a frame of its own. As the last refinement, you'll add a frame break to flow the second paragraph into the text frame next to the map.

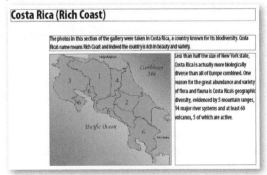

The appearance of the final layout.

6.   Position the Type tool cursor just in front of the word "Less" in the second text frame. Right-click/Ctrl-click, and from the contextual menu, choose Insert Break Character > Frame Break to jump the to the last text frame.

7.   Press Esc to select all the frames in the story and show the text threads linking them together. Save and close the file.

8.   With *no* documents open, choose View > Extras > Show Text Threads to set this as the default. Now, whenever you have linked text frames, the text threads will show.

Managing Text Flow

In the last exercise, you learned how to manually thread text frames. If you're adding a large volume of text to your document that extends across multiple pages, the process of manually loading the text cursor for each new text frame can become tedious and time consuming. With assistance from a modifier key, you can streamline the process a bit and save yourself some time.

As you edit, text may become overset, or you may end up with empty pages. You can manage these changes manually, or you can let InDesign help by setting up a couple preferences. If you set the preferences with no document open, all new documents will be affected.

In this section, you'll learn some tips for managing text flow and document pages, and for maximizing the help InDesign can provide.

Exercise 17.2: Managing Text Flow

The measurements in this exercise are given in points (pt). As far as InDesign is concerned, points and pixels are equivalent. So, if your Preferences are set to use pixels, you don't need to change anything. If you're using a different unit of measure, you can type in the measurements we've supplied, followed by "pt," and InDesign will do the unit conversion for you.

Note: Default print documents in InDesign appear in the Pages panel as two-page spreads, referred to as facing pages. In a document with facing pages, page 1 starts on the right, as it would in a book, pages 2 and 3 are paired, as are 4 and 5, etc. This can be a little disconcerting if you try to scroll vertically from one page to the next. From page 1, you would scroll to page 3, for example. Navigating from one page to another by double-clicking a page in the Pages panel lets you target the page you want to go to without the frustration of scrolling up and down and left and right to position the desired page in the document window.

Deselect the Facing Pages checkbox in the New Document dialog to set up a document with single pages.

1. Go to File > New > Document and select Default from the Document Preset dropdown. Click OK.

2. Press Ctrl+D/Command+D, navigate to the chapter_17_exercises folder, and double-click **advice_from_caterpillar.txt** to load it into the cursor.

3. Position the loaded text cursor somewhere in the middle of the page and click once to place the text.

    Notice that the text fills the page below the point where you clicked, and extends to the left and right margins of the page. When you place text by clicking, rather than dragging to define a text frame, the text frame boundaries automatically conform to the margin and column definition that was set in the New Document dialog. If the page setup had specified multiple columns, the placed text would have flowed to fill the column you clicked.

    Also note that each paragraph of the placed text is followed by two paragraph returns. In typography, this is a *huge* no-no. Removing the extra returns manually can be time consuming and annoying. Good thing InDesign can take care of it for you.

4. Press Ctrl+Z/Command+Z to undo the text placement, and then press Esc to clear the loaded text cursor.

5. Press Ctrl+D/Command+D again, but, this time, check the Show Import Options checkbox at the bottom left of the Place dialog. Browse to and select the **advice_from_caterpillar.txt** file, and then click Open.

6. In the Extra Carriage Returns section of the Text Import Options dialog, check the Remove Between Paragraphs checkbox. The file was created on a Mac, so, choose Macintosh Roman from the Character Set dropdown. Click OK.

When placing text, InDesign can automatically remove extra returns between paragraphs and strip formatting done in Microsoft Word to start fresh.

7. Save the document as **ex17_2.indd** in the chapter_17_exercises folder.

8. Position the loaded text cursor at the upper left margin of the page. This time, hold down the Alt/Option key and click once to place the text.

   When you held down the Alt/Option modifier key, the text cursor icon changed to a broken squiggle ( ) (a technical term), indicating that you were about to semi-autoflow your text. Semi-autoflow places your text in the clicked column and then automatically reloads the cursor so you can selectively place the remaining text. Also, note that InDesign removed the extra paragraph returns.

9. With the cursor loaded, click the New Page button at the bottom of the Pages panel. When the empty page appears, hold down the Shift key and click at the upper left margin of the new page in the document window to autoflow the loaded text.

   You may have noticed that the squiggle for the autoflow cursor was continuous and unbroken ( ). With autoflow, the remaining text flows through your document, inserting additional pages as required, to make a total of four pages.

   InDesign can also remove empty pages for you as you edit your document.

Note: You can also add pages from the Pages panel menu. Choose Insert Pages and then specify how many pages you want to add, where in the document you want to add them, and which master to apply.

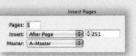

10. Go to Edit > Preferences > Type (Windows) or InDesign > Preferences > Type (Mac). Check the Smart Text Reflow checkbox, uncheck Limit to Master Text Frames, and check Delete Empty Pages. Click OK to close the Preferences dialog.

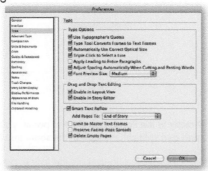

Adjust just a few preferences, and InDesign will automatically add and remove pages for you as the amount of text in your document changes.

Note: Setting the Smart Text Reflow preference with a document open applies it to the active document only. To make Smart Text Reflow a global preference, set it with no documents open.

11. Double-click on page 1 in the Pages panel. When the page appears in the document window, double-click the text frame on page 1 to switch to the Type tool. Press Ctrl+A/Command+A to select the entire story.

12. Go to Object > Text Frame Options (Ctrl+B/Command+B). When the Text Frame Options dialog opens, set the number of columns to 2. Note that from this dialog, you have the option to set column width, the width for the gutter between columns, inset spacing, and vertical justification. (New with CS5 is the Balance Columns checkbox.) Click OK to close the dialog. You should now have 3 pages in the document.

13. With the entire story still selected and the Paragraph controls active in the Control panel, add 8 pt space after ( ) and deselect the Hyphenate checkbox. Switch to the Character controls and format your text using Myriad Pro Regular, 10 pt with default leading.

14. With the text still selected, open the Paragraph Styles panel (Window > Styles > Paragraph Styles). Alt-click/Option-click the New Style button at the bottom of the panel. Name the style "body". Be sure to check the Apply Style to Selection checkbox, and then click OK.

15. Still on the first page, triple-click the first line to select the title "Advice from a Caterpillar" and style it as follows: Myriad Pro Regular 30 pt, all caps (TT), and set the tracking to 75 pt ( ) to give the title more emphasis. Make the font color green.

    Next to the column controls on the Paragraph section of the Control panel is a new InDesign CS5 feature: span columns. It used to be that if you wanted a header to span multiple columns, it was necessary to create a separate text frame. Span columns makes it possible to have multi-column headers in the same text frame as the body of your content. Span columns actually has a dual function; in addition to spanning columns, it can split them too—to create 2-, 3-, and 4-column text, all in the same text frame.

16. With the "Advice from a Caterpillar" text still selected, press Shift+Ctrl+C/Shift+Command+C to center it. If necessary, switch to the Paragraph controls on the Control panel. Choose Span 2 from the Span Columns dropdown and add 20 pt space after to the title paragraph to separate it from the body content.

Directly in the Paragraph Control panel, you can span and split columns, all in the same text frame.

Text wrap is another great feature to simplify the layout process, making text within a frame flow around other graphical elements. To illustrate this, you'll create a pull quote, content that is "pulled out" of the body content for emphasis.

17. Select the Rectangle tool and click once on the document. In the Rectangle dialog, enter 195 px for both width and height and click OK. Press V to switch to the Selection tool, and click once on the rectangle to select it.

18. Click the arrow to the right of the Fill Swatch () on the Control panel, and choose a fill color. If desired, adjust the tint at the top of the panel. (We chose a 30% green fill.) From the Control panel, choose a stroke color and stroke weight. We chose a 3 pt, 100% green stroke.

19. Select a corner style from the Corner Options dropdown on the Control panel and adjust the corner radius to 18 px.

You can set object corner options from the Control panel.

20. Double-click on the body text to switch to the Type tool. Then, select the text in the third body paragraph on the first page that reads "at least I know who I was when I got up this morning, but I think I must have been changed several times since then." Press Ctrl+C/Command+C to copy, and hold down the Ctrl/Command key to switch temporarily to the Selection tool and click the green rectangle. Release the modifier key and when you see the parentheses on either side of the Type tool cursor (🔲), click once to activate the text frame. Press Ctrl+V/Command+V to paste the quote.

21. Press Ctrl+A/Command+A to Select All and format the pull quote using Minion Pro Bold Italic, 16 pt, 30 pt leading, center-aligned. Press Ctrl+B/Command+B to bring up the Text Frame Options dialog and choose Center from the Vertical Justification dropdown. Click OK to close the dialog.

22. Using the Selection tool, drag the formatted text frame onto the document page and center it over the gutter between the text columns. You'll know the pull quote is centered when you see a magenta smart guide appear through the X marking the center of the frame as you drag.

Align the X in the center of the pull quote to the smart guide indicating the center of the page and the gutter between the columns.

23. To get the body text to wrap around the pull quote, go to Window > Text Wrap. When the Text Wrap panel opens, choose the Wrap Around Object Shape button and set the Offset to 18 pt. Leave Wrap To set to Both Right & Left Sides.

Note: The stroke weight dropdown is just to the right of the fill and stroke swatches on the Control panel.

In the image above, the Control panel fill and stroke controls are on the left and the stroke weight and stroke type controls are on the right.

Note: If you don't see the magenta guide as you drag the pull quote over the center of the page, press Ctrl+U/Command+U to turn on smart guides. Alternatively, go to View > Grids & Guides > Smart Guides.

With Text Wrap, you can choose to wrap text around the object bounding box or the object shape. You can also have the text jump the object, or jump to the next column.

There will no doubt come a time when you need to convert a print document for on-screen display, or vice versa. InDesign has a convenient feature called Layout Adjustment for just such a purpose. Though not always a completely perfect solution, it can certainly provide you with a solid start in the conversion process.

24. Go to Layout > Layout Adjustment, and, when the dialog opens, check the Enable Layout Adjustment checkbox. Leave the other default settings and click OK to close the dialog.

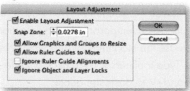

When Layout Adjustment is turned on, InDesign will automatically reflow your text and graphics when you change margins and page orientation.

25. Go to File > Document Setup. When the dialog opens, deselect the facing pages checkbox. Change the Page Orientation from portrait to landscape and click OK (Orientation: ▢ ▢). You can see that for this simple layout, the pages reflow perfectly to the new dimensions.

26. Double-click the words "A-Master" in the Pages panel to bring the master page into view. From the Pages panel menu, select Master Options for "A-Master," and, when the dialog opens, change the Number of Pages to 1.

27. With the master still active, go to Layout > Margins and Columns. With the Make all settings the same link linked, enter 50 px in any of the fields and press Tab. Unlink the link, enter 100 px in the Bottom margin field, and click OK.

Because A-Master is applied to all the document pages by default, the new margins are applied throughout the document.

28. With nothing selected on the page, Go to Window > Styles > Paragraph Styles. Double-click the body style, and, when the Paragraph Styles dialog opens, select Basic Character Formats from the options on the left. Change the font size to 12 pt and the leading to 13 pt to make the text easier to read on screen.

29. Go to Type > Show Hidden Characters, and then go to page 2 of the document.

Note that each paragraph of the Father William poem starts with a number of spaces, making it tough to control the formatting of the text. You'll use InDesign's robust Find/Change feature to eliminate the extra spaces.

30. Press Ctrl+F/Command+F or go to Edit > Find/Change to open the Find/Change dialog. Place your cursor in the Find What text field and press the Spacebar six times. Leave the Change To field blank and ensure that either Story or Document is selected from the Search dropdown. Click Find. InDesign finds and selects the first group of six consecutive spaces. Click Change to confirm that the command does what you were looking to do, and then click Change All.

31. An alert pops up to notify you that InDesign made 15 replacements. Delete two of the six spaces from the Find What field of the dialog (you want to find groups of four spaces). Click Change All. Click Done to close the dialog.

32. With the Type tool, click once to position the cursor directly before the beginning of the Father William poem. It begins at the bottom of the second column on the first page. In the Pages panel, double-click on page 2. Hold the Shift key and click just after the last line of the poem, "down the stairs." It should be near the top of the second column. With the entire poem selected and the Paragraph controls active on the Control panel, choose Split 2 from the Span Columns dropdown.

33. Format the selected text with Myriad Pro Italic, green. Keep the text selected.

In looking at the layout, the columns you just created feel a little crowded. You can tune the spacing in the columns more finely by accessing the Span Columns options.

34. From the Control panel menu, choose Span Columns. When the dialog opens, check the Preview checkbox. Set Space Before Split to 12 pt, Inside Gutter to 20 pt, and Outside Gutter to 9 pt. Click OK to close the dialog.

Using the Span Columns dialog, when you split columns in a text frame, you can set the width for inside and outside gutters, as well as space before and space after.

Since so much of this document is quoted text, the alignment of the quotations inside the paragraph margins is really glaring in the ragged appearance it creates. You can easily fix that using InDesign's Optical Margin Alignment.

35. With the Type tool cursor active in the text frame, go to Type > Story. When the Story panel opens, check the Optical Margin Alignment checkbox and then set the overhang amount to the size of your story font (12 pt).

Note: Hidden characters are visual indicators of spaces, paragraph returns, tabs, etc. They give you a little bit of a look behind the curtain so you can see more of what's actually going on in your document.

You can find a free 5-page guide to Hidden Characters at InDesignSecrets.com: http://indesignsecrets.com/free-guide-to-indesign-special-characters.php

You can play with this a bit, but, for best results, it's generally recommended that you match the overhang setting to the size you've selected for your font.

The Story panel enables you to create hanging punctuation using Optical Margin Alignment. The result is that quotation marks, periods, commas, dashes, and the edges of letters such as "W" and "A", hang outside the text margins to give the appearance of better alignment.

36. Save and close the file.

Type on a Path

Flowing type in InDesign isn't restricted to enclosed frames; you can flow type on an open or closed path as well.

Exercise 17.3: Type on a Path

Note: Holding the Shift key constrains the proportions of a shape and also constrains lines and transformations to angles that are multiples of 45°.

Holding the Alt/Option key while dragging a shape draws that shape outward from the center.

Hold down the Spacebar before you let go of the shape (while drawing), and you can drag to reposition it!

1. Go to File > New Document, choose Web for Intent, and 900 x 700 for Page Size. When the document opens, select the Ellipse tool (L). (Click and hold the Rectangle tool and then, when the tool submenu appears, click on the Ellipse tool to select it.)

The little arrows throughout the interface are indicators that there are hidden tools or controls that you can click the arrows to discover. This is true for tools on the Tools panel, menus, and pretty much any other icon you may encounter that displays a tiny arrow at the lower right.

2. Close to the center of the document window, click and start dragging outward with the Ellipse tool. As you're dragging, hold down the Alt/Option key and then add the Shift key to draw a perfect circle from the center. Ensure that your circle has a stroke so you can see it on the page.

3. With the circle selected on the page, set its width and height to 234 px in the Control panel. Alt-drag/Option-drag to duplicate the circle.

Note: You can temporarily switch to a tool by holding its keyboard shortcut key.

4. Select the Type tool and mouse over the edge of the first circle. (Don't click.) Note the parentheses that appear on the Type tool cursor. The parentheses indicate that InDesign recognizes a closed path and will flow text into the contours of the shape if you click. (⟨Ⅰ⟩) (Don't click.)

5. From the Tools panel, click and hold the Type tool to expose the other tools it's hiding, and then select the Type on a Path tool (⟨⟩). Mouse over the path again and note that a little plus sign appears on the Type on a Path

---

cursor to indicate that it recognizes the path (⌐). Click to activate the path and type "Round and round."

6. Press Ctrl+A/Command+A to Select All, and then press Ctrl+D/Command+D. Browse to the chapter_17_exercises folder, select **path_text_txt**, and click Open to replace the existing text and flow the loaded text onto the circle.

7. If necessary, zoom in on the circle (Ctrl+/Command+) and switch to the Selection tool. With the circle selected and the Stroke swatch active, click the / key on your keyboard to set the stroke color to None.

On a closed path, if the text is overset, the in and out ports of the text frame are positioned right on top of each other. A close look will reveal that there are two vertical lines indicating the text frame boundaries, each with its corresponding port. If you mouse over either line, your cursor will change to a line with a teeny tiny right or left-facing arrow. Dragging the arrow shortens or lengthens the text path and, depending on which line you choose, repositions the beginning or end of the text on the path. As with any overset text, clicking the red plus sign will load your cursor and allow you to thread the text.

When type is overset on a closed path, the in and out ports of the text frame sit right on top of each other.

There is a third line, the center line, somewhat harder to locate, that indicates the center of the text frame. It's always located directly across from the in and out ports before they're repositioned. The center line also acts as a control point to reorient the entire frame on the path. Dragging the center line along the path repositions the frame. If you drag the line up or down, you can flip the orientation of the text to the inside or outside of the path.

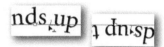

Dragging the center line of the type on a path text frame up or down flips the orientation of the type on the path.

8. Locate the right edge of the text frame, and, when you see the right-facing arrow, drag to the right to scale the text frame. Locate the center point of the frame and drag it in toward the center of the circle to flip the orientation of the text to the inside of your circle.

9. Click the out port (the red plus sign) and then mouse over the inside of the second circle. When you see the link icon on the cursor, click to place the remaining text inside the circle. Press Ctrl+B/Command+B, and, when the Text Frame Options dialog opens, adjust the Inset Spacing to 70 px and set Vertical Justification to Center.

Next you'll relink the text, but first you need to break the existing link.

10. Click one of the out ports of the second circle and then position the loaded cursor somewhere over the inside of the circle. When the cursor icon changes to an unlocked link (see the screenshot), click to remove the threaded text from the inside of the circle. The out port of the original circle should have a red plus sign again.

To break a thread between text frames, use the Selection tool and click a connecting port to load the text cursor. Then, when you see the broken link icon, click somewhere in that frame to break the connection.

When the link is broken, the text will be overset again, and you'll need to reload the cursor in order to thread it to another frame.

11. Double-click the Pencil tool to open the Pencil Tool Preferences dialog, and drag the Smoothness slider to around 80%. Leave the Keep Selected and Edit Selected Paths checkboxes checked, and keep the default value of 12 in the proximity text field. Click OK to commit your settings and close the dialog.

The Pencil Tool Preferences let you control the rendering of freeform pencil paths. The lower the Fidelity, the more closely the path will follow the exact movement of your mouse as you draw, resulting in more points on the path. The higher the Smoothness, the smoother the curves. This does not necessarily result in a reduction of points, however. If you leave the Keep Selected checkbox checked, along with the Edit Selected Paths checkbox, you can keep redrawing the path until you get it the way you want it, as long as you start redrawing the path within the pixel distance specified in the slider.

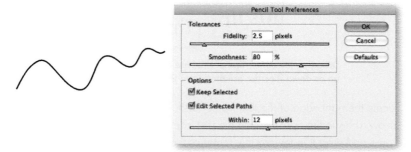

A path drawn with the Pencil tool and the Pencil Tool Preferences dialog.

12. Choose a stroke color and set the fill color to None. Click and drag with the Pencil tool to draw a curving path on the page. Press Shift+T to select the Type on a Path tool, position the mouse over the path where you want the text to begin, and click when you see a plus on the Type tool cursor ( ).

13. When the blinking Type cursor appears on the pencil path, hold the Ctrl/

Command key to switch temporarily to the Selection tool, and click to select the circle with the type on the path. Still holding the modifier key, click the red plus sign at the circle text out port to load the cursor.

14. With the overflow text from the circle loaded into the cursor, click the pencil path you just drew to thread the text from the circle to the curve. Don't worry if the text is still overset. This exercise was just for practice.

15. Save the file as **ex17_3.indd** in the chapter_17_exercises folder, and close it.

In this exercise, you explored several ways to work with threading type on a path. You created a closed path and flowed type around it, and then drew an open path onto which you threaded the text.

Nested Styles

Nested styles are a wonderful time saving feature when you have a volume of text that requires a pattern of repetitive formatting. Catalogs and directories are perfect candidates for nested styles, where each entry may have distinct formatting for each of its component elements.

Nested styles are really just an assemblage of Character styles, separated by specific delineators and held in a paragraph definition. This being the case, it is easiest to create nested styles by first creating each component Character style in the context of an example paragraph. When the Character styles are all defined and assigned, you can then save the Paragraph style, detailing the assembly instructions in the Drop Caps and Nested Styles section of the Paragraph Styles dialog.

Exercise 17.4: Nested Styles

1. From the chapter_17_exercises folder, open **ex17_4_ end.indd** and check it out. Open the Paragraph and Character Styles panels (Window > Styles > Character/Paragraph Styles) and explore the paragraphs to see how they're constructed. Double-click the style definitions in the panel to explore the details. When you've finished investigating, keep the file open for reference. Open **ex17_4_start.indd** and save it as ex17_4.indd.

   The first step in creating a nested Paragraph style is to set up each of the Character styles comprising it. In this example, you'll be setting up separate styles for the book title, author, the number of pages, the word "Publisher," the publisher name, the date of publication, and the ISBN numbers. Seven Character styles is a lot, so by the time you're done creating them, you should be a pro.

2. With the Type tool, select the book title in the first paragraph, including the colon. Set the font to Myriad Pro Black, 11 pt, 10 pt leading, small caps (Tr), green. Open the Character Styles panel and Alt-click/Option-click the New Style button at the bottom of the panel. Name the style "Title," check the Apply Style to Selection and Preview checkboxes, and click OK to close the dialog.

Note: For each Character style you'll be creating, select [None] from the Based On dropdown in the Character Styles dialog.

3. Select the balance of the first line, up to the opening parenthesis before the number of pages. Set the font to Myriad Pro Regular 10 pt, 10 pt leading, black. Save the formatting as a Character style named "Author."

4. Select the number of pages including both parentheses. Set the font to Myriad Pro Italic, 10 pt, 10 pt leading, black. Save the formatting to a Character style named "Pages."

5. Select the word "Publisher" as well as the colon on the second line, and set the font to Myriad Pro Regular, 10 pt, 10 pt leading, black. Save the formatting to a Character style named "Publisher title."

6. Select the Publisher name and set the font to Myriad Pro Italic, 10 pt, 10 pt leading, black. Save a Character style named "Publisher."

7. Select the date, including the parentheses, and set the font to Myriad Pro Regular, 10 pt, 10 pt leading, black. Capture the formatting in a Character style named "Date."

8. Select the ISBN numbers, the entire last line of text. Set the font to Myriad Pro Regular, 10 pt, 10 pt leading, black. Create a Character style named "ISBN."

Several of the styles you've just defined share the same definition, and, in actuality, there is no reason not to reuse the same Character style multiple times in a Nested Paragraph style. The number of Character styles used in the exercise is really to drive home the point that you can get as elaborate as you like when creating nested styles. Of course, you want to be careful not to use so many font variations on your page that you cheapen the look of your document.

9. Select the entire paragraph by clicking four times, and Alt-click/Option-click the New Style button at the bottom of the Paragraph Styles panel. Name the new style "TotalBook" and ensure that the Apply Style to Selection checkbox is checked.

10. Select Basic Character Formats on the left of the panel. Set the font face to Myriad Pro and the font style to Regular. Set the size and leading to 10 pt and the case to Normal.

When you create a Paragraph style from selected text, a number of the default settings in the Paragraph Styles dialog are garnered from the first character in the selection.

Note: If you try to set the Left Indent value before setting the First Line Indent to 0, you'll get an error message telling you that indents cannot extend outside the text frame.

11. In the Character Color section of the panel, select the Black color swatch. Select Bullets and Numbering from the left of the panel, and set the List Type on the right to None. From the Indents and Spacing section, first set First Line Indent to 0, and then set Left Indent to 0. Set Space After to .125.

Here's where it all comes together. Now you get to assemble the Character styles to define the paragraph. The structure of the paragraph requires seven nested styles in all. This would be the case even if you hadn't made separate Character style definitions for each element in the paragraph.

Printed and bound by CPI Group (UK) Ltd, Croydon, CR0 4YY

21/10/2024

01777096-0012

12. Select Drop Caps and Nested Styles from the left of the window and click the New Nested Style button on the right. From the Character Style dropdown that appears in the Nested Styles section of the window, choose the Title Character style. You get to choose whether to apply the style up to the delimiter or including it. In this case, you want to apply the Title style to the colon as well as the text, so leave the default choice of through. There is only one colon before you want the style to change, so you'll leave the default value of 1. If you wanted to change the value, you could simply type a different number into the field. Since the colon is the delimiter, type it into the last field for the first Character style, replacing the word "Words."

Note: A delimeter is a character or sequence of characters that mark the beginning or end of a measure of data. In the case of nested styles, colons, periods, spaces, etc. would all be considered delimiters.

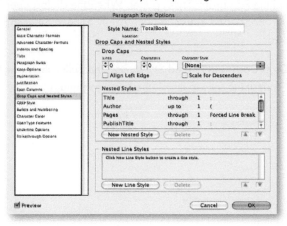

The Drop Caps and Nested Styles section of the Paragraph Styles dialog.

13. Click the New Nested Style button again, and set the Character style to Author. Since you want the Author style to apply up to the parenthesis enclosing the number of pages, choose up to from the next dropdown, leave 1 selected, and type an opening parenthesis as the delimiter.

14. Add the remaining Character styles and settings to match the image below, and then click OK to close the Paragraph Styles dialog.

Title	through	1	:
Author	up to	1	(
Pages	through	1	)
PublishTitle	through	1	:
Publisher	up to	1	(
Date	through	1	)
ISBN	through	1	Forced Line Break

The seven Nested styles assembled to create the TotalBook Paragraph style.

15. To test your creation, select the next two paragraphs with the Type tool and apply the TotalBook Paragraph style. Awesome, right?! To test the style further, type the paragraph in the note at the right, which has the same delimiters. You could copy one of the paragraphs that are already there instead, but then you wouldn't get to see how cool it is that the styles change automatically as you type. Be sure to end each line with a soft return (Shift+Enter/Shift+Return).

Note: The Singularity Is Near: When Humans Transcend Biology: by Ray Kurzweil (672 pages)

(soft return)

Publisher: Penguin (Non-Classics); (September 26, 2006)

(soft return)

ISBN-10: 0143037889, # ISBN-13: 978-0143037880

The elaborate style you just built requires that each book entry be one single paragraph with the lines divided by soft returns. Another way to approach such a formatting challenge is to compose three separate nested Paragraph styles, one for each line of the book information. As part of a style definition, InDesign allows you to specify the style to apply to the following paragraph. Using this feature, you can sequence the nested Paragraph styles to achieve the same visual result as with the TotalBook style.

16. With the Type tool cursor anywhere in the line of text that begins with "The Presence of the Past," Alt-click/Option-click the New Style button at the bottom of the Paragraph Styles panel. When the dialog opens, name the new style "Book" and ensure that the Apply Style to Selection checkbox is checked.

17. Select Drop Caps and Nested Styles, and then click the New Nested Style button. Format the style to match the following image:

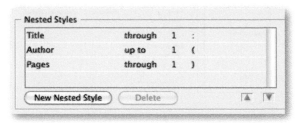

Nested styles for the Book Paragraph style definition.

18. Create another Paragraph style and name it "Publisher." Add the following nested styles:

Nested styles for the Publisher style definition

Note: Once you apply a Paragraph style, if you add a return somewhere inside the styled paragraph, the new paragraph will be the same style as the original. This is the case even if the nested Paragraph style definition specifies a different Paragraph style for the Next Style. Next Style only applies to new lines, not text that has been broken with a return.

19. Create a third Paragraph style and name it "ISBN." Set the font to Myriad Pro Regular, 10 pt, 10 pt leading. Still in the Paragraph Styles dialog, select General, and choose Book from the Next Style dropdown. Click OK to close the dialog.

20. In the Paragraph Styles panel, double-click the Book style. When the dialog opens, in the General section, choose Publisher from the Next Style dropdown. Set the Next Style for the Publisher style to ISBN.

21. To test the styles, select all three paragraphs from the Sequential Nested Styles Paragraphs section of the document (the three paragraphs together

look like the single paragraphs above). In the Paragraph Styles panel, Right-click/Ctrl-click the Book style and choose Apply "Book," then Next Style.

With lots of styles in your document, sorting through them to find the style you're looking for can get to be rather tedious. Style groups can help to keep things organized.

22. From the bottom of the Paragraph Styles panel, Alt-click/Option-click the New Style Group button (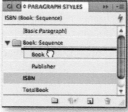). When the Style Group Options dialog opens, name the style group "Book Sequence." Drag the Book, Publisher, and ISBN styles into the folder.

You can keep your styles organized using style groups (the folder icon), and dragging your styles into them. Alternatively, select all the styles you want included in the group, Right-click/Ctrl-click, and choose New Group from Styles from the contextual menu.

In this exercise, you got comfortable with making Character styles and assembling them to create two flavors of nested Paragraph styles. You also learned to use the Next Style feature in the Style Option dialog to have InDesign automatically change from one style to another as you enter text.

CHAPTER SUMMARY

This chapter was all about text: flowing it, formatting it, and making it conform to your design. To aid your typographical work, you made use of several helpful InDesign features including:

- The ability to show and hide text threads
- The ability to show hidden characters
- The robust Find/Change dialog

You flowed text through multiple text frames manually, and also used the autoflow and semi-autoflow modifier keys to speed the process. You then stepped outside the box to flow type onto closed and open paths, and learned to adjust the orientation of that type on the path.

In your management of text flow and layout you

- Adjusted margins and columns on master pages to affect the document universally
- Adjusted margins and columns on individual document pages
- Employed optical margin alignment to achieve a more pleasing appearance of text alignment
- Became familiar with the Text Wrap panel, wrapping text around a pull quote
- Worked with the new span columns dialog to span and split columns within a single text frame
- Set up the Smart Text Reflow preference to have InDesign add and remove pages automatically with the flow of text in your document
- Converted a print document for on-screen display

In the course of your explorations you:

- Set application preferences by adjusting settings with no open documents
- Worked with the Pencil tool and set Pencil tool preferences
- Refined your work with Paragraph styles: creating nested styles and utilizing the next style feature in the style definition dialog
- Employed style groups to organize the definitions in the Paragraph Styles panel

Now that you have firm footing in your work with text, the next chapter provides a blueprint for developing multi-page documents. Employing the Pages and Layers panels, you'll establish a solid structure for any document you build.

• Chapter 18

MULTI-PAGE DOCUMENT LAYOUT

This chapter covers the nuances of setting up a multi-layered, multipage document, helps you to avoid possible pitfalls you may encounter in the process, and offers an introduction to anchored objects. The tools and techniques you'll learn in this chapter lay the groundwork for print and interactive documents alike.

Multi-page Layout

Throughout the book, you've been working with multi-page interactive documents. You may have noticed that the files are built so that each page has its own named layer. You may have also noticed that while the named layers are always visible in the Layers panel, the object sublayers only appear when the page that contains them is active in the document window. Because objects appear and disappear based on the active page, you will save yourself *lots* of time trying to figure out where things are if you separate the objects in your document into page-specific layers.

Working with Master Pages

If you're creating a multi-page interactive document, it's likely that you will employ master pages for the portions of the interface that remain consistent from page to page. When using master pages, you may encounter a rather strange anomaly where items on certain document pages appear grayed out or disappear.

Items on master pages can obscure content on other layers as a result of the stacking order of objects in the Layers panel.

This happens when objects on an inactive page overlap objects on the active page and are positioned above them in the layer stacking order. This anomaly can be somewhat alarming if you don't know what's causing it. The best way to avoid the problem is to establish a separate layer for the master page objects, as for each of the document pages, and then position it appropriately in the Layers panel. Most often, the master page layer will best be positioned at the bottom of the layer stack. There are occasions, however, where some master page objects need to appear above the contents of the document pages, while other master page objects need to be positioned below them.

A perfect example of such a scenario is when you have a master page containing both a navigation bar with dropdown menus, and background interface elements. The background elements need to be positioned beneath the contents of the document pages, but, in order for the dropdown menus to be visible, the navbar needs to be positioned above them.

One way to resolve this issue is to create two layers for the master page objects: one for the background and one for the navbar. You would then position the navbar layer at the top of the layer stack, and the background layer at the bottom.

In addition, you might elect to use nested master pages. The foundation master would contain the background interface elements, while the child master would inherit the background, and then add the navigation buttons. The benefit to this approach is the clear separation created between the general interface and the navigation elements, allowing you to work on one without concern about inadvertently changing the other. You would still need to create two distinct layers, though, one for each of the masters, and they would still need to be appropriately positioned at the bottom and the top of the layer stack.

Exercise 18.1: Working with Master Pages

This exercise walks you through setting up a multi-page site with a skeleton navigational structure using nested master pages. You'll set up named layers for each document page and customize some of the page content. Along the way, you'll create precisely sized and positioned rectangles with rounded corners; place, reposition, and scale images; work with transparency and effects; add drop caps to text; over-ride master page items; and relink images in the Links panel.

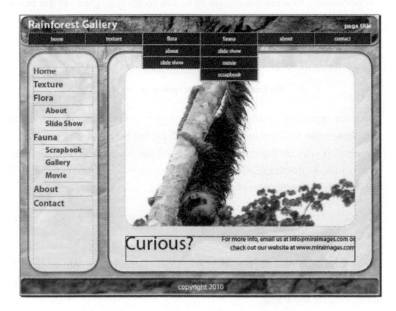

The exercise project: a multi-page site using multiple master pages.

1. Open **ex18_1_end.indd** and explore it a bit. Check out the master pages in the Pages panel and the layer structure in the Layers panel. When you're done looking through the file, keep it open for reference.

   For this project, as you can see, the interface is constructed of stacked rectangles containing the same placed image with varying transparency settings.

2. Go to File > Open, choose the web 900 x 700 preset you created on page 34, and save it as ex18_1.indd in the chapter_18_exercises folder.

3. Double-click on A-Master in the Pages panel to open it in the document window. Select the Rectangle tool (M), and click the upper left square of the Reference

---

Point proxy on the Control panel (▦). Position the Rectangle tool crosshair at the upper left corner of the document page and click once to open the Rectangle dialog. Set the rectangle width to 900 px and the height to 700 px, and then click OK.

4. The upper left corner of your rectangle should be aligned with the upper left corner of the document page. If the alignment is perfect, both the X and Y values on the Control panel will be 0. If necessary, select and replace the X and Y values with 0.

Note: If the Corner Options dropdown is not visible on the Control panel, it may be that your application window is simply not wide enough to show all the controls you've chosen to display on the panel. Instead, you can access the Corner Options dialog by going to Object > Corner Options.

5. With the rectangle still selected, select the Rounded Corner option from the Control panel, and set the corner radius to 22 px. Next, press Ctrl+D/ Command+D (File > Place), and navigate to the chapter_18_exercises > links folder. Select **bark.jpg** from the links folder and click Open. With the cursor loaded, click once on the rectangle to place the image inside it.

6. Right-click/Ctrl-click on the rectangle and choose Fitting > Fill Frame Proportionally to scale the image to fill the rectangle. Then set the object transparency to 50% on the Control panel.

The Control panel Transparency controls.

7. Click the upper left corner of the page again with the Rectangle tool, and this time, enter 900 px for width and 75 px for height. Once again, round the corners and set the corner radius to 22 px. Place the **bark.jpg** image, and again, Right-click/Ctrl-click to open the contextual menu. Choose Fill Frame Proportionally from the Fitting options.

The image fills the new rectangle, but it would look better if its position precisely matched the background image.

8. Press V on your keyboard to switch to the Selection tool. Mouse over the rectangle, and, when the target appears in its center, click it to select the image inside the frame.

The bounding box of the image should extend from edge to edge of the rectangle and nearly to the bottom of the page. You're going to scale the image to match the background.

9. Holding down the Shift key, click and drag the lower right corner of the image down and to the right, until its bottom edge is flush with the bottom of the page.

Scale the image in the second rectangle to match the dimensions of the page background. The scaled image will be wider than the page.

10. Click off the page content to deselect the image, and then select the rectangle. Apply a 2 px, solid, paper-colored stroke to the rectangle.

Next, you'll apply an effect to just the stroke of the rectangle.

11. Click the *fx.* button on the Control panel and choose Bevel and Emboss from the Effects dropdown. When the dialog opens, deselect the Bevel and Emboss checkbox to remove the effect from the object. Select Stroke from the Settings For dropdown, and re-check the Bevel and Emboss checkbox to apply the effect to the stroke. Select Emboss from the Style dropdown and set Size to 8 px. Leave the other default settings and click OK to close the dialog.

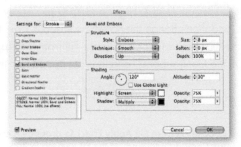

The settings for the effect applied to the stroke of the rectangle.

With the rectangle positioned at the 0,0 point, and the stroke centered on the rectangle, the effect on the stroke isn't visible at the top of the page. You'll realign the stroke and reposition the rectangle to better show the effect.

12. With the rectangle still selected, go to Window > Stroke or click the ☰ icon in the Panel dock. When the Stroke panel opens, click the center button in the Align Stroke section of the panel (Align Stroke: ▢▢▢) (the Align Stroke to Inside button). Then set the Y coordinate in the Control panel to 1 to move the rectangle down on the page and better show the effect.

13. Go to Window > Styles > Object Styles, or click the ⬚ button in the Panel dock. When the Object Styles panel opens, Alt-click/Option-click the New Style button at the bottom of the panel. In the New Object Style dialog, name the style "interface." Check the Apply Style to Selection and Preview checkboxes, and then click OK to close the dialog.

14. Create another rectangle 900 px wide and 45 px high. On the Control panel, select the bottom left square of the Reference Point proxy. Enter 0 for the X coordinate and 700 for the Y coordinate. In the Object Styles panel, click interface to style the rectangle. Change the corner radius to 10 px on the Control panel.

The object style you created set the stroke color, weight and alignment, rounded corners, and the bevel and emboss effect you'll need for the rest of the interface elements. While you'll make some adjustments to the formatting after the style is applied, the interface style takes care of the bulk of the object formatting for you.

Next, you'll place and manually scale the bark image in the rectangle to match the background image.

15. Switch to the Selection tool and place **bark.jpg** in the rectangle. Click the target in the rectangle to select the placed image, hold down the Shift key, and drag the image up until its bottom is flush with the bottom of the rectangle. Still holding the Shift key, mouse over the upper right corner of the image. When the cursor changes to a diagonal double-pointed arrow, click and drag up and to the right until the top of the image is flush with the top of the page.

16. Click off to deselect the image and switch back to the Rectangle tool (M). Create a rectangle for the side nav that is 178 px wide by 552 px high. Select the upper left square of the Reference Point proxy on the Control panel, and position the rectangle at X:18 px and Y:90 px. Apply the interface Object style, and then change the corner radius to 43 px, the stroke color to black, and the fill color to [Paper]. Choose Fill from the Apply Effect To dropdown on the Control panel, and then set opacity for the fill to 70%.

Choose Fill from the Apply Effect To dropdown on the Control panel and set the fill opacity to 70%.

17. Create one more rectangle, for the main content of the page. Make it 664 px wide by 552 px high. Position it at X:218 px and Y:90 px and apply the interface Object style. Change the stroke to black, the fill to [Paper] and the fill opacity to 70%. Switch to the Selection tool and click off the page content to ensure that nothing is selected.

18. Go to View > Entire Pasteboard and press Ctrl+D/Command+D. From the chapter_18_exercises > links folder, select **sloth.jpg**. Click Open to load your cursor and then click somewhere on the pasteboard (outside the page) to be sure the image is placed outside any of the existing rectangles.

19. Set the dimensions of the image to 576 px wide by 397 px high in the Control panel, position it at X:263 and Y:130, and apply rounded corners with a radius of 30 px. Right-click/Ctrl-click on the image and choose Fitting > Fill Frame Proportionally from the contextual menu. Check the Auto-Fit checkbox on the Control panel so all new images placed in the frame will fit perfectly.

20. For the text content on the page, create a rectangle that is 576 px wide by 64 px high and position it at X:262 px and Y:544 px.

21. Select the Type tool and click inside the rectangle to convert it to a text frame. In the Control panel Character controls, set the font to Myriad Pro Regular, 16 pt with 21 pt leading. Go to Type > Fill with Placeholder Text to add filler text to the frame.

22. On the Control panel, switch to the Paragraph controls and click the Justify with Last Line Aligned Left button (▤).

Note: If you're feeling ambitious, you could create an Object style to handle the formatting of your placed images. Alt-click/Option-click the New Style button at the bottom of the Object panel, and name the style "perfectFit." Check the Auto-Fit checkbox and choose Fill Frame Proportionally from the Fitting dropdown. Choose the center point in the Reference Point proxy and click OK.

Frame Fitting Options

☑ Auto–Fit

Content Fitting

Fitting: Fill Frame Proportionally

Align From: ⊞

Managing Styles from the Control Panel

Sometimes, InDesign will remember a style you applied to an object, character, or paragraph, and apply that style automatically. If you accidentally highlight a style with no object selected, it becomes the new default. Should you encounter this behavior, you can correct it by ensuring that nothing is selected in your document, and then setting your Character and Object styles to [None] and your Paragraph style to [No Paragraph Style].

You can reset your styles from their individual panels or from the Control panel. There are Control panel dropdowns for Paragraph and Character styles that appear in the panel when the Type tool or Note tool is active. There is also a dropdown for Object styles that appears when any of the other tools are selected. Clustered with each of the styles dropdowns are all the controls and menu items you could need for managing your styles.

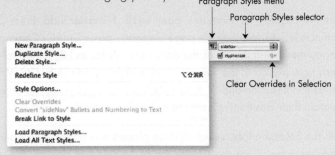

Paragraph Styles menu

Paragraph Styles selector

Clear Overrides in Selection

Control panel Paragraph style controls.

Control panel Character style controls.

Clear Overrides

Clear attributes not defined by style.
Click to reset disabled categories to [None]

Control panel Object style controls: The Object style controls enable you to set default styles for text frames and graphic frames.

---

23. To make the first letters of the paragraph into drop caps, enter 2 in the Set Drop Cap Number of Lines text box ( ) Then enter 9 for the Drop Cap Number of Characters ( ). (This will cause the text to be overset. Don't worry about it; this is just for the sake of the exercise.) Position the Type tool cursor after the last letter of the drop caps, and switch to the Character controls. Select 100 from the Kerning dropdown ( ) to create some separation between the drop caps and the body of the text.

24. Switch back to the Control panel Paragraph controls. Click the button to the right of the list buttons, and select New Paragraph Style from the popup menu. Name the style "body" and click OK to close the dialog.

You'll copy and paste the remaining master page elements from a separate document.

Note: If you double-click the body style in the Paragraph Styles panel, you'll see that the style not only captured the standard formatting, but captured the drop caps as well.

25. From the chapter_18_exercises, open **ex18_1_master.indd**. Press Ctrl+A/Command+A to select all the page elements, press Ctrl+C/Command+C to copy them, and then click the document tab for ex18_1.indd to return to it. Switch to the Selection tool and press Alt+Shift+Ctrl+V/Option+Shift+Command+V (Edit > Paste in Place) to paste the objects and maintain their positioning from the original document.

26. With the Selection tool, select all three placed text boxes, and open the Swatches panel. Click the T at the top of the panel to activate the text fill color, and then choose the [Paper] swatch to change the text color to white ( ). Save your document.

That's it for the first master page. Next you'll set up the second master, and then the pages for the site. If you were to make this into a functional site, you would have to flesh out the navigation after setting up the site pages. For this exercise, we'll call it quits after setting up the skeleton structure of the site.

27. Right-click/Ctrl-click anywhere in the Master section of the Pages panel (at the top of the panel), and choose New Master from the contextual menu. When the dialog opens, change the name of the new master to "Navbar," and choose A-Master from the Based on Master dropdown. Click OK to create the master and close the dialog.

Note: Ctrl+Shift+click/Command+Shift+click releases the clicked item from the master so you can edit it.

When you base one master page on another, changes to the parent master update automatically in the child.

The new master appears in the document window and looks exactly like the first one. Try selecting any of the objects on the page, though, and you'll see that, like all master page items, the objects are locked by default.

The new master will contain a navbar with dropdown menus. You'll want the navbar objects to be above the other objects in the layer stacking order, so you'll put them on their own layer. Rather than building the navbar from scratch, we made life easy for you with navbar graphics to copy and paste from another file.

28. In the Layers panel, click once on Layer 1, pause for just a moment, and click again to activate the Layer name. Change the name to "Interface." Alt-click/Option-click the New Layer button at the bottom of the panel, and, when the dialog opens, change the layer name to "TopNav." Click OK to close the dialog.

29. With the TopNav layer active, from the chapter_18_exercises folder, open **ex18_1_navbar.indd**. Select All (Ctrl+A/Command+A), and copy the objects on the page. Return to ex18_1.indd. With the TopNav layer active in the Layers panel and the B-Navbar master active in the Pages panel, paste the navbar objects in place (Edit > Paste in Place).

30. By default, since A-Master was the original document master, it's applied to the existing document page. To apply the Navbar master instead, select it in the Pages panel, and drag it onto the page 1 icon in the bottom section of the panel. Release the mouse when you see the grabber hand with a highlight around it on the page 1 icon.

To apply a master to a page, drag the master onto the page icon in the Pages panel.

The document you're creating will have a total of nine pages. You can add them all at once using a menu command.

31. Right-click/Ctrl-click anywhere in the bottom section of the Pages panel and choose Insert Pages from the contextual menu. Enter 8 for the number of pages, confirm that B-Navbar is the selected master, and click OK to close the dialog.

The Insert Pages dialog lets you specify how many pages you wish to add to a document, where you want them added, and which master you want to apply.

Before making changes to any of the document pages, you'll set up your layer structure and create a layer for each page of the document.

32. In the Layers panel, select the Interface layer, and then click the New Layer button nine times. Double-click each layer and rename it according to the following list. Start with the layer just above Interface, and work your way up.

1. Home
2. Texture
3. Flora: About
4. Flora: Slide Show
5. Fauna: Slide Show
6. Fauna: Movie
7. Fauna: Scrapbook
8. About
9. Contact

The Layers panel with layers organized by page.

Now you'll make some changes to the content on a couple pages to see how the layer structure works.

Note: Master page items are indicated by a dashed outline.

32. On the first page of the document, Ctrl+Shift+click/Command+Shift+click on the photo of the sloth to override the master page item. Open the Links panel (Window > Links or 🔗 in the Panel dock) and click to twirl down the arrow next to sloth.jpg.

Note that there are only two instances of the sloth image in your file, despite the fact that it appears on nine document pages and two master pages. Also note that to the right of each image file name is a page number hyperlink that will take you right to that instance of the image. The A next to the first instance indicates that the image is placed on A-Master.

33. From the Links panel, select the **sloth.jpg** image instance on page 1 and then click the Relink button (🔗) at the bottom of the panel. Navigate to the chapter_18_exercises > links folder and open **butterfly.psd**. Select the image on the document page with the Selection tool, and then drag the blue square in the selection column of the Layers panel into the Home layer.

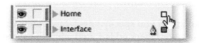

You'll want to relocate objects that you override from the master layer to their respective page layers in order to keep things organized and make them easier to manage.

34. Ctrl+Shift+click/Command+Shift+click the body text to unlock it, and then double-click it with the Selection tool to activate the Type tool cursor in the text frame. Select the drop cap letters and replace them with the word "Butterflies" followed by a space. To have the entire word appear in drop caps, change the Drop Cap Number of Characters to 11 in the Paragraph controls on the Control panel. With the Type tool cursor positioned after the space you entered, set the kerning to 100 in the Control panel Character controls.

35. Ctrl+Shift+click/Command+Shift+click to override the page title text, triple-click to select it, and then type in the word "Home" to replace it.

36. Press Esc to switch to the Selection tool, and then press Ctrl+A/Command+A to select all the objects on the page. Drag the blue square in the Layers panel selection column up to the Home layer.

Here's a quirky text behavior you can get when left alignment is combined with drop caps.

37. Go to the last page of the document and override the body text. Change the drop cap text to "Curious?, " followed by a space, and then delete the remainder of the text. In the Control panel Paragraph controls, choose Align Right (≣) and type "Contact us at info@yourwebmail.com." Press Shift+Enter/Shift+Return to create a soft return and type "Check out our website at www.Interactive-InDesign.com."

38. Override the page title text and replace it with the word "Contact." Open the Layers panel, locate the selected text sublayer, and drag it onto the Contact layer.

39. Still in the Layers panel, drag the Interface layer to the top of the stack to see the strange behavior you can encounter when objects from other pages obscure objects on the active page.

The text frame on the Contact page, as well as a portion of the top navbar, will appear faded out on the page.

40. Drag the Interface layer back to the bottom of the stack. If you like, continue to override and edit the master page items and move frames to their proper layers. Save your document, and then close all three open files.

Anchored Objects

While anchored objects are unlikely to be a mainstay of your interactive work, for documents with multiple pages and content that needs to travel with specific passages of text, anchored objects are the best. Besides, they're just too cool not to get a mention. Anchored objects flow with the text to which they're anchored. By far the coolest aspect of anchored objects is that they also work with objects like sidebars, which can be made to flow from one page to the next and maintain their position relative to the document spine. Like everything else, the easiest way to understand anchored objects is to work with them, and that's what you'll do in the next exercise.

Note: When you drag multiple items from one layer to another in the Layers panel, InDesign reverses their stacking order. If the stacking order of the objects in the layer is important, you'll need to drag them to the new layer individually rather than as a group.

Note: You can highlight the content from the blinking Type tool cursor to the end of the text (including overflow) by pressing Ctrl+Shift+End/Command+Shift+End. On a Mac Laptop, press Command+Shift+FN+ right arrow.

Note: If you entered a hard return rather than a soft return, both paragraphs would have Drop Caps. You would then have to remove the drop caps from the formatting of the second paragraph.

Exercise 18.2: Working with Anchored Objects

In this exercise, you'll place inline, above line, and custom-aligned anchored objects.

1. Open **ex18_2_end.indd** from the chapter_18_exercises folder. Note the images in the text frame on page 1. Click the next button at the lower left of the document window to navigate to page 2, and note the position of the sidebar. If you like, keep the file open for reference, and open ex18_2_start.indd. Save it as ex18_2.indd.

2. On page 1 of the document, click once on the purple area of the sidebar with the Selection tool (on the right side of the page). Press Ctrl-X/Command-X to cut it. Press T to switch to the Type tool. Then position your cursor in front of the words "You are old....." (fourth line from the bottom of the second column). Press Ctrl+V/Command+V to paste the sidebar. The text disappears from the first page, having jumped to the second. No cause for alarm; just click the Next button at the bottom left of the document window to get to page 2.

3. Press Esc to switch to the Selection tool, and click once to select the sidebar. Then, go to Object > Anchored Object > Options. When the dialog opens, choose Custom from the Position dropdown and check the Preview checkbox. The sidebar disappears from the second page, jumping back to the first.

4. In the Anchored Object Options dialog, check the Relative to Spine checkbox and click the upper right corner of the right Anchored Object Reference Point proxy. Because the Relative to Spine checkbox is checked, the upper left point is selected automatically. Choose Page Margin from both the X Relative To and Y Relative To dropdowns. The upper left and upper right Anchored Position reference points are selected automatically. Click OK to close the dialog and then navigate back to page 1 of your document.

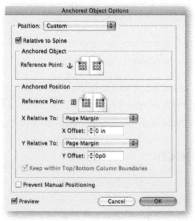

The custom settings view of the Anchored Object Options dialog.

5. Holding the Shift key to maintain vertical alignment, click on a purple portion of the sidebar (not the picture at the bottom), and drag it to the right. Position it between the right edge of the page margin and the decorative border of the page.

The bottom of the sidebar should be aligned to the bottom margin of the page, and you should see a dotted blue line connecting the sidebar to the place where you pasted it in the text frame. Note that the line connects to the sidebar at its upper right corner, the corner you specified as the reference point in the Anchored Object Options dialog. (If you don't see the dotted line, go to View > Extras > Show Text Threads.)

An anchored object can be positioned outside of a text frame and still travel with the text to which it's anchored.

6. Select the image of the Mad Hatter on the pasteboard and cut it (Ctrl+X/Command+X). Switch to the Type tool, click just after the text "So you think you're changed, do you?" near the top of the second column, and press Enter/Return on your keyboard. Press Ctrl+V/Command+V to paste. The sidebar does its disappearing trick and the Mad Hatter is tucked cozily in the column.

7. Navigate to page 2 of the document to see that the sidebar located itself on page 2 in the same position relative to the document spine that it had on page 1. Pretty smart sidebar, wouldn't you say? And a pretty fancy trick too.

8. Return to page 1. Hold down the Ctrl/Command key to switch temporarily to the Selection tool, and click once to select the image of Alice and the Caterpillar on the pasteboard. Release the modifier key, and cut the image.

9. Click once with the Type tool cursor, just after the last line of the first paragraph in the first column, which ends with "sleepy voice," and paste.

   Alice has a nice new home, and the Mad Hatter repositions himself as the text to which he's anchored to flows to make room for Alice.

10. Switch to the Selection tool and click once on Alice. Go to Object > Anchored Object > Options and select the Above Line radio button. Choose Center from the Alignment dropdown, set Space Before to 0p5 and Space After at p7. Click OK to close the dialog. Alice is centered in the column, with space between her and the text above and below her.

That's it for anchored objects. This book couldn't have been created without them. By the way, anchored objects aren't limited to text and graphic frames; buttons can be anchored too.

Note: If your leading isn't set to Auto, InDesign will not automatically make room on the new line to accommodate a placed image. As a result, the placed object may overlap the text. You can adjust this by choosing the Jump Object option in the Text Wrap panel (Window > Text Wrap).

CHAPTER SUMMARY

This chapter gave you what you need to know to set up a multi-page document using master pages. You learned how to:

- Create master and nested master pages
- Organize the Layers panel for multi-page documents
- Add pages to a document
- Apply a master to document pages
- Create inline, above line, and custom-aligned anchored objects

You also learned some new skills, including how to:

- Manage styles from the Control panel
- Add drop caps to text
- Add placeholder text
- Set stroke alignment

Additionally, you had the opportunity to revisit some skills you learned earlier in the book, including:

- Creating precisely sized and positioned rectangles
- Placing, repositioning, and scaling images
- Working with transparency and effects
- Relinking images in the Links panel
- Working with Object styles
- Creating rounded corners
- Working with fitting options
- Using the Zoom Out shortcut

Your understanding of InDesign wouldn't be anywhere near complete without an understanding of its graphical capabilities. The next chapter digs more deeply into some of InDesign's drawing tools, and then continues on into the rich and enchanting world of color.

● Chapter 19

SHAPES AND COLOR

While InDesign is renowned as an exceptional print layout application, its robust graphical capabilities are not nearly as well recognized. This chapter provides a taste, a tease, and an invitation to further explore the rich set of drawing tools and features InDesign has to offer. You'll make and assemble shapes, and indulge in the delicious feast of color you can whip up from InDesign's stock of color resources. This chapter is purely a recipe for play; so, let the fun begin!

Creating Custom Shapes

While an extraordinary tool for layout and rich with tools for animation and interactivity, InDesign is also a wonderful tool for creating graphical elements from scratch. It includes a pretty robust selection of drawing tools that include the shape tools, the Line tool, and the Pen, Pencil, Smooth and Erase tools. These tools, combined with the power of the Pathfinder panel, make it possible to do lots of graphical work directly in InDesign without ever needing to leave the application.

The shortcuts to help you draw with the shape tools in InDesign will be quite familiar if you're already working with Photoshop and/or Illustrator: the Alt/Option key to draw a shape (Illustrator) or selection (Photoshop) from the center, the Shift key to constrain aspect ratio, and the Spacebar to reposition an object as you draw.

The Pathfinder panel in InDesign makes it possible to combine multiple shapes to achieve a complex result that would be nearly impossible to draw manually. The InDesign Pathfinder buttons function similarly to the Shape Modes buttons in the Illustrator Pathfinder panel. With buttons to add, subtract, intersect and exclude, the sky's the limit to what you can create. The big difference between the Illustrator and InDesign tools is that Illustrator provides the option to keep the shapes you're combining editable. In InDesign, the result is a fixed object.

Exercise 19.1: Using the InDesign Drawing Tools

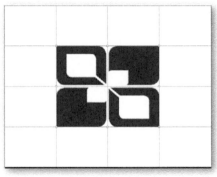

This exercise walks you through drawing a complex shape with InDesign, putting together the pieces that make it possible to create logos and graphics that will make you proud.

Before getting to the work of drawing, you'll first enlist InDesign to set up guides which will assist you in the process.

Note: The Create Guides dialog enables you to fit guides to either the page dimensions or the area defined by the page margins. Since the exercise document has no margins, either setting has the same effect.

1. Create a new document using the Web 900 x 700 preset you set up on page 34 and save it as **ex19_1.indd** in the chapter_19_exercises folder.

2. Go to Layout > Create Guides, and, when the dialog opens, check the Preview checkbox so you can see what the guides will look like on the page. Set the Number for both Rows and Columns to 4, and set both Gutter values to 0. Then click OK to close the dialog.

 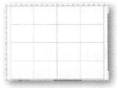

The Create Guides dialog enables you to set a custom grid of guides on your page. The image to the right shows the result of the settings in the dialog at the left.

3. Double-click the Fill swatch on the Control panel and choose any color from the Color Picker. We chose RGB red.

4. Press M on your keyboard to select the Rectangle tool, and then position the crosshair cursor at the intersection of the topmost horizontal guide and the leftmost vertical guide (X: 225 px, Y:175 px).

5. Hold down the mouse and start dragging down and to the right. Still holding the mouse, press the up arrow key once and then press the right arrow key once to create a total of four rectangles. Continue dragging to the intersection of the bottommost and rightmost guides, and then release the mouse.

6. Press V on your keyboard to switch to the Selection tool, and then press Ctrl+Shift+A/Command+Shift+A to deselect all. Select the upper right rectangle and click the yellow square at its upper right to turn on Corner Options. A yellow diamond appears at each corner of the rectangle. Hold down the Shift key, click on the diamond at the upper left corner, and drag to the right until the smart guide tooltip reads 40 px.

Click the yellow square at the upper right of a shape to turn on Corner Options. Hold down the Shift key and drag a diamond to shape an individual corner.

7. Select the lower right diamond on the same rectangle, hold down the Shift key, and drag left to set a radius of 40 px.

8. Select the lower right rectangle. If the Corner Options controls are visible on the Control panel, Alt-click/Option+click the ▯ icon. Otherwise, go to Object > Corner Options. When the dialog opens, set a corner radius of 40 px for the upper right and lower left corners, and set the corner style to rounded. Be sure to set the other corner radius values to 0.

You can set options for the individual corners of an object in the Corner Options dialog.

9. Select the upper left rectangle and round its upper right and lower left corners to a radius of 40 px.

10. Select the lower left rectangle and round its upper left and lower right corners to 40 px. Save your file.

The four rectangles after the corners have been adjusted.

11. Press Ctrl+A/Command+A to select all four rectangles, and then press Ctrl+C/Command+C to copy them. Press Alt+Shift+Command+V/ Option+Shift+Ctrl+V or Right-click/Ctrl-click and select Paste in Place from the contextual menu. With the duplicate rectangles still selected, click the arrow next to the Fill swatch on the Control panel and change the color to [Paper].

12. Deselect All, and then select the upper right and lower left white rectangles with the Selection tool. On the Control panel, check to be sure that the center point is selected in the Reference Point proxy and that the Constrain proportions for scaling link is locked for the scaling percentages. Enter 40 in the Scale X field and press Tab to uniformly scale the white rectangles and to center them on top of the colored rectangles.

13. Select the upper left rectangle, enter 60 in the Scale X field on the Control panel, and press Tab to scale the rectangle to 60% of its size. The white rectangle should be centered on the rectangle below it.

14. Select the lower right rectangle and scale it to 60% as well.

15. Click M to select the Rectangle tool and click once on the document. When the Rectangle dialog opens, enter 10 for width and 190 for height, and then click OK.

16. Switch to the Selection tool and drag the rectangle to center it vertically between the rectangles on the left and the rectangles on the right. Mouse over a corner of the rectangle, and, when the cursor changes to a double-sided arrow, drag to rotate it to the left by 50°. Alternatively, enter 50 in the Rotation Angle field on the Control panel.

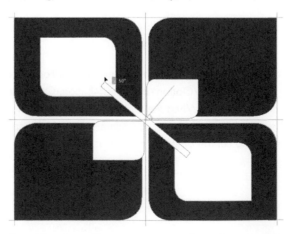

InDesign's drawing tools enable you to create and transform shapes with precision.

17. Hold down the Shift key and click on each of the four colored rectangles to select them. Open the Pathfinder panel by clicking the ▣ icon in the Panel dock, or go to Window > Object & Layout > Pathfinder.

18. Click the first icon (▣) in the Pathfinder section of the panel (Add) to join the rectangles into a compound shape. Then click on the pasteboard to deselect it.

19. Shift-click to select each of the five white rectangles (including the skinny one), and then join them using the Pathfinder Add command.

20. Select both compound paths, and click the second icon (▣) in the Pathfinder section of the panel (Subtract). The white shapes are subtracted from the colored shapes to create a new compound shape. Save the file and keep it open for the next exercise.

The moral of this lesson is that you don't have to be able to draw to create graphics with InDesign. If you can visually break objects into shapes, you can "draw." So let yourself play and see what kind of wonderful things you come up with.

The InDesign Color Palette

If you're looking for colors in InDesign, don't be fooled by the meager selection of colors in the Swatches panel. A bit misleading at first glance, the Swatches panel actually gives you access to a complete collection of swatch books with thousands of colors to choose from. While the swatch book colors are CMYK and are oriented for use in print, they can easily be converted to RGB in the process of adding them to the Swatches panel. The swatch books can be likened to the paint chips you find at a hardware store. Regardless of what you see on your screen, if you use specific color book colors in your print document, your print provider will know what colors to match. Given the wide variability in color display from one computer monitor to another, the objective color standard provided by the color books is critically important for print, to ensure predictable output. When creating documents for electronic delivery, you have greater freedom. Any color you can create on screen is fair game.

With that flexibility in mind, for interactive design, you can take full advantage of the spectrum of color available through the Color panel. The Color panel enables you to choose a color model, build color by number, or select colors from the color ramp.

InDesign's color resources don't stop with the Swatches and Color panels, though. Tucked away and out of view is the Kuler panel, with rich palettes containing enough color choices to boggle the mind. The Kuler panel (Window > Extensions > Kuler) provides access to thousands of 5-color themes shared by an online community of designers. A trip to the Kuler panel is like stepping into a kaleidoscopic time warp. The minutes pass imperceptibly as whole worlds of color unfold. In other words, give yourself some time to play. Kuler is live and interactive, and you can transfer its colors directly to your Swatches panel. The colors and themes are completely editable, so you can use them as a jumping off point for themes of your own. If you'd rather "do it yourself," its Create panel lets you do just that, with a selection of six color harmony rules to assist in developing your palettes. Of course, you too can choose to share your color themes with the Kuler community, if you're so inclined.

Note: You can transfer Kuler colors directly to the Swatches panel in all the Creative Suite 5 applications except Dreamweaver.

Exercise 19.2: Playing with Color

This exercise will familiarize you with the color resources in InDesign, and teach you how to use them. Perhaps even more important, it'll give you a chance to indulge in playing with color, just for the sheer fun of it.

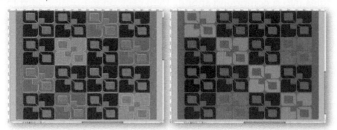

The palette of colors you can create in InDesign is virtually unlimited!

1. To get a sense of where this lesson is going, feel free to open ex19_2_end.indd from the chapter_19_exercises folder to check it out. In fact, if you want to jump straight to playing with color and don't want to mess with setting up the document, save it as ex19_2.indd and skip to step 21 of this exercise on page 323. Otherwise, if you don't have the file from the previous lesson open, go to the chapter_19_exercises folder and open **ex19_2_start.indd**. Whichever file is open, save it as ex19_2.indd.

   First, you'll set up a grid pattern with the shape you created in the previous lesson. You'll then save the page with the grid to a master page, so you can make as many pages to play with as you like. Then you'll get busy with color.

2. Switch to the Selection tool and, if necessary, unlock the Constrain proportions for width and height link in the Control panel. Select the shape on the page and change the width to 200 px and the height to 172 px in the Control panel.

3. Go to View > Grids & Guides > Delete All Guides on Spread.

4. With the shape still selected, select the upper left square of the Control panel Reference Point proxy and enter 0 for both the X and Y values. This will position the shape at the upper left corner of the page.

5. Go to Edit > Step and Repeat, and, when the dialog opens, check the Preview checkbox. Set the number of columns and rows to 4, the Vertical Offset to 177 px and the Horizontal Offset to 205 px. Check the Create as a grid checkbox to create a uniformly spaced 4 x 4 grid, and then click OK.

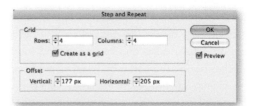

The Step and Repeat command enables you to duplicate objects with a specified offset.

6. Press Ctrl+G/Command+G to group the objects and, in the Align section of the Control panel, select Align to Page. Click the Align vertical centers and Align horizontal centers buttons to center your design, and then press Ctrl+Shift+G/Command+Shift+G to ungroup the objects.

Note: If the Alignment tools aren't visible on the Control panel, go to Window > Object & Layout > Align to open the Align panel.

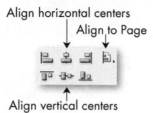

Align horizontal centers

Align to Page

Align vertical centers

The Align controls on the Control panel.

7. To create a rectangle that will serve as the background, press M to select the Rectangle tool, and click once on the page. In the Rectangle dialog, enter 900 px for Width and 700 px for Height and then press Enter/Return to close the dialog.

8. If necessary, add a fill to your rectangle, and you'll see that it covers the other shapes. Press Shift+Ctrl+[/Shift +Command+[to send the rectangle to the bottom of the object stack. Alternatively, you could Right-click/Ctrl-click and choose Arrange > Send to Back from the contextual menu. Use the Align controls to center the rectangle on the page. Save your document.

   Next, you'll start building your color palette from the color books, and then set up the color pattern for the design.

9. Click the ▦ icon in the Panel dock or go to Window > Color > Swatches. To better see all the colors you'll be adding to the Swatches panel, choose Small Swatch from the panel menu. The swatches should appear as a collection of color squares, rather than as a list of named colors.

10. Next, choose New Color Swatch from the panel menu. From the Color Mode dropdown, choose Pantone Solid Coated. When the color book swatches appear, scroll through the list to find a color you like. and double-click to select it. We chose Adobe Red: Pantone 485.

    The name of the color book you chose will appear in the Color Mode dropdown.

11. If you wish to convert the color to RGB, choose RGB from the Color Mode dropdown. Ensure that Process is selected in the Color Type dropdown, and click Add to add the color to your swatches. Choose five more colors from any combination of the color books and add them to your swatches.

    IMPORTANT! *Do not* choose randomly from the color books if you are creating CMYK documents for print. This workflow is for RGB documents *only*!

12. Click the second shape in the first row with the Selection tool. Hold the Shift key, and click every other shape as shown in the screenshot on the following page.

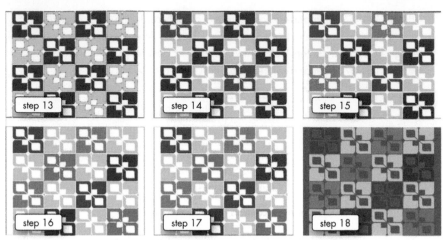

The color progression represented in steps 12-18.

13. Press Ctrl+G/Command+G to group the selected shapes, and then choose a fill color from one of the swatches you added. Feel free to try some colors we used, just to get things set up (R=192 G=196 B=204).

Note: Feel free to work with a simpler 3-color palette and skip steps 14-17.

14. Deselect All, and then select the first shape in the first row and the third shape in the third row. Group them and apply a different fill color (R=88 G=69 B=99).

15. Deselect All, and then select the third shape in the first row and the first shape in the third row. Group them and apply a third fill color (R=116 G=142 B=149).

16. Deselect All, and then select the second shape in the second row and the fourth shape in the fourth row. Group them and apply a fourth fill color (R=114 G=107 B=129).

17. Deselect All, and then select the fourth shape in the second row and the second shape in the fourth row. Group them and apply a fifth fill color (R=51 G=63 B=78).

18. Deselect All. Click just to the left or right of the shapes to select the background rectangle and then apply the sixth fill color (R=73 G=98 B=108).

    Don't get crazy about getting your colors perfect at this point. You've just begun to explore, and you'll be expanding your color selection shortly.

    Before building out your palette, you'll first save your layout to a master page so you can create multiple pages for experimentation.

Note: You need to double-click on page 1 to make it the active page in the document window, or else the pages you add will be added to the master page spread.

19. In the Pages panel, Right-click/Ctrl-click page 1, and choose Save as Master from the contextual menu. InDesign adds a new master page with a default name of B-Master, and it becomes the active page in the Pages panel.

20. Double-click on the page 1 in the Pages panel, and then select Insert Pages from the panel menu. Enter 3 in the Pages field, select B-Master from the Master dropdown, and then press Enter/Return to close the dialog. InDesign adds three color-coded pages to your document with your shape grid on them.

The Insert Pages dialog can be accessed from the Pages panel menu.

21. To unlock the master page objects so you can change the object colors, Right-click/Ctrl-click page 2 in the Pages panel and choose Override All Master Page Items (Alt+Shift+Ctrl+L/Option+Shift+Command+L). Do the same to unlock the objects on pages 3 and 4, and you'll be ready to go.

Note: When working with master pages, it's generally best to override page items on an item-by-item basis. The file for this exercise is a specialized case.

    The sheer number of colors in the color books can be a little daunting, particularly when it comes to trying to choose an entire palette. As an alternative, Kuler is a phenomenal tool for finding ready-made palettes or for providing a starting point to create a palette of your own.

22. Go to Window > Extensions > Kuler, and, if necessary, click the Browse button at the top of the panel. Eye candy, right? This is just the beginning! Click the ⬍ ⬇ buttons at the lower left of the panel to scroll through the themes. If you want to look further, click the dropdowns just above the color swatches to choose a different theme category and sorting filter. When you find a theme you like, click to highlight it, and then click the Add selected theme to swatches button (⊞) at the bottom of the panel. Add at least three themes to your swatches.

Note: To take advantage of Kuler, you need to have an internet connection.

The Kuler panel is a feast for the eyes, and an awesome design tool for selecting colors.

23. With one of your themes selected in the Kuler panel, click the Edit theme in Create panel button (✑) at the bottom of the panel.

    If you've worked with Live Color in Illustrator, the Kuler Create panel should look familiar. You can use it to modify colors in a selected theme, or you can develop a theme from the fill or stroke color of a selected object. The Selected Rule dropdown lets you choose from six color harmony rules: Analagous, Monochromatic, Triad, Complementary, Compound, and Shades. You can also customize a color combination independent of the rules.

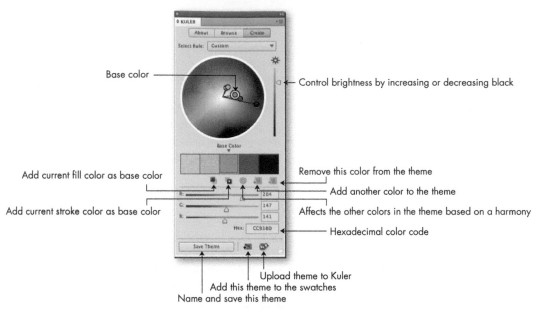

Base color
Control brightness by increasing or decreasing black

Base Color

Add current fill color as base color
Remove this color from the theme

Add current stroke color as base color
Add another color to the theme

Affects the other colors in the theme based on a harmony

R: 204
G: 147
B: 141
Hex: CC938D
Hexadecimal color code

Save Theme

Upload theme to Kuler
Add this theme to the swatches
Name and save this theme

The Kuler Create panel.

24. Select any of the markers in the color wheel and drag to see the change in color. If you come up with a theme you'd like to keep, press the Add this theme to swatches button at the bottom of the panel.

25. Select a color other than the existing base color from the swatches under the color wheel, and then click the Affects the other colors in the theme based on a harmony button. This makes your selected color the new base color.

26. Select a color harmony rule from the Select Rule dropdown to create a new color theme. Then, save it to the Swatches panel.

27. Double-click on page 2 in the Pages panel to make it the active page in the document window, and go to town! Just play for a bit and enjoy. When you've finished playing, there's even more to explore.

28. Double-click on page 3. After unlocking the master page items, press Ctrl+A/ Command+A to select everything on the page. Hold the Shift key and click the background rectangle with the Selection tool to deselect it. Press Ctrl+Shift+G/ Command+Shift+G to ungroup the shapes and then go to Window > Object & Layout > Pathfinder. Click the Add button to join all the shapes into one large compound shape.

29. With the new shape selected, go to Window > Color > Gradient or click the icon on the Panel dock. Click just below the color ramp to activate the gradient and fill the shape. Select each of the gradient markers in turn, open the Swatches panel, and Alt-click/Ctrl-click a color to assign it to the marker. Click just below the color ramp to add another color marker, and then assign a color to it as well. Choose Radial from the Type dropdown and drag the markers to shift the radius of the gradient colors. Drag the diamonds to shift the transition point between colors. When you're happy with your gradient,

Note: For each new page of shapes, be sure to unlock all the objects on the page before trying to play with the colors. Choose Override All Master Page Items from the Pages panel menu.

choose New Gradient Swatch from the Swatches panel menu. Name the gradient according to the colors you selected (RedPurpleRadial, for example) and click OK to add it to Swatches panel.

30. Select the Gradient tool (G) from the Tool panel, position the cursor in the center of the shape, and drag it to one of the corners. Experiment with dragging the gradient different lengths and from different starting points in the shape. Select Linear from the Type dropdown to see how it changes the look of the design.

31. Select the background rectangle on the page and create a gradient fill for it. If you settled on a Linear gradient for the compound shape, try a radial gradient for the rectangle. Add the gradient to the Swatches panel.

Depending on your color selection, this could create something beautiful or a visual nightmare. Just remember, for now, it's about play and discovery.

32. Select the compound shape, click the arrow to the right of the Stroke swatch on the Control panel, and choose a stroke color. Adjust the stroke weight as you see fit.

OK, we know we're pushing the boundaries of good design, or maybe we just made a plunge over the edge, but this is about the color. The point is to explore possibilities that you might not otherwise give yourself the freedom to explore. So let go of the preconceptions and have fun with it!

33. Click the *fx.* button on the Control panel and choose Basic Feather from the Effects dropdown. When the Effects dialog opens, set Feather Width to 12 px, Choke to 21% and Corners to Rounded. Check the Preview checkbox and adjust the settings to your taste. Don't click OK yet.

You can feather objects using the Effects dialog.

34. Choose Transparency from the options at the left of the panel and explore the different Blending modes. When you find a combination you like, click OK to close the dialog.

The color possibilities available in InDesign are truly unlimited, so indulge yourself by taking the time to play.

Note: Without delving too deeply into issues of color in the print world, it's important here to make the distinction between spot and process colors. After all, we don't want you to get yourself into an inadvertent pickle when sending a job to your print provider.

When a job is printed on an offset press, typically it's run through the press four times, with one plate for each of the process colors: cyan, magenta, yellow and black. Spot colors are colors that either can't be created by combining the process inks, or that are premixed for use as corporate branding colors, for example, or to eliminate the need for all four plates. Often, a job is printed with only two colors, to cut the number of required plates from four to two, and thereby cut the printing cost.

A number of the color books available from the New Color Swatch dialog are for spot colors (the Pantone Solid color books, for example) and you don't want to select them randomly since each spot color represents an additional plate that could add substantial cost to your print job.

While useful in creating RGB palettes, Mixed Ink and Mixed Ink Groups are especially relevant for print. They make it possible to create an entire palette by combining a spot color with another spot or any of the process colors. So, even with a 2-color job, you can have a broad spectrum of colors to use in your design.

You're probably starting to get the idea that the color variations available to you in InDesign are endless. And the truth is, there's still more. The Color panel lets you make precise refinements with separate color channel and tint controls that encompass RGB, CMYK, and Lab color. You can also capture color from anywhere on your page with the Eyedropper tool (I). Two other little known features are the Mixed Ink and Mixed Ink Group options, which let you develop individual colors or an entire palette from selected process and spot inks.

The next section of the exercise will familiarize you with these options.

35. Choose New Swatch from the Swatches panel menu, and then choose PANTONE solid coated from the Color Mode dropdown. If you have a particular pantone color you need to find, you can type its number in the PANTONE field. Type in "262" and click the Add button. Then, type in "3302" and click Done to close the dialog.

36. Choose New Mixed Ink Group from the Swatches panel menu. When the dialog opens, click in the square to the left of PANTONE 262 C and PANTONE 3302 C to select the spot colors for the Mixed Ink Group. For both colors, enter 10 for the Initial ink percentage, 10 for Repeat, and 5 for Increment. Note that the number of swatches to be generated is 121. Press Preview Swatches to see the palette that will be generated, and then click OK to close the dialog and add the colors to the Swatches panel.

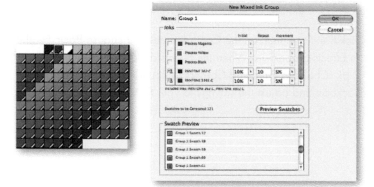

InDesign can generate custom palettes for you through the Mixed Ink Group dialog. Mixed Inks and Mixed Ink Groups can only be created using combinations of spot inks and the four process inks (CMYK).

Since the Swatches you just created were generated from spot inks, now you'll convert them to RGB.

37. Select the first spot color in the Swatches panel, hold down the Shift key, and click on the second spot color. Choose Swatch Options from the panel menu. Choose RGB from the Color Mode dropdown and Process from the Color Type dropdown. Click OK to convert the spot colors to RGB.

The mixed ink swatches are converted to CMYK when you convert the spot colors to RGB. Now you'll convert them to RGB too.

38. Select the first mixed ink color, hold down the Shift key, and select the last. Convert the Color Mode from CMYK to RGB in the Swatch Options dialog and click OK.

39. Double-click on page 4 in the Pages panel to make it the active page in the document window, and use your color group swatches to color the pattern.

    The Color panel (Window > Color > Color) displays either the stroke or fill color of the selected object. From this view of the panel, you can change the color tint by dragging the slider, clicking in the Tint Ramp, or entering a value in the Tint Percentage field. If you're coming to this panel, more often than not you'd be looking to choose colors rather than to adjust a tint. For print, you're better off sticking with color book colors, since they're calibrated to an objective standard. For interactive and web design, the Color panel gives you access to a huge spectrum of color in a conveniently compact package.

40. With one of the object groups selected, click the ⬛ icon in the Panel dock or go to Window > Color > Color. Choose RGB from the Color panel menu to bring up the RGB color panel. Select the value in the R, G, or B field and use the up and down arrows on your keyboard to change the value in the color channel incrementally.

    Alternatively, you can type a value in any of the fields, or click the color ramp to select a different color. You can also drag the individual color channel sliders. To choose a lighter or darker color, hold down the Shift key and drag one of the sliders to move all the sliders at once. Right-click/Ctrl-click the ramp for quick access to the panel menu, and to add the selected color to the Swatches panel. Alt-click/Option-click the ramp to add the selected color to the stroke if the fill is active or vice versa. Shift-click the ramp to cycle through the RGB, CMYK, and Lab Color models.

41. Play to your heart's content, and, when finished, save and close the files.

Note: Just because color is such fun, we've set up a gallery at www.Interactive-InDesign.com where you can submit your color experiments from this exercise. We ask for your name, a title for your piece (if you have one), and that you send the file in JPEG, PNG, or GIF format. From the Home page, click the Gallery link on the left.

To export a JPEG directly from InDesign, go to File > Export and choose JPEG from the Format dropdown. Browse to the location you want to save your file, name it, and click Save.

CHAPTER SUMMARY

In this chapter, you dug deeper into InDesign's graphic capabilities and had an opportunity to play with shape and color. You learned to develop a color palette using:

- The Swatches panel
- Color books
- Kuler
- The Color Panel
- Mixed Ink Groups

You also became more familiar with master pages and the Pathfinder panel, and learned how to:

- Save a page as a master page
- Override master page items
- Change the view of the Swatches panel
- Save and create themes in Kuler
- Work with blending modes
- Create gradients
- Work with the Basic Feather effect

Above all else, hopefully you had a lot of fun!

The next section ties everything together. Let it be your guide to navigating the sometimes unpredictable output process. The provided tips and tricks will help ensure that your documents perform reliably and deliver the results you intend to achieve.

Part 7

OUTPUT: PROCESSES, PITFALLS, AND PERFORMANCE

This final part of the book provides you with everything from the rudiments of choosing the best export settings for output to Interactive PDF, SWF, and Flash Professional (FLA), to a guide for navigating the perils and pitfalls, curiosities, and quirks you'll encounter in finalizing your interactive projects. Now that you understand how to use the tools to create amazing interactivity, this section is a must-read to help refine your workflow and optimize your final result.

● Chapter 20

OUTPUT

The mechanics of actual output, whether to Interactive PDF, SWF, or FLA for Flash Professional, are relatively straightforward. You just need to be aware of what the various export settings mean, as well as their implications and some of the standard conventions. This chapter walks you through all those details so the export process itself will become the easiest part of your workflow.

Introduction

Your project is finished, you've tested it throughout the development process, and now it's ready for export. This is the easy part, once you understand the options in the PDF, SWF and FLA export dialogs. This chapter shepherds you through, and provides recommendations and guidelines for the output of your projects.

All exports start by going to File > Export. The Format dropdown at the bottom of the window gives you quite a few options from which to choose, but to create interactive documents, you'll only be choosing from three: Adobe PDF (Interactive), Flash Player (SWF), and Flash CS5 Professional (FLA).

Adobe InDesign Tagged Text
Adobe PDF (Interactive)
Adobe PDF (Print)
EPS
Flash CS5 Professional (FLA)
✓ Flash Player (SWF)
InCopy Document
InDesign Markup (IDML)
JPEG
Rich Text Format
Text Only
XML

To export your file to Interactive PDF, SWF, or FLA, first go to File > Export and then choose from the Format dropdown at the bottom of the dialog.

Export to SWF

Before jumping directly into the details of SWF export, we should probably take a few minutes to explain how SWF files are displayed on the web. In order to view a SWF in a browser, it needs to be embedded in an HTML page. The HTML page and the SWF file will ultimately reside on the server where your website is hosted. When you export your interactive document to SWF, you can choose to create only the SWF, or you can have InDesign generate both the SWF as well as an HTML page to contain it. This is great, since the page InDesign generates checks to see which version of the Flash player is being used in the browser, and provides a message if the user needs to update to a newer version. It's also great because it means you don't have to figure out how to make the page yourself! While helpful that InDesign does the work for you, in some instances you may want to adjust the position of the SWF on the page, or possibly change the HTML background color. You'll want to check out the next chapter to learn how to tweak a couple lines of HTML code to get your page looking the way you want it.

Note: For information on how to get your SWF and HTML page onto your site, check in with your hosting service. They should be able to guide you through.

Since you'll be dealing with multiple files when you export your SWF for the web, you must be certain to *keep the related files together*. Along with the SWF and HTML page, separate files for each SWF, sound, video, and SWF video controller you've included in your document will be exported to a folder called "resources." This folder needs to travel with the SWF and HTML page, and the relative position of all these files in the file hierarchy needs to be maintained in order for things to play properly. This means that you must resist any temptation to add subfolders to the resource folder, or to rename any of the associated files after the fact. You can create a folder to contain the SWF, HTML page, and the resource folder, as long as you take that folder into account when linking the HTML page in your site. The only file you can safely rename without breaking your project is the HTML file itself. If you intend to use your interactive project as the home page of your site, you'll need to rename your HTML page **index.html** (all lower case). The index page needs to be placed direct to the top level folder in your site in order to be recognized by the browser as your home page. This means that you can't use the containing folder mentioned above if you want your home page to be found.

As for the export itself, you may remember, that in the second chapter we made mention of the balancing act between quality, performance, and speed that is a constant consideration when developing for the web. Speed is inversely proportional to file size: the smaller a file, the faster it downloads, the speedier the delivery. You can impact file size by adjusting the export settings for compression and resolution of the images you use in your file. The goal is to achieve the smallest possible file size, using the greatest possible compression, while maintaining acceptable quality.

When working with Flash, file size is not the only factor to influence performance; the complexity of the animation in a file can also have a dramatic impact. Some animations require more processing power than others, putting so much demand on the system to perform all the necessary calculations that the movie may not play smoothly. This is just one more reason to test your projects on multiple machines with different capabilities to ensure that you don't encounter unanticipated and unpleasant surprises. If you're having issues with the performance of your file, you may need to simplify the animations you've employed in your project. Unfortunately, this may mean changing or even eliminating some of your animation. You'll have to make the call as to whether the tradeoff is warranted.

Adobe provides a number of excellent resources for web and interactive development (and for working with print as well), at http://www.adobe.com/products/creativesuite/design/crossmedia_resources/ Click both the Web and Interactive tabs to get the specifics, and to download white papers rich with information.

When exporting your Flash file, frame rate is another consideration that can affect both performance and file size. Remember that video and animation are really a series of still frames shown in rapid sequence to create the illusion of motion over time. The number of frames per second (fps) is referred to as the frame rate (as you learned in Adobe Media Encoder on page 220. It's standard wisdom that the higher the frame rate, the smoother the appearance of the animation. This is true up to a frame rate of 30 fps. Beyond that, humans are unable to perceive any difference in smoothness of play, so frame rates beyond 30 fps achieve no more than a drain on the processor. Back in the day, 12 fps was the default Flash frame rate, but, as processors have improved, there is hot debate as to whether a frame rate of 24 fps or 30 fps is preferable. 35 mm movie cameras use a standard exposure rate of 24 frames per second, and it's arguable as to whether there is a perceptible difference in smoothness of play between 24 fps and 30 fps. Much of the animation you'll create in your projects won't require a frame rate that high. If your animations are complex enough to tax a processor, frankly, it won't matter what frame rate you set; the processor will only play the frames at the rate it can process them. Also, higher frame rates may translate to larger files, since the file requires more frames to fill each second, which may translate to more keyframes. Once again, we're back to the balance between quality and performance. A good rule of thumb when you need to optimize your project is this: use the lowest frame rate that delivers an acceptable result.

It's important to know that, despite all the steps you take to optimize your Flash export, the SWF files generated by InDesign are bloated in comparison to what you could achieve directly in Flash Professional. Sad, but true. With the CS5 version of InDesign, Adobe focused on adding all kinds of cool features, and didn't concentrate directly on file optimization. Hopefully, as the interactive capabilities of the product evolve, we'll see improvement in file optimization as well.

Now that you have a basic understanding of some of the considerations surrounding your export choices, let's get on with the business of the actual export. There are lots of controls in the SWF Export dialog, but there's no reason to get overwhelmed. It's really very simple and, most likely, you'll find a group of settings that work for you and use them pretty routinely. The rest of the settings are good to know about for the occasion when your reliable standards don't get the job done.

The Export SWF dialog has two tabs. When it first opens, it displays the General tab, and the settings here are pretty self-explanatory.

The General tab of the Export SWF dialog with recommended settings.

In the Export section of the dialog, you can choose to export a Selection (this will come in handy in the next chapter), All Pages in the document, or a Range of pages you specify. This is also where you choose whether to have InDesign generate an HTML page, so you can view your SWF in a browser. It's always a good idea to check the View SWF after Exporting checkbox, so you can see right away if there are any issues you need to address. This checkbox only appears if you choose to generate the HTML page.

For the Size section of the dialog, the Scale value of 100% will render your project with the original document dimensions. You can elect, instead, to scale the movie to fit any of the standard predefined web dimensions in the Fit To dropdown, or set a width or height of your own. InDesign will scale your document proportionally, so whatever value you enter in the Width field will dictate the value for the Height field and vice versa. You want to be careful that you don't scale your document *up* to a point where the image resolution will end up being less than 72 ppi. Scaling your document down won't pose resolution issues, but if you shrink your page by too large a percentage, the image quality may suffer, and text could become very hard to read.

| 1280 x 800 | 100% | 800 x 600 | 300 x 234 |
| (328 KB) | (307KB) | (270 KB) | (160 KB) |

You can modify the output size of your document in the export dialog. For an image-heavy document, you can see that page size has a big impact on SWF file size.

Of all the options on the General tab, perhaps the most obscure are the Background choices. The default Background setting is Paper Color. Typically, the paper color in an InDesign document is white. Be aware, though, that you can change the paper color in InDesign, just as you would change any other swatch color. Just double-click the [Paper] swatch in the Swatches panel to access the color controls, and make your changes in the Swatch Options dialog. With Paper Color selected for the Background option in the Export SWF dialog, whatever the paper color is in your document will be the background color of your exported SWF.

The Transparent option is a bit more curious. You can actually export your SWF as if it had no background, with all its content floating freely atop the HTML page that contains it. Choosing the Transparent option disables Page Transitions and the Interactive Page Curl.

Exported with paper color background.

Exported with transparent background.

The gray color in the transparent SWF on the right is the background color of the HTML page showing through the semi-transparent background graphic in the SWF.

In the Interactivity and Media section of the dialog, you'll want to be sure to select the Include All radio button. The Appearance Only radio button wipes out all the interactivity in your file, which kind of defeats the whole purpose of creating an interactive document in the first place, right? It captures the Normal state appearance of any buttons, posters from included videos, and the state of any animated elements as they appear in the layout at the time of export. The Appearance Only button is activated when the Rasterize Pages and/or Flatten Transparency options are selected on the Advanced tab of the dialog.

The Page Transitions dropdown allows you to override any Page Transitions you applied to your document, and apply the selected transition to every page instead. The From Document option exports the document with the selection of Page Transitions you applied manually in the development process.

The last checkbox enables you to add an interactive page curl. You can add this effect regardless of whether you include other page transitions. You learned all about page transitions on page 206 and the Interactive Page Curl on page 208.

Outside of the document dimension settings, all the options that impact the size of your final file reside on the Advanced tab of the Export SWF dialog.

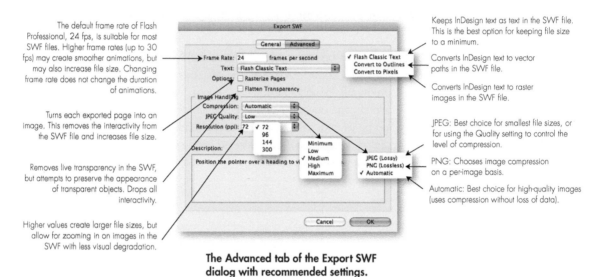

The default frame rate of Flash Professional, 24 fps, is suitable for most SWF files. Higher frame rates (up to 30 fps) may create smoother animations, but may also increase file size. Changing frame rate does not change the duration of animations.

Turns each exported page into an image. This removes the interactivity from the SWF file and increases file size.

Removes live transparency in the SWF, but attempts to preserve the appearance of transparent objects. Drops all interactivity.

Higher values create larger file sizes, but allow for zooming in on images in the SWF with less visual degradation.

Keeps InDesign text as text in the SWF file. This is the best option for keeping file size to a minimum.

Converts InDesign text to vector paths in the SWF file.

Converts InDesign text to raster images in the SWF file.

JPEG: Best choice for smallest file sizes, or for using the Quality setting to control the level of compression.

PNG: Chooses image compression on a per-image basis.

Automatic: Best choice for high-quality images (uses compression without loss of data).

The Advanced tab of the Export SWF dialog with recommended settings.

The default frame rate for export is 24 fps, which is the same as the default for Flash Professional. In many cases, changing the frame rate will have no impact at all on the size of your exported SWF. Of course, it doesn't hurt to do a little experimentation, since every little bit of optimization counts. The rule of thumb is to use the lowest possible frame rate that produces an acceptable result.

For the Text options, typically your best choice will be Flash Classic text. This is true for a couple reasons. First, this option results in the smallest file size. Second, the text is searchable and can therefore be picked up by search engines.

Rasterize Pages and Flatten Transparency both wipe out the interactivity in your file. Obviously not the choice for exporting an interactive file.

We did some testing to determine the effect of frame rate and image compression on file size to give you a real-life reference for the impact of the different options. While the results will most likely vary from one file to another (this is a fact of life in web and interactive development) for the one file we tried, we found no change at all in file size with export at frame rates of 12 fps, 24 fps, and 30 fps. You can check out the files in the chapter_20_exercises > frame_rate folder.

Note: For a file with vector shapes only, changing the JPEG compression options will have no effect at all.

As you might expect, the differences in size between image-heavy SWFs exported using the various compression options were quite dramatic. In all our testing, for an image-heavy file, we found that Automatic is the compression option that produces the best results. With Automatic selected, the biggest factor governing the size of the SWF file was the level of JPEG compression. For image-laden files, we recommend starting with Low to see if the quality of the output is acceptable. If it looks fine to you, the next step would be to try Minimum to see if the result is workable. Remember, you want the smallest possible file that passes the quality test. If the output from the Low setting isn't usable, try Medium next, going up the ladder until you achieve an acceptable product.

Compression Option	SWF File Size
PNG	3.1 MB
Auto: JPEG Maximum	1.4 MB
Auto: JPEG High	401 KB
Auto: JPEG Medium	311 KB
Auto: JPEG Low	262 KB
Auto: JPEG Minimum	201 KB

This chart provides a comparison of the different compression settings available for export to SWF. The exported file was a one-page, 900 px x 700 px, image-heavy document.

The last option on the Advanced tab is where you select the resolution of the exported images included in your file. Remember that 72ppi is the standard resolution for images published to the web, and the optimal resolution with regard to file size.

Exercise 20.1: Exploring the SWF Export Options

This exercise takes you on a tour of files demonstrating the various export options.

1. From the chapter_20_exercises folder, open **ex20_1_start.indd**. Go to File > Export and choose Flash Player (SWF) from the Format dropdown at the bottom of the dialog. Navigate to the chapter_20_exercises folder, name the file **home_low.swf** in the Save As field, and click Save.

2. In the Export SWF dialog, select the following settings on the General tab: All Pages, Generate HTML File, View SWF after Exporting, Scale: 100%, Paper Color, Include All. Since this is a single-page document, you can ignore the transitions and interactive page curl. Of course, given that the document is only one page, the links won't work.

3. Switch to the Advanced tab and use the following settings: Frame Rate: 24 fps, Flash Classic Text, Compression: Automatic, JPEG Quality: Low, Resolution: 72 ppi. Click OK to export your SWF.

4. An HTML page with your exported SWF opens in the browser. Note the quality of the images in the file, and keep the file open. Keep the browser open for the rest of the exercise.

    Not so tough, right? Like we said, the export is the easy part. Now you'll look at files exported using different compressions to see how they differ in appearance.

5. From the browser, go to File > Open File. Navigate to the chapter_20_exercises > output > compression options folder, and select **home_auto_min72.html**.

6. When the file opens in the browser, observe the quality of the images. This file is more compressed than the file you exported, and the quality of the images is definitely not passable. If you have enough screen real estate, you might want to arrange the browser windows so you can compare the files side-by-side. Close home_auto_min72.html if necessary to make room, but keep the browser and your exported file open.

7. In your browser, go again to File > Open File. Browse to the chapter_20_exercises > output > compression options folder and open **home_auto_medium72.html**.

8. Compare this file to the file you exported to decide if the difference in quality justifies the difference in file size (approx 50KB).

    As a point of reference, it used to be a standard goal that the combined file size of the contents of a web page add up to a total of no more than 35K.

9. Close the HTML files, but keep the browser open.

    Now that you've had a chance to see the effects of compression on your SWF file, you'll take a few minutes to look at the results of the different text export options.

10. From the chapter_20_exercises > output > text_options folder, open **home_raster_txt_auto72.html**, **home_outline_txt_auto72.html**, and **home_flash_txt_auto72.html** in your browser. You should now have three files open, each representative of one of the text export options. Compare the appearance of the text in the files.

    Lastly, you'll take a look at a file that was exported with a transparent background.

11. From the chapter_20_exercises > output folder, open **transparent.html**. Note the gray of the HTML page background showing through the background of the SWF.

12. Close the open HTML files, quit the browser and return to InDesign. Close the ex20_1.indd file to complete the lesson.

Export to Interactive PDF

Throughout the book, when referring to an exported PDF, the term *Interactive PDF* has been used rather than the term *PDF*. One reason for this is that, with the release of InDesign CS5, there's an export dialog dedicated expressly to Interactive PDF. Adobe's choice to separate print from interactive PDF export is mostly a good thing in that the Interactive PDF export options are fewer and much simpler to navigate than those for print. We say *mostly* a good thing because, with the settings fixed as they are, if you're working with documents that use multi-page spreads, you don't have the option to export the pages of those spreads as individual, sequential pages. When exporting to PDF for print, you have one very special checkbox option (Spreads) that isn't available from the Interactive PDF Export dialog. The Spreads checkbox in PDF print export allows you the choice of whether a spread exports as individual pages or maintains its integrity as a spread. For Interactive PDF, the caution is this: if you have spreads you want to export as individual pages, be sure to change the document and master page definitions to single rather than facing pages. (See page 290 to learn how.) Go to File > Export and choose Adobe PDF (Interactive) from the Format dropdown at the bottom of the dialog to access the Export to Interactive PDF dialog.

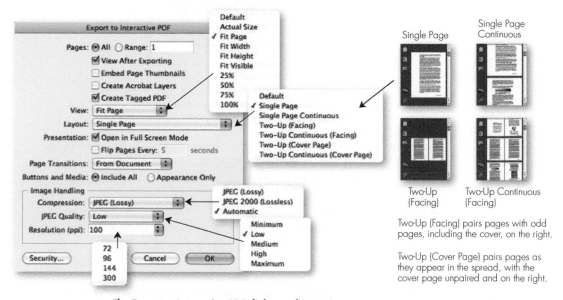

The Export to Interactive PDF dialog and its options.

The choices you'll make in the top half of the dialog have mostly to do with the display of the document rather than with optimization. You can choose to export your entire document, or a range of pages. It's always a good idea to check the View After Exporting checkbox so you can verify that your document performs as expected. Page thumbnails add to file size, so, if file optimization is a priority, you won't want to include them in your file. If you check the Create Acrobat Layers checkbox, the layers in your InDesign document will carry over to your PDF, and you can add Show/Hide actions in Acrobat Professional that will turn the layer visibility on and off. A number of the interactive capabilities in InDesign actually existed first in Acrobat, with media support and buttons, as well as tools to create interactive forms. You can in fact, extend a PDF exported from InDesign, using any of the interactive tools in Acrobat. But that's for another book.

Continuing with the export dialog, you'll want to check the Create Tagged PDF checkbox. Tagging your PDF provides it with additional structure, which makes it accessible to screen readers and, therefore, compliant with the Americans with Disabilities Act (section 508). The additional structure provided by tagging also helps to resolve a number of quirky typographical issues that can arise in the conversion process.

The export dialog provides a host of options for page view and layout. For an Interactive PDF, it's a safe bet that you'll want your entire page to fit in the document window, so, for View, choose Fit Page. For Layout, Single Page will most likely be your best option, since it shows one page (or one spread) at a time. You may choose to check the Open in Full Screen Mode checkbox, but be forewarned: before a document set to Full Screen Mode opens, it first puts up an alert to warn of potential danger. It might be a little scary to someone opening your document who isn't familiar with the drill.

Before a PDF set to Full Screen Mode opens, Acrobat and Reader display the above alert.

A really cool feature is that you can set your document pages to flip automatically every couple seconds. Just check the Flip Pages Every checkbox, and enter a number in the Seconds field. Perfect for a self-running presentation: just set it an forget it.

The page transition options are the same as for SWF export. You can use the transitions you set in the document, or choose one transition to apply to every page. For the Buttons and Media option, you'll want to Include All or you'll lose all the interactivity you set up in your document.

When exporting to Interactive PDF, just as with SWF, file size is an important consideration, particularly if you intend to deliver your document via the web. The principles governing your compression choices are the same, and the controls in the Export to Interactive PDF dialog are similar to those for exporting to SWF. For Compression, you can choose Automatic, JPEG (Lossy), or JPEG 2000 (Lossless). The JPEG quality settings are the same as in the SWF export dialog.

The issue of resolution in optimizing an Interactive PDF is not as clear cut as it is with SWFs. While SWFs exported from InDesign don't zoom in size in a browser window, zooming in a PDF enlarges the images on the page. Zooming beyond the limits of the image resolution (100% magnification for a file with images at 72ppi) results in degradation of image quality and ultimately pixelization. Therefore, a resolution higher than 72 ppi is required to enable zooming above 100% while maintaining image quality. As expected, the increase in resolution comes at the price of a larger file. Once again, you're confronted with the tradeoff between file size and quality. You need to weigh how much you want your audience to be able to zoom in against the time the larger file will take to download. If you want people to be able to zoom, a good rule of thumb is to use a resolution anywhere from 100 ppi to 150 ppi. As an alternative to the preset resolution settings, you can type your preferred value in the Resolution field.

We exported the same test document to Interactive PDF that we used for the SWF export, and applied the different image handling options to provide a baseline comparison of file size. You can see the results in the table below. The blue highlighted rows indicate files that were exported with automatic compression, low JPEG quality, and different resolutions. The other files were all exported at 72 ppi.

Compression Option	Resolution	PDF File Size
JPEG 2000	72	930 KB
Automatic Maximum	72	930 KB
Automatic Low	300	889 KB
JPEG Maximum	72	651 KB
Automatic Low	144	623 KB
Automatic High	72	586 KB
JPEG High	72	578 KB
Automatic Low	96	573KB
Automatic Medium	72	569 KB
Automatic Low	72	553 KB
JPEG Medium	72	553 KB
Automatic Minimum	72	537 KB
JPEG Low	72	537 KB
JPEG Minimum	72	520 KB

Comparison of file size resulting from export of a one-page, image-heavy file with different compression settings.

Exercise 20.2: Exporting to Interactive PDF

In this exercise, you'll set print preferences for buttons, export an Interactive PDF, and compare several files exported using different compression options.

1. Go to the chapter_20_exercises folder and open **ex_20_2_start.indd.** Save it as ex_20_2.indd.

2. Go to File > Export, and choose Adobe PDF (Interactive) from the Format dropdown at the bottom of the Export dialog. Browse to the chapter_20_exercises folder and save the file as **home_low_100.pdf.**

3. In the Export to Interactive PDF dialog, choose the following settings: Pages: All, View After Exporting, Create Tagged PDF, View: Fit Page,

Use these settings for your export.

Layout: Single Page, Open in Full Screen Mode, Flip Pages Every 3 Seconds, Page Transitions: Fade, Buttons and Media: Include All, Compression: Automatic, JPEG Quality: Low, Resolution: 100. Uncheck Page Thumbnails and Create Acrobat Layers.

4. Click the Security button at the bottom of the dialog. Check Require a password to open the document, and enter "1234" in the Document Open Password field. Check Use a password to restrict printing, editing and other tasks and enter "5678" in the Permissions Password field. Choose None from both the Printing Allowed and Changes Allowed dropdowns, and deselect Enable copying of text, images and other content. Leave the other two check boxes checked and click OK to export your PDF.

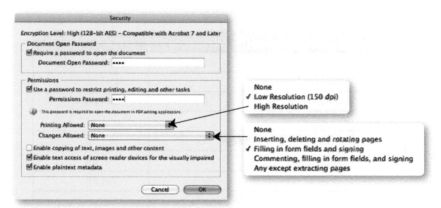

The Security dialog enables you to set passwords for opening and making changes to the document. If you apply both a Document Open Password and a Permissions password, the Permissions password can also be used to open the document. The Document Open Password, however, can only be used to open the document.

5. Enter "1234" in the first Password dialog and click OK. Then enter "5678" in the second Password dialog and click OK. Click OK in the Export Interactive PDF dialog to generate your PDF.

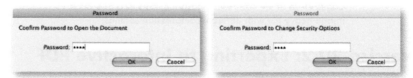

Before InDesign exports the document, it asks you to confirm the security passwords.

6. Before Acrobat Professional or Adobe Reader opens, you will be prompted to enter a password to open the document. Enter "5678," the Permissions password for the document, which also acts as a master password, and then click OK.

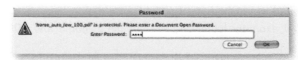

You can use the Permissions password to open the document and to change the document Security settings.

7. The Full Screen alert pops up to scare you. Check the Remember my choice for this document checkbox, and click Yes to open the document.

8. The document opens in Full Screen Mode, and the pages should change with a Fade transition every three seconds until the end of the presentation is reached. Click the links in the sidebar nav to see that they are functioning properly, and then press Esc, or Ctrl+L/Command+L on your keyboard to exit Full Screen Mode.

9. Press Ctrl+/Command+ to zoom in as many times as necessary to reach a magnification of at least 150%. You should see the magnification percentage displayed in the Select and Zoom toolbar, located below the Tasks toolbar at the top of your screen. Alternatively, you can select the Zoom tool on the toolbar and drag a marquee around an area you'd like to zoom in on. You can also press the + button on the toolbar, manually enter a zoom value in the magnification percentage field, or click the tiny black arrow to its left to choose a predefined percentage. The images should still be crisp and clear at 150% magnification. Close the file.

The Select and Zoom toolbar in Acrobat 9 Professional.

10. If you'd like to compare the results of the different compression options for yourself, go to the chapter_20_exercises > output > pdf_output folder and open **home_jpg_min_72.pdf**, **home_jpg_med_72.pdf** and **home_jpg_max_72.pdf**.

11. Go to Window > Tile > Vertically to arrange all three documents side-by-side. Select 200% from the preset magnifications for each window, and then select the Hand tool ( ) in the first window. Click and drag the page to position the white flower in the window. Do the same in the other two windows to compare the quality of the images.

Comparison of image quality in PDFs exported to JPG: Low, JPEG: Medium and JPEG: Maximum.

12. Change the magnification for each document to 100% to see how the images appear at their natural size.

Even at the same resolution, you can see the dramatic difference in image quality.

13. Close all three documents. Navigate to the chapter_20_exercises > output > pdf_output folder. Hold down the Ctrl/Command key and click to select **home_auto_low_72.pdf, home_auto_low_96.pdf, home_auto_low_144.pdf,** and **home_auto_low_300.pdf**. Go to Window > Tile > Vertically to arrange the documents and compare the image quality at different magnification percentages. When you're finished exploring, close all the files, quit Acrobat or Reader and return to InDesign. Close the ex_20_2.indd file to complete the lesson.

Export to Flash Professional (FLA)

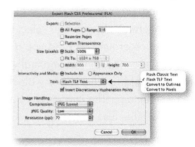

The Export Flash CS5 Professional (FLA) dialog.

Overall, the Export Flash CS5 Professional (FLA) dialog should feel familiar, with similar page selection, compression, and raster and transparency options to what you've seen in the Export to SWF and Export to Interactive PDF dialogs. The primary difference, and certainly one worthy of mention, is the Flash TLF Text option (Text Layout Framework).

Flash TLF Text allows you to take advantage of the robust new Text Layout Framework capabilities in Flash Professional CS5. Threaded text frames from InDesign are rendered intact with margins, leading, and more, transferred faithfully to your FLA file, and remain fully editable in Flash Professional. Not every InDesign text feature carries over—drop caps and text wrap, for example—but a rich set of text formatting options do. The other text export options are Flash Classic Text, which creates searchable text and compact export, Convert to Outlines, and Convert to Pixels.

When you export your document to FLA, each spread from your InDesign file is converted to a separate movieClip in its own frame on the Flash timeline. The spread-to-movieClip scenario makes it easy to move each spread's movieClip to its own layer in the timeline, and reposition it as required for sequencing or animation.

Note: To complete this exercise, you'll need to have Flash CS5 Professional installed on your system.

If you included video or audio files in your InDesign document, the poster you selected for the video appears in the FLA as a static image. Any media exported with your document from InDesign is captured in a Resources folder named after the file so you can easily restore them to your Flash file. (example: ex20_3_Resources). Buttons you create in InDesign keep their states and appearance but any actions you add are lost when exporting to FLA.

Exercise 20.3: Exploring Export to Flash Professional (FLA)

You'll export an InDesign file to FLA, and compare two FLA files to see the results of different InDesign layouts.

1. Open **ex20_3_start.indd** from the chapter_20_exercises folder and save it as ex20_3.indd. If necessary, open the Pages panel (Window > Pages), and make note that the file has six pages. Double-click on A-Master and, with the Selection tool, click the words on the sidebar nav to see that they are each individual text fields. Note that the page header, footer, Sidebar, and main content areas all have transparency applied to create the dimensional effect.

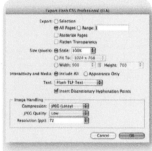

Use these settings for your export.

2. Go to File > Export and choose Flash CS5 Professional (FLA) from the Format dropdown at the bottom of the dialog. Navigate to the chapter_20_exercises > fla folder and Save the file as **ex20_3.fla**.

3. In the Export Flash CS5 Professional dialog, enter the following settings: Export: All Pages, Scale: 100%, Interactivity and Media: Include All, Text: Flash TLF Text, Insert Discretionary Hyphenation Points, Compression: JPEG (Lossy), JPEG Quality: Low, Resolution (ppi): 72. Then click OK to export your FLA.

4. Open Flash CS5 Professional and go to File > Open. Browse to the chapter_20_exercises > fla folder and open **ex20_3.fla**.

5. When Flash CS5 Professional opens, check to be sure that the Essentials workspace is selected. The Workspace Switcher is located at the upper right of the application window, just as it is in InDesign.

6. Select the Library tab (it's shared with the Properties tab) at the top of the Panel Dock, at the right of your screen. Scroll through the library to see the huge number of objects that have been created in the conversion of your InDesign file to Flash. Scroll back to the top of the Library and click on the item at the top of the list. Use the down arrow on your keyboard to display each of the images one-by-one.

    As you click through, you'll notice that any objects that were on your master page in InDesign are repeated for each spread that was in the document. You'll also notice that every instance of every InDesign effect applied to the interface objects is converted to multiple images in the FLA.

    There are two *really* important lessons to learn from this:

    1) It's best not to use master pages when designing for export to FLA. If there are objects that should appear on each spread, put them in their own layer in your InDesign document and remove any master page objects.

---

2) It's best not to use transparency when designing for export to FLA. If transparency is a critical part of your design, wait until the file is in Flash to add it.

3. Take a look at the Timeline (at the bottom of the screen), and note that there are six keyframes (the black dots in the Timeline), one for each of the document spreads. Click and drag the pink rectangular Playhead (just above the keyframes on the Timeline) back and forth between the frames to see each of your InDesign spreads. Drag the playhead to frame 4 on the timeline where you see that the Two-Toed Sloth text needs to be adjusted.

4. Click the Properties tab at the upper right of the application window. If necessary, switch to the Selection tool ( ) from the Tool panel at the far right of the interface. Double-click on the overset "2-Toed Sloth" text to go into Editing Mode, and then click once again in the text frame to select it. You'll know you're in Editing Mode if the breadcrumb editing path at the upper left of the document window says Scene 1 Spread_4.

5. Mouse over the lower right edge of the text frame. When the cursor changes to a double-sided diagonal arrow, hold down the mouse and drag down and to the right until the right edge of the text box text reaches the "i" in lives, and the bottom is close to the baseline of the bottom line of text. When you release the mouse, the overset plus sign disappears, and the complete text is properly displayed. If you have trouble dragging the corner, select the text frame, Right-click/Ctrl-click on it, and choose Arrange > Bring to Front from the contextual menu.

While Flash TLF text frames work similarly to text frames in InDesign, the translation is not always exact.

6. Click the blue arrow to the left of the breadcrumb editing path to exit Editing Mode and return to the main timeline. The editing path now reads "Scene 1."

7. Go to Control > Test Movie > in Flash Professional. The following alert will pop up to warn you that you need to make a change to the file to enable it to stream. Click OK to dismiss the alert and play your movie.

Note: The alert warns you that with the settings as they are, the entire SWF will have to download before the movie will play. If you choose Flash Classic Text rather than TLF text when you export from InDesign, you will avoid the alert.

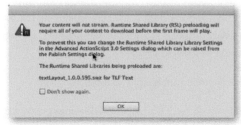

When you export from InDesign to Flash Professional with the TLF Text export option selected, Flash will display an alert to let you know that adjustments need to be made in order for the movie to stream.

8. The movie opens and plays. You can see that, without adding ActionScript to control it, it revolves continually through the frames. Close the movie and return to Flash Pro.

   To make the movie workable, it's necessary to add ActionScript (which is outside the scope of this book). If you'd like to see what the movie could look like with ActionScript, buttons that work, and some of the extraneous images removed, check out **ex20_3_end.fla** in the chapter_20_exercises > fla folder.

   Now, you'll open a file that had no transparency but had video and audio added to it before it was exported from InDesign.

9. Still in Flash Pro, go to File > Open and browse to the chapter_20_exercises > fla folder. Ensure that the All Readable Documents is selected in the Enable dropdown at the bottom of the dialog.

   Before you open the FLA file, you'll take a moment to see what's in the Resources folder that was exported in the conversion from InDesign to Flash Pro.

10. Double-click on the **ex20_3_video_Resources** folder to see the video, SWF and audio files inside. Back out of the Resources folder and open **ex20_3_video.fla**. Check out the Library to see how few objects there are compared to the ex20_3.fla file that you opened earlier.

    Admittedly, this file was created from only one spread, compared to six spreads in the previous file. But with no transparency, the image bloat seen in the other file is gone. If this had been a multi-page document with its top nav on a master page, Flash would have duplicated the nav buttons on each spread. To optimize the file, the duplicate buttons would need to be removed.

11. Close all the FLA files, quit Flash Pro, and return to InDesign. Close ex20_3.indd to complete the lesson.

Packaging Your Document

When you've completed your document, whether it be for print or interactive, it's always a good idea to package it, for archival purposes if nothing else. Packaging a document creates a folder containing a copy of the InDesign document, with all its assets collected in a Links folder, all fonts in a Document fonts folder, and a text file called Instructions.txt. The text file can be used for special instructions and contact information. For print providers who don't use a PDF workflow, you'd send a packaged file to them with everything they might need to print your job. For any type of project, packaging and burning a copy to CD, or saving externally in some other way, is important to keep the project and its component pieces safe and in one place. Should your computer crash or some other type of catastrophe occur, your packaged file has everything necessary, short of the program itself, to reconstruct your project. The project package includes all your media files as well.

Packaging a file is easy, particularly if you stay on top of any Preflight errors as they arise. (To learn all about using the Live Preflight feature, check out Customizing the Preflight Panel for Interactivity on page 37.) Just go to File > Package, and the Summary window of the Package dialog will pop up to tell you of any potential problems in your document.

Note: If you were sending your document to print, you'd want to check the Colors and Inks window of the Package dialog to verify that your document didn't contain unintended spot colors.

The Summary window always flags RGB images. For interactive projects, this is irrelevant. You can just ignore the warning. If the project is destined for print, check with your Print provider. 40 - 60% of print shops in North America no longer see RGB content as a problem for plate making or high-end printing.

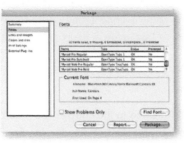

The Package dialog is one more place, in addition to the Links panel (page 39) and the Preflight panel, where you can verify that your files meet your minimum resolution and color space requirements. You can also check for missing fonts, spot colors, print settings, and plug-ins. Most importantly, you can use the Packaging process to create an archival version of your document.

Exercise 20.4: Packaging Your Document

1. Open **interactive_indesign_end.indd** from the chapter_20_exercises folder. Go to File > Package.

2. Review the summary to note that all but one of the document images are RGB.

3. Click the word "Fonts" at the left of the dialog, and then scroll through the list of fonts on the right.

   To change a font in the document, click the Find Font button at the lower right of the dialog. (For more on using the Find Font dialog, check out page 69.)

Note: Effective resolution is the resolution after an image has been scaled.

4. Click Links and Images at the left of the dialog, and scroll through the links. Click any linked image to see that the bottom of the dialog displays both the actual and effective image resolution. If you see two resolution values, rather than one, under either of the resolution headings, it means your image has been non-proportionally scaled.

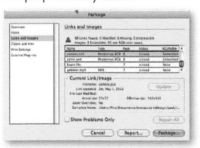

Every item linked to or embedded in your document is listed in the Links and Images window of the Package dialog.

5. Click Package. If you've not saved the final version of your file, an alert will pop up to inform you that the document must be saved before packaging. Click Save.

6. The Printing Instructions dialog pops up next. This is where you can add any instructions and contact information that would be helpful, either for your print provider in completing the job, or as project information for archiving. For the exercise, just click Continue.

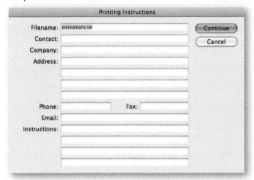

The Printing Instructions dialog enables you to provide relevant information about the job to your print provider, or store relevant information for archiving.

Note: Font Licensing: Legally, as with most software, you only have the right to use fonts for which you have the proper licensing. It is illegal to copy and distribute them outside the provision of your licensing agreement. Check the terms of your agreement with your font vendor to find out the particulars. Licensing for Adobe fonts typically allows for installation of purchased fonts on up to five computers. When you purchase InDesign or any of the Adobe Suite products, you also purchase the rights for all fonts installed with the applications.

7. To save the folder, navigate to the chapter_20_exercises folder. Replace the space in the folder name with an underscore to minimize potential problems with delivery of the file. For print, many print shops will have you send your files via FTP. A space in the folder name could result in the file not showing up on the FTP server. Dismiss the Font Licensing Restrictions alert when it pops up.

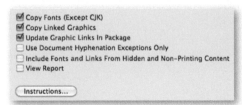

It's always a good idea to check the Copy Fonts checkbox. This will include a copy of the document fonts in the package. There are multiple versions of many fonts, with subtle differences in letter spacing and alignment. These differences could result in unanticipated reflow of text and other issues.

Note: If you don't check View Report in the export dialog, InDesign doesn't give you any notification that the file has been successfully packaged. It just does the job.

8. In Windows Explorer or Finder, navigate to the chapter_20_exercises folder. Locate and double-click on interactive_indesign_endFolder to open it. Double-click the Links folder to see that it contains all the links from the file, including the media files.

9. Jump out of the Links folder and double-click the Document fonts folder to see that all the fonts from the file have been collected and saved.

10. Return to InDesign and close interactive_indesign_end.indd to complete the exercise.

Note: If all the links in your document are broken (if you moved the folder containing your linked images before packaging, for example), and you package the document anyway, InDesign won't create a Links folder.

CHAPTER SUMMARY

This chapter took you from your finished InDesign document to a finished product. You learned how to output to Interactive PDF, SWF, and FLA. In the process, you got an understanding of a variety of compression options, factors that affect file size, and the tradeoff between file size and compression that is a constant consideration in development for web and interactive.

Additionally, you learned how to best prepare a document for FLA export and some of the steps to take for best results, including:

- Putting any elements that belong on every spread on a layer of their own, and avoiding the use of master page items.

- Avoiding use of transparency and effects in the InDesign document. (You can add effects once the document is in Flash Pro.)

Last, but not least, you learned how to package a document, useful for delivery to your print provider, but especially important for archival purposes.

Now that you have the mechanics of export under your belt, the next chapter fills you in on how best to develop your files to get the results you expect. It's chock full of important workarounds and tips to navigate some just plain weird things you may encounter. It's an essential guide to help you get around the stumbling blocks without having to stumble (as much).

● Chapter 21

PREPARING FOR OUTPUT

This chapter is one of the most important in the book, providing tips and workarounds for known issues, and helping you to avoid problems before they arise. While you've been learning how to push the boundaries of InDesign's interactive features, this chapter will spell out some of its limitations and help you work with them to your best advantage.

Introduction

While it would be ideal to be able to create one interactive document that would function equally well for print, SWF, Interactive PDF, and FLA, the fact is, they are different animals, with different strengths and limitations. While it is indeed possible to incorporate workarounds in your file that accommodate assorted output requirements, you may find it more efficient to create separate versions of the file, specific to your output destination. Whichever approach you choose, knowing the quirks you may encounter can inform your design process and maximize the cross-functionality you can achieve throughout development.

Adding Animation to an Interactive PDF

You should already be aware that animation you create in the InDesign Animation panel doesn't carry over when your document is exported to Interactive PDF. This is not as much of a crisis as it might first appear, since export of your InDesign files to Interactive PDF supports export of placed SWFs files. How do you get the SWF files? What's lovely is that you can export the animation you create in InDesign directly to SWF, and then place that SWF back in InDesign for export to Interactive PDF. Pretty cool trick, yes?

Exercise 21.1: Adding Animation to an Interactive PDF

Depending on the complexity of the animation on the page, you can export an entire spread to SWF and then place it back in InDesign, or can export and place only the animated elements. In this exercise, you'll export a multi-state object and the buttons that control it to SWF, place it back in the spread, and then export to Interactive PDF.

1. Navigate to the chapter_21_exercises folder, open **ex21_1_start.indd,** and save it as ex21_1.indd.

2. The multi-state object on the page is grouped with the buttons that control it. With the Selection tool, click once on the red flower to select the group.

3. Go to File > Export and choose Flash Player (SWF) from the Format dropdown at the bottom of the Export dialog.

4. Save the file as **multistate.swf** in the chapter_21_exercises folder.

5. In the Export section at the very top of the SWF Export dialog, confirm that the Selection radio button is active and the Generate HTML File and View SWF after Exporting checkboxes are unchecked. Leave the other default settings on the General tab, and switch to the Advanced tab. Set Compression to Automatic and JPEG Quality to Low. Leave Frame Rate set to 24 fps, set Resolution to 72, and leave the other checkboxes unchecked. Leave the Flash Classic Text selected and press OK to export.

6. When the export is complete, If necessary, open the Layers panel (Window > Layers), click once on the flora page 2 layer to highlight it, and click the

Create New Layer button () at the bottom of the panel. Double-click the layer name and rename the layer "SWF" in the Layer Options dialog.

7. Press Ctrl+D/Command+D (File > Place), browse to the chapter_21_exercises folder, and select **multistate.swf**.

8. With the SWF layer highlighted in the Layers panel, to place the SWF, click once with the loaded cursor on the upper left corner of the multi-state object group (the red flower group).

Position the Place cursor at the upper left of the multi-state object group and click once to place the SWF.

The placed SWF is indicated by a box filled with diagonal lines and an icon in the upper left.

If a placed SWF is not set to play on page load, and you haven't set a poster to customize its display, the SWF icon in the upper left corner will display in the PDF. Not pretty. Time for a trip to the Media panel to set things up to look the way you want them to.

9. With the SWF still selected, go to Window > Interactive > Media or click the ▤ button in the Panel dock to open the Media panel. Check the Play on Page Load checkbox and, from the Poster dropdown, choose From Current Frame.

Set the SWF to Play on Page Load and choose From Current Frame for the poster.

10. In the Layers panel, click the eyeball icon to the left of the flora page 2 layer to hide it.

Since PDFs don't understand multi-state objects, they capture the first state of a multi-state object as a poster. If you don't hide the layer, the poster will show during the initial portion of the SWF animation, when the flower grows to fill the screen.

11. Go to File > Export and choose Adobe PDF (Interactive) from the Format dropdown at the bottom of the Export Interactive PDF dialog. Browse to the chapter_21_exercises folder and save the file as **ex21_1.pdf**.

12. When the Export to Interactive PDF dialog opens, be sure the View After Exporting checkbox is checked. Choose Actual Size from the View dropdown and uncheck Open in Full Screen Mode. Set Compression to Automatic, JPEG Quality to Low, and Resolution (ppi) to 72. Click OK to export the file.

The export settings to test your PDF with the placed SWF.

13. When the ex21_1.pdf file opens in Acrobat 9 or Adobe Reader 9, observe the initial animation.

When Acrobat opens, you may need to scale the document window in order to see the entire page. The Actual Size setting you used in export ensures that the PDF page, and therefore the SWF it contains, are displayed at full size. Unfortunately, when Acrobat scales a document to fit in view, any SWF or video files on the document pages retain their original dimensions. The result can be inadvertent cropping of your media content. This is one more reason why it's important to determine your project dimensions with your target audience in mind.

You'll see this cropping behavior in the next step of the exercise.

14. Click the tiny black arrow to the right of the Magnification Percentage field at the top of the screen, and choose 50% from the dropdown. The navigation buttons for the flower slide show disappear. Then choose 100% from the dropdown, and the navigation buttons reappear. (If necessary, adjust the position of the page on the screen to see the navigation buttons.)

15. Click the Next button and then the Previous button to see that they function as intended.

16. Close the file, but leave Acrobat open and return to InDesign. Close ex21_1.indd to complete the exercise.

PDF Peculiarities

Show/Hide actions are a mainstay of interactivity, and you've had a lot of experience with them throughout the exercises in the book. One of the strange behaviors you may encounter when exporting your interactive document to PDF is with elements that should be hidden appearing above other elements. You'll check out a file that exemplifies this behavior so you can see what we mean.

It's possible that this anomaly occurs due to a problem in processing objects with transformations, such as rotation and scaling, in combination with transparency, when converting to PDF. The folks at Adobe were as perplexed by the behavior as we were. In any case, we figured out a workaround, which is what you'll explore in the next exercise.

Exercise 21.2: PDF Show/Hide Anomalies

1. Switch to Acrobat 9 Professional or Adobe Reader 9 and open **ex21_2_start.pdf** from the chapter_21_exercises folder. Click the thumbnail image buttons on the arc to see what happens.

   You may recognize this file from Exercise 9.4 on page 163. In that exercise, you exported to Flash and everything worked fine. But, as you click through the buttons in the PDF, it quickly becomes clear that there's big trouble in PDF paradise.

2. Close the file, leave Acrobat or Reader open, and return to InDesign.

3. Check to be sure that the Interactive Modified workspace you set up in Chapter 3 (page 27) is active, and that the Pages, Buttons, and Layers panels are stacked and open for easy access.

4. If necessary, open the Layers panel (Window > Layers) and twirl down the arrow on the fauna page layer to show its object sublayers. Then, twirl down the arrow on the fauna images layer to see each of the image button sublayers.

5. Click in the selection column of the faunaImg2 object layer to select the first button containing a large image. If necessary, open the Buttons panel to see the button details. Scroll through the Visibility list in the Buttons panel to see that, when you click on the button, it is set to hide only itself. The thumbnail buttons are ignored.

6. Click the eyeball to the left of the fauna images layer to hide it, and click the first thumbnail image button on the document to select it. Scroll through the Visibility section of the Buttons panel. You'll see that the button hides all the large images, with the exception of the image that matches its thumbnail.

   The strange visibility behavior can be resolved by hiding everything that shouldn't show, including the thumbnails, rather than leaving the thumbnail buttons set to "ignore." Then, when a large image button is clicked, it needs to be hidden and all the thumbnail buttons need to be made to show.

The stacked Pages, Buttons, and Layers panels.

Note: Since the document has only one page, you won't really need to use the Pages panel. To make more room, you can mouse over the divider between the Pages and Buttons panels, and drag up to make the Pages panel shorter. For even more room, you can collapse the Pages panel by double-clicking on the word "Pages."

7. With the first thumbnail still selected, in the Visibility section of the Buttons panel, click to highlight faunaBtn9 (you may have to scroll through the list to find it). Hold down the Shift key and click faunaBtn2 to select it, and all the buttons in between. Click the Hide button just below the list to hide all the thumbnails.

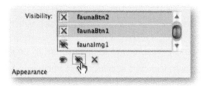

In the Buttons panel, select all the thumbnail buttons and hide them.

8. Select the next thumbnail image button on the document, and with faunaBtn1-faunaBtn8 still selected in the Visibility section of the Buttons panel, click the Hide button.

9. Repeat for each button thumbnail and then show the fauna images layer in the Layers panel. If necessary, expand the fauna images layer and click in the Selection column to select faunaImg2.

10. In the Visibility section of the Buttons panel, note that all the thumbnail buttons are still selected. Click the Show button.

11. Repeat for each of the remaining faunaImg layers and then save the document in the chapter_21_exercises folder.

12. Go to File > Export and choose Adobe PDF (Interactive) from the Format dropdown at the bottom of the Export dialog. Verify that Compression is set to Automatic, JPEG Quality to Low, and Resolution to 72 (ppi). The View After Export checkbox should still be checked. Click OK to export the file.

13. An alert will pop up to warn you of a potential issue. Click OK to dismiss it and complete the export.

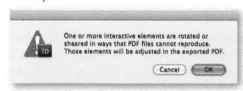

Click OK to dismiss the alert and complete the export.

14. Test your buttons in the PDF to see that you've resolved the issue.

The moral of the story is, for PDF export, if you want to take advantage of Show/Hide actions, hide everything in the document that shouldn't be seen, and don't "Ignore" anything that's part of the interactivity of the document.

Note: Although not recommended, you do have an option to include legacy media in your InDesign file for export to PDF (not for SWF or FLA). Legacy media that's supported includes MOV, AVI, MPG video, and AIFF and WAV audio files. Using legacy media requires that QuickTime be installed on the system, which could be problematic for Windows users. (If iTunes is installed, Quicktime is installed with it.) Since Flash runtime is built into Acrobat 9 and Reader 9, Flash Media, rather than legacy media, is the preferred, and more universal, option.

Buttons and PDF File Size

Since file size is a concern for Interactive PDFs, it's important to know that buttons on master pages are repeated on every spread of an exported PDF as individual objects, as they are when exported to FLA. To decrease file size and eliminate unnecessary overhead in your file, you can take advantage of the interactive form capabilities in Acrobat Professional to generate multiple instances of the same button.

As you would when preparing a file for export to FLA, remove all buttons from the master page in your InDesign document, and position them instead on the first page of your document. When the export to Interactive PDF is complete, you can then replace the buttons by duplicating them in Acrobat Professional. As mentioned earlier, the form features in Acrobat (which include buttons) have been supported for many versions. Keep in mind, though, that if you've included Flash media in an Interactive PDF exported from InDesign, you must use Acrobat or Adobe Reader 9 or later for the media to play.

Exercise 21.3: Optimizing Buttons in an Exported PDF

In this lesson, you'll export a properly prepared file to Interactive PDF and then duplicate its buttons in Acrobat Professional.

Note: Acrobat Professional is required to complete this exercise.

1. Open **ex21_3_start.indd** from the chapter_21_exercises folder. Click through the pages using the Next Page button at the bottom left of the document window to see that the side nav buttons appear on only the first page. If necessary, open the Buttons panel and click each of the buttons on page 1 to see that they have a Go To Destination action applied with Zoom set to Actual Size.

2. Go to File > Export (Ctrl+E/Command+E) and choose Interactive PDF from the Format dropdown at the bottom of the dialog. Name the file **ex21_3.pdf** and save it in the chapter_21_exercises folder.

3. In the Export Interactive PDF dialog, be sure that View File After Export is selected, set View to Actual Size, and choose your other export settings. Click OK to export the file.

4. If Reader is set as your default PDF viewer, you'll need to manually open Acrobat Professional and then open **ex21_3.pdf**. With the file open in Acrobat Pro, use the Next and Previous buttons just above the document window to click through the document pages, and then return to page 1. Note that page 1 is the only page in the document with buttons.

Note: Acrobat doesn't recognize an InDesign button with only one state as a button. It interprets it as a hyperlink. If you want Acrobat to be able to duplicate buttons for you, be sure to add a Rollover state to your text buttons even, if you make no change.

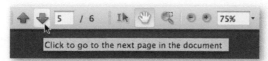

Use the blue arrows in Acrobat to navigate through the document pages.

5. Go to Forms > Add or Edit Fields to enter Form Editing mode. The Fields Navigation pane is at the far left of the screen, with each of the button names listed under Page 1. The buttons themselves are highlighted on the page.

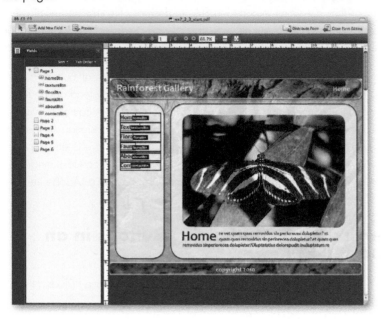

Form Editing mode in Acrobat 9 Professional. The Fields Navigation pane on the left lists all the form fields in the document.

6. Click homeBtn in the Fields pane, hold down the Shift key, and click contactBtn to select both buttons, and all the buttons in between. Right-click/Ctrl-click on one of the button names and select Duplicate from the contextual menu.

7. In the Duplicate Field dialog, select the From radio button. Enter 2 in the first text field and 6 in the second. Click OK to duplicate the buttons. All the buttons, on all the pages, appear in the Fields Navigation pane.

Right-click/Ctrl-click a field in the Fields pane to access the Duplicate Field dialog.

8. Click the Close Form Editing button at the upper right of the application window (Close Form Editing) and test your buttons.

9. Save your file as **ex21_3_end.pdf**, and close it. Quit Acrobat and return to InDesign.

Adjusting a SWF HTML Page

Don't know about you, but we're not big fans of the default gray background color for the HTML page that's generated when you export to SWF. We also find it somewhat disconcerting that sometimes the SWF is in the upper left corner of the page, and sometimes it's in the middle with space at the top. One situation in which this seems to occur is when the interactive page curl is applied. No worries, the fix is actually easy, if looking at code doesn't make you too squeamish. You can make a few really simple adjustments to get things to look the way you want them to.

If you have Dreamweaver, you'll be able to play around and see your results as you work. If not, you can use any text editing application, and then test your HTML page in the browser. It'll take a little more back and forth, but it'll be a worthwhile investment of time. Before your HTML page will open in a text editor, you may first need to save it as a .txt file, in order for it to display properly as plain text. You'll make your corrections, and then save the result with a .html extension. The portion of the code you need to change is toward the bottom of the page, so it's easy to find.

Exercise 21.4: Adjusting a SWF HTML Page

In this exercise, you'll export two SWFs, one with and one without page curl, to see the difference in the resulting HTML code. You'll then modify the code to change the position of the SWF on the page, and change the page background color.

1. Open **ex21_4_start.indd** from the chapter_21_exercises folder. Go to File > Export (Ctrl+E/Command+E) and choose Flash Player (SWF) from the Format dropdown at the bottom of the Export dialog. Name the file **ex21_4.swf**.

2. In the Export SWF dialog, for the first export, choose All Pages, Generate HTML file, View SWF after Exporting, Scale 100%, Paper Color, Include All, From Document, and Include Interactive Page Curl. Keep the default Advanced settings.

    When the page opens in the browser, note that the movie is offset from the top and left edges of the browser window.

3. Right-click/Ctrl-click on the gray area of the HTML page and choose View Page Source (or View Source, or Source, etc.; different browsers use somewhat different commands). OK, it's a lot of code, but you needn't sweat it. The part you're concerned with is really simple. Scroll down to the bottom of the page.

4. Before deconstructing the code to understand the changes you can make, return to InDesign and export the file again. Use the same settings except this time, be sure to deselect the Include Interactive Page Curl checkbox. Save the file as **ex21_4_no_curl.swf**.

5. When the second page opens in the browser, note that the SWF is aligned to the upper left of the page. View the source code, scroll down to the bottom of the page, and position the two pages of code side-by-side for comparison.

Use these export settings.

```
<body bgcolor="#999999">                          <body bgcolor="#999999">
<!--url's used in the movie-->                    <!--url's used in the movie-->
<!--text used in the movie-->                     <!--text used in the movie-->
<script language="JavaScript" type="text/ja       <script language="JavaScript" type="text/ja
<!--                                              <!--
var hasRightVersion = DetectFlashVer(requir       var hasRightVersion = DetectFlashVer(require
if(hasRightVersion) {  // if we've detected        if(hasRightVersion) {  // if we've detected
        // embed the flash movie                          // embed the flash movie
        AC_FL_RunContent(                                 AC_FL_RunContent(
                'codebase', 'http://downloa                       'codebase', 'http://downloa
                'width', '900',                                  'width', '1176',
                'height', '700',                                 'height', '976',
                'src', 'ex7_2_4_no_curl',                        'src', 'ex7_2_4_curl',
                'quality', 'high',                               'quality', 'high',
                'pluginspage', 'http://www.                      'pluginspage', 'http://www.a
                'align', 'middle',                               'align', 'middle',
                'play', 'false',                                 'play', 'false',
                'loop', 'false',                                 'loop', 'false',
                'scale', 'showall',                              'scale', 'showall',
                'wmode', 'window',                               'wmode', 'window',
                'devicefont', 'false',                           'devicefont', 'false',
                'id', 'ex7_2_4_no_curl',                         'id', 'ex7_2_4_curl',
                'bgcolor', '#999999',                            'bgcolor', '#999999',
                'name', 'ex7_2_4_no_curl',                       'name', 'ex7_2_4_curl',
                'menu', 'true',                                  'menu', 'true',
                'allowFullScreen', 'true',                       'allowFullScreen', 'true',
                'allowScriptAccess','sameDo                      'allowScriptAccess','sameDom
                'movie', 'ex7_2_4_no_curl',                      'movie', 'ex7_2_4_curl',
                'salign', ''                                     'salign', ''
```

Color Key	Reference
	Background Color
	SWF Dimensions
	File Reference
	Alignment
	Play Settings

HTML source code for the same SWF exported with and without interactive page curl. The width and height values for the SWF are different, even though the same movie was exported for both files. The color key in the image above is used throughout the following explanation, so you can easily identify the referenced portions of the code.

The highlighted sections of the code above are what you're going to look at changing. The first thing to note is that the dimensions allocated for the SWF in the file are different depending on whether or not the interactive page url is selected in the export settings. Strange! In the exercise example, the original SWF was 900 x 700 (see the ▪ highlighted section on the image above). When exported with the page curl, the size of the block containing the SWF is instead, 1176 x 976 (▪). Regardless of the dimensions of this SWF block, the SWF is centered in it by default, and the bgcolor (▪) near the bottom of the code is applied to it. InDesign makes the bgcolor for the HTML page (at the very top of the code), and the bgcolor for the SWF block (the bgcolor in the body of the code) the same, so you can't tell without looking at the code what's really going on. If you change either or both of the bgcolors, you can create the appearance of a frame around your SWF, depending on the dimensions you assign to the SWF containing block. Since the SWF is centered in the block by default, the size of the block contributes in part to the position of the SWF on the page.

The exported SWF above has an interactive page curl. The HTML page background was changed to black. The dimensions of the block containing the SWF in the HTML page were changed to 940 x 740 (from 1176 x 976), and its color was changed to white to create the appearance of a 20 pixel frame.

You can easily adjust the position of the SWF inside the block by assigning one of the following values to salign (■): (example: **'salign', 't'** where t = top middle).

Value	Position
t	Top Middle
b	Bottom Middle
l	Left Vertical Middle
r	Right Vertical Middle
tr	Top Right
tl	Top Left
br	Bottom Right
bl	Bottom Left

To align the position of the SWF inside its containing block, assign one of the values above to salign as follows: 'salign', 'tl'.

To change a background color, enter a hexidecimal value for either or both of the bgcolor options. To learn all about Hex colors, check out page 13, but maybe we can save you some time by reminding you that the Hexadecimal value for white is #FFFFFF and black is #000000.

The last thing we'll mention is that, if you ever need to swap out the SWF in a particular HTML file, that can easily be done by replacing all the references to the file name in the code (■). There's an additional file reference that doesn't show in the code example above, which occurs in the title tag. To see where the title tag value shows up on the page, take a look at the tab in the screenshot of the browser window on the previous page. In this case, the page title we assigned to the document is "Flower Gallery" The title tag has nothing to do with whether your SWF plays or not, but it is seen by your audience when they open your page, and it becomes the title of saved bookmarks or favorites. It would be best to enter a name you want people to see as opposed to the default page title assigned by InDesign, which reflects the file name.

To save you the time of opening and editing the code, we've provided an example for you to look at.

6. In your browser, go to File > Open File and browse to the chapter_21_exercises folder. Open **ex21_4_end.html** and view the source code. Scroll to the bottom of the page and note that the background colors for the page and the SWF block have been changed, as have the SWF block dimensions. The SWF has been aligned to the top of its block and the page title has been changed to Flower Gallery. When you've seen all the changes to the code, you can close the file, quit the browser and return to InDesign.

Note: When modifying code, it's critically important that you leave any quotation marks as you found them. Without the proper quotes, the code won't work.

Unless you want to keep playing, you can quit InDesign. You've completed the last exercise in the book!

Parting Shots

In efforts to give you everything we've got, this next little bit covers just a few odds and ends we want to make sure you know about before wrapping things up.

Multi-state Objects

You already know how cool multi-state objects are (Multi-state Objects starting on page 189), but you may not have realized that you can include video in them. Things get a little dicey, though, if you assign a controller. You're better off making your own buttons to start and stop the video.

SWF Export

It's possible that, when exporting to SWF, an object with transparency overlapping an interactive element may cause the interactivity to be lost.

Export to FLA

This has already all been said, but here it is again all in one place. When exporting to FLA, stay away from transparency and master page items, since they add dramatically to file size. Remember that movies export as a poster only, with all the media files saved to a separate Resources folder. Don't waste your time adding actions to buttons or creating hyperlinks since they won't work in the exported FLA.

For files exported to FLA, you're better off placing Illustrator artwork than copying and pasting it. Placed Illustrator files are treated as a single image when exported to FLA, but artwork that's copied and pasted is treated as lots of individual objects. If you'd rather copy and paste, go to Preferences > Clipboard Handling and check the Prefer PDF When Pasting, and Copy PDF to Clipboard checkboxes. This will ensure that you Illustrator artwork is placed as one object.

Another interesting thing to know when exporting to FLA: an image placed multiple times (rather than copied and pasted) is treated as one object to which all of its instances refer. Objects that are copied and pasted are treated as unrelated elements.

Transitions and Page Curl

Objects using certain animation presets don't play well with page transitions or the interactive page curl. For example, an object with a Fade in animation will be visible as the page is turned or as the page transition plays. The animations presenting this sort of issue are Appear, Fade In, the Fly-in presets, Zoom in 2D and Swoosh. Avoid page transitions when using these animations.

PDF

Try as we might, we couldn't get the dropdown menus that work so beautifully in SWF to work in Interactive PDF. Sorry, no workaround for this one.

When you scale a PDF in Acrobat that has a SWF in it, the PDF scales but the SWF does not.

If using Flash media in your Interactive PDF, you might want to consider a prominent message informing your audience that Acrobat or Reader 9 or above is required to properly view the file.

Conclusion

Well, we've said all we have to say. It's our greatest hope that the book has served you well, and that you now have the know-how and the inspiration to create engaging interactive projects.

In the course of your exploration and design you'll encounter issues and make discoveries that we haven't—and when you do—we'd like to hear about it. Don't just send us your tortures; share your triumphs too. You can post your InDesign adventures on our blog at www.interactive-indesign.com.

CHAPTER SUMMARY

This chapter was about tying together all the loose ends and addressing some of the issues you may encounter in your interactive work with InDesign. You learned how to properly prepare your files for output, and covered topics including:

- Adding animation to an Interactive PDF
- Correcting Interactive PDF show/hide issues
- Duplicating buttons in Interactive PDFs to minimize file size
- Adjusting the position of a SWF on an HTML page
- Adjusting the background color of an HTML Page

Last but not least, you picked up a bunch of tips and troubleshooting techniques, including:

- Using video in multi-state objects
- Cautions about page transitions, page curls, and transparency
- How best to work with Illustrator artwork for export to FLA
- The do's and don'ts of designing for export to FLA
- Working with issues around transparency and interactivity when exporting to SWF

Now that you've completed the book, check out the resources in the next few pages. We put together a list of shortcuts you'll find useful and a checklist for optimizing your interface. ENJOY!

Default Keyboard Shortcuts

....

RESOURCES

For easy reference, in the next few pages you'll find the following goodies: a consolidated list of the keyboard shortcuts found throughout the book (with a few extra thrown in for good measure), a checklist of recommended steps for optimizing the interface, and URLs for a couple priceless InDesign treasure troves.

Default Keyboard Shortcuts

File Menu

Place… –- Ctrl+D/Cmd+D

Edit Menu

Copy – Ctrl+C/Cmd+C

Cut – Ctrl+X/Cmd+X

Deselect All – Shift+Ctrl+A /Shift+Cmd+A

Find/Change… – Ctrl+F/Cmd+F

Paste – Ctrl+V/Cmd+V

Paste in Place – Alt+Shift+Ctrl+V/Opt+Shift+Cmd+V

Redo – Shift+Ctrl+Z/Shift+Cmd+Z

Select All – Ctrl+A/Cmd+A

Step and Repeat… – Alt+Ctrl+U/Opt+Cmd+U

Undo – Ctrl+Z/Cmd+Z

Layout Menu

Go to Page… – Ctrl+J/Cmd+J

Arrange: Bring Forward – Ctrl+]/Cmd+]

Arrange: Bring to Front –Shift+Ctrl+]/Shift+Cmd+]

Arrange: Send Backward – Ctrl+[/Cmd+[

Arrange: Send to Back – Shift+Ctrl+[/Shift+Cmd+[

Fitting: Fill Frame Proportionally – Alt+Shift+Ctrl+C/Opt+Shift+Cmd+C

Fitting: Fit Content Proportionally – Alt+Shift+Ctrl+E/Opt+Shift+Cmd+E

Group – Ctrl+G/Cmd+G

Lock – Ctrl+L/Cmd+L

Select: Container – Escape

Select: Content – Shift+Escape

Select: First Object Above – Alt+Shift+Ctrl+]/Opt+Shift+Cmd+]

Select: Last Object Below – Alt+Shift+Ctrl+[/Opt+Shift+Cmd+[

Select: Next Object Above – Alt+Ctrl+]/Opt+Cmd+]

Select: Next Object Below – Alt+Ctrl+[/Opt+Cmd+[

Text Frame Options… – Ctrl+B/Cmd+B

Ungroup – Shift+Ctrl+G/Shift+Cmd+G

Product area : View Menu

Actual Size – Ctrl+1/Cmd+1

Extras: Hide Text Threads – Alt+Ctrl+Y/Opt+Cmd+Y

Fit Page in Window – Ctrl+0/Cmd+0

Fit Spread in Window – Alt+Ctrl+0/Opt+Cmd+0

Grids & Guides: Smart Guides – Ctrl+U/ Cmd+U

Hide Rulers – Ctrl+R/Cmd+R

Screen Mode: Presentation – Presentation Mode: Escape, Shift+W

Screen Mode: Set Presentation Background to Black – Presentation Mode: B

Screen Mode: Set Presentation Background to Gray – Presentation Mode: G

Screen Mode: Set Presentation Background to White – Presentation Mode: W

Zoom In – Ctrl+/Cmd+

Zoom Out – Ctrl–/Cmd–

Product area : Window Menu

Object & Layout: Align – Shift+F7

Text Wrap – Alt+Ctrl+W/Opt+Cmd+W

Product area : Object Editing

Decrease scale by 1% – Ctrl+,/Cmd+,

Decrease scale by 5% – Alt+Ctrl+,/Opt+Cmd+,

Product area : Text and Tables

Align center – Shift+Ctrl+C/Shift+Cmd+C

Align force justify – Shift+Ctrl+F/Shift+Cmd+F

Align justify – Shift+Ctrl+J/Shift+Cmd+J

Align left – Shift+Ctrl+L/Shift+Cmd+L

Align right –Shift+Ctrl+L/Shift+Cmd+L

Apply bold – Shift+Ctrl+B/Shift+Cmd+B

Apply italic – Shift+Ctrl+/Shift+Cmd+I

Apply normal – Shift+Ctrl+Y/Shift+Cmd+Y

Decrease baseline shift – Text: Alt+Shift+Down Arrow/Opt+Shift+Down Arrow

Decrease kerning – Text: Alt+Shift+Left Arrow/Opt+Shift+Left Arrow

Decrease tracking – Text: Alt+Left Arrow/Opt+Left Arrow

Decrease leading – Text: Alt+Up Arrow/Opt+Up Arrow

Decrease point size – Shift+Ctrl+,/Shift+Cmd+,

Increase baseline shift – Text: Alt+Shift+Up Arrow/Opt+Shift+Up Arrow

Increase kerning – Text: Alt+Shift+Right Arrow/Opt+Shift+Right Arrow

Increase tracking – Text: Alt+Right Arrow/Opt+Right Arrow

Increase leading – Text: Alt+Down Arrow/Opt+Down Arrow

Increase point size – Shift+Ctrl+./Shift+Cmd+.

Product area : Tools

Apply Color – ,

Apply Gradient – .

Apply None – /

Apply default fill and stroke colors – D

Direct Selection Tool – A

Ellipse Tool – L

Hand Tool – H

Line Tool – \

Pen Tool – P

Pencil Tool – N

Rectangle Tool – M

Rotate Tool – R

Scale Tool – S

Selection Tool – V, Text: Escape

Swap fill and stroke activation – X

Swap fill and stroke colors – Shift+X

Save all – Alt+Shift+Ctrl+S/Opt+Shift+Cmd+S

Toggle Character and Paragraph Modes in Control Panel – Alt+Ctrl+7 Opt+Cmd+7

Recommended Preference Settings

With no document open:

1. Go to Preferences > Units & Increments and adjust the following:
   - Ruler Units: Pixels
   - Size/Leading: 1 pt
   - Baseline Shift: 1 pt
   - Kerning/Tracking: 10\

2. Go to Preferences > Display Performance
   - Greek Type Below 0
   - Vector Graphics, slide to High Resolution

3. Go to Edit > Spelling > Dynamic Spelling

4. Go to Edit > Spelling > Autocorrect

5. Go to View > Extras > Show Text Threads

6. Change your default font: set font family, font size, paragraph formatting, etc.

7. Change the [Basic Paragraph] Paragraph style
   - Turn on Optical Kerning
   - Turn off Hyphenation

8. Choose Panel Options from the Pages panel menu. In the Panel Options dialog, uncheck Show Vertically in the Pages section at the top of the dialog

9. Add common colors to the Swatches panel

InDesign Web Resources

http://www.indesignusergroup.com/: Access to the international network of InDesign user groups where you can connect with other InDesign enthusiasts

http://tv.adobe.com/product/indesign/: Video tips, tricks, features and more, straight from Adobe

http://indesignsecrets.com/: A website dedicated to everything InDesign. Lots of tutorials, resources, podcasts, videos and more

http://forums.adobe.com/community/indesign/indesign_general: Discussion threads relating to a wide range of InDesign topics

http://www.adobe.com/support/indesign/: Tutorials, issues, white papers and more

http://www.indesignmag.com/: InDesign magazine is a bimonthly periodical devoted entirely to all the wonderful things you can do with Adobe InDesign

Index

3D space animation, 171–175
4-color process printing, 10

A

ABCs (Adobe Beginner classes), 220
Acrobat Document Properties window, 258
Actions, 23, 59, 362
   Animation actions, 141, 144, 184
   Go To Destination actions, 98, 116, 119
   Go to Next State actions, 193
   Go To Page actions, 73, 116
   Go To Previous State actions, 193
   Go To State actions, 196
   Go To URL actions, 61, 90, 123, 202
   Show/Hide actions, 89, 91, 114, 120,
     339, 355
   Sound actions, 61–62, 243
   Video actions, 239
Actions dropdown menu, 181
Actual Size setting (PDF export), 354
Add Cue Point button, 230
Add New Action button, 61
Add Objects to State option, 196
Add Swatch button, 64
Add to Autocorrect List dialog box, 33
Adobe Acrobat Document Properties
   window, 258
Adobe Beginner classes (ABCs), 220
Adobe Forums Web site, 369
Adobe Media Encoder (AME), 215–232
   audio compression, 219–220
   cue points, 229–231
     adding, 230
     guidelines of, 229
   import & export file formats, 220–221
   Metadata Export panel, 231
   queue clean up, 231
   trimming and cropping, 227–229
   video, 216–218
     compression, 218–219
     frame rates and standards, 217–218
     interlaced and progressive video, 216–217
   working with, 221–226
Adobe Premiere Pro, 219
Adobe Web site, 369
Advanced search, 49–51

Advanced Television Systems Committee
   (ATSC), 217
Align controls, 112, 132, 173, 236, 321
Align Horizontal Centers button, 173,
   236, 321
Align Left button, 186, 259
Align panel, 25, 29, 132, 173, 178, 186, 321
   Distribute spacing, 132, 178
Align to dropdown menu, 132, 173, 236
   Align to Page, 132, 236, 321
   Align to Selection, 178, 182
Align Vertical Centers button, 132, 173,
   236, 321
All Readable Documents option, 347
AME. *See* Adobe Media Encoder
Americans with Disabilities Act, 340
Anchored objects, 311–313
   Alignment dropdown menu, 313
   Anchored Object Options dialog box, 312–313
Animation panel, 23, 128–132, 140, 154, 159
   161–162, 174, 181, 184, 352
   Animate dropdown menu, 137–138, 140,
     161, 166, 202, 238
animations, 127–188
   adding to PDF files, 352–354
   Animation panel, 128–132, 140, 154, 159,
     161–162, 174, 181, 184
   buttons, 180–184
   continuous loops, 175–176
   continuous scroller, 176–180
   custom motion paths, 152–162
   easing and duration, 130–136
   effects, 152
   letters, 148–151
   motion paths, 137–140
   motion presets, 129–130
   moving through 3D space, 171–175
   multiple objects and closed paths, 167–171
   multiple objects and open paths, 163–167
   off-center, 184–187
   timing, triggering events, and buttons,
     140–145
   transitions, 152
Appearance Only button, 335–336
Application Frame, 27
Apply Style to Selection checkbox, 118, 260